Measuring and Accounting for Environmental Public Goods

NBER
NATIONAL BUREAU *of* ECONOMIC RESEARCH

Studies in Income and Wealth
Volume 82

NBER
NATIONAL BUREAU *of* ECONOMIC RESEARCH

Measuring and Accounting for Environmental Public Goods

A National Accounts Perspective

Edited by **Nicholas Z. Muller, Eli P. Fenichel, and Mary Bohman**

The University of Chicago Press

Chicago and London

The University of Chicago Press, Chicago 60637
The University of Chicago Press, Ltd., London

Published 2025
Printed in the United States of America

34 33 32 31 30 29 28 27 26 25   1 2 3 4 5

ISBN-13: 978-0-226-83935-6 (cloth)
ISBN-13: 978-0-226-83936-3 (e-book)
DOI: https://doi.org/10.7208/chicago/9780226839363.001.0001

Library of Congress Cataloging-in-Publication Data

Names: Conference on Research in Income and Wealth (2023 : Alexandria, Va.) creator | Muller, Nicholas Z., editor | Fenichel, Eli P., editor | Bohman, Mary, editor
Title: Measuring and accounting for environmental public goods : a national accounts perspective / edited by Nicholas Z. Muller, Eli P. Fenichel, Mary Bohman.
Other titles: Studies in income and wealth
Description: Chicago ; London : The University of Chicago Press, 2025. | Series: Studies in income and wealth ; volume 82 | Revised versions of papers presented at the Conference on Research in Income and Wealth titled "Measuring and Accounting for Environmental Public Goods: A National Accounts Perspective," held in Alexandria, VA, on March 16–17, 2003.—Acknowledgements page. | Includes bibliographical references and index.
Identifiers: LCCN 2024042364 | ISBN 9780226839356 (cloth) | ISBN 9780226839363 (ebook)
Subjects: LCSH: Natural resources—Accounting—Congresses | Natural resources—United States—Congresses | Environmental economics—United States—Congresses | LCGFT: Conference papers and proceedings
Classification: LCC HC85 .C658 2023 | DDC 333.7068/1—dc23/eng/20241031
LC record available at https://lccn.loc.gov/2024042364

♾ This paper meets the requirements of ANSI/NISO Z39.48-1992 (Permanence of Paper).

Relation of the Directors to the Work and Publications of the NBER

1. The object of the NBER is to ascertain and present to the economics profession, and to the public more generally, important economic facts and their interpretation in a scientific manner without policy recommendations. The Board of Directors is charged with the responsibility of ensuring that the work of the NBER is carried on in strict conformity with this object.

2. The President shall establish an internal review process to ensure that book manuscripts proposed for publication DO NOT contain policy recommendations. This shall apply both to the proceedings of conferences and to manuscripts by a single author or by one or more co-authors but shall not apply to authors of comments at NBER conferences who are not NBER affiliates.

3. No book manuscript reporting research shall be published by the NBER until the President has sent to each member of the Board a notice that a manuscript is recommended for publication and that in the President's opinion it is suitable for publication in accordance with the above principles of the NBER. Such notification will include a table of contents and an abstract or summary of the manuscript's content, a list of contributors if applicable, and a response form for use by Directors who desire a copy of the manuscript for review. Each manuscript shall contain a summary drawing attention to the nature and treatment of the problem studied and the main conclusions reached.

4. No volume shall be published until forty-five days have elapsed from the above notification of intention to publish it. During this period a copy shall be sent to any Director requesting it, and if any Director objects to publication on the grounds that the manuscript contains policy recommendations, the objection will be presented to the author(s) or editor(s). In case of dispute, all members of the Board shall be notified, and the President shall appoint an ad hoc committee of the Board to decide the matter; thirty days additional shall be granted for this purpose.

5. The President shall present annually to the Board a report describing the internal manuscript review process, any objections made by Directors before publication or by anyone after publication, any disputes about such matters, and how they were handled.

6. Publications of the NBER issued for informational purposes concerning the work of the Bureau, or issued to inform the public of the activities at the Bureau, including but not limited to the NBER Digest and Reporter, shall be consistent with the object stated in paragraph 1. They shall contain a specific disclaimer noting that they have not passed through the review procedures required in this resolution. The Executive Committee of the Board is charged with the review of all such publications from time to time.

7. NBER working papers and manuscripts distributed on the Bureau's web site are not deemed to be publications for the purpose of this resolution, but they shall be consistent with the object stated in paragraph 1. Working papers shall contain a specific disclaimer noting that they have not passed through the review procedures required in this resolution. The NBER's web site shall contain a similar disclaimer. The President shall establish an internal review process to ensure that the working papers and the web site do not contain policy recommendations, and shall report annually to the Board on this process and any concerns raised in connection with it.

8. Unless otherwise determined by the Board or exempted by the terms of paragraphs 6 and 7, a copy of this resolution shall be printed in each NBER publication as described in paragraph 2 above.

Contents

Prefatory Note

This volume contains revised versions of the papers presented at the Conference on Research in Income and Wealth titled "Measuring and Accounting for Environmental Public Goods: A National Accounts Perspective," held in Alexandria, VA, on March 16–17, 2023.

We are grateful for support for this project from the Alfred P. Sloan Foundation through grant #G-2020-13874, and from the Bureau of Economic Analysis. Support for the general activities of the Conference on Research in Income and Wealth is provided by the following agencies: Bureau of Economic Analysis, Bureau of Labor Statistics, the Census Bureau, the Board of Governors of the Federal Reserve System, the Statistics of Income/Internal Revenue Service, and Statistics Canada.

We thank Mary Bohman, Eli P. Fenichel, and Nicholas Z. Muller, who served as conference organizers and as editors of the volume.

Acknowledgments

The editors and conference organizers received excellent support from NBER and University of Chicago staff. Helena Fitz-Patrick (NBER) provided valued guidance as we navigated the steps to publication. She also greatly improved the book through her editing. Chad Zimmerman, Executive Editor at the University of Chicago Press, coordinated the reviews and publication approvals. Brett Maranjian (NBER) worked with us to organize the conference and ensured that we had a flawless two days of papers and conversation. In addition, we benefited from Katharine Abraham's insights and contributions from Dylan Rassier on the initial planning of the conference.

Introduction

Nicholas Z. Muller, Eli P. Fenichel, and Mary Bohman

This NBER Conference on Research on Income and Wealth (CRIW), focused on measuring and accounting for environmental public goods using a national accounts perspective, was originally proposed by V. Kerry Smith and Richard T. Carson, two long-standing leaders in environmental economics. In part, the motivation was to coincide with the 50th anniversary of William D. Nordhaus and James Tobin's seminal paper "Is Growth Obsolete" (1972). The papers in this volume, along with much of the related literature since the 1970s, depend on the conceptual basis established by Nordhaus and Tobin. However, as methods, models, computing power, and data availability have improved, both the scope and the depth of the work on environmental accounting has grown, as evidenced by the papers in this volume. Hence, this research represents a new research agenda that has been a long time in the making. At the same time, the new research responds to policymakers' calls for linked economic-environmental statistics to track progress and make decisions about climate, air, water, and other sectors (OSTP et al. 2023).

Measurement of the economy is a core concern for the field of economics, though the question of what the economy encompasses is not separable from what gets measured. Human activities have always been sensitive to environmental change (Brander and Taylor 1998; Hsiang, Burke, and Miguel

Nicholas Z. Muller is the Lester and Judith Lave Professor of Economics, Engineering, and Public Policy at Carnegie Mellon University, and a research associate of the National Bureau of Economic Research.

Eli P. Fenichel is the Knobloch Family Professor of Natural Resource Economics at the Yale School of the Environment.

Mary Bohman is the former Acting Director and Deputy Director of the Bureau of Economic Analysis.

2013), but in the past 70 or so years it has become overwhelmingly clear that economic activity influences environmental change affecting production and income. Meanwhile, the role of economic measurement has expanded to provide information for fiscal and monetary policy. These applications, while clearly important, are a mere subset of the questions that motivated assessments of national income and welfare. For fundamental questions related to economic progress, output or market consumption are not sufficient metrics and welfare consistent measures are also needed (Jorgenson 2018). As Nordhaus and Tobin (1972) argue, "There are other serious consequences of treating as free things which are not really free. This practice gives the wrong signals of the direction of economic growth." Therefore, economic measurement requires us to think of the biosphere as a collection of often mispriced assets that provide services to the economy and that exist within its boundaries.

The origins of accounting for natural resources extend deep into human history.[1] The Magna Carta has rules for the management of game and fishes, suggesting some measure of accounting. By the early 1900s, academics such as Fisher (1906) defined fish as wealth and argued that "it would be wrong, however, that because we cannot value them accurately, public parks or freeman cannot be called wealth." This influenced political leaders of the time. For example, Theodore Roosevelt (1910) argued, "The nation behaves well if it treats the natural resources as assets which it must turn over to the next generation increased, and not impaired, in value; and behaves badly if it leaves the land poorer to those who come after it." During and after the Great Depression, the United States, the United Kingdom, and other countries began developing national income accounts to provide a systematic unified overview of the economy. During the development of national accounts in the 1940s and World War II, natural resources and the environment were not considered major concerns. Factory output and "paying for the war" (Coyle 2015) were the primary areas of focus. In the years after the war, welfare economics developed a richer understanding of the importance of natural resources and contributions of the environment to welfare (Banzhaf 2019; Krutilla 1967).

Modern discussion about environmental-economic accounting was pushed to the fore by the anti-growth stance of Meadows et al. (1972) and a rejoin by Nordhaus and Tobin (1972). In 1992, following a flurry of theoretical developments (including Weitzman 1976; Maler 1991; Solow 1986), the United States Bureau of Economic Analysis (BEA), the US agency responsible for the US national accounts, initiated a set of environmental and economic satellite accounts, first published in 1994.[2] In 1993, the international

1. The origins of writing, counting, and coins are all tied up with early methods of accounting for livestock and ownable natural resources (Evertt 2017).

2. *Satellite accounts* is a term of art that refers to a subsection or articulating accounts that relate to the main national income and product accounts.

community published revised guidelines to the international standard for the System of National Accounts (SNA). These revisions included a new treatment of natural resources, such as non-produced and non-financial biological assets. In 1994, the US Congress directed the Department of Commerce (which houses the BEA) to suspend production of the integrated environmental and economic satellite account pending a peer review of the methods.[3] The following, year in 1995, the US Congress passed the 1995 Paperwork Reduction Act, which overhauled the US Statistical System, reformed the office of the Chief Statistician of the United States, within the Office of Management and Budget, and gave that position the authority to coordinate efforts like the integrated environmental and economic satellite account. Meanwhile, the National Research Council of the National Academies of Science published "Nature's Numbers" (Nordhaus and Kokkelenberg 1999) satisfying Congress's instructions. Around the same time, research at the World Bank was beginning to develop approaches to adjustments in net savings for the environment (Hamilton and Clemens 1999).

In the decade following "Nature's Numbers," there was another flurry of activity. The World Bank (2005), the National Research Council (2005), the National Bureau of Economic Research (Nordhaus 2006), and US Government Accountability Office (2007) all published reports emphasizing the importance of including natural resources and the environment in the national income and product accounts. Some of these reports provided specific guidelines, but all left details to be resolved. At the same time, academic research continued to advance (Arrow et al. 2004; Arrow et al. 2003; Sefton and Weale 2006). In 2008, the SNA were again revised (European Commission et al. 2009), with little change to the instructions for including natural resources and the environment. These revisions included passage 1.46, "Natural resources such as land, mineral deposits, fuel reserves, uncultivated forests or other vegetation and wild animals are included in the balance sheets provided that institutional units are exercising effective ownership rights over them, that is, are actually in a position to be able to benefit from them. Assets need not be privately owned and could be owned by government units exercising ownership rights on behalf of entire communities. Thus, many environmental assets are included within the SNA." However, these revisions do not provide detailed guidance on how to include such environmental assets. This difficulty led to the System of Environmental-Economics Accounting (SEEA) Central Framework (United Nations et al. 2014) and the start of a SEEA experimental ecosystem accounting process (United Nations et al. 2021).[4] Research continued to evolve, featuring

3. US House of Representatives. (n.d.). H. Rept. 103–708 (Conference Report) accompanying the Departments of Commerce, Justice, and State, the Judiciary and Related Agencies Appropriations Act, 1995 (Pub. L. 103–317). US Government Publishing Office, 61.

4. The physical flow accounting in the SEEA ecosystem accounts became an international standard in 2021, but the valuation component is still considered experimental.

advances in empirical measurement (Muller 2014; Muller et al. 2011; Arrow et al. 2012; Fenichel and Abbott 2014; Fenichel et al. 2016). At around the same time the World Bank and the United Nations Environment Programme started the Changing Wealth of Nations (2011) and Inclusive Wealth (2012) reports. These go beyond environmental-economic statistics. However, their grounding is clearly in the tradition of environmental-economic statistics. By this point there was already a growing international push to augment existing national accounts to consider the environment and perhaps other policy goals (Stiglitz et al. 2010).

The SEEA process led to many countries developing environmental-economic accounting experiments and programs. In 2011, The European Union passed regulation (EU) 691/2011 establishing a requirement for member states to begin developing some environmental economic accounts and to report to EuroStat. These accounts focused mostly on industrial flows deemed to be related to the environment, including waste products. They also included air emissions accounts. This process continues to expand with a growing number of accounts required.[5] In 2014 the United Kingdom started its natural capital accounts and included those as official experimental accounts in the 2020 Blue Book of statistics. The need for national economic statistics to inform measures beyond output continued to become clear from an academic perspective (Jorgenson 2018) and a policy perspective as the OECD and UN both embarked on ambitious "Beyond GDP" agendas. The Dasgupta Review (2021) further accelerated interest in environmental-economic accounting. In 2023, the United States renewed its effort in environmental economic accounting through the development of a US strategy (OSTP et al. 2023).

The papers in this volume advance the conceptual and empirical basis for adding natural capital to the suite of economic and environmental statistics that inform public policy. They provide insights into valuation of natural capital including the need to address heterogeneity in measurement across types of capital, heterogeneity of geography, and in the distribution of individuals. Cropper and Park's paper builds on Maureen Cropper's keynote address at the conference. All the other papers are accompanied by brief comments and reflection from a discussant.

The first three papers advance the conceptual measurement of environmental-economic accounts following the SEEA framework and provide directions for use.

Cropper and Park tackle the issues associated with incorporating local air

5. "Environmental accounts—establishing the links between the environment and the economy." Eurostat. Last edited on October 12, 2023. ISSN 2443–8219. https://ec.europa.eu/eurostat/statistics-explained/index.php?title=Environmental_accounts_-_establishing_the_links_between_the_environment_and_the_economy#Introduction_to_environmental_accounting, and "Green Deal: pioneering proposals to restore Europe's nature by 2050 and halve pesticide use by 2030." Press release, June 22, 2022. European Commission, Brussels. https://ec.europa.eu/commission/presscorner/detail/en/ip_22_3746.

pollution, greenhouse gases, and water pollution into the national accounts. The authors focus on data needs and modeling approaches required to develop satellite accounts for air pollution. For greenhouse gases, the authors focus on issues pertaining to valuation using the social cost of carbon. Their work on water pollution emphasizes the more primitive state of data inventories and the ability to connect such emissions to monetary damage.

Agarwala et al. develop a framework to use natural capital accounts as a tool for forward-thinking policy challenges in order to address issues such as inequality, productivity, and net zero transition. The authors develop and report empirical estimates of productivity growth in the United Kingdom adjusted for environmental pollution damage. They also provide a simple model to incorporate risk to natural capital assets from degradation or loss. Nicholas Muller provides a discussion. Similarly, in the spirit of providing a tool for policymakers to predict future well-being, McLaughlin et al. introduce a new database of historical Genuine Savings (GS), an indicator of sustainable development. GS derives from the theoretical work on wealth accounting, and addresses shortcomings in conventional metrics of economic development by incorporating broader measures of saving and investment, including human capital (education) and natural resource depletion. This article provides consistent historical estimates of GS since 1850 for 25 countries and compares the estimates to other economic indicators to assess the ability of GS to predict future well-being. Stefanie Onder provides a discussion.

To provide consistent data to incorporate heterogeneity into analysis of economic-environmental issues, Colmer and Voorheis introduce a new prototype of a microdata infrastructure: the Census Environmental Impacts Frame (EIF). The EIF provides detailed individual-level information on demographics, economic characteristics, and address-level histories—linked to spatially and temporally resolved estimates of environmental conditions at the micro (individual) level—for most residents in the United States over the past two decades. This linked microdata infrastructure provides a unique platform for advancing our understanding about the distribution of environmental amenities and hazards, when, how, and why exposures have evolved over time, and the consequences of environmental inequality and changing environmental conditions. They discuss the opportunities and limitations of these new data. The authors conclude with a measurement example showing the difference in exposure to tree canopy at the individual level versus aggregation to the Census Block Group level. This paper points to one possible direction of the rich future for environmental-economic statistics. Corbett Grainger provides a discussion.

The next four chapters look to apply lessons learned and develop strategies to implement specific environmental-economic accounts. These papers investigate developing estimates tied to the SEEA Central Framework (SEEA-CF). The analysis is also consistent with US strategy.

Addicott turns his attention to developing an environmental-economic account for geologic beach structures. He analyzes the role of geographic heterogeneity as a key determinant of the value and productivity of natural assets with a study of coastal beaches. To address differences in the arrangement of sand along the coastline, he conducts three case studies using high-resolution, remotely sensed data and information on property attributes and transactions. He draws on these estimates to assess how estimates of beach width—a coastal environmental attribute—can provide a way forward for natural capital accounting. This analysis could possibly link to future implementation of a coastal ecosystem account aligned with the National Strategy to Develop Statistics for Environmental-Economic Decisions, a strategy for developing natural capital accounts and other environmental-economic statistics. Justin Contat provides a discussion.

Fixler et al. develop a proof-of-concept environmental activity account for the United States to quantify the environmental goods and services sector (EGSS) devoted to protecting, rehabilitating, or managing the environment. They follow the principles and methods outlined in the SEEA-CF and draw on the US Bureau of Economic Analysis (BEA) satellite account approach. Their analysis provides insights into classification, measurement challenges, and data gaps. Their estimates roughly track comparable European country statistics, and the authors conclude that additional work and resources would result in high-quality US statistics. They identify methodological improvements that are needed to advance this sort of account for the United States. David Evans provides a discussion.

Warziniack et al. create a first set of forest natural capital accounts following the SEEA-CF and demonstrate how these accounts can be integrated with general equilibrium models of the economy to capture the integrated ecological processes that constitute a forest and the associated ecosystem services. They focus on the Colorado River Basin and estimate the direct implications of deforestation for the forest industry and indirect impacts on the economy through water treatment costs and the carbon stock. Andie Creel provides a discussion.

The Wielgus et al. paper builds on work by the US National Oceanic and Atmospheric Administration (NOAA) and BEA to build a Marine Economy Satellite Account (MESA). They draw on extensive NOAA data and research to develop approaches to incorporate natural capital considerations using the SEEA-CF framework. Wielgus et al. identify three key aspects of natural capital that require measuring both additions and reductions in natural capital stocks: offshore oil and gas, commercial fishing, and beach recreation. Andrew Scheld provides a discussion.

The papers in this volume raise several cross-cutting themes, two of which are highlighted here. A foundational concept of the national income and product accounts is the expression of economic activity in monetary units. Conversion of the disparate goods and services that comprise output into a common unit of account critically enables aggregation into (and subsequent reporting of) our commonly cited barometers of economic activity: value-added, gross output, and gross domestic product. It would be meaningless, and potentially misleading, to simply aggregate and report physical units of goods produced.

Valuation, or conversion of physical stocks and flows into monetary units, is also necessary in the context of natural capital accounting. Consider the task of tracking emissions of carbon dioxide and primary particulate matter; each of these pollutants impacts distinct aspects of the economy including public health and premature mortality risk, natural disasters and risks to man-made capital, agricultural yields, and species loss. Yet, firms, industries, and economies commonly produce these pollutants. So, the problem facing natural capital accountants is analogous to that facing national income accountants. Physical flows must be converted to a common unit of account to measure pollution damage.

In the context of the national accounts, valuation mostly relies on market prices.[6] Despite the conceptual and practical appeal of using market prices to value economic activity, this approach does not always work in the context of natural capital accounting. If the entities being tracked in natural capital accounts are not traded in markets, then quite clearly, no market prices exist.[7] In such cases, economists turn to nonmarket valuation techniques. These now well-established tools are categorized into two groups: revealed and stated preference approaches. The former extracts evidence on the value of the natural environment from related market transactions (see Addicott). The value of parkland can be estimated by its effect on proximate property transactions. Stated preference tools ask people directly about the value they place on the natural environment using highly structured surveys. Participants may be asked about their willingness-to-pay to reduce mortality risk. While both approaches have been used widely and critically evaluated in the academic literature (Johnston et al. 2017; Bishop et al. 2020; Bateman and Kling 2020; Lupi et al. 2020; Evans and Taylor 2020) and in policy contexts, it is critical to recognize that these tools *estimate* values. In contrast, reliance on market prices (as is more common in the national accounts) depends, more straightforwardly, on observing and gathering pricing data and appropriately summarizing such data.

Despite these important differences, valuation suffers from key shortcomings in the national accounts and the natural capital accounting contexts. First, prices often reflect averages rather than true *marginal* values. This is

6. Valuation for owner occupied housing is imputed. Hedonics are used to value the various components of computers.

7. Consider that reduced populations of a particular species due to habitat loss may not be directly recorded in markets if that particular species is not the subject of exchange. For example, while well-defined prices exist for harvested bluefin tuna, they do not for the Greenland shark. However, the shadow value of the loss of species may influence other prices in the market. For example, the loss of bats from disease can reduce agricultural yields and thus total volumes and possibly prices (Manning and Ando 2022).

because they are most often recorded from observing total value added over a period of time and dividing by observed quantities transacted. Consider that prices of, say, food or gasoline used in the accounts necessarily reflect averages over both time and space. Likewise, values derived from either of the nonmarket valuation approaches above embody sample averages. Second, uniform application of these average values to marginal and inframarginal units of goods and services produced renders aggregates as fundamentally disconnected from microeconomic conceptualizations of welfare, namely, producer and consumer surplus.[8]

Heterogeneity is a ubiquitous feature in economic and environmental data. This raises the following question: how to deal with goods and services that are similar, but not quite the same? The US national accounts use the North American Product Classification System (NAPCS) to decide what goods get grouped together.[9] In this system, for example, fluid milk, non-frozen yogurt, and cheese are all separate products. However, distinctions within these product categories are lost; cheese is cheese whether it is artisanal or mass produced. Cat food and dog food are separate goods, but all other types of pet food are combined into a single category. These sorts of decisions are the result of a deliberative process that has not happened for many environmental goods or services.

That lack of an agreed-upon approach to aggregating services makes addressing heterogeneity in environmental economic accounts challenging. But that is not the only reason heterogeneity matters. For example, Colmer and Voorheis point out that matching individuals to natural capital, and its associated services, is scale dependent. Addicott attempts to address this challenge using attributes of detailed remote sensing and property value data along with numerous aggregation decisions. Furthermore, while numerous goods and services are considered to be the same anywhere in the United States, services from the environment are not (Muller and Mendelsohn 2007; Plummer 2009; Addicott and Fenichel 2019).

The differences among goods and services within the market boundary are measured by their prices. However, when prices are imputed, the analyst needs to consider potential quality differences within a type of service. For example, in the context of estimating pollution damage, one of the central determinants of such damage is the value of mortality risk reductions, or the Value of a Statistical Life (VSL). Considerable empirical evidence suggests that the VSL-income elasticity is positive. Hence, the VSL varies along the income distribution.[10] While this result is intuitive, it presents particularly thorny issues for natural capital accounting. One strategy is to

8. Index number theory can be used to realign the concepts, when the focus is on specific changes (Diewert 1992).

9. North American Product Classification System, US Census Bureau. https://www.census.gov/naics/napcs/.

10. This result is observed across countries with different income levels and across different income groups within countries.

employ the observed income elasticity to impute group-specific values and group-specific damages from pollution exposure. An alternative approach is to rely on a sample average value, a uniform VSL, for instance, and to calculate group-specific damages holding the valuation parameter fixed. While the former may be supported or informed by empirical research, it raises two issues that must be addressed. First, using population subgroup-specific values in a cross-sectional setting departs from standard practice by government agencies conducting policy analysis to use an average value. Second, this tack gives the impression that the practice of natural capital accounting attributes greater weight to outcomes amongst higher income groups. The research in this volume provides context and analysis showing the need for future research to address these issues in the context of the natural capital accounts (for example, Colmer and Voorheis).

This conference took place in March 2023 as the international statistical community worked to prepare guidelines for the 2025 revisions to the SNA that update the 2008 standards. The United Nations Statistical Commission (UNSC) met in late February and early March 2024 and approved a framework for most of the proposed changes (United Nations Statistics Division 2024). New measures of natural resource depletion and a broader discussion of sustainability, along with considerations of human and natural capital, will be included in the revision.

The 2025 revisions raise the importance of net measures of domestic product by recommending more visibility for net domestic product adjusted for both consumption of fixed capital and depletion of natural resources.[11] This shift in emphasis provides incentives for countries to increase investments in measuring natural capital. In addition, the 2025 SNA recommendations propose expanding coverage in areas that will support development of specific natural capital and environmental services accounts. For example, they propose to explicitly include renewable energy resources (such as solar and wind electricity generation), and the recommendations provide more consistency in delineation and calculation of net present values for mineral and energy resources by aligning with the SEEA central framework.

The 2025 revisions and advances in SEEA have the potential to expand the number of countries producing natural capital and environmental services accounts. The most recent analysis of the adoption of SEEA (2023 Global Assessment) indicated that 90 countries currently implement at least part of the SEEA framework. The categories published by the largest number of countries are energy accounts, followed by environmental production and management expenditures and air emissions.[12] The categories published by the largest number of countries are energy accounts, followed by air emis-

11. 2025 System of National Accounts Draft for Global Consultation, United Nations, https://unstats.un.org/unsd/nationalaccount/snaupdate/2025/Draft_2025SNA.pdf.

12. 2023 Global Assessment Results, System of Environmental Economic Accounting, United Nations, https://seea.un.org/news/findings-2023-global-assessment-environmental-economic-accounting.

sions, environmental protection and management expenditure, material flow and water accounts. The US has not released official statistics using the SEEA framework, but has published a National Strategy to produce environmental-economic statistics consistent with SEEA (OSTP et al. 2023).

The conference and this volume provide papers from US agencies that fall under the National Strategy to develop US accounts for environmental services (Fixler et al.), marine (Wielgus et al.) and forestry (Warziniack et al.). Each of the papers illustrates the challenges, especially those involving data, to develop the accounts. However, all the authors conclude that work to date shows promise for producing the accounts and they identify specific data needs and challenges.

This conference's cross-cutting theme of valuation represents an important component of the 2025 SNA and SEEA plans. While not yet included in official statistics, these plans place a priority on developing methods to value ecosystem services that can be replicated across different locations within and across countries. Challenges to adoption include the heterogeneity of services by location in addition to determining appropriate valuation methods. The Addicott and Colmer and Voorheis papers address relevant strategies and were discussed earlier in this introduction.

The papers and comments in this volume build on the Nordhaus and Tobin paper published more than 50 years ago as well as the intervening advances in methods, models, data, and computing power. The demand by policymakers to include links between the environment and economic activity has grown over this same period. Notably in 2025 as this book is published, the new SNA guidelines provide expanded coverage for environmental accounts as well as more detailed guidance. These papers inform ongoing challenges tied to valuation of nonmarket assets as well as heterogeneity across both market and nonmarket goods and services. They also provide pilots to measure natural capital for key sectors. Throughout the volume, authors raise issues for future research that we hope shapes future work. With all the research and statistical development underway, the next conference on this topic will not need to wait 50 years.

For acknowledgments, sources of research support, and disclosure of the authors' material financial relationships, if any, please see https://www.nber.org/books-and-chapters/measuring-and-accounting-environmental-public-goods-national-accounts-perspective/introduction-measuring-and-accounting-environmental-public-goods-building-expanded-national-accounts.

References

Addicott, Ethan T., and Eli P. Fenichel. 2019. "Spatial Aggregation and the Value of Natural Capital." *Journal of Environmental Economics and Management* 95: 118–32.
Arrow, Kenneth, Partha Dasgupta, Lawrence Goulder, Gretchen Daily, Paul Ehrlich, Geoffrey Heal, Simon Levin, Karl-Goran Maler, Stephen Schneider, David Starrett, and Brian Walker. 2004. "Are We Consuming Too Much?" *Journal of Economic Perspectives* 18 (3): 147–72.
Arrow, Kenneth J., Partha Dasgupta, and Karl-Goran Maler. 2003. "Evaluating Projects and Assessing Sustainable Development in Imperfect Economies." *Environmental and Resource Economics* 26: 647–85.
Arrow, Kenneth J., Partha Dasgupta, Lawrence H Goulder, Kevin J Mumford, and Kirsten Oleson. 2012. "Sustainability and the Measurement of Wealth." *Environmental and Development Economics* 17: 317–53. doi: 10.1017/s1355770x12000137.
Banzhaf, Spencer. 2019. "The Environmental Turn in Natural Resource Economics: John Krutilla and 'Conservation Reconsidered.'" *Journal of the History of Economic Thought* 41: 27–46.
Bateman, Ian J., and Catherine L. Kling. 2020. "Revealed Preference Methods for Nonmarket Valuation: An Introduction to Best Practices." *Review of Environmental Economics and Policy* 14 (2): 240–59.
Bishop, Kelly C., Nicolai V. Kuminoff, H. Spencer Banzhaf, Kevin J. Boyle, Kathrine von Gravenitz, Jaren C. Pope, V. Kerry Smith, and Christopher D. Timmins. 2020. "Best Practices for Using Hedonic Property Value Models to Measure Willingness to Pay for Environmental Quality." *Review of Environmental Economics and Policy* 14 (2): 260–81.
Brander, James A., M. Scott Taylor. 1998. "The Simple Economics of Easter Island: A Ricardo-Malthus Model of Renewable Resource Use." *American Economic Review* 88 (1): 119–38.
Coyle, Diane. 2015. *GDP: A Brief but Affectionate History*. Revised and expanded edition. Princeton University Press.
Dasgupta, Partha. 2021. *The Economics of Biodiversity: The Dasgupta Review*. London: HM Treasury.
Diewert, W. Erwin. 1992. "Exact and Superlative Welfare Change Indicators." *Economic Inquiry* 30: 565–82.
European Commission, International Monetary Fund, Organisation for Economic Co-operation and Development, United Nations, and World Bank. 2009. System of National Accounts 2008. European Commission, International Monetary Fund, Organisation for Economic Co-operation and Development, United Nations, World Bank.
Evans, M. F., and L. O. Taylor. 2020. "Using Revealed Preference Methods to Estimate the Value of Reduced Mortality Risk: Best Practice Recommendations for the Hedonic Wage Model." Published online September 29, 2020. *Review of Environmental Economics and Policy* 14 (2): 282–301.
Evertt, Caleb. 2017. *Numbers and the Making of Us*. Cambridge, MA: Harvard University Press.
Fenichel, Eli P., and Joshua K. Abbott. 2014. "Natural Capital from Metaphor to Measurement." *Journal of the Association of Environmental and Resource Economists* 1 (1): 1–27.
Fenichel, Eli P., Joshua K. Abbott, Jude Bayham, Whitney Boone, Erin M. K. Haacker, and Lisa Pfeiffer. 2016. "Measuring the Value of Groundwater and Other Forms of Natural Capital." *Proceedings of the National Academy of Sciences* 113 (9): 2382–2387. doi: 10.1073/pnas.1513779113.

Fisher, Irving. 1906. *The Nature of Capital and Income*. Norwood, MA: Norwood Press.
Hamilton, Kirk, and Michael Clemens. 1999. "Genuine Savings Rates in Developing Countries." *The World Bank Economic Review* 13 (2): 333–56.
Hsiang, S. M., M. Burke, and E. Miguel. 2013. "Quantifying the influence of climate on human conflict." *Science* 341 (6151): 1235367.
Johnston, Robert J., Kevin J. Boyle, Wiktor (Vic) Adamowicz, Jeff Bennett, Roy Brouwer, Trudy Ann Cameron, W. Michael Hanemann, Nick Hanley, Mandy Ryan, Riccardo Scarpa, Roger Tourangeau, and Christian. A. Vossler. 2017. "Contemporary Guidance for Stated Preference Studies." *Journal of the Association of Environmental and Resource Economists* 4 (2): 319–405.
Jorgenson, Dale W. 2018. "Production and Welfare: Progress in Economic Measurement." *Journal of Economic Literature* 56 (3): 867–919.
Krutilla, John V. 1967. "Conservation Reconsidered." *American Economic Review* 57 (4): 777–86.
Lupi, Frank, Daniel J. Phaneuf, and Roger H. von Haefen. 2020. "Best Practices for Implementing Recreation Demand Models." *Review of Environmental Economics and Policy* 14 (2): 302–23.
Maler, Karl-Goran. 1991. "National Accounts and Environmental Resources." *Environmental and Resource Economics* 1: 1–15.
Manning, Dale T., and Amy Ando. 2022. "Ecosystem Services and Land Rental Markets: Producer Costs of Bat Population Crashes." *Journal of the Association of Environmental and Resource Economists* 9 (6): 1235–1277.
Meadows, D. H., D. L. Meadows, J. Randers, W. Behrens III. 1972. *The Limits to Growth: A Report to The Club of Rome*. New York: Universe Books.
Muller, Nicholas Z. 2014. "Boosting GDP Growth by Accounting for the Environment." *Science* 345 (6199): 873–74.
Muller, Nicholas Z., and Robert Mendelsohn. 2007. "Measuring the Aggregate Damages of Air Pollution in the United States." *Journal of Environmental Economics and Management* 54: 1–14.
Muller, Nicholas Z., R. O. Mendelsohn, and William D. Nordhaus. 2011. "Environmental Accounting: Methods with an Application to the United States Economy." *American Economic Review* 101: 1–30.
National Research Council. 2005. *Beyond the Market: Designing Nonmarket Accounts for the United States*. Washington, DC: National Academies Press.
Nordhaus, William D. 2006. "Principles of National Accounting for Nonmarket Accounts." In *A New Architecture for the U.S. National Accounts*, edited by Dale W. Jorgenson, J. Steven Landefeld, and William D Nordhaus. Chicago: University of Chicago Press.
Nordhaus, William D., and Edward C. Kokkelenberg. 1999. *Natures' Numbers: Expanding the National Economic Accounts to Include the Environment*. Washington, DC: National Research Council.
Nordhaus, William D., and James Tobin. 1972. "Is Growth Obsolete?" In *Economic Research: Retrospect and Prospect* 5: 1–80. National Bureau of Economic Research.
OSTP, OMB, and DOC. 2023. *National Strategy to Develop Statistics For Environmental-Economic Decisions: A U.S. System of Natural Capital Accounting and Associated Environmental-Economic Statistics*. Edited by the Office of Science and Technology Policy, Office of Management and Budget, and Department of Commerce. Washington, DC: The White House.
Plummer, Mark L. 2009. "Assessing Benefit Transfer for the Valuation of Ecosystem Services." *Frontiers in Ecology and the Environment* 7 (1): 38–45.

Roosevelt, Theodore. 1910. "Conservation: Speech at Denver before the Colorado Live Stock Association." In *Compilation of the Messages and Speeches of Theodore Roosevelt*, edited by Alfred Henry Lewis. https://web.archive.org/web/20190503022606/http://theodore-roosevelt.com/images/research/txtspeeches/692.pdf.
Sefton, J. A., and M. R. Weale. 2006. "The Concept of Income in a General Equilibrium." *Review of Economic Studies* 73: 219–49.
Solow, Robert M. 1986. "On the Intergenerational Allocation of Natural Resources." *Scandinavian Journal of Economics* 88 (1): 141–49.
Stiglitz, Joseph E., Amartya Sen, and Jean-Paul Fitoussi. 2010. *Mis-measuring Our Lives: Why GDP Doesn't Add Up*. The report by the Commission on the Measurement of Economic Performance and Social Progress. New York: The New Press.
United Nations, European Union, Food and Agriculture Organization of the United Nations, International Monetary Fund, Organisation for Economic Co-operation and Development, and The World Bank. 2014. System of Environmental Economic Accounting 2012—Central Framework. United Nations.
United Nations et al. 2021. System of Environmental-Economic Accounting—Ecosystem Accounting (SEEA EA). New York: White cover publication, pre-edited text subject to official editing. https://seea.un.org/ecosystem-accounting.
United Nations Statistics Division, Intersecretariat Working Group on National Accounts. 2024. List of 2025 SNA Chapters. https://unstats.un.org/unsd/nationalaccount/snaupdate/2025/chapters.asp.
UNU-IHDP and UNEP. 2012. *Inclusive Wealth Report 2012, Measuring Progress toward Sustainability*. Cambridge: Cambridge University Press.
U.S. Government Accountability Office. 2007. Measuring our Nation's Natural Resources and Environmental Sustainability. GAO-08–127SP. October. Washington, DC: United States Government Accountability Office. https://www.gao.gov/assets/gao-08-127sp.pdf.
Weitzman, M. L. 1976. "On the Welfare Significance of National Product in a Dynamic Economy." *Quarterly Journal of Economics* 90 (1): 156–62.
World Bank. 2011. The Changing Wealth of Nations. Washington, DC: World Bank.
World Bank. 2005. *Where Is The Wealth Of Nations? Measuring Capital for the 21st Century*. Washington, DC: World Bank.

1

Incorporating Air and Water Pollution into the National Income and Product Accounts

Maureen L. Cropper and Yongjoon Park

1.1 Introduction

The concept of extending the National Income and Product Accounts to include the environment has been discussed for decades (Ahmad et al. 1989; Nordhaus and Kokkelenberg 1999). Much of the emphasis has been on valuing natural capital (e.g., water resources, forests and minerals); however, other studies have focused on pollution (Muller et al. 2011). In this paper we discuss the possibility of developing satellite accounts for local and global air pollution and water pollution. This would include core emissions accounts which describe emissions of key air and water pollutants by sector but also monetary estimates of the damages associated with these emissions.

Why is this important? The externalities associated with air and water pollution in the United States are substantial. Carbon dioxide (CO2) emissions in the US in 2020—5.8 gigatons of CO2—imposed damages of $1.12 trillion dollars (2020 USD) if valued using the USEPA's Social Cost of Carbon (USEPA 2022). The damages associated with air pollution from electric utilities were estimated to be $245 billion in 2010 (2014 USD), but fell to $133 billion in 2017 (2014 USD) (Holland et al. 2020). The value of damages

Maureen L. Cropper is Distinguished University Professor at the University of Maryland, a senior fellow of Resources for the Future, and a former member of the Board of Directors of the National Bureau of Economic Research.

Yongjoon Park is an assistant professor in the Resource Economics Department at the University of Massachusetts Amherst.

We thank Katherine Abraham, Matthew Chambers, David Evans, Eli Fenichel, Charles Griffiths, Peter Maniloff, Al McGartland, Nick Muller, and Scott Wentland for helpful comments. For acknowledgments, sources of research support, and disclosure of the authors' material financial relationships, if any, please see https://www.nber.org/books-and-chapters/measuring-and-accounting-environmental-public-goods-national-accounts-perspective/incorporating-air-and-water-pollution-national-income-and-product-accounts.

from local air pollution were 6.4 percent of GDP in 1999 but fell to 3.2 percent of GDP in 2008 due to improvements in air quality (Muller 2014). Measuring and valuing these externalities will help us as a nation determine how we are progressing in terms of our impacts on the environment.

In this paper we focus on developing satellite accounts for local air pollutants, including the criteria air pollutants,[1] greenhouse gases, and water pollution. In the case of local air pollution, we discuss the resources required to establish core air emissions accounts and the steps required to translate emissions into ambient pollution concentrations and value the impacts of ambient air pollution. Our discussion relies heavily on the pioneering work of Muller et al. (2011), whose evaluation of Gross External Damages associated with air pollution offers important insights into this process. We also discuss recent estimates by the USEPA of emission damages by sector for the criteria air pollutants (USEPA 2023a). In the case of greenhouse gas emissions, the Bureau of Economic Analysis has constructed pilot supply and use tables for the United States in 2017 (Chambers 2023). We present these estimates and discuss how they could be valued using the USEPA's Social Cost of Carbon.

Water pollution is more challenging. Whereas EPA constructs emissions inventories for greenhouse gas emissions and for the criteria air pollutants, inventories for water pollutants such as biochemical oxygen demand (BOD), phosphorus, and nitrogen are more difficult to establish. Progress is being made in modeling non-point source emissions and in estimating their impacts, but the ability to do this on a national scale is not as complete as for air pollution. We discuss what information is currently available to estimate the emissions and impacts of common water pollutants.

When discussing the value of air and water pollution damages we focus on methods currently employed by the USEPA. These methods, while consistent with the best practices of environmental economists, are not necessarily in agreement with the methodology of the National Income and Product Accounts (NIPA). We note areas where the two approaches may not be consistent with each other and where further research is required.

1.2 Satellite Accounts for Local Air Pollutants

Constructing satellite accounts for local air pollutants requires assembling a Core Emissions Account reporting emissions of key pollutants for industries and households. Table 1.1 illustrates a Core Emissions Account (United Nations 2016) for six common air pollutants. Nitrogen oxides (NOx), carbon monoxide (CO), sulfur dioxide (SO2), and fine particulate matter (PM2.5) are criteria pollutants. Ammonia (NH3) may combine with

1. The criteria air pollutants are carbon monoxide (CO), sulfur dioxide (SO2), nitrogen dioxide (NO2), ozone (O3), lead (Pb), and particulate matter (PM10 and PM2.5).

Table 1.1 **Core air emissions account (unit: tonnes)**

	Industries					Households		
	Agriculture	Mining	Manufacturing	Transport	Other	Transport	Heating	Other
Panel A: Local Air Pollutants								
NOx	69.4	6.0	37.9	259.5	89.0	38.0	12.1	1.3
CO	41.0	2.5	123.8	46.2	66.2	329.1	51.2	5.7
VOC	5.2	6.5	40.0	16.4	27.2	34.5	29.4	3.2
PM	7.0	0.1	8.5	9.3	4.4	6.0	2.8	0.5
NH3	107.9		1.7	0.2	0.9	2.3	11.4	1.2
SO2	2.7	0.4	28.0	62.4	8.1	0.4	0.4	0.1
Panel B: Greenhouse Gases								
Carbon Dioxide	10,610.3	2,602.2	41,434.4	27,957.0	82,402.4	18,920.5	17,542.2	1,949.1
Methane	492.0	34.1	15.8	0.8	21.9	2.4	15.5	1.7
N2O	23.7		3.5	0.8	2.6	1.0	0.2	0.1
F-GHGs			0.3		0.4			
Sulphur Hexafluoride								
Nitrogen Triflouride								

Source: Core Account 1 (United Nations 2016)

Note: This table illustrates the generation of air emissions by industries and households, by type of substance. Air emissions are broken down by industry sectors (i.e., agriculture, mining, manufacturing, and transport) and by household purposes (i.e., transport, heating, other). Pollutants are grouped by local and greenhouse gases. The reported local pollutants include nitrogen oxides (NOx), carbon monoxide (CO), volatile organic compounds (VOC), particulate matter (PM), ammonia (NH3), and sulfur dioxide (SO2). The reported pollutants for greenhouse gas emissions include carbon dioxide, methane, and nitrous oxide (N2O), fluorinated greenhouse gases (F-GHGs), sulphur hexafluoride, and nitrogen triflouride.

NOx and SO2 to form PM2.5; VOCs, when combined with NOx, form ground-level ozone (O3). The table also shows greenhouse gas emissions, including carbon dioxide, methane, and nitrous oxide (N2O), which are discussed in the next section.

The USEPA's National Emissions Inventory (NEI), which is published every three years, produces estimates of local air pollutants for both stationary and mobile sources. Estimates are produced for individual stationary sources (e.g., a power plant), and for area sources (e.g., dry cleaners and agricultural operations), road sources and off-road sources at the county level.

To monetize the impacts of these emissions requires translating emissions into changes in ambient air quality, estimating the effects of changes in ambient air quality on health and other end points, and then valuing these impacts. Using the 2002 NEI, Muller et al. (2011) estimated the impacts of the local pollutants listed in table 1.1 on mortality, morbidity, agricultural and timber yields, visibility. and recreation. We describe their results and discuss the insights that these estimates provide.

1.2.1 Muller, Mendelsohn, and Nordhaus Estimates of Gross External Damage

The goal of Muller, Mendelsohn, and Nordhaus (2011) was to provide a framework for estimating the externalities associated with air pollution. To do this, they combined the 2002 NEI with an Integrated Assessment Model (APEEP), which translated emissions of each of six pollutants, by county, into changes in ambient pollution throughout the United States.[2] The impacts of these pollutant changes were estimated using damage functions for various end points, and the damages valued in 2000 dollars.

To illustrate, suppose that a ton of PM2.5 is emitted at ground level in Los Angeles County.[3] A source-receptor matrix translates this emission into changes in ambient PM2.5 in Los Angeles County and in all other counties affected by this release. Together with data on population, the incidence of various health end points and dose-response functions, the impact of this ton can be translated into changes in mortality and morbidity in each county whose ambient air quality is affected by the ton emitted. These marginal changes in health end points can, in turn, be valued, and summed, to estimate the health damages caused by the ton of PM2.5 emitted at ground level in Los Angeles County. Damages associated with other impacts (e.g., on agriculture or on visibility) can be added to health damages.

Figures 1.1–1.3 show the outputs of the APEEP model for three pollutants: PM2.5, SO2 and VOCs (Muller and Mendelsohn 2009). Figure 1.1

2. APEEP, which translates emissions of PM2.5, PM10, VOCs, SO2, NOx, and NH3 into ambient concentrations, has also been used to estimate and value air pollution damages in Muller and Mendelsohn (2007) and Muller and Mendelsohn (2009).

3. In APEEP the impact of a ton of emissions depends on the height at which it is emitted, as well as the geographic location at which it is emitted.

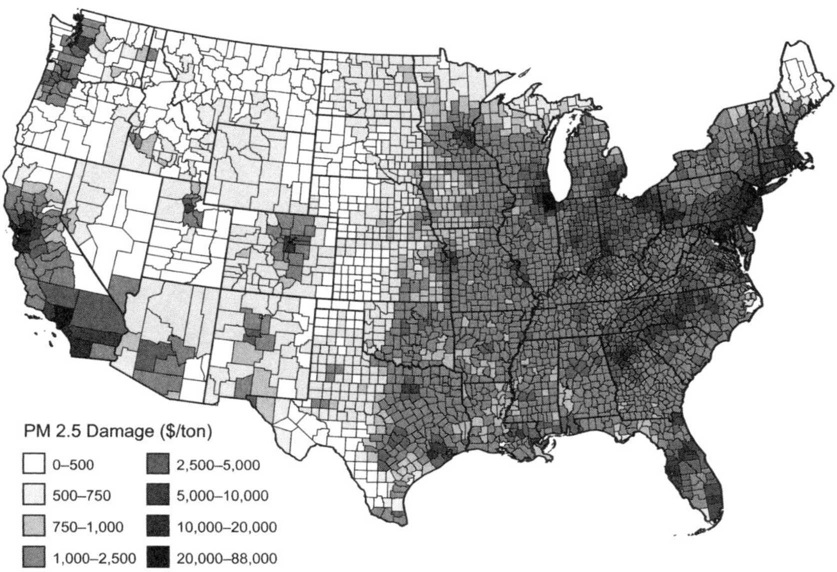

Figure 1.1 Marginal damages from ground-level PM2.5 emitted in 2002
Source: Muller and Mendelsohn (2009)
Note: This figure illustrates the geographical variation in marginal damages due to PM2.5 emitted in 2002. The unit of damage is dollar per ton per year, in 2000 USD.

shows the damages from emitting a ton of PM2.5 at ground level in each county in the US in 2002. Damage categories reflected in these estimates include mortality, morbidity, and damages to agriculture, forestry, and recreation. A ton of PM2.5 emitted at ground level in Los Angeles County imposes damages in excess of $20,000 (2000 USD). Damages from emitting PM2.5 are greatest when estimated in densely populated areas. The damages per ton of SO2 (figure 1.2) and per ton of VOCs (figure 1.3) are less than for PM2.5. This reflects the fact that the health effects associated with PM2.5 are greater than for SO2—although SO2 may combine with ammonia to form PM2.5. VOCs combine with NOx to form ground-level ozone (O3); however, the health damages associated with O3 (per μg/m3) are less costly than for PM2.5 (per μg/m3).

Muller et al. (2011) also identify the sectors responsible for the largest air pollution damages and the damage categories that account for the majority of damages. Table 1.2 presents estimates of Gross External Damages (GED) by sector, as well as the ratio of GED to value added by sector. Electric utilities—dominated in 2002 by coal-fired power plants—account for one-third of total GED. Together, agriculture and forestry, electric utilities, transportation, and manufacturing account for 78 percent of GED. Table 1.3 elaborates on the damages of emissions from coal-fired power

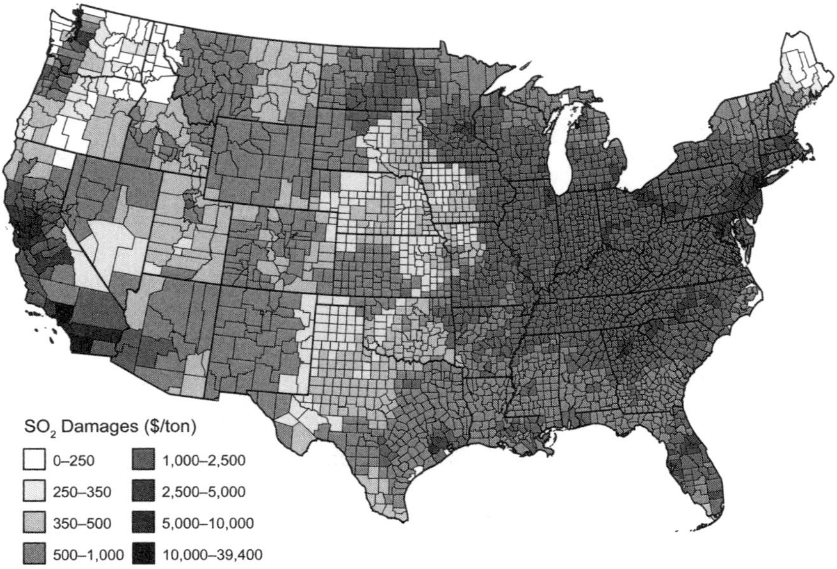

Figure 1.2 Marginal damages from ground-level SO2 emitted in 2002
Source: Muller and Mendelsohn (2009)
Note: This figure illustrates the geographical variation in marginal damages due to SO2 emitted in 2002. The unit of damage is dollar per ton per year, in 2000 USD.

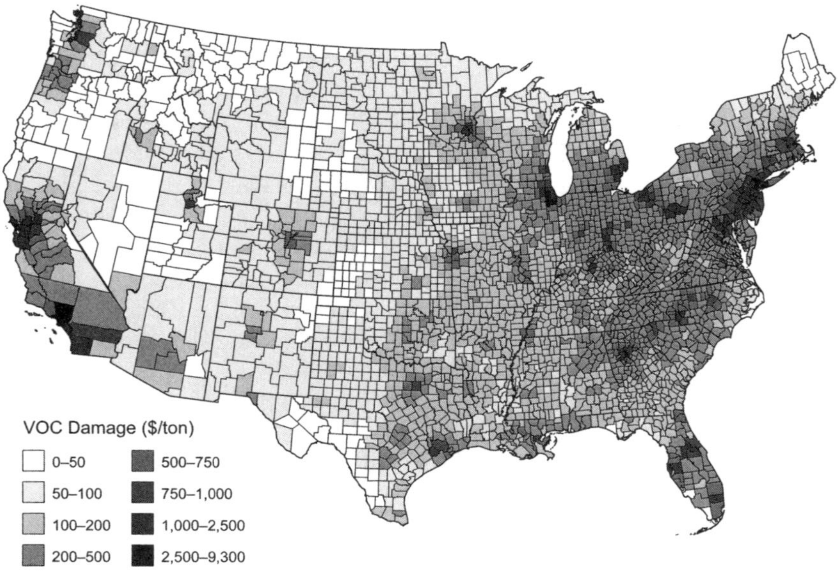

Figure 1.3 Marginal damages from ground-level VOCs emitted in 2002
Source: Muller and Mendelsohn (2009)
Note: This figure illustrates the geographical variation in marginal damages due to VOCs emitted in 2002. The unit of damage is dollar per ton per year, in 2000 USD.

Table 1.2 Gross External Damages and GED/VA ratio by sector

Sector	GED	GED/VA
Agriculture and forestry	32.0	0.38
Utilities	62.6	0.34
Transportation	23.2	0.10
Administrative, waste management, and remediation services	10.7	0.08
Construction	14.7	0.03
Arts, entertainment, and recreation	2.2	0.03
Accommodation and food services	4.2	0.02
Mining	3.3	0.02
Manufacturing	26.4	0.01
Other services	1.0	0.01
Wholesale trade	1.2	0.00
Retail trade	1.7	0.00
Information	0.0	0.00
Finance and insurance	0.0	0.00
Real estate services	0.0	0.00
Professional, scientific, and technical services	0.0	0.00
Management	0.0	0.00
Educational services	0.0	0.00
Health care services	0.7	0.00
Total all sectors	184.0	

Source: Table 1 of Muller et al. (2011)

Note: The table presents data on Gross External Damages (GED) and its ratio to Value Added (VA) for different sectors of the economy in the year 2002. GED is measured in billions of dollars per year (in 2000 USD).

plants. The table reports damages by pollutant and also by category of damage. Emissions of SO2, which are converted into PM2.5, account for 86 percent of power-plant damages. Damages, by category, are dominated by premature mortality, which accounts for 95 percent of damages.

How is premature mortality valued? Muller et al. (2011) value premature mortality using the USEPA's estimate of the Value per Statistical Life (VSL). The VSL is the amount that people would pay to reduce their risk of death by a small amount, aggregated over risks that sum to one statistical life. For example, if each of 10,000 people would pay $200 to reduce their risk of death by 1 in 10,000, the VSL equals 10,000 x $200 or $2 million. EPA's estimate of the VSL is based primarily on hedonic labor market studies, which measure the compensation that workers receive for working in riskier jobs. The VSL is, therefore, based on market prices. EPA's estimate of the VSL, in 2000 dollars, is $6.3 million (USEPA 2023a). The VSL, as applied by EPA, does not vary with age at death: it values the death of a 40-year-old the same as the death of a 70-year-old.

The estimates of GED in tables 1.2 and 1.3 value premature deaths by life-years lost. Muller et al. (2011) take the USEPA's VSL and divide it by the discounted remaining life expectancy of a 40-year-old (the average age of workers in compensating wage studies) to compute a Value per Statisti-

Table 1.3 **GED for coal-fired power plants by pollutant and type of damage**

Pollutant/welfare end point	SO2	PM2.5	PM10	Nox	VOC	NH3	Total
Mortality	44.2	3.53	0	2.75	0.03	0.09	50.6
Morbidity	1.64	0.03	0.12	0.18	0	0	1.97
Agriculture	0	0	0	0.37	0	0	0.37
Timber	0	0	0	0.02	0	0	0.02
Materials	0.06	0	0	0	0	0	0.06
Visibility	0.22	0.01	0.02	0.02	0	0	0.26
Recreation	0	0	0	0	0	0	0
Total	46.12	3.57	0.14	3.34	0.03	0.09	53.4

Source: Table 4 of Muller et al. (2011)

Note: The table shows the gross external damages (GED) of emissions from coal-fired power plants in the year 2002. The table reports damages by pollutant and also by category of damage. The damage is measured in billions of dollars per year (in 2000 USD).

cal Life Year (VSLY). Premature deaths are valued using the number of life years lost multiplied by the VSLY. How does this affect estimates of GED, compared to using a VSL that does not vary with age? Using the VSLY, total air pollution damages are 184 billion 2000 USD (1.8 percent of 2002 GDP). Using the VSL, air pollution damages increase to 460 billion 2000 USD (4.4 percent of 2002 GDP). These figures illustrate the importance of how mortality is valued in estimating air pollution damages.

1.2.2 USEPA Estimates of Air Pollution Damages per Ton of Pollutant

In 2022, EPA released estimates of the cost per ton of pollutant for 21 sectors and five pollutants using the 2017 NEI.[4] Air quality modeling was used to estimate source-receptor matrices for each sector-pollutant combination at a 12 × 12 km resolution (USEPA 2023a). To illustrate, figures 1.4–1.6 show estimated impacts of emissions from oil and gas extraction on annual average PM2.5 and maximum daily 8-hour ozone (averaged over the summer ozone season), and the estimated impacts of emissions from woodburning stoves on annual average PM2.5. Oil and gas extraction in areas around extraction sites (figure 1.4) was estimated to raise ambient PM2.5 by as much as 0.2 μg/m3, and in some cases, 0.3 μg/m3. To put these numbers in perspective, the annual average PM2.5 standard is 12 μg/m3. The impact of woodburning stoves on PM2.5 (figure 1.6) is even greater, raising PM2.5 by over 0.3 μg/m3 in some areas. The impacts of oil and gas extraction on ground-level ozone (figure 1.5) extend over larger areas than the PM2.5 impacts because ozone can travel for hundreds of miles. In Texas and surrounding states, ozone concentrations were estimated to increase by 5 ppb. To put this in perspective, the 8-hour ozone standard is 70 ppb.

The impacts of changes in ambient concentrations on pollution damage

4. See USEPA (2023a, 2023b).

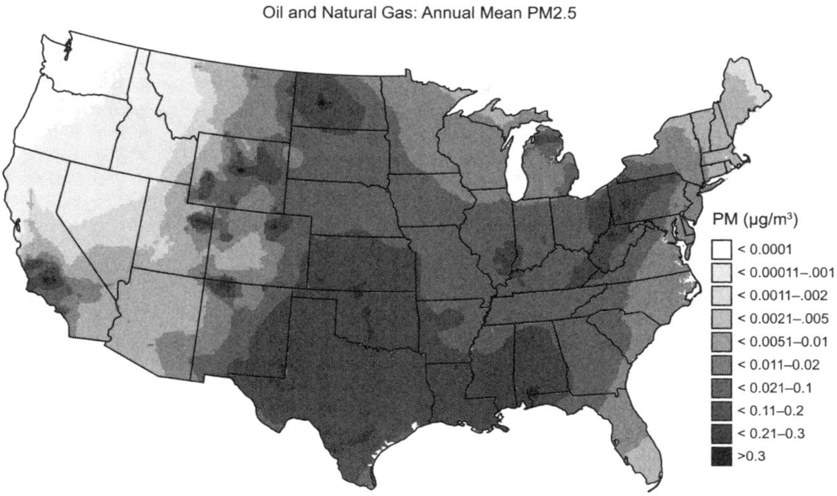

Figure 1.4 Impact on ambient PM2.5 of oil and gas extraction

Source: USEPA (2023a)

Note: This figure visualizes the estimated impacts of emissions from oil and gas extraction on annual average ambient PM2.5 in the United States, measured in µg/m3.

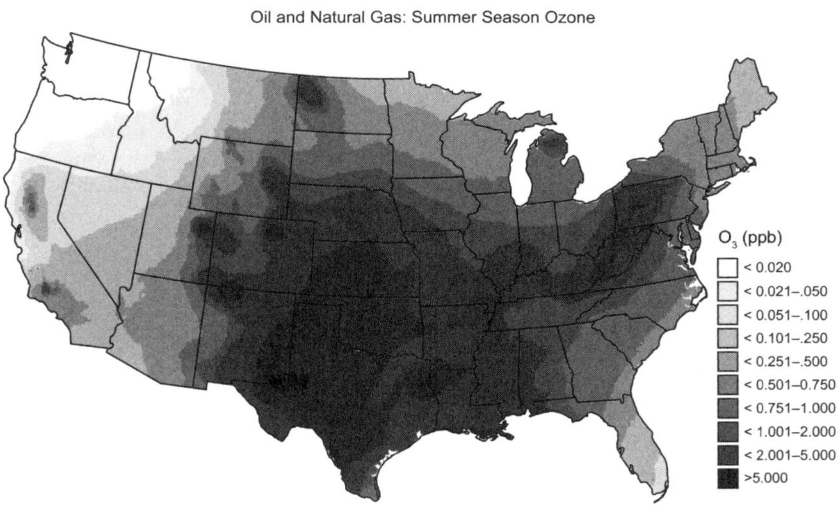

Figure 1.5 Impact on ambient ozone of oil and gas extraction

Source: USEPA (2023a)

Note: This figure visualizes the estimated impacts of emissions from oil and gas extraction on the average of daily maximum 8-hour ambient ozone during the summer ozone season, measured in ppb.

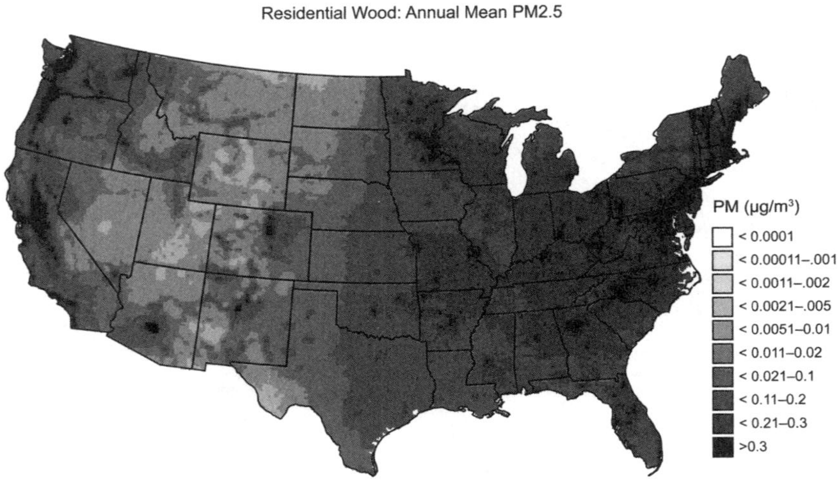

Figure 1.6 Impact on ambient PM2.5 of woodburning stoves
Source: USEPA (2023a)
Note: This figure visualizes the estimated impacts of emissions from woodburning stoves on annual average ambient PM2.5 in the United States, measured in µg/m3.

were also estimated at a 12 × 12 km resolution using the USEPA's BenMAP, an Integrated Assessment Model that links changes in ambient air pollution concentrations to health and other end points and then values these end points (Sacks et al. 2018; USEPA 2023b). Although BenMAP covers all of the pollutants and end points in table 1.2, over 98 percent of the monetized damages associated with emissions come from the mortality impacts of PM2.5 and ozone. These impacts were monetized using a VSL of 10.7 million 2016 dollars.

Table 1.4 illustrates estimated pollution damages by sector and pollutant. PM2.5 damages come from directly emitted PM2.5, or from secondary PM2.5, formed when SO2 or NOx combines with ammonia. Air quality modeling has been used to trace secondary PM2.5 back to its precursors. The same has been done for ozone precursors. Marginal damages associated with emissions of each pollutant have been averaged across all locations in the United States. Marginal health damages associated with any pollutant are greater if the emissions occur near densely populated areas. This explains the high damages per ton of directly emitted PM2.5 for residential wood stoves (see figure 1.6) and refineries compared to oil and natural gas extraction (see figure 1.4). The lower damages per ton for ozone precursors reflect the fact that the mortality impacts of ozone are lower per unit than for PM2.5 (USEPA 2023a). The higher damages associated with NOx

Table 1.4 **Summary of the total damages (mortality and morbidity) per ton in 2025, by sector**

	PM2.5-Related Benefits				Ozone-Related Benefits	
Sector	Direct PM2.5	SO2	NOx	NH3	NOx	VOC
Oil and Natural Gas	\$97,900	\$19,400	\$8,080	\$23,900	\$44,900	\$1,680
Oil and Natural Gas Transmission	\$138,000	\$29,800	\$13,700	\$73,400	\$61,200	\$7,490
Pulp and Paper	\$145,000	\$39,300	\$11,200	\$51,100	\$75,700	\$2,130
Refineries	\$368,000	\$50,900	\$23,100	\$112,000	\$57,500	\$11,500
Residential Woodstoves	\$473,000	\$34,600	\$33,100	\$200,000	\$39,000	\$12,300
Synthetic Organic Chemical	\$140,000	\$42,800	\$17,000	\$71,200	\$70,300	\$5,540
Taconite Mining	\$60,600	\$32,800	\$9,230	—	\$45,800	\$29,600
Electricity Generating Units	\$137,000	\$73,000	\$6,400	—	\$111,000	—
Brick Kilns	\$227,000	\$44,000	\$26,900	\$130,000	\$78,800	\$10,700
Cement Kilns	\$157,000	\$42,300	\$14,600	\$63,900	\$68,900	\$16,900
Coke Ovens	\$281,000	\$53,500	\$25,600		\$61,500	\$33,400
Ferroalloy Facilities	\$151,000	\$45,300	\$15,600		\$95,900	\$7,230
Industrial Boilers	\$192,000	\$42,300	\$15,200	\$85,600	\$64,800	\$13,200
Integrated Iron & Steel	\$384,000	\$53,700	\$23,600	\$190,000	\$69,900	\$13,300
Internal Combustion Engines	\$166,000	\$38,700	\$10,700	\$75,300	\$54,800	\$8,510
Iron and Steel Foundries	\$261,000	\$54,300	\$24,000		\$84,700	\$7,410

Source: USEPA (2023b)

Note: The table illustrates pollution damages (mortality and morbidity) per ton of directly emitted PM2.5 and PM2.5 precursors produced by sector in 2025. Similar figures are produced for ozone precursors. The unit is 2016 USD and 3 percent of the discount rate is used for this calculation.

precursors of ozone reflects the fact that in many areas, ozone production is NOx limited.[5]

1.2.3 Implications for the NIPA

The material we have reviewed suggests that the United States should be able to construct preliminary satellite accounts for local air pollutants. Constructing satellite accounts for local air pollutants requires estimates of emissions of each pollutant by sector. It should be possible to do this for the criteria air pollutants using the National Emissions Inventory, which is issued every three years. Monetizing these damages requires that emissions estimates be made at a fine enough spatial scale to be translated into levels of ambient air pollution which can, in turn, be monetized and valued. Air quality modeling can then be used to translate damages back to the source of emissions. This is currently being done by the USEPA, focusing on the

5. Ground-level ozone is formed when oxides of nitrogen (NOx) combine with volatile organic compounds (VOCs) in the presence of sunlight. When NOx is the limiting factor in this reaction, we say that ozone is NOx limited. In this case, reducing NOx will reduce ozone formation.

impact of emissions of directly emitted PM, NOx, SO2, VOCs, and ammonia on PM2.5 and ground-level ozone.

As noted above, premature mortality accounts for the vast majority of monetized damages from local air pollution, and is valued using the Value per Statistical Life, estimated based on compensating wage studies. This raises two issues. The VSL values the present value of lost utility from dying in a particular year. Thus, it values the present value of a flow of damages from pollution and represents the value of a stock. In the NIPA, the flow of services from a durable good (a stock) are not credited to GDP in the year the good is produced; rather, the flow of services from the stock are credited to GDP in the year in which they occur. Thus, there is a stock-flow issue that must be addressed.

The second issue deals with the extrapolation of the VSL from compensating wage studies to the general population. Compensating wage studies measure the value that workers place on mortality risks—i.e., the amount they must be compensated to bear additional risk of death on the job. The fact that this value is based on market transactions is acceptable to the NIPA; however, it measures the value to the people who bear the risks. It is not clear that this value may be extrapolated to people who do not bear the risks, as an estimate of the value they place on mortality risks.

1.3 Satellite Accounts for Global Air Pollution

EPA produces annual estimates of global air pollutants, including carbon dioxide, methane, and nitrous oxide, implying that it is possible to construct a core air emissions table (see table 1.1) for greenhouse gas (GHG) emissions. A pilot supply and use table (table 1.5) prepared by the Bureau of Economic

Table 1.5 **2017 Supply and Use table for GHGs**

Sector	Total GWP	Sector	Total GWP
Agriculture	611.83	Professional	15.79
Mining	300.02	Management	9.79
Utilities	2152.34	Administrative	180.61
Construction	46.49	Education	7
Manufacturing	1,028.84	Health Care	22.85
Wholesale	67.66	Entertainment	2.54
Retail	91.91	Hospitality	34.64
Transportation	657.49	Other Services	18.88
Information	8.1	Government	33.25
Finance	9.61	Households	1,108.21
Real Estate	24.03	Total Supply	6,431.87

Source: Table 1 of Chambers (2023)

Note: This supply and use table shows the sources of greenhouse gas emissions in 2017 by sector. Units, reflecting global warming potential (GWP) are megatonnes of CO2 equivalent.

Analysis (Chambers 2023), shows the sources of GHG emissions in 2017, by sector. Utilities, manufacturing, and households together account for two-thirds of the 6.4 billion tons of CO2e emitted in 2017. Note that in table 1.5, emissions of individual GHGs have been weighted by their global warming potential.[6] Of the 6.4 billion tons of CO2e emitted in 2017, 79 percent came from carbon dioxide, 11 percent from methane, and 6 percent from nitrous oxide (USEPA 2022).

These emissions could be valued using the USEPA's Social Cost of Carbon, Social Cost of Methane, and Social Cost of Nitrous Oxide (USEPA 2022). To explain how these estimates are calculated, we focus on the Social Cost of Carbon (SCC). The SCC measures the present value of the net damages from emitting a ton of CO2 in a particular year. Due to the long residence times of CO2 in the atmosphere—30 percent of a ton of CO2 emitted today will remain in the atmosphere in the year 2300 (Joos et al. 2013)—estimating the SCC requires predicting what the world will look like in the future. EPA's estimates of the SCC follow the approach suggested by the National Research Council (National Academies of Sciences, Engineering, and Medicine 2017): A socioeconomic module is used to construct probability distributions over future paths of population, per capita GDP and GHG emissions; a climate module translates future emissions paths into paths of mean global temperature, downscaled to estimate regional temperatures and impacts on sea level rise; a damages module relates changes in temperature associated with a pulse of CO2 to damages along each socioeconomic pathway. Along each pathway, damages are discounted to the present, to yield a probability distribution of SCC values. The mean of this distribution, referred to as the SCC, is used to value CO2 emissions.

EPA's most recent estimates of the SCC rely on different sources for their damage estimates: the RFF GIVE model (Rennert et al. 2022), the Data-driven Spatial Climate Impact Model (DSCIM) damage estimates from the Climate Impact Lab (Climate Impact Lab), and a meta-analysis of damage estimates by Howard and Sterner (2017). These damage estimates encompass the impacts of temperature on mortality, on agriculture, on sea level rise, energy and labor productivity. These damages are global damages. The impacts of temperature on premature mortality, which comprise 73 percent of damages in DCSIM model and 47 percent of damages in the GIVE model, are valued using a VSL of 10.05 million 2020 USD, which is extrapolated to other countries based on per capita GDP, using an income elasticity of one.

Estimates of the SCC provided by all three models are given in table 1.6. EPA discounts future damages along each socio-economic pathway using a

6. Global warming potential (GWP) measures how much energy a ton of GHG will absorb over a given time period; i.e., how much radiative forcing it will generate, relative to a ton of carbon dioxide (CO2). The CO2e of a gas is calculated by weighting its mass by its GWP.

Table 1.6 **Social cost of CO2, 2020–2050**

	Damage Module		
Emission Year	DSCIM	GIVE	Meta-Analysis
2020	190	190	200
2030	230	220	240
2040	280	250	270
2050	330	290	310

Source: USEPA (2022)

Note: This table shows the estimates of the Social Cost of Carbon in 2020–2050 using three different models: (i) the Data-driven Spatial Climate Impact Model (DSCIM); (ii) damage estimates from the RFF GIVE model; and (iii) a meta-analysis of damage estimates by Howard and Sterner (2017). The unit is 2020 USD per metric tons of CO2. A near-term Ramsey discount rate of 2 percent is used for the calculations.

Ramsey formula.[7] Parameters of the formula are chosen so that near-term discount rates equal 1.5 percent, 2 percent or 2.5 percent. The preferred estimates of the SCC, shown in table 1.6, use Ramsey parameters tied to a 2 percent near-term discount rate. The SCC in 2020, averaged across the three models, is $193 (2020 USD). This implies that the damages associated with US emissions of CO2 in 2020 were approximately 1.12 trillion dollars. Note that the SCC increases over time because the CO2 emitted occurs in a warmer, richer world. To illustrate: the SCC associated with a ton emitted in 2030 is $230 (2020 USD) and $267 (2020 USD) for a ton emitted in 2040.

Social costs have also been estimated for methane and nitrous oxide. Due to the greater GWP of these gases, and the fact that their impacts occur closer to the present, the social cost of a ton of methane emitted in 2020 is $1,648 and the social cost of a ton of nitrous oxide emitted in 2020 is $54,139.

1.3.1 Implications for the NIPA

The methods used to estimate and value damages in computing the SCC raise issues similar to those discussed in valuing local pollutants, as well as new issues. Because the SCC values the damage from emitting a ton of CO2 today as the present value of the flow of damages it generates, i.e., using a stock concept, this raises the stock-flow issues discussed above. In terms of the categories of damages valued, heat-related mortality is valued using the US VSL, extrapolated to other countries using an income elasticity of one. This raises the extrapolation issues discussed above. It is also important to

7. The Ramsey formula discounts damages at time t to the present using a discount rate = $\rho + \eta g(t)$, where g(t) is the rate of per capita income growth at time t. Criteria for choosing the parameters ρ and η are described in USEPA (2022).

check that all damage estimates reflect marginal prices, rather than consumer surplus.[8]

A more serious issue from the perspective of the NIPA is whether it is appropriate to include in the satellite account damages from US CO2 emissions that occur in other countries. The damages from local air pollution discussed in section 1.2 are damages from emissions in the United States that occur in the United States. Damages in the USEPA's SCC are global damages. Whether these can be included in satellite accounts remains to be determined.

1.4 Satellite Accounts for Water Pollution

Constructing satellite accounts for water pollution requires estimates of water pollutants by sector. Table 1.7 shows a physical supply table for gross releases of substances to water, by sector, including BOD, suspended solids, heavy metals, phosphorous, and nitrogen. What are the sources of such releases in the United States? The National Pollutant Discharge Elimination System (NPDES) covers emissions from point sources, including animal feeding operations, fish farms, industrial operations, including mining and oil and gas drilling, stormwater discharges, and municipal wastewater treatment facilities. Discharges from these sources are collected in Discharge Monitoring Reports (USEPA 2023c), available by state and year.

Substances released to water from non-point sources (e.g., agricultural runoff) are often modeled using EPA's Hydrologic and Water Quality System (HAWQS).[9] HAWQS simulates the effects of management practices for a variety of crops, soils, natural vegetation types, and land uses, to generate estimates of sediment, pathogens, nutrients, BOD, dissolved oxygen, pesticides, and water temperature. Currently, HAWQS is not used to generate annual estimates of non-point source releases, by state and sector, similar to the data that are available in the NPDES.

To estimate the impact of all releases to rivers and streams on ambient water quality, releases from point sources may be added to HAWQS and the model used to generate estimates of ambient water quality (e.g., dissolved oxygen, total suspended solids, BOD, nitrogen, phosphorous and fecal coliform). This is usually done at the watershed level.[10] The change in damages associated with a change in ambient water quality is then estimated

8. Estimates of agricultural damages in the GIVE model reflect consumer and producer surplus associated with changes in yields from temperature changes.

9. Hydrologic and Water Quality System (Version 2.0 BETA), A National Watershed and Water Quality Assessment Tool, https://hawqs.tamu.edu/#/.

10. Currently, about 30 percent of eight-digit hydrologic unit code (HUC-8) watersheds in the United States and about 25 percent of four-digit HUCs have been calibrated in HAWQS (USEPA 2017a; USEPA 2017b).

Table 1.7 **Physical supply table for gross releases of substances to water**

	Generation of gross releases to water			Accumulation	Flows with the rest of the world	Flows from the environment	Total supply
	Sewerage Industry	Other Industries	Households	Emissions from fixed assets			
	Emissions received by the environment						
BOD	5,594	11,998	2,712				20,304
Suspended solids							
Heavy metals							
Phosphorus	836	1,587	533				2,956
Nitrogen	10,033	47,258	1,908				59,199

Source: United Nations (2012)

Note: Table 1.7 is a physical supply table for gross releases of substances to water by sector. The figures are reported in tonnes.

and valued using BenSPLASH: the water quality counterpart to BenMAP (Corona et al. 2020).

Valuing changes in ambient water quality is more difficult than valuing changes in air quality. The majority of monetized air pollution damages are associated with two pollutants—PM2.5 and ozone—and over 90 percent of monetized damages are associated with the mortality impacts of these pollutants. Measures of water quality such as dissolved oxygen, total suspended solids, BOD, nitrogen, phosphorous, fecal coliform, are associated with a variety of end points: improved commercial and recreational fishing, improved swimming and boating, improved aesthetic benefits, and ecosystem services. Whereas the same exposure-response functions relating PM2.5 to mortality can be applied to everyone in the United States, the impact of dissolved oxygen on commercial fishing will vary from one location to another, as will the recreational benefits of cleaner water.

To deal with the multiplicity of pollutants and benefit categories, BenSPLASH combines six measures of water quality—dissolved oxygen, fecal coliform, nitrogen, phosphorous, BOD, and total suspended solids—into a water quality index (WQI). Stated preference valuation functions are combined in a meta-regression to estimate willingness to pay for changes in the WQI (USEPA 2015). Specifically, EPA has combined 51 stated preference studies that value water quality changes affecting ecosystem services provided by water bodies, including recreational fishing, boating and swimming, aquatic life support, and nonuse values.[11] Willingness to pay is computed for all households within the watershed where changes in water quality are evaluated (Corona et al. 2020).

BenSPLASH uses benefits transfer and stated preference studies to derive a valuation function for water quality benefits that can be applied nationally. Because the NIPA rely on market transactions as measures of value, stated preference estimates would not be admissible in the satellite accounts. Alternatives that have been proposed to measuring water quality benefits using market prices have focused on examining the capitalization of water quality into housing prices (Guignet et al. 2019; Keiser and Shapiro 2018), and impacts of water quality on commercial fisheries. These approaches cannot, however, capture all of the benefits of improved water quality.

1.5 Conclusion

The purpose of this paper has been to provide a brief review of the data that are available on emissions of air and water pollutants in the United States and the attempts that have been made to value the damages associ-

11. Nonuse values represent the benefits of knowing that a resource continues to exist even though an individual may never use it personally. Nonuse values are generally estimated using stated rather than revealed preference methods.

ated with these pollutants. This is only the beginning of constructing satellite accounts for air and water pollution. We have not discussed the expenditures by consumers and firms that are made to reduce pollution, nor have we discussed which categories of damages are already incorporated in the National Income and Product Accounts (e.g., damages to commercial fisheries from water pollution), although these could also be incorporated in satellite accounts.

Quantifying pollution emissions and valuing pollution damages would, however, serve to highlight the importance of these externalities, most of which are not captured in the National Income and Produce Accounts. They would also serve as a complement to the environmental activity accounts being developed by the BEA (Fixler et al. 2023), which value economic activities whose "primary purpose is to reduce or eliminate pressures on the environment."

One way to begin would be to create satellite accounts for local and global air pollution. For local air pollution, emissions of criteria air pollutants or their precursors are available through the National Emissions Inventory by sector and geographic location. EPA currently provides estimates of the mortality and morbidity damages from these pollutants, for 21 sectors. In the case of greenhouse gas emissions, the BEA has already produced a proof-of-concept Physical Flows Account for GHGs (Chambers 2023). These emissions could be valued using the federal Social Cost of Carbon, Social Cost of Methane, and Social Cost of Nitrous Oxide, although adjustments to current estimates of the Social Cost of Carbon, Social Cost of Methane, and Social Cost of Nitrous Oxide would likely be necessary, for reasons discussed above. Producing physical flows accounts for water pollution emissions and estimates of their damages is, however, a task for the future.

References

Ahmad, Y. J., S. El Serafy, and E. Lutz. 1989. *Environmental Accounting for Sustainable Development*. Washington, DC: World Bank.

Chambers, M. 2023. "Proof of Concept for a U.S. Air Emissions Physical Flows Account." BEA Working Papers, April. Washington, DC: Bureau of Economic Analysis.

Climate Impact Lab. "Data-Driven Spatial Climate Impact Model User Manual, Version 092022." Data-driven Spatial Climate Impact Model User Manual, Version 092022. Accessed 11/02/2023. https://impactlab.org/research/dscim-user-manual-version-092022-epa/.

Corona, J., T. Doley, C. Griffiths, M. Massey, C. Moore, S. Muela, B. Rashleigh, W. Wheeler, S. D. Whitlock, and J. Hewitt. 2020. "An Integrated Assessment Model for Valuing Water Quality Changes in the U.S." *Land Economics* 96: 478–92.

Fixler, D., Julie L. Hass, Tina Highfill, Kelly Wentland, and Scott Wentland. 2023. "Accounting for Environmental Activity: Measuring Public Environmental

Expenditures and the Environmental Goods and Services Sector in the US." National Bureau of Economic Research.
Guignet, D., M. T. Heberling, M. Papenfus, O. Griot, B. Holland, D. Guignet, M. T. Heberling, M. Papenfus, O. Griot, and B. Holland. 2019. "Property Values and Water Quality: A Nationwide Meta-Analysis and the Implications for Benefit Transfer." Working Paper.
Holland, S. P., E. T. Mansur, N. Z. Muller, and A. J. Yates. 2020. "Decompositions and Policy Consequences of an Extraordinary Decline in Air Pollution from Electricity Generation." *American Economic Journal: Economic Policy* 12: 244–74.
Howard, P. H., and T. Sterner. 2017. "Few and Not So Far Between: A Meta-analysis of Climate Damage Estimates." *Environmental & Resource Economics* 68: 197–225.
Joos, F., R. Roth, J. S. Fuglestvedt, G. P. Peters, I. G. Enting, W. von Bloh, V. Brovkin, et al. 2013. "Carbon Dioxide and Climate Impulse Response Functions for the Computation of Greenhouse Gas Metrics: A Multi-Model Analysis." *Atmospheric Chemistry and Physics* 13: 2793–2825.
Keiser, D. A., and J. S. Shapiro. 2018. "Consequences of the Clean Water Act and the Demand for Water Quality." *Quarterly Journal of Economics* 134: 349–96.
Muller, N. Z. 2014. "Boosting GDP Growth by Accounting for the Environment." *Science* 345: 873–4.
Muller, N. Z., and R. Mendelsohn. 2007. "Measuring the Damages of Air Pollution in the United States." *Journal of Environmental Economics and Management* 54: 1–14.
———. 2009. "Efficient Pollution Regulation: Getting the Prices Right." *American Economic Review* 99: 1714–39.
Muller, N. Z., R. Mendelsohn, and W. Nordhaus. 2011. "Environmental Accounting for Pollution in the United States Economy." *American Economic Review* 101: 1649–75.
National Academies of Sciences, Engineering, and Medicine, Division of Behavioral and Social Sciences and Education, Board on Environmental Change and Society, and Committee on Assessing Approaches to Updating the Social Cost of Carbon. 2017. *Valuing Climate Damages: Updating Estimation of the Social Cost of Carbon Dioxide*. Washington, DC: National Academies Press.
Nordhaus, W. D., and E. C. Kokkelenberg. 1999. *Nature's Numbers: Expanding the National Economic Accounts to Include the Environment*. Washington, DC: National Academies Press.
Rennert, K., F. Errickson, B. C. Prest, L. Rennels, R. G. Newell, W. Pizer, C. Kingdon, et al. 2022. "Comprehensive Evidence Implies a Higher Social Cost of CO2." *Nature* 610: 687–92.
Sacks, J. D., J. M. Lloyd, Y. Zhu, J. Anderton, C. J. Jang, B. Hubbell, and N. Fann. 2018. "The Environmental Benefits Mapping and Analysis Program—Community Edition (BenMAP–CE): A Tool to Estimate the Health and Economic Benefits of Reducing Air Pollution." *Environmental Modelling & Software* 104: 118–29.
United Nations. 2012. SEEA-Water System of Environmental Economic Accounting for Water. Department of Economic and Social Affairs, Statistics Division, New York.
———. 2016. SEEA System of Environmental Economic Accounting—Technical Note: Air Emissions Accounting. July.
USEPA. 2015. Benefit and Cost Analysis for the Effluent Limitations Guidelines and Standards for the Steam Electric Power Generating Point Source Category (Appendix H).
———. 2017a. "HAWQS v1.0 Calibration Process." Accessed 11/02/2023. https://hawqs.tamu.edu/content/docs/calibration/HAWQS-Calibration-Methodology.pdf#/.

———. 2017b. “HAWQS (Hydrologic and Water Quality System).” Accessed 11/02/2023. https://www.epa.gov/waterdata/hawqs-hydrologic-and-water-quality-system.

———. 2022. Report on the Social Cost of Greenhouse Gases: Estimates Incorporating Recent Scientific Advances. National Center for Environmental Economics, Office of Policy, September.

———. 2023a. Estimating the Benefit per Ton of Reducing Directly-Emitted PM 2.5, PM 2.5 Precursors and Ozone Precursors from 21 Sectors. USEPA Office of Air and Radiation, September.

———. 2023b. “Sector-Based PM2.5 Benefit Per Ton Estimates.” USEPA BenMAP. Accessed 11/02/2023. https://www.epa.gov/benmap/sector-based-pm25-benefit-ton-estimates.

———. 2023c. “ICIS-NPDES Permit Limit and Discharge Monitoring Report (DMR) Datasets.” ICIS-NPDES Permit Limit and Discharge Monitoring Report (DMR) Datasets. Accessed 11/02/2023. https://echo.epa.gov/tools/data-downloads/icis-npdes-dmr-and-limit-data-set.

2

Measuring for the Future, Not the Past

Matthew Agarwala, Diane Coyle, Cristina Peñasco, and Dimitri Zenghelis

2.1 Introduction: The Measurement Challenge and Missing Capitals

Climate change has been described as "the greatest market failure the world has ever seen" (Stern 2007). It results from a combination of multiple and dynamic market failures, with implications for every field of economics, including labor, health, finance, fiscal and monetary stability, and productivity. Yet the climatological and ecological fundamentals are largely absent from the statistics that economists might use to model and assess the consequences of climate change or biodiversity loss. Economic analysis is significantly inadequate if trade statistics ignore the depletion of natural capital, asset pricing models ignore ecological risks, and productivity measurement ignores risks and impacts due to air pollution and temperature extremes. Useful economic models and predictions need appropriate data.

The conventions, definitions, and assumptions that underpin conventional economic measurement largely reflect the System of National Account's (SNA) origins as a framework for macroeconomic policy developed in a wartime context (Coyle 2014). They exclude many natural assets because they lie outside the asset boundary (because they are not owned) or the production boundary (because the activities in question are not carried out by an institutional unit with ownership rights) or because they cross national

Matthew Agarwala is a senior research associate at the Bennett Institute for Public Policy at the University of Cambridge.

Diane Coyle is the Bennett Professor of Public Policy at the University of Cambridge and codirector of the Bennett Institute for Public Policy.

Cristina Peñasco is an associate professor in public policy at the Department of Politics and International Studies at the University of Cambridge.

Dimitri Zenghelis is a special advisor at the Bennett Institute for Public Policy at the University of Cambridge.

boundaries and ownership rights are not feasible (SNA 2009, 1D). This framework was developed at a time when natural resources seemed relatively abundant, and when—for many people—the natural world seemed stable. Measurement of changes in the environment outside the SNA production and asset boundaries were not a pressing concern.

The situation has changed dramatically since the 2008 revision of the SNA. The effects of human activity on economically vital aspects of the natural world are demonstrable and unsustainable. Even as the 2025 revision of the SNA is under way, there have been significant changes in economic measurement. The Dasgupta Review on the Economics of Biodiversity forcefully stated the case for incorporating measures of natural capital into economic statistics (Dasgupta 2021). It is also reflected in the development of the System of Environmental Economic Accounting (SEEA) as the formal UN standard for natural capital accounting, the UN's Statistics Commission's 2021 adoption of statistical standards for ecosystem accounting, and the development of natural capital accounts by some National Statistical Offices (NSOs), including the United Kingdom and the United States.

The revision of the System of National Accounts underway and due for publication in 2025 has a focus on missing capitals, natural capital prominent among them. However, the formal standard will be the start of the process of developing natural capital accounts; the United States has only recently announced it will begin work on natural capital accounts. The task is immense and will require new sources of data and data collection techniques. The spatial aspects will be challenging. However, a backwards-looking snapshot, constrained by production and asset boundaries that exclude important components of nature, omits information which may be relevant to forward-looking economic decisions. The collection of physical natural capital data, and the valuation of natural capital assets using (inevitably imperfect) shadow prices is essential if the aim of gathering statistics is, rather than enabling an autopsy of the economy, to diagnose its ills and help decision-makers address them.

Such initiatives are motivated by a growing recognition that a new, or at least substantially extended, economic and measurement framework is needed. Responding to global demand for going "Beyond GDP," governments from Canada to New Zealand are compiling well-being statistics, and there are advocates for using direct well-being measures (such as life satisfaction) as a policy target (De Neve et al. 2020). The UN's Inclusive Wealth Reports and World Bank's Changing Wealth of Nations series measure wealth across most major economies, with the World Bank extending this to consider social capital for the first time in 2021[1] (World Bank 2021).

1. World Bank (2021) notes the importance of social capital in determining economic outcomes and explores how it could be measured, but due to a lack of measurement and valuation, social capital is not incorporated into the core accounts at this time. Dasgupta (2021, 325) presents social capital as an enabling asset that adds value to natural, human, and physical capital by facilitating their use.

The COVID-19 pandemic underscored the importance of recent initiatives to incorporate health into human capital measures (Kraay 2019). Other suggestions include dashboards or suites of indicators (including those in several of the Sustainable Development Goals). While these approaches all have different merits, policymakers and businesses need statistics that can act as a forward-looking guide to enable diagnosis and action. This points to a limitation not only of the rear-view mirror of the national accounts, but also of many of the alternative proposals, which are also snapshots of the recent past. Comprehensive asset stock statistics directly and consistently correspond with SNA flow measures, allowing a richer assessment of the functional relationship and returns to assets in the production function.

Taking an inclusive wealth approach to economic measurement is not just about extending accounting boundaries to incorporate a broader slice of economic activity: it entails thinking critically about the whole suite of assets on which that activity relies, how their stocks are changing, and how they will contribute to well-being in the future. Natural capital accounting can provide a forward-looking tool of exactly this kind, combining environmental and economic knowledge (Vardon et al. 2022). Advantages of such an approach include that assets embed a concern for the future because their current value is determined by expected risk-adjusted future flows of capital services, and the net change in assets determines the economy's productive capacity over time. Furthermore, it responds to the demands to go "Beyond GDP," because an increase in net inclusive wealth (or equivalently net investment) is invariably associated with an increase in social welfare, including for future generations. This is a formal equivalence because intergenerational well-being will depend on the flow of consumption at all future dates, which will depend on the stock of assets and the capital services they provide (Dasgupta and Mäler 2000).

An important characteristic of natural capital accounting concerns the geographical scope of the statistics. Environmentally relevant spatial scales are unlikely to coincide with the national or subnational boundaries used for conventional economic measurement. These are relevant because policy and business decisions concern these political geographies. Important elements of natural capital—referred to as "global public goods" (Arrow et al. 2012)—cross nation state boundaries. For example, critical marine fish stocks move through national and international waters; 60 percent of the world's fresh water flows through transboundary lake and river basins (UN-Water 2021); and air pollution, greenhouse gas emissions, and climate change are also obvious examples. In these cases, accounting systems fitted to national borders may conceal rather than reveal important changes in the natural capital on which economies rely.

The boundaries issue also highlights distributional questions. If inclusive wealth is to function as a better, forward-looking measure of social welfare, its distributional aspects are important, and distributional criteria ought in principle to be reflected in shadow prices. Climate change and biodiversity impacts are exacerbating and creating inequalities within and between countries. Natural capital—like other forms of public wealth—is more important to people with low monetary incomes and wealth. Indeed, Drupp et al. (2018) show that more equal societies place higher value on environmental public goods and that the nonmarket benefits of environmental policy disproportionately benefit the poor. However, more deprived communities tend to be located within lower-quality natural environments which exacerbate inequalities associated with tighter environmental constraints and reduced access to environmental services (Mullin et al. 2018).

A wealth-based measurement framework will only improve economic and environmental policies and outcomes if the required data are collected and used in mainstream economic analyses. This requires at least three conditions to be satisfied. First, accounts recording the stocks of natural, social, human, and physical capital must be produced at regular intervals. Second, these wealth accounts must be fully consistent with the social accounting matrices that already underpin the macroeconomic models used for such purposes. Finally, a decision must be made by analysts and policymakers to utilize the data in economic analyses. This final step—deciding to use the information—is often overlooked. Much of the wealth accounting world has operated under an "if we build it, they will come" model. But there is an inertia in economic statistics that favors the status quo. We therefore highlight below several potential avenues for economists to use data on natural capital to better understand mainstream economic questions relating to risk, inequality within and between countries, and productivity.

In the next section we develop a simple model to introduce the risks associated with depletion into the valuation of natural capital assets. The SEEA adopts the SNA convention of using exchange or market prices for valuation purposes, but these differ by definition from the appropriate shadow (or "accounting" prices in the context of environmental externalities. There is a large and growing literature on appropriate valuation methods (see for example Bateman et al. 2002; Atkinson et al. 2012; Fenichel and Abbott 2014; Islam et al. 2019). Our contribution here, in the context of using natural capital accounts as a tool for forward-thinking, is to provide a simple model to incorporate risk to the assets from degradation or loss. We then turn to three areas of immediate policy interest to suggest how natural capital accounts can shed important light on the nature of the policy challenge and potentially improve outcomes: inequality, productivity, and net zero transition.

2.2 Incorporating Risk in Natural Capital Measurement

The established body of knowledge concerning theories of capital, asset pricing, and risk management can usefully be brought to bear on questions of environmental-economic relevance. Horan et al. (2018) posit natural capital as part of a portfolio of assets, noting that efficient portfolio management would require the risk-free return on assets to be equal to the return that could be earned by investing in a numeraire capital stock (for example a tradable AAA-rated government bond with a face value). But in addition to the uncertainties and dynamics that govern conventional asset pricing, natural capital entails nonmarket capital services, variously encompasses public, quasi-public, and private good characteristics, and is additionally subject to ecological complexities and dynamics—all of which complicate valuation. Here we set out a simple model to begin thinking about how risk might be incorporated into the measurement and valuation of natural capital.

Consider the national statistician tasked with reflecting the value of forest natural capital within the national account. It is one thing to report that a country has 1 million ha of pristine forest, but another thing altogether to know there is a 50 percent chance it burns within the next 30 years. If we have scientific projections of how natural capital stocks might be at risk, how might this be reflected in a wealth account? We could focus on the return on risk-adjusted capital, noting that the capital stock is at risk but assuming that the returns per unit of forest are constant. Alternatively, we could consider a scenario in which the capital remains intact, but that the value of the ecosystem service flows generated by it are at risk. In this case, the variable of interest is the risk-adjusted return on capital. Finally, we could imagine a scenario where both the capital stock and the ecosystem service flows are at risk, in which case we may be interested in the risk-adjusted return on risk-adjusted capital. The challenge is how one might formalize these issues such that the relevant risks could be reflected within a natural capital account.

We begin by asking how the risk of ecosystem collapse translates into economic risks. We want to derive the adjustment that accountants should make to the value they attribute to ecosystem assets. In our simple model, time is continuous, denoted by $t \geq 0$. Suppose an ecosystem (such as a forest) of size K, yields a *flow* of benefits of P dollars *per unit of forest* to the firm. Forest ecosystems generate a wide range of economically valuable environmental goods and services, including air purification, nutrient cycling, timber production, carbon storage, and as a place for outdoor recreation. P reflects the combined contribution of this suite of services to welfare. But the relevant shadow prices are not readily observed, meaning that in practice, natural capital and ecosystem service accounts rely on estimations and proxies. In addition, UN SEEA guidelines require the use of market-equivalent values within national natural capital accounts for consistency with the SNA. If market data are used as the basis for estimating P, and if the market has already identified, aggregated, and priced in all potential risks to the forest, then adding an additional risk parameter into the model could double count some risk. However, it is unlikely that current market prices fully reflect the risks of ecosystem collapse so we need to suggest how risk could be accounted for.

We begin by assuming P is constant. We will later assume that P increases exponentially, to reflect the idea that natural capital will become increasingly scarce relative to produced capital. The discount rate the firm applies to future benefits from the forest is $r > 0$ per unit of time.

So as long as the ecosystem remains intact, the flow of benefits from it is PK at each moment (in the case where P is constant). If the firm is certain that the ecosystem would remain unblemished forever, it would be worth PK/r. But because ecosystems are being degraded generally, the firm's projection is that its supply source will collapse at an unknown date before T years from now. We study the case where the distribution of this risk is uniform: at $t = 0$, there is a constant probability rate $1/T$ of the ecosystem being destroyed in the interval of time $[0, T]$.

Bayesian updating implies that, conditional on the forest surviving until time t, the probability that it will be destroyed at any date in the interval $[t, T]$ is $1/(T - t)$. Viewed from $t = 0$, the probability that the forest will survive until t, is thus $(T - t)/T$. The *hazard rate* at t is $1/(T - t)$, which goes to infinity as t tends to T. We can now apply this to calculate the risk-adjusted shadow value of the pristine forest.

As the probability that the forest will exist until t is $(T - t)/T$, the expected worth of the ecosystem is:

$$(1) \qquad PK\left(\int_0^T \frac{e^{-rt}(T-t)}{T}\,dt\right) = \left(\frac{PK}{r}\right)(1 - e^{-rT}) - \left(\frac{PK}{T}\right)\left(\int_0^T (te^{-rt})dt\right).$$

Write the risk adjusted value of K as a function of T as $F(T)$. Then integrating the final term on the right-hand side to equation (1) by parts yields:

$$(2) \qquad F(T) = \left(\frac{PK}{r}\right)\left(1 - \frac{(1 - e^{-rT})}{rT}\right).$$

The risk adjustment term is thus R:

$$(3) \qquad R = \left(1 - \frac{(1 - e^{-rT})}{rT}\right).$$

It is straightforward to confirm that $\mathrm{d}F(T)/\mathrm{d}T > 0$. Thus, $F(T)$ is a monotone increasing function of T in the interval $[0, \infty)$. Moreover, $F(T) \to 0$ as $T \to 0$ and $F(T) \to PK/r$ as $T \to \infty$. Both limits are intuitive. Moreover, the risk-adjustment factor, R, lies between 0 and 1, exactly as one would expect.

An extension of the model involves abandoning the assumption that P is a constant. With the world's rainforests being razed to the ground to make way for cattle ranches, plantations, and mines, we would expect the benefits from K to increase over time relative to our assumed *numeraire*, market income. The simplest assumption is that P increases exponentially at rate $\beta > 0$, that is, $P(t) = P(0)e^{\beta t}$. To be concrete, assume $r > \beta$. It is now simple to confirm that:

$$F(T) = \left(\frac{PK}{(r - \beta)}\right)\left(1 - \frac{(1 - e^{-(r-\beta)T})}{(r - \beta)}T\right).$$

That is, the risk adjusted shadow price of capital is the *higher* the *larger* is β. That too is exactly what intuition would suggest.

Returning to equation 2, the risk-adjustment in this simple model could be applied either to the shadow price P or as an adjustment to the stock, K. The result is general and not restricted to the random death process we consider here: the associated risk factor is a number lying between 0 and 1 and can be deployed either on P or K.

Future work could explore how P might change with income. If income rises through time, then a standard Ramsey decomposition would imply a higher discount rate. If one abstracts the pure rate of time preference and assumes an income elasticity of unity (as is commonly the case) this should be proportionate to growth. This would imply a falling current stock value for the forest in proportion to increased income growth assumptions through time. Of course, if the impact of natural capital loss is non-marginal, say because of the systemic effect of all the forests burning at once, then income may not rise through time and would need to be modeled endogenously in line with the risk of catastrophe.

An important question remains over the potential sign and magnitude of the climate beta.[2] Early investigations asserted that large income losses from extensive warming suggest a higher benefit from mitigation investments, and thus a negative climate beta (Howarth 2003; Weitzman 2007; Sandsmark and Vennemo 2007). In contrast, Nordhaus (2011) indicates that carbon intensive growth and technological progress could deliver greater consumption, emissions, and warming, leading to a greater return on mitigation investments. Thus consumption and mitigation benefits would be positively correlated, yielding a positive climate beta. Dietz et al. (2018) use DICE to model climate beta explicitly, finding that upward pressure on β arising from uncertain technical progress dominates downward pressure on β arising from uncertain climate sensitivity and damages. That is, in line with Nordhaus (2011), they find that emission reductions actually increase the aggregate consumption risk borne by future generations (Dietz et al. 2018, 260).

Alternatively, rising incomes could lead to increased substitution (say from burning trees for fuel to renewable electricity), or could even change preferences toward greater consideration for natural capital conservation. While evidence suggests that substitutability of natural capital with other forms of capital may be low to moderate (Cohen et al. 2019; Yamaguchi and Managi 2019), higher income may facilitate a greater access to resources

2. The authors are grateful to Professor Joe Stiglitz for raising this intriguing question.

that can help adapt to or mitigate the risks associated with the loss of natural capital. For example, the company may be able to invest in alternative sources of water or energy or use their financial resources to develop new technologies that reduce their reliance on the natural resources stock in the forest. In those cases, under the assumption of a decreasing marginal utility of income, in more rapidly growing economies there will be more income in the future and the negative impact on human welfare will be marginally less.

Our simple model brings accounting for risks to natural assets into natural capital accounting, which will be needed for a fuller welfare accounting. An advantage of natural capital accounting is that it forces other areas of economic analysis to begin to incorporate previously omitted but growing environmental risks. Future work could explore systemic risks, highlighting interactions and correlations between natural and other forms of capital.

2.3 Natural Capital Accounts and Inequality Within Countries

The Dasgupta Review (2021) laid down the gauntlet for economists to demonstrate how natural capital accounts can shed light on mainstream economic challenges. We consider three ways in which natural capital accounting is relevant to current policy challenges. The first of these concerns the interactions between natural capital, environmental policies, and inequality.

The credibility and usefulness of natural capital accounts will depend on their ability to improve understanding of the distributional consequences arising on the one hand from changes in natural capital, and on the other hand from environmental policies that aim to preserve natural capital. The distributional aspects are important both within and between countries. Up to a quarter of inclusive national wealth in developing countries consists of natural capital, while in OECD high-income countries it represents around 3 percent of national wealth. However, the value of natural capital in the latter is three times that of lower income countries (World Bank 2021). The available evidence suggests that of all the asset classes, natural capital is the only one that is in sustained, world-wide decline (Dasgupta 2021, World Bank 2021).

This decline contributes to inequality in at least two ways. First, poor, marginalized, and vulnerable groups may be more directly exposed to the physical risks associated with natural capital depletion: they may be less likely to hold insurance against floods, droughts, and fires; their livelihoods may be more dependent on primary agricultural commodities or even directly dependent on local natural capital for food; and losses in natural capital may constitute a greater proportional loss of total wealth than for higher income groups. We return in the next section to the global distributional question.

Second, lower-income and marginalized groups may be more exposed to the negative trade-offs associated with environmental policies that will safeguard nature if, for example, their tools and skills are less transferable in the shift toward a net zero and nature positive economy. By systematically reviewing the outcomes and trade-offs of decarbonization policies, Peñasco et al. (2021) show that while regulatory, economic, and financial policy instruments are generally associated with positive environmental, technological, and innovation outcomes, many policies supporting the deployment of renewable energy are also associated with short- to medium-term negative effects on distributional outcomes. For instance, 12 of the 13 studies they reviewed identified regressive effects from feed-in tariffs, a result that held across 40 geographical contexts for which data were available. Similarly, 63 percent of studies reviewed found negative distributional impacts from energy taxes.

We can expect that if people perceive environmental policies as a threat to their own income or well-being, public acceptance will be low and the transition to net zero will be impaired. Distributional and economic aspects are at the core of that public acceptance. If decarbonization policies are perceived to be unfair or lead to job losses, this could delay action, which scientific evidence suggests we cannot afford. A common critique of net zero policies is that they may reduce competitiveness, raise prices, and exacerbate inequalities. But the evidence suggests that unabated climate change already is and will continue to exacerbate existing inequalities within and between countries, and will create new ones.

On the other hand, clean technologies afford opportunities for greater efficiency and productivity in the use of resources. One study suggests that transitioning to a decarbonized energy system by 2050 would save at least $12 trillion globally in comparison to the current scenarios of fossil fuel use (Way et al. 2022). How those savings are distributed represents another source of concern. From a political economy perspective, climate and environmental policy implementation and the process of global decarbonization requires the access to minerals like cobalt, lithium, or rare earth among many others whose production is concentrated in few countries, even to a larger extent than oil and gas (IEA 2021). In this sense inequality and perceived distributional concerns may remain at the core of the energy transition if not considered adequately. Indicators like energy access, energy dependency, energy security, or the environmental, biodiversity, and competitiveness effects experienced at sites of extraction are indicators that can shed light on the distributional impacts of decarbonization policy (Newell and Mulvaney 2013; Mercure et al. 2021).

There are several implications derived from the evaluation of distributional impacts of policies aiming to improve our natural environment. Much of the available evidence has used metrics such as the impacts on income and wealth distribution to analyze the progressive or regressive effects of the implementation of certain types of policies in particular for societal groups such as vulnerable households. Less common, however, is assessment of distributional impacts associated with the possible co-benefits of reducing environmental damage, including for example food security, energy security, or improved physical health (Kortetmäki and Järvelä 2021); and indeed improved accessibility to natural capital and/or environmental goods (Montenegro et al. 2021). The latter is more difficult to quantify, but neglecting this dimension in assessment and evaluation of the impacts of environmental policies can generate myopic results in regards to their effects on inequality of different policies (Montenegro et al. 2021).

A wealth-based approach can shed further light on longer-term questions of distribution and inequality. Given the variety of distributional impacts associated with natural capital assets and the policies essential to protect them, an array of indicators will be necessary in two fronts: first, in *ex ante* assessments of the impacts of climate change and the cost-benefit consideration of the adoption of certain environmental policies; and second, in *ex post* evaluations of such impacts, either the co-benefits or trade-offs. These can differentially impact the consumers of the affected goods or services, either those households or firms with different income levels, revenues and/or situated within different regions in one country or in different countries (Montenegro et al. 2021). Some studies have explored the impact on consumers (their spending on energy as a percentage of total expenditure) and the differences in the ability of large and small firms (including renewable energy producers of various sizes) to thrive under a range of policies. Age too is an important yardstick: policies may affect intergenerational equity. Internationally, energy transition may affect countries at different levels of development.

Fuller natural capital accounts would help shed light on the distributional effects across time and space of policies such as land reform or climate action. While great progress has been made in the production of natural capital accounts, in the context of the SEEA-EEA, the resulting accounts are not yet fully delivering on this potential use. Several extensions could be considered. These include natural capital valuation approaches that reflect regional- and asset-specific risks (as set out in section 2.2) or the use of equity weights designed to reflect within-country differences in access to natural capital and associated ecosystem services such as improved air quality (Bond and Basu 2021; Mullin et al. 2018; HM Treasury 2022).

2.4 Natural Capital and Inequality between Countries

Globalization has opened markets, facilitated the spread of people, ideas and culture, and lifted millions out of poverty. But it has also ushered in an era of unprecedented natural resource depletion and environmental change. Many current development challenges deal with the intersection of the benefits of economic activity and the costs of environmental degradation. International trade plays an important role. It separates the location of production from that of consumption and drives a wedge between those who demand natural resources, the countries that govern them, and those who experience the associated social, economic, and environmental consequences (Dupuy 2011; Dupuy and Agarwala 2014). Measurement systems that fail to account for this "offshoring" of natural capital consumption may provide a distorted picture of national and global sustainability and make it harder to address the global collective action problem.

Most wealth accounting efforts employ territorial accounts that describe trends in natural capital stocks within a country's national borders and are therefore relevant for calculating domestic per capita natural capital depletions. Trade enters solely through the effect of net exports on national savings. We argue that because international trade is a large and in general still growing share of the global economy, rising from just 24 percent of gross world product in 1961 to 64 percent in 2011 (World Bank 2018), there is justification for reexamining the extent to which territorial natural capital accounts are fit for purpose when measuring national and global sustainability in an increasingly globalized world. Indeed, the influential Sarkozy Commission noted that a measurement approach "centered on national sustainabilities may be relevant for some dimensions of sustainability, but not for others" (Stiglitz et al. 2009, 77).

Atkinson et al. (2012) and Agarwala (2020) propose the development of complementary natural capital accounts, one from the traditional production, or territorial-based perspective, and another from the consumption-based perspective. Production-based accounts record resource depletions that take place within a country's borders, regardless of where those resources are ultimately consumed. Consumption-based accounts record resource depletions embodied within a country's final demand, regardless of where in the world those depletions actually took place. The need for consumption-based accounts has been firmly established in the carbon accounting literature, partially to explore various interpretations of "responsibility" for CO_2 emissions (Davis et al. 2011; Steininger et al. 2016; Afionis et al. 2017). Atkinson et al. (2012) and Agarwala (2020) extend this debate to a much wider range of natural capital assets, including oil, coal, gas, minerals, fisheries, and timber. Examining both sets of accounts simultaneously provides a more complete understanding of an economy's impact on both national and global sustainability, provides insight into dependencies on domestic versus global resource stocks, and is crucial to understanding resource security concerns and identifying opportunities for joined-up bilateral and international resource policy.

The presence of transboundary externalities (and therefore imperfect markets for natural capital resources) means that merely relying on import prices in adjusted savings metrics would systematically bias any individual country's measured progress toward national versus global sustainability (Oleson 2011; Atkinson et al. 2012; Wiedmann et al. 2015; Steininger et al. 2016). Of course, if natural capital resources embodied in international trade were priced at their theoretical shadow price, this would not be an issue because genuine savings measures account for net exports. But when natural capital is traded below its shadow price, this adjustment fails. If natural resources are exchanged on international markets at prices that deviate from their optimum shadow price, then international trade implicitly entails transfers of "virtual sustainability" between resource exporters and importers. The more natural capital is traded internationally, the more important this distortion becomes: UNEP (2015) shows that in physical terms, resource extraction increased 1.8-fold from 1980 to 2011, but that resource trade increased by a factor of 2.5 over the same period, indicating the distortion is accelerating.

Using the GTAPv9 140 country, 57 sector multi-regional input-output model, Atkinson et al (2012) and Agarwala (2020) compute the value of per capita natural capital depletions across oil, coal, gas, mineral, forestry, and fishery resources. Greenhouse gas emissions are not included. Figures 2.1a-b depict per capita production- and consumption-based depletions. Figure 2.1c illustrates the difference between per capita production and consumption depletions (specifically, production minus consumption).[3]

There are several striking features of these maps. First, figures 2.1a-b convey different stories about the impact of national economies on global natural capital. The highest per capita production based depleting countries consist mainly of major oil producing nations such as Qatar ($9,384), Kuwait ($8,676), Brunei Darussalam ($6,405) and Norway ($5,866). Australia ($1,222), Canada ($938) and Russia ($707) also fall in the top 20. Countries with the highest consumption-based depletions per capita include Luxembourg (£1,188), Iceland ($1068), and Kuwait ($889). The difference map (figure 2.1c) can be interpreted as the magnitude of the "policy blind spot" (Steininger et al. 2016) that would arise if policies were informed by either the production or consumption account rather than both. Negative (positive) values indicate per capita resource net importers (exporters).

Accounting for natural capital across borders becomes even more important when we consider global public goods with transnational externalities. We know that greenhouse gases reduce wealth, but the question remains, *whose?* Consider the following sequence: coal extracted in Malaysia is burned in China to produce goods that are consumed in the United Kingdom. The associated climate change increases extreme weather, reducing productive capacity in Bangladesh. What happens to inclusive wealth along this chain of events? Accounts have been developed that attribute the carbon externality at various points along the supply chain: the country of extraction, com-

3. All values are in 2011 US dollars. Chloropleth class breaks (color categories) correspond to a boxplot distribution. The values for the six color classifications are defined as follows (min, p25 – 1.5*iqr), (p25 – 1.5*iqr, p25], (p25, p50], (p50, p75], (p75, p75 + 1.5*iqr] and (p75 + 1.5*iqr, max], where iqr = interquartile range.

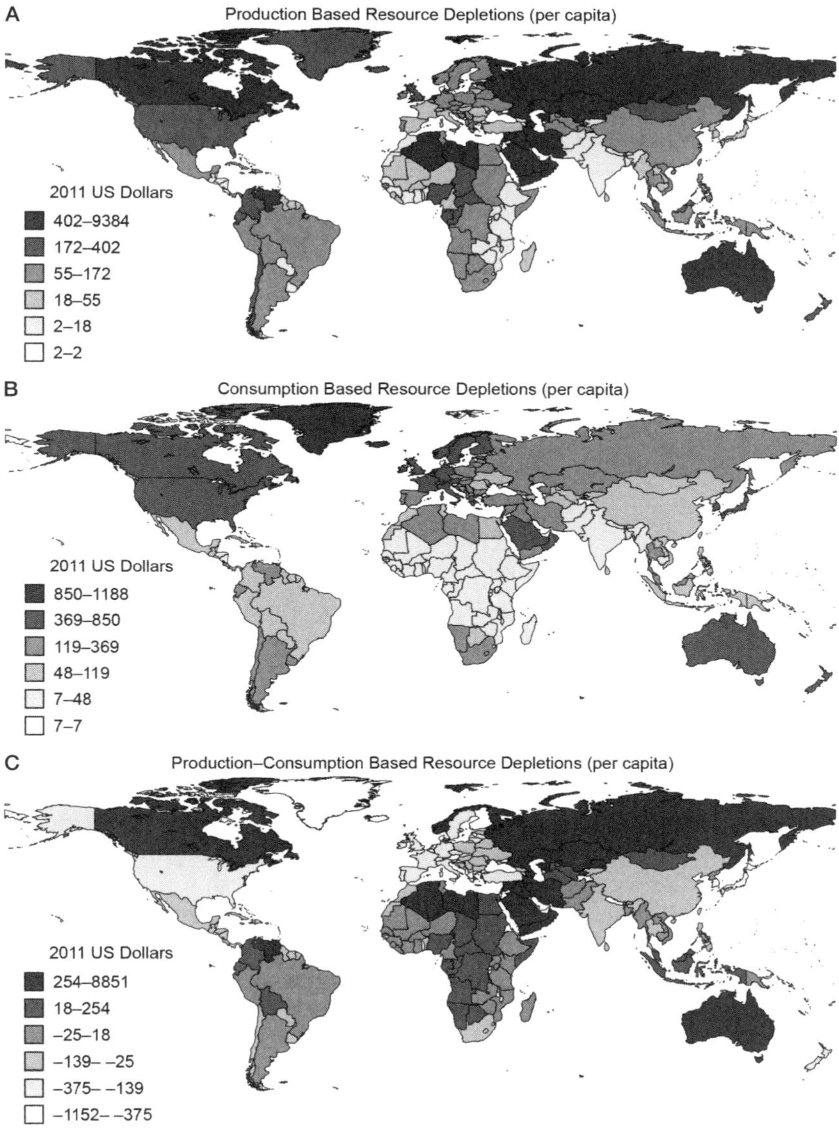

Figure 2.1 Production and consumption accounts for natural resource depletion

Figures 2.1a-b show per capita production and consumption-based resource depletions. Fig. 2.1c shows the difference (production minus consumption) in per capita resource depletions. Resources include forestry, fisheries, coal, oil, natural gas, and other mining (metal ores, uranium, gems). Values in 2011 USD. Greenhouse gas emissions are not included.

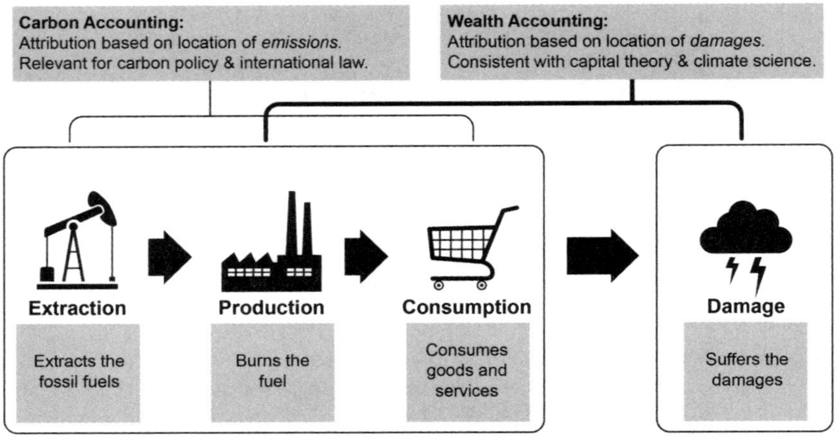

Figure 2.2 From carbon accounting to wealth accounting across borders
Source: Agarwala (2020).

bustion, or final demand (Davis et al. 2011). But this ignores a critical step: the country in which the damages are ultimately realized (see figure 2.2).

In practice, carbon and natural capital accounting procedures deduct the value of emissions from the country in which they are released. But for the theory of inclusive wealth, this would be appropriate only under the restrictive and scientifically unrealistic condition that climate externality exactly coincided with the location of emissions. Arrow et al. (2012) show that in the presence of transboundary externalities, the appropriate adjustment to each nation's wealth would reflect the domestic damages generated by global emissions rather than the emissions generated domestically. Returning to our example, this means measured wealth in Bangladesh would fall owing to decisions taken in Malaysia, China, and the United Kingdom. This is unfair, but in the absence of international compensation for greenhouse gas emissions, it provides a far more accurate depiction of the relationship between emissions and domestic versus global sustainability. Damage-based accounts require country-level estimates of the climate impacts arising from the marginal ton of greenhouse gas emissions. This remains an important obstacle, but initial progress shows that integrated assessment models and, increasingly, macroeconometric climate models, can be used (Arrow et al. 2012; UNU-IHDP 2012; Agarwala 2020). In theory, damage-based accounts could be constructed wherever countries impose externalities upon each other through their management of global public goods, but the complexity of the measurement and valuation challenges will vary across types of natural capital.

Constructing natural capital accounts from production-, consumption-, and damage-based perspectives reveals different, yet equally important, trends in natural capital depletion. Focusing exclusively on production accounts opens the potential for "leakage" and ignores opportunities to influence resource management along the supply chain. Moreover, the suite of accounts developed here enables us to provide greater insight into the global nature of sustainability. Production, consumption, and damage accounts are useful complementary tools for understanding the natural capital impacts and dependencies of nations.

2.5 Natural Capital Accounts and Productivity Measurement

A major challenge faced by many economies is the slowdown in productivity growth since the mid-2000s. Compared to the prior long-run trend, this growth slowdown accounts for an output shortfall totaling around 20 percent of GDP depending on the country.

One obstacle to enacting policies to combat climate change and protect natural capital is that they are often perceived to reduce growth and productivity. This perception has been challenged (see section 2.6 below). One problem is that the standard approach to measuring productivity adopts a private goods perspective, permitting by assumption the "free disposal" of bad outputs. But if production activities generate externalities, then relying on market-based measures of output will distort the measurement of productivity. The development of environmentally adjusted measures of national income is not new (Nordhaus and Tobin 1973; Repetto et al. 1996; Muller 2014), but the exercise here is to show how these can inform mainstream policy issues such as productivity growth.

Viewed against the backdrop of climate change, the exclusion *by assumption* of carbon emissions from productivity analyses is hard to defend. To investigate the relationship between productivity growth and natural capital, Agarwala and Martin (2022) utilize the richness of UK natural capital and sectoral production data to construct environmentally adjusted productivity measures for the United Kingdom, deducting the value of greenhouse gas and air pollution emissions from the value of output. As in Muller (2014), they focus on greenhouse gas and air pollutant emissions because of the availability of high-quality emissions data, the high economic impact of greenhouse gas and pollution emissions, and the ability to directly attribute emissions to economic activities within the national accounts. Extending beyond the calculation of a "green GDP" measure, they use this adjusted-GVA to calculate environmentally adjusted labor productivity measures. Emissions prices are taken from UK government documentation and are reflected in table 2.1.[4]

4. The UK Department for Business, Energy, and Industrial Strategy (BEIS) adopts a "target-consistent" carbon price rather than a social cost of carbon. This is partially due to the difficulties of estimating the SCC. Rather than estimating the SCC, the marginal abatement cost approach relies on government to set a policy target such as reaching net zero emissions by

Table 2.1 **Summary of emissions and pollutants, including data sources**

Category	Type	Price data source	Price per tonne in base year	Assumed price growth per year	Total fall in volume 1990–2019
Greenhouse gases	All	BEIS	£241 (2020)	1.5%	41%
Acid rain precursors	Nitrogen oxide (NO_x)	Defra	£6,383 (2017)	2%	67%
	Sulphur dioxide (SO_2)	Defra	£13,206 (2017)	2%	95%
	Ammonia (NH_3)	Defra	£7,923 (2017)	2%	17%
Other pollutants	Non-methane volatile organic compounds	Defra	£102 (2017)	2%	68%
	Particulate matter (PM2.5)	Defra	£73,403 (2017)	2%	78%

Source: Agarwala and Martin (2022)

GVA was adjusted downwards by deducting the product of the relevant prices and quantities. This drove some industries (manufacturing of coke and petroleum products and air transport) to post net negative GVA for the entire assessment period. However, most industries saw faster productivity growth after adjusting for bad outputs, reflecting reductions over time in per unit emissions. At the aggregate scale, environmentally adjusted labor productivity growth was higher (see figure 2.3).

The general result that environmentally adjusted productivity growth will be higher than conventionally measured productivity growth can be expected to hold in countries where the emissions intensity of output has been falling over time (Muller 2020; Agarwala and Martin 2022). However, the opposite can be expected in countries where the emissions intensity of output has risen (Mohan et al. 2020). There are some important limitations to the case studies presented here. Focusing on production-based emissions ignores leakage and offshoring effects, and future work should encompass multi-regional input-output analysis to reflect this. At least as important is the fact that household production falls outside the production boundary, so their results based on GDP-adjustment exclude energy use and associated emissions by consumers (for example in personal transport and home heating). Whilst this aligns their results more closely with mainstream economic statistics, these are clearly important omissions that future work should seek to address. Such extensions will require, and are made possible by, the regular publication of natural capital accounts with sufficient sectoral detail.

2050, and then estimating the cost of achieving it. There are still uncertainties—around changing targets, the availability of abatement technologies, and their costs, but proponents of this approach argue that such uncertainties are far smaller than those encountered in estimating the SCC (Dietz and Fankhauser 2010; Stern and Stiglitz 2021)

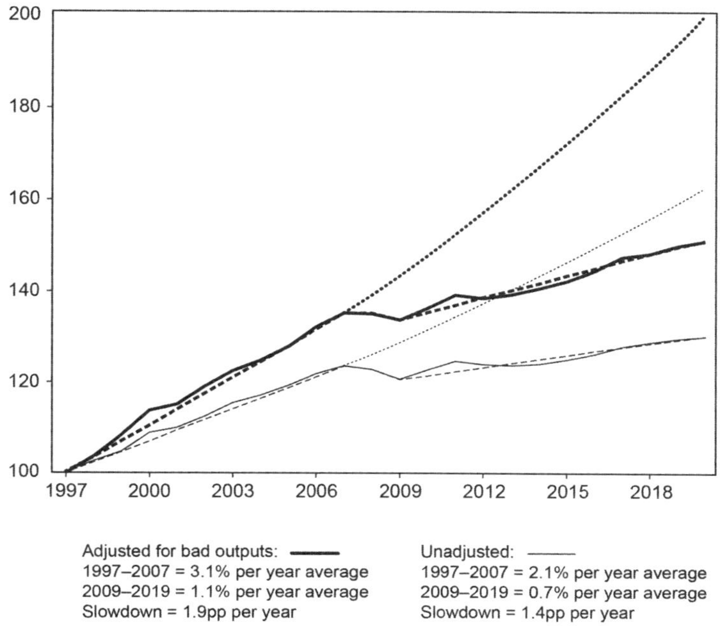

Figure 2.3 Whole economy labor productivity, with and without adjustment for bad outputs, with pre-GFC-downturn trends, 1997 to 2020

Notes: Pre-Great Financial Crash-downturn trend calculated as the compound average annual growth rate from 1997 to 2007. Projection assumes this rate of growth continues from 2007 onwards.

2.6 Natural Capital and Macro Transition Policies

Measurement of natural capital will create a clearer picture of the scale and pace of the depletion of natural assets and the flow of services they provide to current economic activity. At the same time, the policy and behavioral responses to resource loss and climate change will affect the valuation of all assets. The shadow prices of natural assets should fall (sometimes dramatically) and their productivity in generating ecosystem services should increase. For instance, the transition to a low-carbon production system risks devaluing or stranding physical, human, and knowledge capital. Wealth accounts including natural capital will provide decision-makers with a clearer picture of the implications of transition policies and their potential to rapidly impact the value of assets.

Historically, economic assessments of the cost and deployment of decarbonization technologies have been pessimistic relative to experience in key sectors such as renewables, electric vehicles, and battery storage (Grubb et al. 2021a). The large gap between projected costs and realised costs suggests that the models being used are not adequate. By ignoring path dependencies in innovation, the cumulative nature of innovation processes, learning-by-doing, and economies of scale in production, distribution and discovery, as well as the role of government in crowding-in private investment, such assessments failed to predict the rapid cost reductions witnessed in renewables generation and battery technologies. Figure 2.4 shows the strong inverse relationship between deployment and clean technology costs.

Conventional analyses that ignore these effects, or treat them as exogenous to the model, generally overstate the cost of climate action, leading to costly policy delay (Penasco et al. 2021; Grubb et al. 2021a). Indeed, delay can itself increase overall decarbonization costs, by postponing the reinforcing feedbacks between deployment and cost reductions, making high cost estimates potentially self-fulfilling (van der Meijden and Smulders 2017).

Economic models need to encompass the self-reinforcing role of expectations and strategic complementarities, whereby the payoff for policymakers, businesses, and consumers from investing in clean technologies, institutions, and behaviors is a function of how many others do likewise. In the longer run, such feedbacks increasingly give new technologies the advantage over incumbents. Commodity-based systems, such as fossil fuels, are subject to diminishing returns to scale, and hence have limited scope for operational costs to fall as demand rises. The cheapest resources to extract and transport are harvested first. By contrast, new technologies are characterized by powerful economies of scale, both in discovery and production costs (Geels et al. 2021).

Acemoglu et al. (2012) build on this understanding to make a powerful theoretical case to suggest that policy to support clean innovation can be temporary. Once the "clean innovation machine" has been "switched on and is running," it can be more innovative and productive than the conventional alternative, with a positive impact on GDP levels and growth. For example, renewable energy generation is already cheaper than incumbent energy technologies (Way et al. 2022). This strongly indicates that economic modeling to inform policy choices needs to move beyond single equilibrium constraints, focusing on static allocative efficiency, to understand the processes which generate dynamic efficiency and multiple equilibria. Capturing and incorporating reinforcing or dampening feedbacks allows modelers to better assess the risk of changing asset valuation alongside the creation of entire new markets and new assets (Aghion et al. 2014). Natural capital accounts are a complementary tool to this dynamic (non-convex, non-marginal and endogenous) systems approach. They help track the large impacts of interventions on valuations.

Natural capital and wealth accounts are more broadly useful for assessing and guiding macroeconomic policies (Agarwala and Zenghelis 2020). Fiscal sustainability requires investing in assets that generate sustainable private and public returns. If public borrowing is used to invest in the productivity

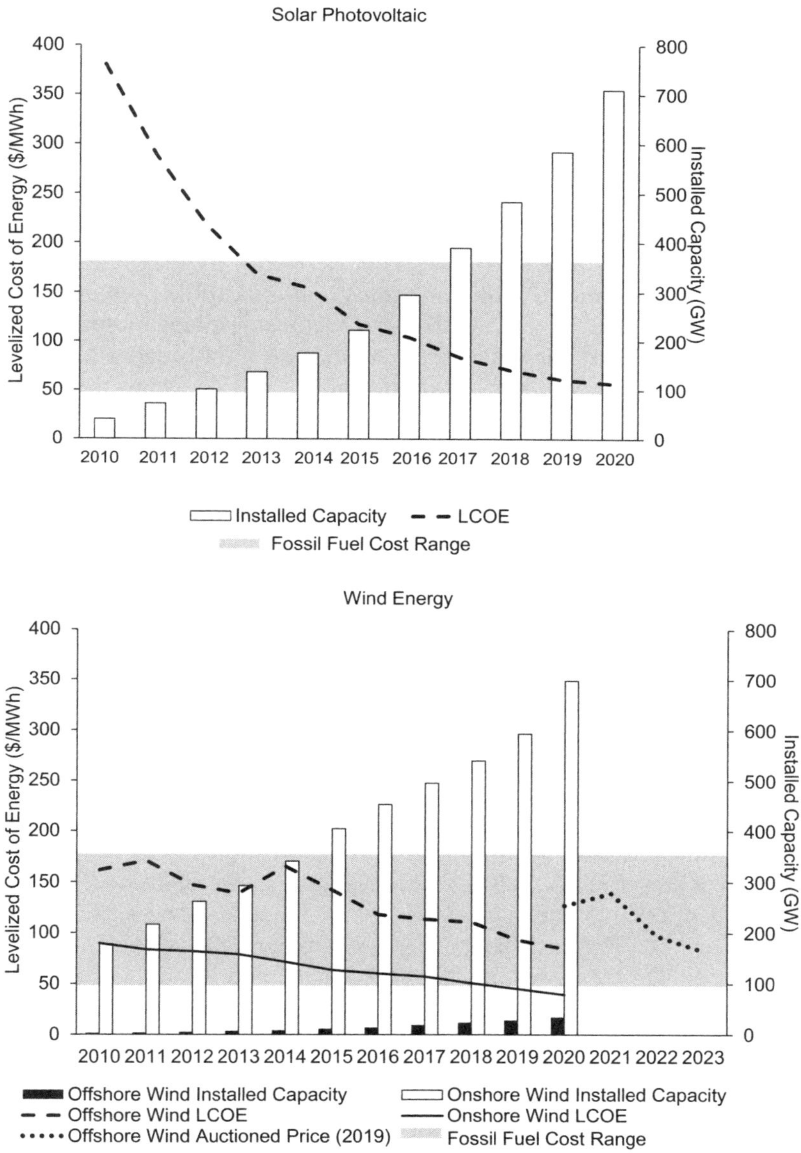

Figure 2.4 The deployment and cost of renewables, 2020 GW

Source: IPCC Sixth Assessment, Chapter 1 Figure 1.2, updated to 2021 as published in Grubb et al. (2021b).

of public assets (Buiter et al. 2020), or to enable private assets to become more productive, it can generate growth and tax revenues that allow debt interest to be repaid (Robins et al. 2020, Agarwala et al. 2021). This means investing in complementary assets that raise productivity and offer the greatest potential (Aghion et al. 2016) in the carbon-constrained markets of the future.

For example, it requires investment in human capital to secure the skills and jobs, and, through R&D, to drive the technologies, processes, and institutions necessary to support the low-carbon economy. By the same token, as part of a comprehensive wealth approach, natural capital accounts can guide investment in assets that are likely to become devalued or stranded. Such macro considerations indicate the need to adopt a broader balance sheet perspective. The inclusive wealth approach to measuring the comprehensive range of assets in which the public and private sectors invest generates a better understanding of the impact of policies and thereby helps inform policy choice at a time of rapid, non-marginal structural change (Zenghelis et al. 2020).

2.7 Conclusion

The origin and purpose of national statistics was to provide a clear view of the evolution of the economy, in order that governments and other decision-makers could make good choices. The original SNA framework was suited to this purpose in the seemingly resource-abundant postwar world. The definitions and standards have continued to evolve during subsequent decades and are currently undergoing another major revision, due to be published in 2025. This will include recognition of the need to measure natural capital, and some other assets in inclusive wealth. We have argued that while welcome, there is a significant challenge ahead, in going beyond the SEEA's use of exchange prices in order to get closer to "true" shadow prices, including adjusting for risk to natural assets; and in the magnitude of the data collection needed. However, we have also shown how natural capital accounts can be used to address some of the policy challenges facing the economy: inequality, productivity slowdown, and the opportunities and risks of the net zero transition.

For acknowledgments, sources of research support, and disclosure of the authors' material financial relationships, if any, please see https://www.nber.org/books-and-chapters/measuring-and-accounting-environmental-public-goods-national-accounts-perspective/measuring-future-not-past.

References

Acemoglu, D., P. Aghion, L. Bursztyn, and D. Hemous. 2012. "The environment and directed technical change." *American economic review* 102 (1): 131–166.

Adler, M. D. 2019. *Measuring Social Welfare: An Introduction*. New York, NY: Oxford University Press.

Afionis, S., M. Sakai, K. Scott, et al. 2017. "Consumption-Based Carbon Accounting: Does It Have a Future?" *Wiley Interdiscip Rev Clim Chang* 8: 1–19. doi: 10.1002/wcc.438.

Agarwala, M., M. Burke, P, Klusak, K. Mohaddes, U. Volz, and D. Zenghelis. 2021. "Climate change and fiscal sustainability: Risks and opportunities." *National Institute Economic Review* 258: 28–46.

Agarwala, M., and J. Martin. 2022. "Environmentally-Adjusted Productivity Measures for the UK." Working Paper No. 028. Manchester, UK: The Productivity Institute.

Agarwala, M., and D. Zenghelis. 2020. Natural Capital Accounts for Macroeconomic Policy. New York, NY: United Nations Statistics Commission.

Agarwala, M. K. 2020. *Natural capital accounting and the measurement of sustainability*. Doctoral dissertation, London School of Economics and Political Science.

Aghion, P., A. Dechezleprêtre, D. Hémous, R. Martin, and J. Van Reenen. 2016. "Carbon Taxes, Path Dependency, and Directed Technical Change: Evidence from the Auto Industry." *Journal of Political Economy* 124 (1): 1–51. doi:10.1086/684581.

Aghion, P., C. Hepburn, A. Teytelboym, and D. Zenghelis. 2014. "Path Dependence, Innovation and the Economics of Climate Change." Centre for Climate Change Economics and Policy/Grantham Research Institute on Climate Change and the Environment Policy Paper & Contributing paper to New Climate Economy.

Arrow, K. J., P. Dasgupta, L. H. Goulder, K. J. Mumford, and K. Oleson. 2012. "Sustainability and the measurement of wealth." *Environment and development economics* 17 (3): 317–353.

Atkinson, G., I. Bateman, and S. Mourato. 2012. "Recent Advances in the Valuation of Ecosystem Services and Biodiversity." *Oxford Review of Economic Policy* 28 (1): 22–47.

Atkinson, G., M. Agarwala, and P. Munoz. 2012. "Are National Economies (Virtually) Sustainable? An Empirical Analysis of Natural Assets in International Trade." In *Inclusive Wealth Report*, 87–117. Cambridge: Cambridge University Press.

Bateman, I. J., R. T. Carson, B. Day, et al. 2002. *Economic Evaluation with Stated Preference Techniques: A Manual*. Cheltenham: Edward Elgar Publishing Limited.

Bond, P., and R. Basu. 2021. "Intergenerational Equity and the Geographical Ebb and Flow of Resources: The Time and Space of Natural Capital Accounting." In *The Routledge Handbook of Critical Resource Geography*, 260–73. New York, NY: e.

Bright, G., E. Connors, and J. Grice. 2019. "Measuring Natural Capital: Towards Accounts for the UK and a Basis for Improved Decision-Making." *Oxford Review of Economic Policy* 35 (1): 88–108.

Buiter, W. H., I. Ball, and D. Detter. 2020. A Stronger Recovery Through Better Accounting. Project Syndicate.

Cohen, F., C. J. Hepburn, and A. Teytelboym 2019. "Is natural capital really substitutable?" *Annual Review of Environment and Resources* 44 (1): 425–448.

Coyle, D. 2015. *GDP: a brief but affectionate history-revised and expanded edition*. Princeton University Press.

Dasgupta, P. 2021. *The economics of biodiversity: The Dasgupta review*. London, UK: HM Treasury.
Dasgupta, P., and K. G. Mäler. 2000. "Net national product, wealth, and social well-being." *Environment and development economics* 5 (1): 69–93.
Davis, S. J., G. P. Peters, and K. Caldeira. 2011. "The Supply Chain of CO2 Emissions." *Proceedings of the National Academy of Sciences* 108: 18554–18559.
De Neve, J. E., A. E. Clark, C. Krekel, R. Layard, and G. O'donnell. 2020. "Taking a Wellbeing Years Approach to Policy Choice." *BMJ* 371.
Dietz, S., and S. Fankhauser. 2010. "Environmental Prices, Uncertainty, and Learning." *Oxford Review of Economic Policy* 26 (2): 270–84.
Dietz, S., C. Gollier, and L. Kessler. 2018. "The Climate Beta." *Journal of Environmental Economics and Management* 87: 258–74.
Drupp, M. A., J. N. Meya, S. Baumgärtner, and M. F. Quaas. 2018. "Economic Inequality and the Value of Nature." *Ecological Economics* 150: 340–45.
Dupuy, L. 2011. "International Trade and Sustainability: A Survey." Université Montesquieu Bordeaux IV.
Dupuy, L., and M. Agarwala. 2014. "International Trade and Sustainable Development." In *Handbook of Sustainable Development*, second ed., edited by G. Atkinson, S. Dietz, E. Neumayer, and M. Agarwala, 399–417. Cheltenham, UK: Edward Elgar.
Ekins, P., and D. Zenghelis. 2021. "The Costs and Benefits of Environmental Sustainability." *Sustainability Science* 16 (3): 949–65.
Fenichel, E. P., and J. K. Abbott. 2014. "Natural Capital: From Metaphor to Measurement." *Journal of the Association of Environmental and Resource Economists* 1 (1/2): 1–27.
Fenichel, E. P., and Y. Hashida. 2019. "Choices and the Value of Natural Capital." *Oxford Review of Economic Policy* 35 (1): 120–37.
Geels, F. W., J. Pinkse, and D. Zenghelis. 2021. "Productivity Opportunities and Risks in a Transformative, Low-Carbon and Digital Age." Working Paper No. 009. Manchester, UK: The Productivity Institute. https://www.productivity.ac.uk/publications/productivity-opportunities-and-risks-in-a-transformative-low-carbon-and-digital-age/.
Global Commission on Adaptation. 2019. *Adapt Now: A Global Call for Leadership on Climate Resilience*. Washington, DC: The New Climate Economy.
Grubb, M., P. Drummond, A. Poncia, W. McDowall, D. Popp, S. Samadi, C. Penasco, K. Gillingham, S. Smulders, M. Glachant, G. Hassall, E. Mizuno, E. Rubin, A. Dechezleprêtre, and G. Pavan. 2021a. "Induced Innovation in Energy Technologies and Systems: A Review of Evidence and Potential Implications for CO2 Mitigation." *Environmental Research Letters* **16** 043007.
Grubb, Michael, Paul Drummond, Jean-Francois Mercure, Cameron Hepburn, Peter Barbrook-Johnson, João Carlos Ferraz, Alex Clark, Laura Diaz Anadon, Doyne Farmer, Ben Hinder, Matt Ives, Aled Jones, Gao Jun, Ulka Kelkar, Sergey Kolesnikov, Aileen Lam, Ritu Mathur, Roberto Pasqualino, Cristina Penasco, Hector Pollitt, Luma Ramos, Andrea Roventini, Pablo Salas, Simon Sharpe, Zhu Songli, Pim Vercoulen, Kamna Waghray, Zhang Xiliang. 2021b. *The New Economics of Innovation and Transition: Evaluating Opportunities and Risks: A Report by the Economics of Energy Innovation and System Transition (EEIST) Consortium*. Oxford, UK: The Economics of Energy Innovation and System Transition (EEIST) consortium. https://www.oxfordmartin.ox.ac.uk/publications/the-new-economics-of-innovation-and-transition-evaluating-opportunities-and-risks/.
Hein, L., K. J. Bagstad, C. Obst, B. Edens, S. Schenau, G. Castillo et al. 2020. "Progress in Natural Capital Accounting for Ecosystems." *Science* 367 (6477): 514–15.

Helm, D. 2019. *Green and Prosperous Land: A Blueprint for Rescuing the British Countryside*. London: William Collins.

Hepburn, C., B. O'Callaghan, N. Stern, J. Stiglitz, and D. Zenghelis. 2020. "Will COVID-19 Fiscal Recovery Packages Accelerate or Retard Progress on Climate Change?" *Oxford Review of Economic Policy* 36 (S1).

HM Treasury. 2022. The Green Book, UK Government. https://www.gov.uk/government/publications/the-green-book-appraisal-and-evaluation-in-central-goverent/the-green-book-2020.

Horan, R. D., E. P. Fenichel, D. Finnoff, et al. 2018. "A Portfolio-Balancing Approach to Natural Capital and Liabilities: Managing Livestock and Wildlife Diseases with Cross-Species Transmission." *Environmental Resource Economics* 70: 673–89. https://doi.org/10.1007/s10640-017-0161-4.

Horcea-Milcu, AI., J. Leventon, J. Hanspach, et al. 2016. "Disaggregated Contributions of Ecosystem Services to Human Well-Being: A Case Study from Eastern Europe." *Regional Environmental Change* 16: 1779–1791. https://doi.org/10.1007/s10113-016-0926-2.

Howarth, R. B. 2003. "Discounting and Uncertainty in Climate Change Policy Analysis." *Land Economics* 79 (3): 369–81.

IEA. 2021. The Role of Critical Minerals in Clean Energy Transitions. Paris: IEA.

IIF. 2021. "Global Debt Monitor. COVID Drives Debt Surge—Stabilization Ahead?" February 17.

Islam, M., R. Yamaguchi, Y. Sugiawan, and S. Managi. 2019. "Valuing Natural Capital and Ecosystem Services: A Literature Review." *Sustainability Science* 14: 159–74.

Kortetmäki, T., and M. Järvelä. 2021. "Social vulnerability to climate policies: building a matrix to assess policy impacts on well-being." *Environmental Science & Policy* 123: 220–228.

Kraay, A. 2019. "The World Bank Human Capital Index: A Guide." *World Bank Research Observer* 34: 1–33.

Lange, Glenn-Marie, Quentin Wodon, and Kevin Carey. 2018. *The Changing Wealth of Nations 2018: Building a Sustainable Future*. Report of the World Bank Group. 10.1596/978-1-4648-1046-6.

Lok, M., E. Benson, M. Gough, S. Ahlroth, O. Greenfield, J. Confino, and W. Wormgoor. 2018. "Natural Capital for Governments: What, Why and How." Capitals Coalition. Available from https://capitalscoalition.org/publication/natural-capital-for-governments-what-why-and-how/.

Mercure, J. F., P. Salas, P. Vercoulen, G. Semieniuk, A. Lam, H. Pollitt . . . and J. E. Viñuales. 2021. "Reframing incentives for climate policy action." *Nature Energy* 6 (12): 1133–1143.

Mohan, A., N. Z. Muller, A. Thyagarajan, R. V. Martin, M. S. Hammer, and A. Van Donkelaar. 2020. "The Growth of Nations Revisited: Global Environmental Accounting from 1998 to 2018." NBER Working Paper No. 27398. Cambridge, MA: National Bureau of Economic Research.

Montenegro, R. C., P. Fragkos, A. H. Dobbins, D. Schmid, S. Pye, and U. Fahl. 2021. "Beyond the energy system: modelling frameworks depicting distributional impacts for interdisciplinary policy analysis." *Energy Technology* 9 (1): 2000668.

Muller, N. Z. 2014. "Boosting GDP Growth by Accounting for the Environment." *Science* 345 (6199): 873–74.

Muller, N. Z. 2020. "Long-Run Environmental Accounting in the US Economy." *Environmental and Energy Policy and the Economy* 1 (1): 158–91.

Mullin, K., G. Mitchell, N. R. Nawaz, and R. D. Waters. 2018. "Natural Capital and

the Poor in England: Towards an Environmental Justice Analysis of Ecosystem Services in a High Income Country." *Landscape and Urban Planning* 176: 10–21.
Narayanan, B. G., A. Aguiar, and R. McDougall. 2015. Global Trade, Assistance, and Production: The GTAP 9 Data Base. Center for Global Trade Analysis, Purdue University.
Newell, P., and D. Mulvaney. 2013. "The political economy of the 'just transition.'" *Geographical Journal* 179 (2): 132–140.
Nordhaus, W. D. 2011. "Estimates of the Social Cost of Carbon: Background and Results from the RICE-2011 Model." NBER Working Paper No. 17540. Cambridge, MA: National Bureau of Economic Research.
Nordhaus, W. D., and J. Tobin. 1973. "Is Growth Obsolete?" In *The Measurement of Economic and Social Performance*, edited by Milton Moss, 509–64. New York: National Bureau of Economic Research.
Oleson, K. L. L. 2011. "Shaky Foundations and Sustainable Exploiters: Problems with National Weak Sustainability Measures in a Global Economy." *Journal of Environment and Development* 20: 329–49. doi: 10.1177/1070496511416747.
Peñasco, C., L. D. Anadón, and E. Verdolini. 2021. "Systematic Review of the Outcomes and Trade-Offs of Ten Types of Decarbonization Policy Instruments." *Nature Climate Change* 11 (3): 257–65.
Repetto, R., D. Rothman, P. Faeth, and D. Austin. 1996. *Has Environmental Protection Really Reduced Productivity Growth? We Need Unbiased Measures*. Washington, DC: World Resources Institute.
Robins, N., J. Rydge, N. Stern, S. Unsworth, A. Valero, and D. A. Zenghelis. 2020. "Strategy, Investment and Policy for a Strong and Sustainable Recovery: An Action Plan." Centre for Economic Performance, London School of Economics.
Sandsmark, M., and H. Vennemo. 2007. "A Portfolio Approach to Climate Investments: CAPM and Endogenous Risk." *Environmental and Resource Economics* 37 (4): 681–95.
Steininger, K. W., C. Lininger, L. H. Meyer, et al. 2016. "Multiple Carbon Accounting to Support Just and Effective Climate Policies." *Nature Climate Change* 6: 35–41. doi: 10.1038/nclimate2867.
Stern, N. 2007. *The Economics of Climate Change: The Stern Review*. Cambridge University Press.
Stern, N., and J. E. Stiglitz. 2021. "The Social Cost of Carbon, Risk, Distribution, Market Failures: An Alternative Approach." NBER Working Paper No. 28472. Cambridge, MA: National Bureau of Economic Research.
Stiglitz, J. E., A. Sen, J-P Fitoussi. 2009. Report by the Commission on the Measurement of Economic Performance and Social Progress. UK Government.
SNA. 2009. System of National Accounts 2008. New York.
UNEP. 2015. *International Trade in Resources: A Biophysical Assessment*. UNESCO, Paris, France.
UNU-IHDP. 2012. *Inclusive Wealth Report 2012: Measuring Progress Toward Sustainability* Cambridge, UK: Cambridge Univ. Press.
UN-Water. 2021. *Summary Progress Update 2021—SDG 6—water and sanitation for all*. Version: July 2021. Geneva, Switzerland.
van der Meijden, G., and S. Smulders. 2017. "Carbon Lock-In: The Role of Expectations." *International Economic Review* 58: 1371–1415. https://doi.org/10.1111/iere.12255.
Vardon, M., P. Lucas, S. Bass, et al. 2023. "From COVID-19 to Green Recovery with natural capital accounting." *Ambio* 52: 15–29.
Ward, T., R. E. Mujica-Mota, A. E. Spencer, et al. 2022. "Incorporating Equity Concerns in Cost-Effectiveness Analyses: A Systematic Literature Review." *Phar-*

macoEconomics 40: 45–64. https://doi-org.ezp.lib.cam.ac.uk/10.1007/s40273-021-01094-7.
Way, Rupert, Matthew C. Ives, Penny Mealy, and J. Doyne Farmer. 2022. "Empirically Grounded Technology Forecasts and the Energy Transition." *Joule* 6 (9): 2057–2082. https://doi.org/10.1016/j.joule.2022.08.009.
Weitzman, M. L. 2007. "A Review of the Stern Review on the Economics of Climate Change." *Journal of Economic Literature* 45 (3): 703–24.
Wiedmann, T. O., H. Schandl, M. Lenzen, et al. 2015. "The Material Footprint of Nations." *Proceedings of the National Academy of Sciences* 112: 6271–6276. doi: 10.1073/pnas.1220362110.
World Bank. 2018. World Bank: World Development Indicators.
World Bank. 2021. *The Changing Wealth of Nations 2021: Managing Assets for the Future*. Washington, DC: World Bank.
Yamaguchi, R., and S. Managi. 2019. "Backward- and Forward-Looking Shadow Prices in Inclusive Wealth Accounting: An Example of Renewable Energy Capital." *Ecological Economics* 156: 337–49.
Zenghelis, D., M. Agarwala, D. Coyle, M. Felici, S. Lu, and J. Wdowin. 2020. "Valuing Wealth, Building Prosperity." Wealth Economy Project first year report. Cambridge, UK: Bennett Institute for Public Policy.

Comment Nicholas Z. Muller

Agarwala, Coyle, Penasco, and Zenghelis (ACPZ) correctly argue that "[u]seful economic models and predictions need appropriate data." (p. 1). This claim encapsulates the motivation for rigorous natural capital accounting and it portends, in a broad sense, the implications of critical and longstanding omissions in official economic statistics. ACPZ dive deeply into specific examples of important gaps in the accounts, focusing on risk-adjusted valuation of natural capital, measurement of both intra-and-inter country inequality, and macro-level labor productivity. This essay will augment the topics raised by ACPZ by examining the implications of omissions of pollution damage for measures of economy-wide growth, monetary policy, and business cycles.

In 2016, Robert Gordon argued that the halcyon days of American growth are over, in part, because essentially all of the fundamental growth-enhancing technological innovations had already occurred and that their stimulative effects were played out (Gordon 2016). In particular, Gordon (2016) showed that following 1970, productivity growth rates[1] in the US economy had fallen from 2.4 percent between 1920 and 1970 to 1.8 percent between 1970 and 2014. Using historical data on air pollution levels in the

Nicholas Z. Muller is the Lester and Judith Lave Professor of Economics, Engineering, and Public Policy at Carnegie Mellon University, and a research associate of the National Bureau of Economic Research.

1. Gordon reports output per person and output per hour worked in figure 1–1 on p. 14. The growth rates quoted here are in terms output per person.

US economy collected from 1957 to 2020, Muller (2020) argued that at least part of this apparent slowdown in productivity growth was due to incomplete economic statistics. In particular, Muller (2020) deducted air pollution damages from Gross Domestic Product (GDP) and tracked annual growth in this adjusted measure. Rather than an attenuation of growth after 1970, this net measure of output grew *more rapidly* after 1970. Why? Following the passage of the federal Clean Air Act Amendments of 1970, the United States invested trillions of dollars in pollution control, fundamentally transforming key aspects of the capital stock and durable goods. The result was a steep decline in pollution levels and damages (Muller 2020). Modest growth in real GDP coupled with falling damages from pollution meant that the net measure of output grew more rapidly than market GDP. Failure to measure pollution damage, or degradation of natural capital, leads to the conclusion that growth attenuated after 1970, whereas a measure of output inclusive of these unpriced, social costs from productive activity reveals entirely different patterns in US growth. Investments in natural capital often yield returns not captured by the conventional income and product accounts.

Muller (2020) reports that, from the late 1950s to 2016, pollution damages fell especially quickly during troughs of the business cycle. Particularly notable reductions in pollution intensity occurred during the sharp contractions during the early 1980s and through the Great Recession. These episodes embodied compositional change in the US economy: the dramatic collapse of steel manufacturing during the late 1970s and early 1980s as well as a marked shift away from reliance on coal-fired power generation during the Great Recession. As a result of these declines in pollution intensity, the adjusted measure of output exhibited less clear troughs. In fact during all recessionary periods from 1957 to 2016, the adjusted measure *grew* by 0.4 percent, whereas GDP shrank by 0.3 percent on an annual basis. The conclusion here is that extending the accounts to include measures of natural capital may influence the rhythm of economic fluctuations which affect important decisions made by investors, policymakers, and the general public.

On the connection between natural capital and economic policy, Muller (2021) shows how monetary policymakers can use information on pollution intensity to adjust their policy rates, thereby moving consumption from high-to-low pollution intensity periods. Specifically, Muller (2021) leverages a New Keynesian framework (Goodfriend 2016) to show how the so-called natural rate of interest (or r*) is influenced by macro-economic changes in pollution intensity. During periods when an economy is becoming more pollution-intensive, this pollution-adjusted interest rate (r_g) falls short of the conventionally-defined r*. And, when an economy is cleaning up r* exceeds r_g. The intuition for the orientation between r* and r_g hinges on the growth effects of pollution damage established by Muller (2014), ACPZ (2023), and Muller (2020). Namely, increasing (decreasing) pollution intensity exerts a drag (boost) on growth when the national accounts can track such phenomena. The upshot from Muller (2021) is that during periods of rapid changes in pollution intensity (e.g., energy transitions, decarbonization, large-scale policy changes), central banks can use r_g to achieve their traditional goals of price stability and full employment while also mitigating pollution damage. Omitting consideration of the growth effects of pollution damage gives rise to the potential for resource allocation mistakes due to biases embedded in r*.

Each of the examples offered in this essay bolster ACPZ's prescient claim that functional economic models depend on apposite data. The core message conveyed here and which is complementary to that of ACPZ is two-fold. First, without a complete representation of economic activity, inclusive of stocks and flows of natural capital, foundational metrics such as real growth rates may be biased. Second, systematic omissions from the official accounts permeate the information environment in which globally significant decisions (such as the calibration of monetary policy) are made.

Finally, ACPZ argue that "the effects of human activity on economically vital aspects of the natural world are demonstrable and unsustainable" (p. 2). That *some* of these "vital aspects" of the natural environment may be deemed *essential* to sustained human development undergirds the both the importance and the urgency of the current efforts to revise the System of National Accounts (SNA) to include measures of natural capital.

For acknowledgments, sources of research support, and disclosure of the author's material financial relationships, if any, please see https://www.nber.org/books-and-chapters/measuring-and-accounting-environmental-public-goods-national-accounts-perspective/comment-measuring-future-not-past-muller.

References

Agarwala, Matthew, Diane Coyle, Cristina Peñasco, Dimitri Zenghelis. "Measuring for the Future, Not the Past." In *Measuring and Accounting for Environmental Public Goods: A National Accounts Perspective*, edited by Mary Bohman, Eli Fenichel, and Nicholas Z. Muller. Chicago, IL: University of Chicago Press. This volume.

Goodfriend, Marvin. 2016. "The Case for Unencumbering Interest Rate Policy at the Zero Bound." *Jackson Hole Economic Policy Symposium*, volume 26.

Gordon, Robert. 2016. *The Rise and Fall of American Growth*. Princeton, NJ: Princeton University Press.

Muller, N. Z. 2014. "Boosting GDP growth by accounting for the environment." *Science* 345 (6199): 873–4.

Muller, N. Z. 2020. "Long-Run Environmental Accounting in the US Economy." *Environmental and Energy Policy in the Economy* 1: 158–91.

Muller, N. Z. 2021. "On the Green Interest Rate." NBER Working Paper No. 28891. Cambridge, MA: National Bureau of Economic Research.

3

Tracing Sustainability in the Long Run
Genuine Savings Estimates, 1850–2018

Eoin McLaughlin, Cristián Ducoing, and Les Oxley

3.1 Introduction

> *To maintain and augment the [Capital] stock that may be reserved for immediate consumption, is the sole end and purpose both of the fixed and circulating capitals. It is this stock which feeds, cloaths, and lodges the people. Their riches or poverty depends upon the abundant or sparing supplies which those two capitals can afford to the stock reserved for immediate consumption.* (Smith, 1776, Book II, chapter I)

Eoin McLaughlin is professor of economics and Head of Research in the Department of Accountancy, Economics, and Finance in the Edinburgh Business School at Heriot-Watt University.

Cristián Ducoing is a senior lecturer in the Department of Economic History at Lund University and a teacher at the Department of Economics, Public University of Navarre.

Les Oxley is a professor of economics at the University of Waikato.

The authors acknowledge the excellent research support by Johanna Fink (johanna.fink@ekh.lu.se) in the database compilation. Previous versions of this paper have been presented at the Swedish Economic History Meeting in Gothenburg October 2021; "The Wealth of Nations in the Post-Covid Era," April 2022; the World Economic History Congress in Paris, July 2022; the Queen's University Centre of Economic History Seminar, September 2022; and the Heriot-Watt Economics seminar, September 2022. Thanks to Eli Fenichel, Nicholas Muller, and Stephanie Onder for their comments on earlier iterations of this draft. These acknowledgments are extensive to all the participants at the "NBER Conference CRIW Measuring and Accounting for Environmental Public Goods: A National Accounts Perspective." This work is funded by the *Riksbanken Jubileunsfond* through the project Genuine Savings as a measure of sustainable development. Towards a GDP replacement. Ref: P19–0048:1 (https://www.rj.se/en/anslag/2019/genuine-savings-as-a-measure-of-sustainable-development.-towards-a-gdp-replacement/). The data utilized in this article are available at the web site genuinesavings.org (https://www.genuinesavings.org/data). For acknowledgments, sources of research support, and disclosure of the authors' material financial relationships, if any, please see https://www.nber.org/books-and-chapters/measuring-and-accounting-environmental-public-goods-national-accounts-perspective/tracing-sustainability-long-run-genuine-savings-estimates-1850-2018.

There is considerable interest from international organizations and policymakers as to how the management of natural resources affects human well-being (e.g., Clark and Harley 2020). For example, the 2021 *Dasgupta Review* argues that "in order to judge whether the path of economic development we choose to follow is sustainable, nations need to adopt a system of economic accounts that records an inclusive measure of their wealth." The concept of *Inclusive* (or *Comprehensive*) wealth measures the value of produced, natural, and human capital in a country and this approach has been adopted by both the World Bank (World Bank 2006, 2011, 2018, 2021) and the UN Environment Programme (UNU-IHDP 2012, 2014, 2018).[1] Inclusive Wealth includes all assets from which people can obtain well-being, either directly or indirectly. Changes in inclusive wealth per capita, whether positive or negative, are indicators of sustainable or unsustainable development (Hanley et al. 2016).

Polasky et al. (2019) call for a greater integration of both economic and sustainable development concepts and ideas. We echo this call. However, we also call more specifically for greater integration of economic history and sustainability science. Due to the work of the late Angus Maddison and colleagues, we are able to utilize GDP estimates as far back as the Middle Ages for some countries. (Bolt and van Zanden 2014; Broadberry et al. 2015). While this has provided invaluable material for studying the sources of economic growth, the economic history community has shown little engagement with sustainable development research and the measurement of inclusive wealth in particular. Seeing inclusive wealth as the foundation of future income, and hence welfare, means that changes in wealth (saving/investment) provide an indication of the feasibility of future, sustainable, development paths (Dasgupta 2001).

The work presented here is the first step toward producing such long-run comprehensive welfare indicators, focusing more on stocks (e.g., wealth), including natural capital, which provide future generations with the capabilities to increase their well-being, rather than on flows (e.g., income), conventionally measured by GDP, which measures annual outcomes without recourse to their long-term implications. If wealth-based methods are to inform sustainable social, economic, and environmental futures, they should, as a minimum, be able to explain the past. We will therefore analyze whether historical experiences can explain variations in past and current levels of comprehensive/inclusive wealth within and across countries and what future sustainable development prospects might look like. If the wealth accounting concept is to complement or replace other indicators, it requires evidence which includes long-run estimates for a wide range of countries and

1. In August 2022 the US government announced a new national strategy for monitoring natural assets. https://www.whitehouse.gov/omb/briefing-room/2022/08/18/a-new-national-strategy-to-reflect-natural-assets-on-americas-balance-sheet/

a standardized empirical methodology (Hanley et al. 2016). The goal of this work is both to illustrate how the concept can be applied to economic history and also to inspire future scholars to expand on this work and develop new estimates to help inform modern debates.

This article introduces a new historical database of Genuine Savings (GS),[2] a widely used modern economic indicator of sustainable development. The database is the first attempt to collect and collate existing estimates by several scholars to create a consistent database with a wide range of geographic coverage. It builds on work by researchers that has been primarily been published in the field of environmental economics (Rubio 2004; Lindmark and Acar 2013; Greasley et al. 2014; Hanley et al. 2016; Greasley et al. 2017). This work is complementary to existing collaborative research programs in economic history, namely the Maddison Project (Bolt and van Zanden 2014), by providing sustainability contextualization to historic income growth. The project also relates to recent work on historical estimates of the Human Development Index (HDI) (Prados de La Escosura 2021), but with a greater emphasis on environmental degradation. Through the creation of a new database we hope to give important historical context to current debates on sustainability. Therefore our estimates of the change in wealth will complement and nuance these research agendas.

The historical focus is necessary to provide evidence as to whether past policies, choices and resultant outcomes, guided by GDP as a welfare enhancing measure, have maximized (or even increased) well-being, *sustainably*. Historical data and outcomes provide important measures to test the robustness of the GS approach. Furthermore, historical data can enhance current metrics and provide a deeper understanding of natural capital, human capital, technological change, and environmental degradation in the long run, to guide policy for the future.[3] Much of the current work on environmental economics considers uncertain, unknown futures, (scenarios or predictions), which may simply never exist.[4] However, insights and data from the past can test alternative modeling approaches to inform policy making in the present and the future. Fenichel et al. (2016) argue that a better understanding of how past changes influence present sustainability outcomes can be used to forecast the impact of future changes in sustainability.

3.2 Economics of Sustainable Development

By the early 1990s, the phrase *sustainable development* had become "pervasive" and was "the watchword for international aid agencies, the jargon of development planners, the theme of conferences and learned papers, and the

2. Interchangeably known as "Comprehensive Investment" and "Adjusted Net Savings."

3. Recent studies are going in the same direction, such as the *Dasgupta Review* and the inclusion of Natural Capital in UN accounting.

4. Climate change uncertainty has received increasing attention since the 2000s (Tol 2003).

slogan of developmental and environmental activists" (Lélé 1991). However, a clear definition of the phrase was elusive, as there were (and are) several, sometimes contradictory, definitions (Pezzey 1992; Dietz and Neumayer 2007).[5] The 1987 *Brundtland Report*, one of the most widely cited interpretations of Sustainable Development (SD) as a concept (Schubert and Láng 2005), defined it as "development that meets the needs of the present without compromising the ability of future generations to meet their own needs" (World Commission on Environment and Development 1987, 43).

The *Brundtland Report* definition therefore has inter- and intra-generational equity considerations and has been the starting point of economists engaging with the concept of SD. For example, Asheim (1994) sees SD as an inter-generational equity issue and defines SD, following the lines of Hartwick (1977), "as a requirement of our generation to manage the resource base such that the average quality of life that we ensure ourselves can potentially be shared by all future generations." Whereas Pezzey (1992) defined SD as "non-declining utility of a representative member of society for millenia into the future." The former definition has become interpreted as a "capabilities-based" and the latter as an "outcome-based" definition of SD (Hanley et al. 2016). The capabilities-based approach views an SD path of an economy as one where the (per capita) real values of changes in capital stocks are non-negative (i.e., constant or increasing). Whereas the means-based approach views an SD path as one where utility or consumption per capita is non-declining. Dasgupta (2001) illustrates the relationship between both approaches and shows how comprehensive wealth, in particular the change in wealth, equates to future well-being.[6] The latter approach to sustainability links future well-being with changes in capital stocks (Pearce and Atkinson 1993; Pearce 2002).

Wealth is seen as the foundation of future income and hence welfare (Weitzman 2003, 2017), as changes in wealth (saving/investment) provide an indication of the feasibility of future sustainable development paths. The intuition here is that wealth underpins future well-being within an economy, as wealth (capital) broadly defined is required to generate future income streams (i.e., GDP) (Arrow et al. 2004, 2012), see figure 3.1. This approach has been the hallmark of recent efforts by the World Bank and the UN Environment Programme (e.g., see World Bank 2006, 2011, 2018, 2021; UNU-IHDP 2012, 2014, 2018).[7]

Dasgupta (2001) defines (*comprehensive*) wealth in terms of manufactured capital, human capital, natural capital, and knowledge. There is a further distinction within this literature in terms of how one perceives aggregate

5. SD is inherently interdisciplinary and, as Qasim (2017) shows, this leads to a wide engagement with the concepts and development of metrics to assess it.

6. This is also elucidated in Arrow et al. (2012).

7. See McLaughlin et al. (2024) for a critical appraisal of conflicting signals from the work of the World Bank and the UN Environment Programme.

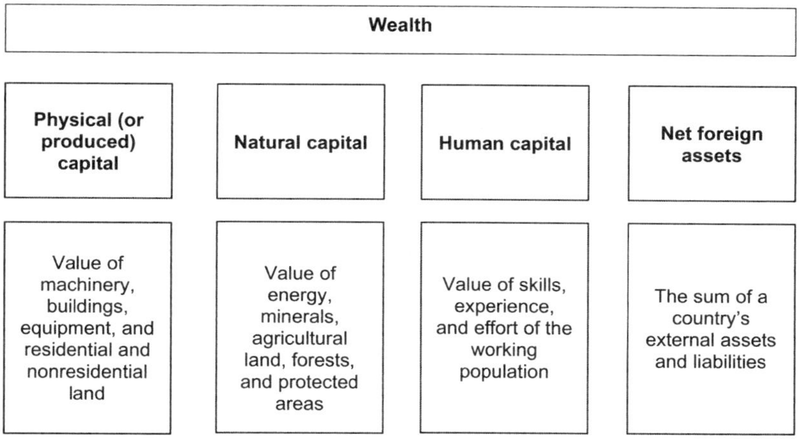

Figure 3.1 Components of wealth

capital. One approach being that SD requires non-declining total wealth (weak sustainability) and another where SD requires non-declining natural capital (strong sustainability). The first approach effectively uses extensions of the Solow (1956) neoclassical growth model to incorporate exhaustible resources (Solow 1974; Dasgupta and Heal 1974; Stiglitz 1974), and assumes perfect substitutability between different types of capital and the monetization of natural capital.[8] Whereas the latter approach deems that a decrease in a physical unit of natural capital cannot be replaced by increase the quantity of other forms of capital (Costanza and Daly 1992).[9] Fenichel and Zhao (2015) show how technological advances can enhance the array of substitution possibilities, yet the extent of substitutability is difficult to determine empirically (e.g., Markandya and Pedroso-Galinato 2007; Cohen et al. 2019), therefore how one chooses to approach sustainable development, from a weak or strong perspective, is a matter of preference. However, if a country fails a weak sustainability test, such as negative genuine savings, it will in all likelihood also fail a strong test as well (Hamilton and Clemens 1999).

The GS approach to sustainability rests firmly on the so-called Hartwick (1977) rule, which shows how consumption can be constant over time by re-investing rents from natural resource extraction into other forms of capital

8. So a $1 decrease in the value of natural capital can be compensated by a $1 increase in human capital for instance.

9. Costanza and Daly (1992) refer to total natural capital which is renewable plus nonrenewable natural capital. Ecosystems are the example given for renewable (or active) natural resources as they can yield a service when harvested (timber) or when left in place (e.g. erosion control). Whereas nonrenewables are passive in that they yield no service until they are harvested.

(i.e., person-made or human). One of the attractions of GS is that, under certain assumptions, it can be used to assess both the capabilities-based and the outcome-based approaches to SD (Hanley et al. 2016). Another attraction is that it is firmly grounded in the system of national accounts (SNA) framework and can be used to measure and compare countries in a consistent manner. At the most basic level, the economics of SD is more welfare orientated and focuses on changes in wellbeing (proxied by per capita consumption) than GDP growth, as it focuses on net savings (investment), and places greater emphasis on natural resource stocks (Ferreira et al. 2008). The GS approach therefore relates to both the idea of wealth accounting, as it is an indicator of how a nation's total wealth changes year-on-year (i.e., a flow) (Hamilton and Hepburn 2017; World Bank 2018), and income accounting (i.e., GDP), as it is built upon the foundations of the SNAs (Hanley et al. 2016). In accounting terms, while both GS and GDP are flows, the distinction between them is clear: GS is a measure of the change in the stock of wealth, whereas GDP is a measure of income that is derived from the stock of wealth (Weitzman 2003).

3.2.1 Existing GS Estimates

Over the past 25 years, starting with Pearce and Atkinson (1993) and Hamilton and Clemens (1999), there have been a series of genuine savings estimates for a range of countries. The time period covered by most estimates range from the 1970s to the present.

Studies have tended to trade off scale and scope, with studies focusing on individual countries being richer in data quality but not directly comparable across countries. Definitions of metrics have also varied with "green" and "genuine" savings measures commonly constructed and used interchangeably (see Hanley et al. 2016 for a review of the empirical literature). There are several studies that have calculated GS for shorter time periods. Some have explicitly compared estimates of GS with measures of Green National Product (Pezzey et al. 2006; Mota et al. 2010). Others have focused on expanding measures of GS to incorporate additional pollutants (Pezzey et al. 2006; Mota and Domingos 2013; Ferreira and Vincent 2005; Pezzey and Burke 2014).[10] At the most extreme, McGrath et al. (2021) incorporate damage costs for local pollutants and find that this changes genuine savings signals (from positive to negative) for several European countries over the period 1990 to 2018.

There have been several estimates of historical GS, the pioneering work was by Rubio (2004), who estimated GS for Mexico and Venezuela from

10. For example Ferreira and Moro (2011) estimate GS for Ireland from 1995–2005, McGrath et al. (2019) build on this work by incorporating additional pollutants and estimate GS for Ireland from 1990–2016.

the 1920s to the 1990s. Later work looked at the experience of developed countries over more than a hundred years, with a focus on Sweden, the United Kingdom, Germany, the United States, and Australia (Lindmark and Acar 2013; Greasley et al. 2014; Hanley et al. 2016; Greasley et al. 2017). More recent work has analyzed GS for countries in the 20th century (Qasim et al. 2020; McGrath et al. 2021). The innovative contribution of Greasley et al. (2014) was to test the predictive power of GS as a forward-looking indicator of sustainable development using the historical experience of the United Kingdom, where GS performs best over long horizons and when TFP was incorporated. These findings were corroborated for the United States, Germany, Australia, and Ireland (Hanley et al. 2016; Greasley et al. 2017; McGrath et al. 2024) although not in the case of Sweden (Lindmark et al. 2018).

Pezzey and Burke (2014) argue that the scale that GS should be analyzed is at a global level. Their contribution is to aggregate national level estimates of GS and incorporate differences in carbon pricing at a global level. The global scale approach was extended by Blum et al. (2017), who incorporated historical estimates of the abovementioned developed countries with estimates for several Latin American countries. Our database expands on this work by extending the range of countries included in the database.

3.3 Methodology

GS, also known as adjusted net saving (ANS), measures the "true" (or "genuine") rate of saving (investment) in an economy after taking into account depreciation of fixed capital, investment in human capital, depletion of natural resources, and damages caused by pollution. Genuine savings, the name used in this article, is an indicator that aims to assess an economy's sustainability based on the concepts of Environmental Economic Accounting (SEEA 1993, 2003, 2014). In effect, GS is tracking the *change* in wealth.

The main formula for calculating GS is as follows:

$$GS = I - \delta K - n - \sigma(e) + m, \tag{1}$$

where I is investment, δK is traditional depreciation of fixed capital, n are resource rents, σ is the damage cost from pollution,[11] and m is human capital. We construct several indicators, as illustrated in figure 3.2, to display and distinguish several aspects of sustainability.

We have largely followed Hamilton and Clemens (1999) and the World Bank (2006, 2011) methodology[12] for calculating GS by estimating a range

11. Emissions minus dissipation
12. This is outlined in Bolt et al. (2002).

1 Gross Savings/ Investment	2 Net Savings	3 Green Savings	4 Green Savings	5 Genuine Savings	6 GST
National income minus consumption/ acquisition of new or existing fixed assets	Gross savings minus depreciation	Net savings minus depreciation of natural capital	Green savings minus pollution damages	Green savings (4) plus investment in human capital	Technology-augmented Genuine Savings, augmented plus the present value of technological change

Figure 3.2 Genuine savings calculations

of increasingly comprehensive measures of year-on-year changes in total wealth over time.[13]

3.3.1 Net National Savings and Investment

The starting point for World Bank (2011) in calculating GS is to estimate national savings as a residual from GDP minus total (private and government) consumption. Then estimates of depreciation are subtracted from this to calculate net savings rates.

Maddison (1992) was a pioneer in the comparative study of historical savings rates, calculating historical savings rates for 11 countries from the 1870s through to the 1980s. However, these are gross savings rates and there is no allowance for depreciation.

For our study we deviate from the Hamilton and Clemens (1999) approach and incorporate net *investment* as an alternative to net *savings*. Here net investment, including overseas investment, reflects changes in a country's physical assets. Estimates of net investment are readily available for various countries, but for some of them we have estimated net investment using gross investment and consumption of fixed capital, or simply annual depreciation of assets (see appendix for a detailed list of sources used).

3.3.2 Natural Capital

To account for the depletion of natural (renewable and non-renewable) resources we subtracted the rent from the depletion of natural resources,

13. Recent work of the World Bank (2018, 2021) has focused primarily on wealth estimates and calculate the change in wealth as a predictor of sustainability. There is only one study which attempted to do this using historic data but viewed GS as a more reliable indicator of sustainability (McLaughlin et al. 2014).

using gross revenues minus average costs of depletion, from net investment.[14] For many European countries (e.g., Great Britain), the bulk of rents from resource extraction originate from fossil fuels (coal, oil, and natural gas). We also considered other resources (metals and mineral ores), but the quantities by and large are negligible compared with the accumulation of other assets. For the United States and Australia, two resource-abundant developed nations, we included data on coal, oil, and gas as well as metal and mineral ores. For Latin American countries, resources considered include metal and mineral ores and fossil fuels. Important sources of natural capital depletion are petroleum (Argentina, Colombia, Mexico), gold (Brazil, Colombia), silver (Colombia), coal (Brazil), and copper (Chile).

In terms of renewable resources, we include changes in forestry. Hamilton and Clemens (1999) do not include net natural growth of living resources and only include forestry that are commercially exploited and acknowledge that this methodological decision biases against sustainability. Here we include net growth to reduce this bias, while the forest stock appreciates it also has biodiversity benefits that would be overlooked if this is omitted. As we do not fully value ecosystems or biodiversity, excluding net forest growth would bias against sustainability even further. However, we are aware that forest growth cannot be readily translated straightforwardly into *biodiversity*.

3.3.3 Human Capital

It is possible to measure human capital created by investment in education and skills (Dasgupta 2001), however within existing national accounting frameworks expenditure on children's education (via teacher salaries) is considered to be consumption, and while some element of capital spending on school building is included in capital formation, this is a small share of annual education expenditure (Hamilton and Clemens 1999). To address this we use education expenditure to proxy the accumulation of human capital to obtain a more inclusive measure of a country's assets.

Admittedly there are limitations to this approach as it is known that education does not perfectly equate with human capital, however, alternatives measurements of human capital stocks, such as discounted life-time earnings, are not available for all countries over the whole of our sample. Furthermore, an additional limitation of this approach is that education expenditure as a proxy for human capital accumulation makes no allowances for appreciation

14. We used the market value of extracted renewables and non-renewable resources as well as the extracted quantities to compute the gross revenues. The average extraction costs were estimated using labor requirement and the average wage of laborers. Similarly, estimates of the value of the change in timber stocks by country was based on changes in area covered with forests, the average quantity of timber per m^3 and the market value of timber. For more recent periods the FAO (2010) provides estimates on the cubic quantities of timber on a given surface area; it is likely that applying this methodology on historical periods overestimates historical forest stocks since we implicitly assume than the high modern tree planting density has existed throughout the period under observation.

of, for instance, on-the-job training and experience, as well as depreciation (aging and mortality) of human capital. Moreover, this approach does not account for international migration whereby migrant recipients benefit from the human capital embodied in immigrants and developing countries may experience losses in human capital through emigration.

Besides data availability and evident flaws and limitations of the expenditure approach, it must be understood that we are measuring the savings to produce further increases in well-being. Under this framework, the reinvestment of resource rents are a valid indicator of *societies' effort* to compensate future generations (Hartwick 1977).

3.3.4 Technological Progress and the Value of Time

Technological change has been an important concept in the theoretical literature (Weitzman 1997, 1999; Arrow et al. 2004, 2012), but there are a number of challenges incorporating a measure of technology into empirical studies.[15] Weitzman (1997) suggests that an adjustment for technological change may be in the region of 40 percent of Net National Product. Thus, omitting a technological progress measure would misstate the degree of sustainability of an economy. In relation to technological progress, although many of the general purpose technologies were invented in the late 19th century (telephones, electricity, combustion engine), it was not until the 20th century that they were adopted en masse; in many cases this meant the use of new natural resources that had been overlooked in the past (oil and natural gas for example) but in turn this led to more efficient use of resources (e.g., improvements in fuel efficiency, see Gordon 2016).

Several studies have used changes in TFP as an indicator of technological progress and incorporated this into the genuine savings framework through the net present value of TFPs contribution to future GDP growth (Pezzey et al. 2006; Mota and Domingos 2013; Greasley et al. 2014; McGrath et al. 2024). We follow this approach and incorporate the effects of exogenous technological progress into our measure of GS by including the present value of TFP growth. Following Pezzey et al. (2006) and Greasley et al. (2014) we calculate the present value of future changes in trend TFP over a 20-year time horizon. This is done to capture the uncertainty over the duration of the value of technological progress.[16]

15. For example, such as how to measure technology, i.e., R&D, patents, energy intensity, total factor productivity.

16. Arrow et al. (2012, table 3) incorporate a measure of TFP but do so by adding the current TFP growth rate to the per capita growth rate of Total (Comprehensive) Wealth. However, this approach only adds 1 year and does not take account of the value of time as an uncontrolled capital stock. The choice of 20 years follows Pezzey et al. (2006) and Greasley et al. (2014). Using the case of Argentina as an example, where the present value of TFP is 10.12 percent over 20 years, if a shorter horizon (10 years) is used, this is reduced to 8.45 percent of GDP, and if a longer horizon (30 years) is used, this increases to 15.87 percent of GDP. Therefore, by choosing a 20-year horizon we err on the side of underestimation of the value of technological progress.

TFP is a central piece of the puzzle to assess sustainable development; this metric, however, is somewhat in conflict with other components of GS. TFP is related to informativeness, intangible assets, institutions, and social capital, and as a consequence the incorporation of TFP brings the risk of "double-counting" the effects equally associated with technology and human capital.

Baier et al. (2006) find that incorporating a measure of human capital reduces the size of the residual. Similarly, Manuelli and Seshadri (2014) argue that better measurements of human capital quantity and quality can further reduce TFP. Moveover, as Bakker et al. (2019) note, 'TFP growth is not a synonym for technological change," and TFP growth may in fact be an over/under estimate of the contribution of technological change to labor productivity growth owing to a misspecified production function. There are also issues relating to specifying a production function which incorporates natural capital. For example, Brandt et al. (2013) find that accounting for natural capital in the production function overestimates productivity in economies undergoing resource booms and underestimates productivity in economies that experience declining natural capital.

This gives us reason to believe that the overlap between human capital accumulation and the value of technology accumulation leads to a slight overestimation of total capital formation. Data limitations and availability prevent us from fully disentangling human capital and technology. We therefore opt to incorporate an unadjusted TFP series in our estimates, however, in the results section we illustrate the effect of TFP appended to green investment to avoid the possibility of double counting as education expenditure is included in GS.

3.3.5 Social Costs of Carbon

Carbon dioxide (CO_2) is a greenhouse gas (GHG) with a lifetime of up to 200 years in the atmosphere and accounts for 75 percent of global warming potential (Stern 2007, table 8.1). The Social Cost of Carbon (SCC) represents "future damage" from of an additional tonne of CO_2 (Rennert et al. 2021). We incorporate a range of prices, related to the damage from CO_2 emissions, in our global estimates.

The crucial factor is that CO_2 is a stock pollutant in that the annual emissions add to the existing concentration in the atmosphere and each unit of emissions increases the marginal damage cost of the pollutant in the future (Kunnas et al. 2014). To account for CO_2 in our sustainability indicator we used the total amount of carbon dioxide emitted and estimates of the social costs of carbon derived from the wider literature.

There is a range of price estimates that we have incorporated, such as the constant \$20 tonne carbon cost of the World Bank metric, \$29 t/c from Tol (2012), \$110 t/c from the Stern Review (Stern 2007). In this paper we have incorporated the last estimates to show the impact of emissions under dif-

Table 3.1 Selected SCC estimations, different sources and methods

Source (Year)	SCC, price per ton (Interval)	Discount rate
World Bank/Fankhauser	US$20.3 (20–30, after 2010)	n/a
Tol (2008)	US$25	2%
US Interim SCC	US$51 (14 to 260)	3%
Stern (2022 and 2007)	US$110 (77 to 124)	2%
Pezzey & Burke Control (2014)	US$131	2–3%
Pezzey & Burke Non Control (2014)	US$1,455	2–3%
Rennert et al. (2022)	US$185 (44 to 413)	2%

Sources: Fankhauser (1994), Tol (2012), Stern (2022, 2007), Rennert et al. (2022) and Pezzey and Burke (2014).

ferent scenarios.[17] and warn against choosing a singular price because of the wide range of estimates.

The current predominant view in the academic literature seems to be that the underlying DICE models are biased downwards (Stern 2022). A recent review by Hänsel et al. (2020) argues for a higher cost of $208 in 2020. The results presented below utilize two estimates of the social cost of carbon by Pezzey and Burke (2014).[18] The first price, $131 t/c, estimated from a DICE model recalibrated to assume that it is economically optimal to control emissions such that warming may be limited to an agreed target of 2°C and a significantly higher price of $1455 t/c which assumes that no controls of CO_2 emissions are implemented. We also incorporate a lower bound estimate of $51 from the US government (2021). Support from these prices can be found in the most recent estimates of SCC based on a new integrated model assessment, and it has resulted in an SCC of US$185 (with a lower bound of US$44 and an upper bound of $413 per CO_2 ton) (Rennert et al. 2022). A summary of the main SSC estimates is presented in table 3.1.

We choose to highlight these contrasting prices as our study shares similarities with Pezzey and Burke (2014) and Pezzey (2024) in that we also attempt to determine if the world is on a "global" sustainability path. These prices are discounted over time as suggested by Tol (2012) and as illustrated by Kunnas et al. (2014).[19] Using the United States as an example, figure 3.3 illustrates our approach to SSC. The left panel discounts $51 SCC while the right panel discounts the $110 (converted to 1990 prices) using different

17. There is a range of 300 estimates published in journals and reports (Tol 2011). Kaufman et al. (2020) reported SCCs between US$0 and US$2000.

18. Although Pezzey (2019) himself warns, "*SCCs attract more attention globally from academics than from policymakers.*"

19. For a more comprehensive overview of data sources used, see the data appendix as well as Blum et al. (2019); Camacho (2014); Greasley et al. (2014); Greasley et al. (2017); Höfeler (2014); Klenk (2013); and Mennig (2015). "Experts Clash over Cost of Carbon" https://www.scientificamerican.com/article/experts-clash-over-cost-of-carbon/text. Accessed September 20, 2022.

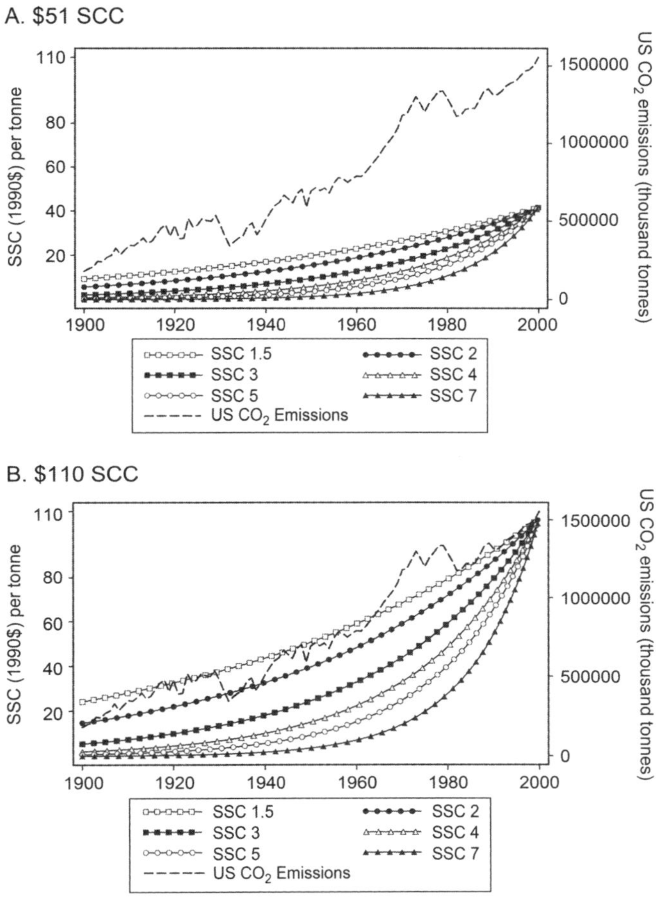

Figure 3.3 SSC example using different discount rates

discount rates, from 1.5 percent to 7 percent.[20] In turn, discounting the same SCC by different discount rates has a dramatic effect on the estimate of the damage cost of US carbon emissions, see figure 3.4. The results below are thus sensitive to both the discount rate as well as the chosen SCC.

Several questions arise from the estimated SCC used in these calculations. The most relevant relates to the discount rate used. In our historical GS the SSC is linearly discounted over time, while there are arguments for using different discount factors or different SSCs at different points in time. In order to address this concern, we have estimated a price variation based on

20. The latter being the preferred discount rate of the Trump administration.

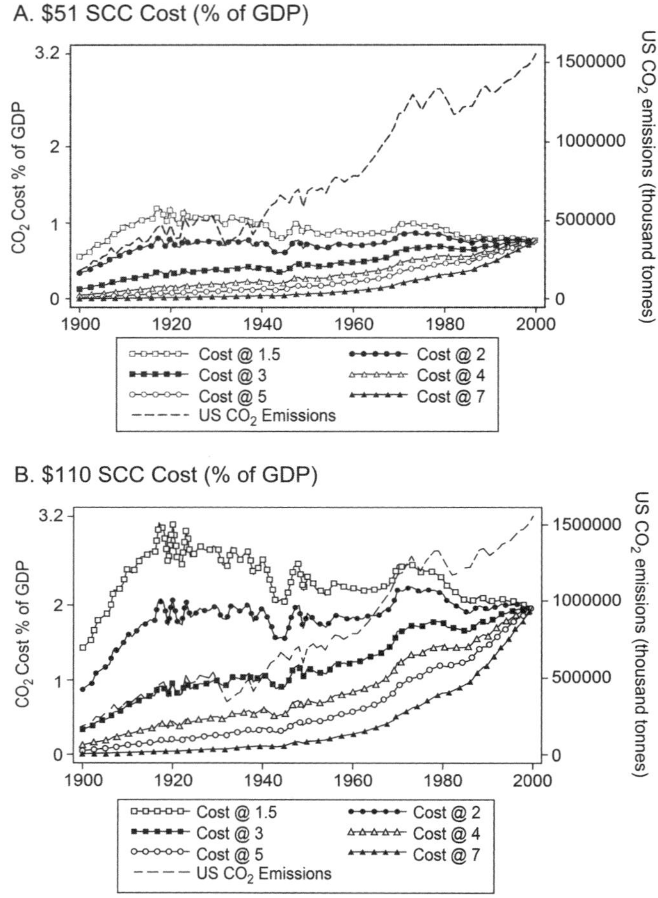

Figure 3.4 SSC example using the United States with $51 and $110

the previous accumulated CO_2 emissions. The difference with the linearly discounted SSC is marginal (between 0.3 percent and 0.5 percent).[21]

3.3.6 International Dollars

Until recently, the World Bank (2006) made comparisons of wealth between countries using market exchange rates. While noting the variance in wealth per capita between developed and developing countries, some of this was attributed to the use of nominal exchange rates (World Bank 2006, 17). The most recent World Bank (2021) attempts to address this issue by adopting Purchasing Power Parities, derived from the International Com-

21. The results of this exercise are included in the appendix.

parison Programme (Deaton and Heston 2010). The issue here is that the prices collected are not necessarily related to the capital stocks that are being measured in wealth accounting and were originally intended to be used in comparing income across countries. Although it is acknowledged that various theoretical and empirical considerations, such as whether using PPP is appropriate in a wealth accounting context; what level of PPP should be used; and how to construct a constant value series based on PPPs, were not addressed in the application of PPPs in a wealth accounting context (World Bank 2021, 83).[22]

While we share the reservations about applying PPPs that are derived for another purpose, using a PPP based series enables comparability across space and time. All units have been deflated using national GDP deflators and have been converted into purchasing power adjusted international dollars following Maddison (2001) and Bolt and van Zanden (2014), expressed as Geary-Khamis dollars ($) in the figures below. Such PPP adjusted estimates are similar to Hanley et al. (2016) and Greasley et al. (2017).

3.3.7 Limitations

A limitation of the construction of GS as outlined above is that it only covers quantifiable indi- cators that can be approximately expressed in monetary units. Thus GS overlooks nonmarket environmental goods and services. As a result the GS metric excludes developments in fisheries, biodiversity, and ecosystem services. It also underestimates pollution damages as it does not incorporate some major pollutants, such SO_2 and NO_x, that were more local in impact.

While historical estimates of biodiversity are available, these indicators are difficult to incorporate in an augmented long-run GS metric until a compromise estimate of their economic value over time is obtained.

Losses in biodiversity are largely the result of changes in land use; the increasing demand for grazing and cropland has encouraged deforestation which in turn has resulted in losses in biodiversity. Estimates of the development of biodiversity suggests that Latin America and the United States, and the majority of the world's countries, experienced losses in biodiversity whereas some countries in Western Europe saw stagnating or even increases in biodiversity.[23] Any future evaluation of the costs of biodiversity loss and

22. Inklaar et al. (2023), in a report commissioned by the World Bank, advocate using multiple deflators (CPI, GDP delfators, PPPs) depending on the purpose of the wealth measure, whether it is seen as the foundation of future consumption or future production. This relates to a well-documented issue surrounding how to deflate consumption when the composition of consumption changes over time, e.g., Palumbo et al., 2006. We highlight the difference between using CPI or GDP deflators in appendices, as CPI and GDP tend to co-move but by different magnitudes changing deflator leads to modest level effects but with no change in the trend of the series.

23. Stock valuations of global ecosystem services are most notable at the end of our period of study, such as Costanza et al. (1997), who estimated the global value of the entire biosphere

SO_2 emissions will lower any sustainability indicator (see Goldewijk 2014 for an overview). Therefore our estimates can be seen as a lower bound estimate of natural capital.

Similarly, there are estimates of SO_2 pollution. The global output of SO_2 increased throughout the 20th century, with the major share of SO_2 being emitted in North America, followed by Western Europe. Total global SO_2 emissions rapidly rose after World War Two, and peaked around 1980. During the late 20th century, environmental regulation combined with fuel-saving technologies and a transition away from fuels with a high-sulphur content helped to lower global SO_2 output (Stern and Kaufmann 1996). The challenge with SO_2 pollution is placing a damage cost on emissions. Unlike CO_2 pollution which is global, SO_2 damages are time and context specific which would require country level estimates SO_2 pollution at various points in time. For example, EEA (2014) estimates of SO_2 damage costs per tonne are based on health damage caused by SO_2. These estimates vary enormously by country.[24] Although both approaches effectively measure health costs through loss in lifetime earnings, the dramatic increase in life expectancy over time raises challenges to this conventional approach.[25]

The absence of monetary evaluations of these phenomena, however, cannot hide the fact that economic growth seems to adversely affect biodiversity and levels of pollution (Dasgupta 2021).

A related issue relates to what is considered a "resource." In some respects this relates to the thorny issue of new goods, goods that did not exist in the past and can distort pictures of growth and inflation (Bresnahan and Gordon 1996). In our study there are several cases of resource discovery and discovery of new uses for once undervalued resources. In our own time this is reflected by the increased demand for lithium in the manufacturing of electric vehicles. Our treatment of "new" environmental resources is to track both production and prices of these goods over time.

3.4 Historical Estimates of Genuine Savings: The New Data Set

As with the majority of economic history research or historical data in the long run, the main group of countries studied have been the developed ones. If we classified these countries by the length of the period already

to be between \$16–54 trillion and \$125–145 in ecosystem services and updated the Costanza et al. (1997) figures from 1997–2011. However, these stock valuations do not enable us to value changes in ecosystem services in the years preceding 1997. Furthermore, there have been increasing use of revealed and stated preference methods to value changes in environmental goods and services. However, these studies have not been applied consistently over time and benefit transfers may not be applicable spatially or temporally for all countries in our study.

24. For example, estimates range from €1,052 in Cyprus to €38,778 in Norway based on value of a life year or from €2,270 in Cyprus to €90,337 in Switzerland based on value of a statistical life.

25. In real terms, the marginal value of an additional year of life when life expectancy is 43 (as it was in 1900), is significantly different to the marginal value of an additional year of life when life expectancy is 79 (as in 2019).

estimated, the United Kingdom has the longest series of GS thanks to the work of Greasley et al. (2014), whose foundation rests on the classic work of UK capital stock estimates (Feinstein 1972, 1978; Feinstein and Pollard 1988). With further estimates of GS available from a number of published studies for several developed countries: the United States, Germany, Australia, France, Switzerland, New Zealand, and Spain (Hanley et al. 2016; Blum et al. 2019; Greasley et al. 2017; Blum et al. 2017; Qasim et al. 2020; Iriarte 2021).

One issue with estimates of GS is the lack of long run data for developing countries. A previous study of Latin American "green" investment over the period 1973–1986 lamented the quality of conventional measures of reproducible capital in Latin American countries (Vincent 2001). In order to overcome this concern, we make use of capital stock estimates for Latin American (Tafunell and Ducoing 2016) and the investment series produced by Tafunell (2013). We also note the availability of the pioneering work of Rubio (2004), who was the first to estimate GS for several Latin American Countries, including Mexico and Venezuela, in the 20th century. Blum et al. (2017) extended these estimates, as well as incorporating four additional Latin American countries (Argentina, Brazil, Chile, and Colombia). Most recently Labat et al. (2018) estimated a long run series for Uruguay (1875–2020).

In this paper we include GS for an additional four countries: Japan, Norway, Portugal, and Denmark.[26] Moreover, the Argentinean and Chilean data have extended a further 20 years back in time from the former estimation mentioned above (Blum et al. 2017).

A summary of the countries presented in this article and the time spans that cover each of the estimates is presented in table 3.2. One of the important contributions of this present paper is the inclusion of long run data-based estimates of GS for more developing countries, which was previously a major issue for comparative economic history and economic development research.

3.4.1 Preliminary Analysis of the New Database

Firstly does the measurement of GS provide us with, as Hamilton and Clemens (1999) call it, "useful new information"? To see if this is the case we compare conventional net national savings (NNS) rates with our measure of resource depletion, shown in figure 3.5. This is effectively a first approximation to the so-called Hartwick (1977) rule, "The investment of current exhaustible resource returns in reproducible capital implies per capita consumption is constant."[27] The 45° line labeled "marginal sustainability" highlights the difference between countries that are sustainable (savings

26. The Denmark data have been estimated from a thesis written by Andrew Pierson.
27. Asheim et al. (2023) generalize the Hartwick rule to account for non-constant population growth.

Table 3.2 **Data sources and period covered of genuine savings estimations**

Country	Period covered	Source
Argentina	1900–2000	Blum et al. (2017)
Australia	1870–2018	Blum et al. (2017); Greasley et al. (2017)
Bolivia	1885–2015	This paper
Brazil	1880–2018	Blum et al. (2017)
Cambodia	1970–2010	Phillipsen + this paper
Chile	1880–2000	Blum et al. (2017) + this paper
Costa Rica	1902–2000	Pollack + this paper
Colombia	1900–2000	Blum et al. (2017)
Germany	1850–2010	Blum et al. (2013)
Great Britain	1850–2010	Greasley et al. (2014)
France	1900–2000	Blum et al. (2017)
Mexico	1900–2000	Blum et al. (2017)
New Zealand	1950–2000	Qasim et al. (2020)
Norway	1870–2000	Fink and Ducoing (2022)
Portugal	1900–2000	This paper
Spain	1950–2010	Iriarte (2021)
Sweden	1850–2010	Lindmark and Acar (2013)
Switzerland	1900–2000	Blum et al. (2017)
Japan	1880–2010	This paper
Venezuela	1935–1985	Rubio (2004)
Uruguay	1875–2015	Labat et al. (2019)
United Kingdom	1765–2000	Greasley et al. (2014)
United States of America	1870–2015	Hanley et al. (2015)

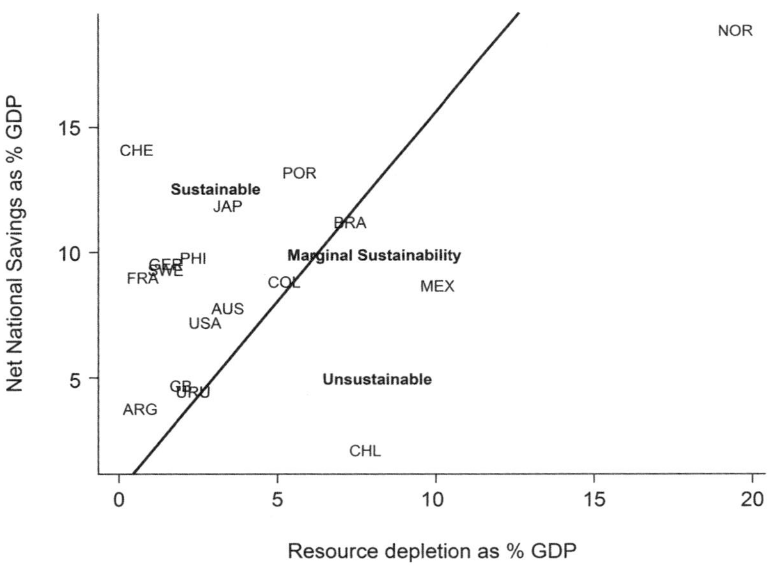

Figure 3.5 Scatter plot of resource depletion and net savings rates, 1950–2000
Source: see table 3.2

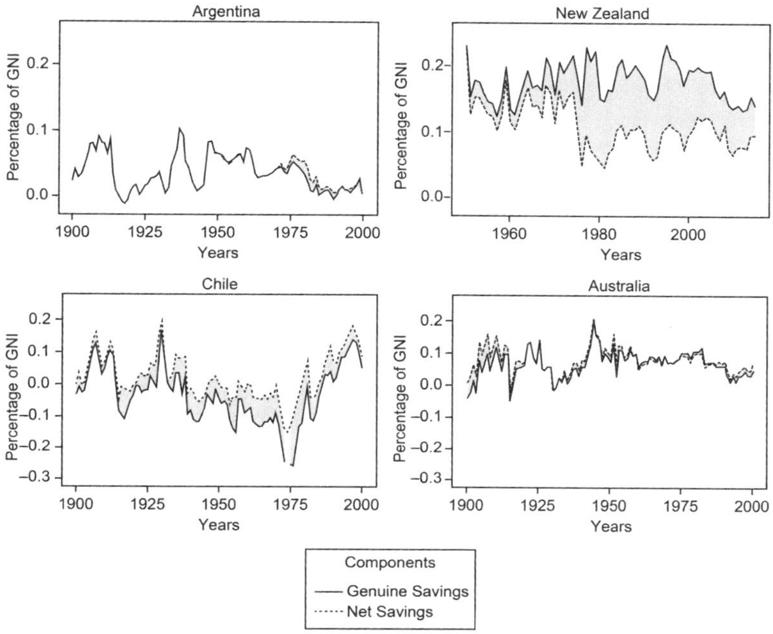

Figure 3.6 Net national savings and genuine savings in Argentina, New Zealand, Chile, and Australia. 1900–2000

Source: See table 3.2

rates > Resource depletion) and countries that are unsustainable (savings rates < Resource depletion). In contrast to Hamilton and Clemens (1999), we do not observe countries with negative net savings rates but we do identify countries that have higher resource depletion than net savings rates and are therefore deemed unsustainable.

The gap between NNS and GS has been called the "depletion rate" by Hamilton and Clemens (1999). If we compare New Zealand with Argentina, two countries with a reasonably well-developed agro-sector, savings rates are mainly positive, but there is a noticeable difference in levels between both countries (see figure 3.6). The case of Chile (bottom left panel in figure 3.6) is a representative example of development in Latin America. Between 1950 and 1990 the average GS per capita was negative, meaning that the extraction of natural resources, mainly copper, was not *re-invested* in either human capital or fixed investment. The experience of Australia stands in contrast to that of Chile. Australia, despite its large mining sector, saw little difference between NNS and GS as resource rents were reinvested to maintain positive genuine savings.

Considering GS alone, figure 3.7 shows all countries using the same scale. Clear trends emerge of savings rates that average 7.8 percent of GDP, rang-

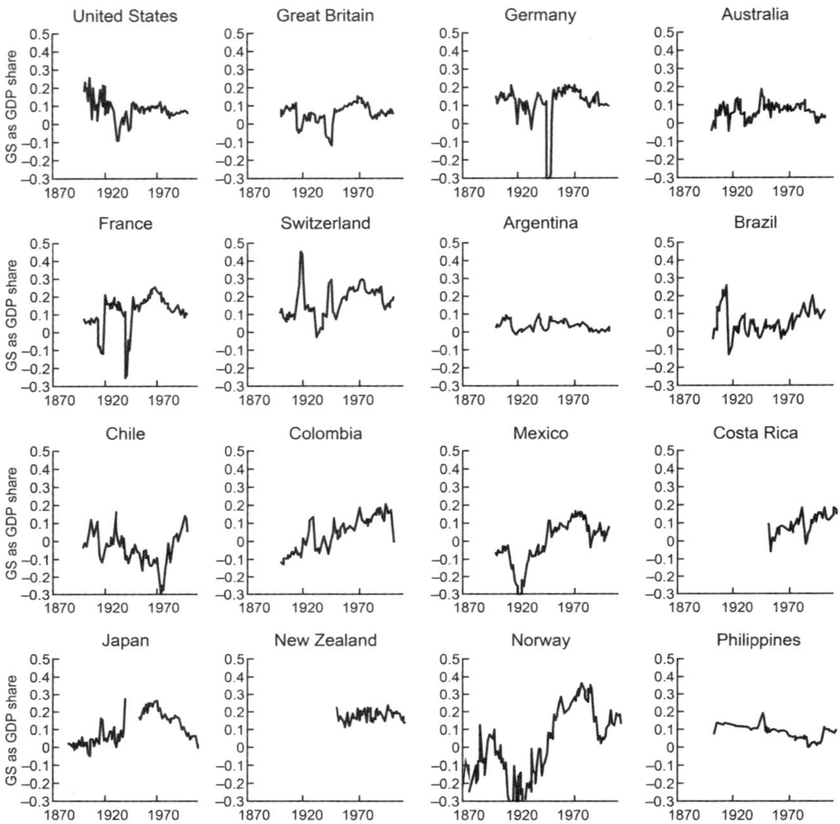

Figure 3.7 Genuine savings as share of GDP, selected countries, 1850–2020
Source: See table 3.2

ing between 69 percent and −68 percent of GDP, in their extreme values.[28] Some countries experience periods of negative GS, such as Brazil, Australia, France, Germany, Britain, the United States, Uruguay, which tended to coincide with well-known macro shocks such as wars and the Great Depression. Others, such as Sweden and Mexico, start the period experiencing negative GS and transition to positive GS. Of the countries two were notable outliers, Chile and Uruguay; the former for persistent negative GS, the latter for its high initial rates of GS and the volatility of the measure. Of the countries in the sample, only New Zealand and Spain do not show signs of negative GS.

The picture is changed when our measure of technological change is incorporated. Figure 3.8 compares GS rates and GSTFP rates for the coun-

28. See table 3.3 for summary statistics for each country.

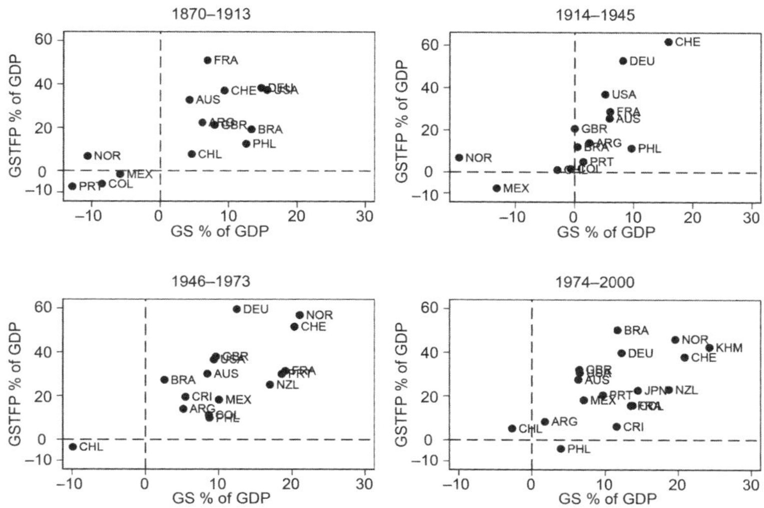

Figure 3.8 Genuine savings incorporating technological change, 1870—2020
Source: See table 3.2

tries in our database. While countries may have episodes of negative GS, this is overcome by positive GSTFP rates. While there are a few exceptions to this, in earlier periods countries had negative GS and low rates of TFP growth which meant that technological progress was unable to compensate for negative GS. On the whole when a measure of technological progress is incorporated it shows a pattern of positive GS indicating that technological progress cannot be omitted in studies sustainable development. This finding is in line with Ferreira and Vincent (2005), who argue that measures of GS are incomplete when sources of economic growth go beyond conventional capital accumulation.

Dasgupta (2009) makes the case that the empirical literature on the sources of economic growth may actually "misdirect" and instead of focusing on GDP growth as an outcome variable, the outcome variable should be the change in well-being. Another aspect to this is that the literature on growth finds conventional investment to be a key driver in growth, but what of comprehensive investment: How do the figures presented here compare to standard narratives surrounding economic growth? Figure 3.9 plots GS (as a percent of GDP) and GDP growth over different time periods.[29]

For three of the sub-periods there is a positive association between GS rates and GDP growth. However, this relationship breaks down during

29. There are two outliers. In 1870–1914 Uruguay has very high GS rates (46.49 percent and 1946–1973 Cambodia with 97.89 percent of GDP; these are excluded from this figure) in the period 1870–1913 but growth is modest.

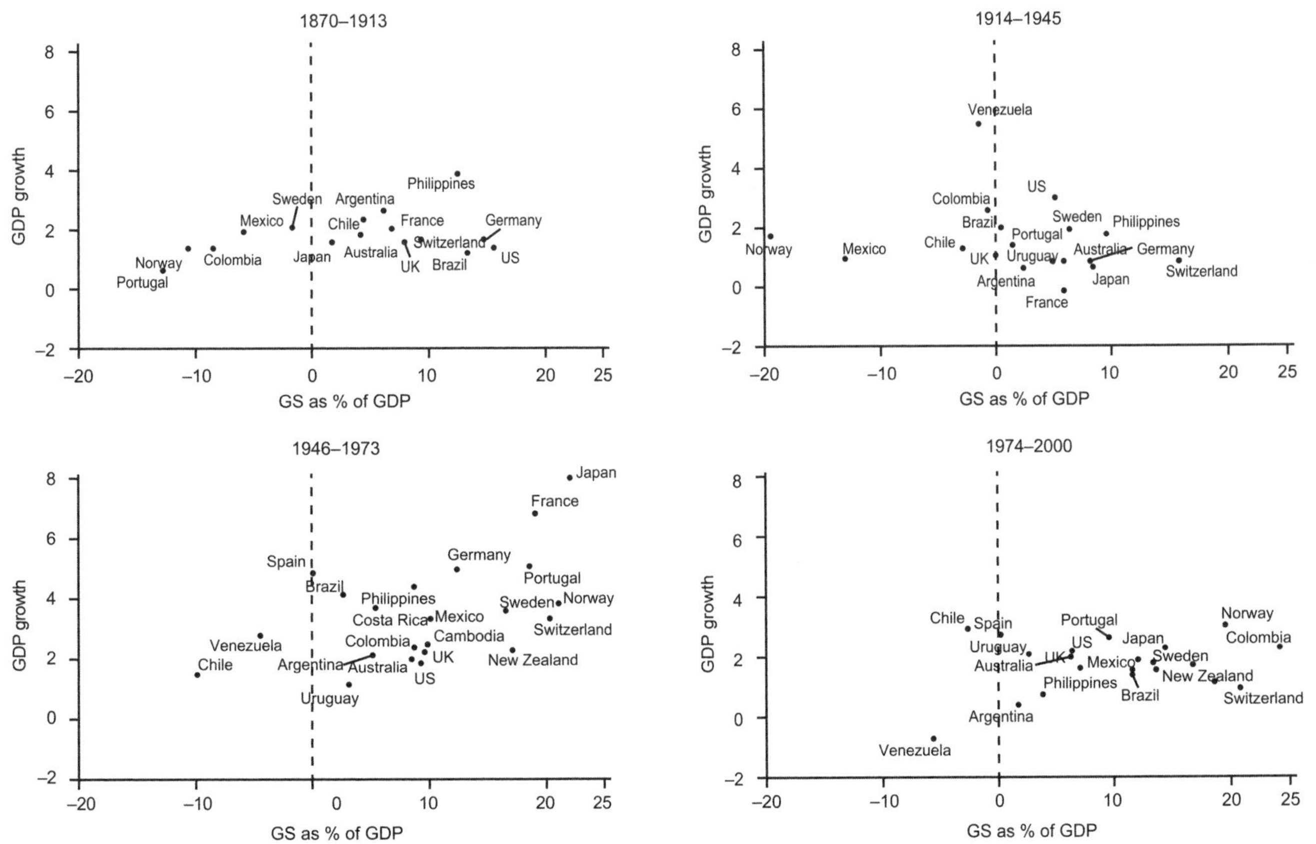

Figure 3.9 GDP growth and savings rates, 1870—2000

Source: See table 3.2 and Maddison database, https://www.rug.nl/ggdc/historicaldevelopment/maddison/?lang=en.

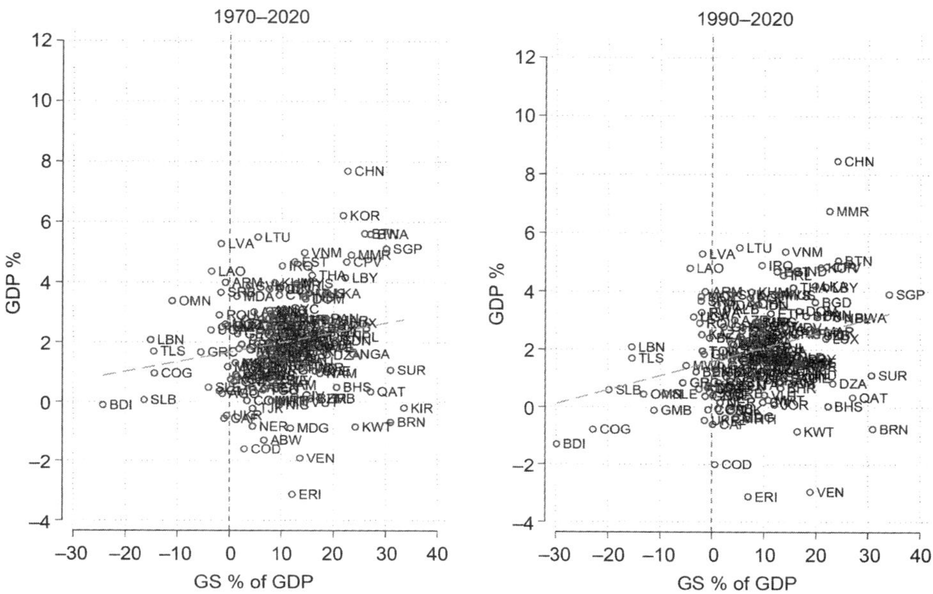

Figure 3.10 GS (% of GDP) and GDP per capita growth

Source: World Development Indicators, https://databank.worldbank.org/source/world-development-indicators.

the interwar period. Several countries experience negative GS rates during the first period, but the number of countries that experienced negative GS declined in each sub-period. Of the countries included in the sample, only Chile and Venezuela persistently displayed negative GS in consecutive periods; this is driven by the resource intensity of their respective economies. On the whole, most countries only experienced short spells of negative GS and reverted to positive growth rates thereafter; the major exception here was Venezuela in the final period 1974–2000. Thus overall, we do find evidence to support the view that countries can experience GDP growth at the expense of growth in (comprehensive) wealth (UNU-IHDP 2018; Yamaguchi et al. 2019); this also becomes evident when using the modern database of the World Bank (see figure 3.10).

The theoretical literature on genuine savings stresses a link between GS and well-being, although in practice this has tended to be defined in monetary units. An exception is Gnégé (2009), who explores the relationship between GS and other measures of well-being such as changes in infant mortality and the Human Development Index, finding a weak positive relationship between the two.[30] Here we focus on the relationship between the

30. Similarly, Blum et al. (2019) explore non-monetary indicators of well-being and find a positive correlation.

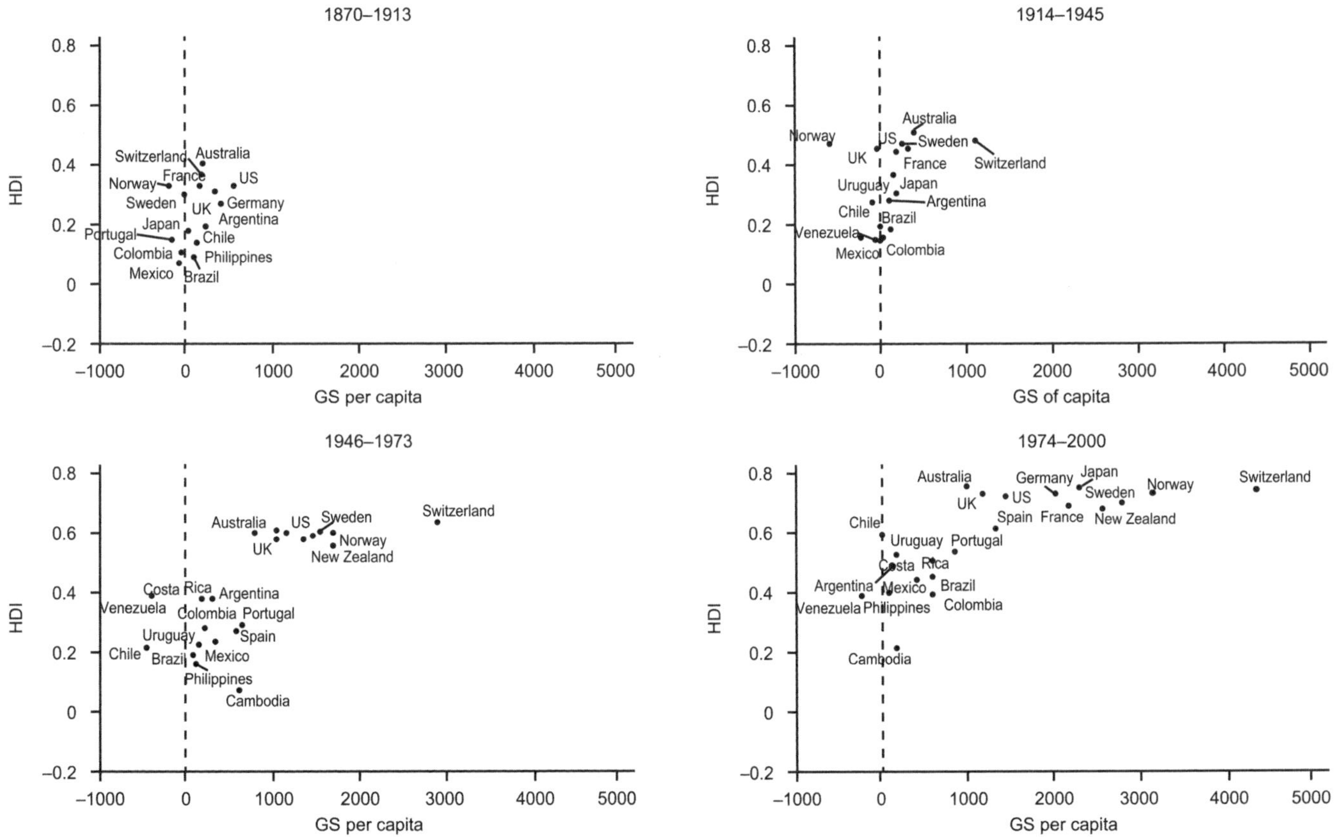

Figure 3.11 HDI and savings rates, 1870—2000

Source: See table 3.2 and Prados de la Escosura database, https://frdelpino.es/investigacion/en/category/01_social-sciences/02_world-economy/03_human-development-world-economy/.

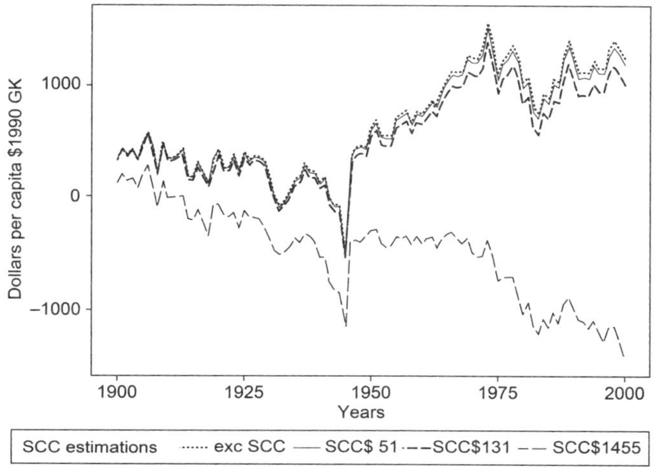

Figure 3.12 Global GS estimations with four different CO_2 cost prices
Source: See table 3.2

GS indicator and the new augmented HDI series (Prados de La Escosura 2021). The initial findings here suggest a weak correlation between GS and HDI initially but that the relationship strengthened significantly over time.

Finally, what are the effects of global pollutants on GS? Figure 3.12 illustrates the effect of including four different SSCs; this is analogous to our GS* above. The SCC represents a range from the distribution in the literature (see discussion above). We include a "price" of $0, which is effectively our benchmark global GS estimate. A $51 SSC shows a slight decrease in the level of GS per capita; doubling the SSC to $131 sees a further decrease in the level of the GS indicator but it is not negative barring the Great Depression and the Second World War. A substantial divergence in the GS metric is noted when the $51 SSC effectively sees a thirtyfold increase ($1,455), the price advocated by Pezzey and Burke (2014). Clearly the GS* metric is sensitive to the price of carbon, but this highlights the challenge of estimating a practical SSC to give policymakers a more realistic impression of likely future damage costs from carbon-intensive economic activity (Kaufman et al. 2020).

3.5 Conclusion

This is the first major compilation of data on historical sustainability trends for a significant sample of countries. Through a standardized methodology, the authors have provided future researchers and the general public a starting point to compare sustainable development from the 19th century to the present day.

Historical estimates of GS help us to trace the main trends in long run sustainability and present new information for policymakers. One powerful and potentially concerning message is the destiny of natural resources rents (and environmental degradation). Figure 3.5 gives a positive message. None of our countries on average experienced negative genuine savings over the period 1950–2000. However, looking at the whole century (figure 3.6), we show that Latin American countries, many of whom had based their economic development on the exploitation of their natural wealth, were unable to maintain a constant rate of savings, thus hampering their future well-being.

Another extremely relevant finding is that the treatment of CO_2 and how it is priced have an enormous impact on the sustainability signal (Pezzey and Burke 2014). The prices shown, namely the high "business as usual" and the lower "control," highlight the messages embodied in their assumptions: if there are no attempts to control emissions into the future, the last 150 years were built on unsustainable practices; if, however, the damaging potential of uncontrolled emissions are accepted and these emissions are optimally "controlled," then the development seen in the last century can be determined to have been on a sustainable path. However, current climate events are closer to the former price.

The preliminary results presented in this article have strong implications for the present and future economic development of the countries considered in this study. A number of studies argue that consumption is a function of (previous) capital accumulation, since the productive basis, i.e., labor, physical and intangible capital, are the productive forces used to generate income. The lessons from these studies are straightforward: current investment in physical capital, and intangible assets such as human capital and technology, may result in higher consumption, wages, and well-being in the future. Likewise, erosion of the productive base due to depreciation of assets, pollution, and depletion of natural resources may limit, or even reduce, future well-being. The implications of this perspective for the "global" economy are clear; if the goal is to ensure future sustainability, the Hartwick rule should be followed. Technological progress, i.e. an increasingly intelligent use of existing assets, can play a significant role in future sustainability. However, in order to use GS in an applied policy framework, further studies and tests must be implemented. The data presented in the article are a crucial input to informed debate.

Appendix

Data Appendix

Summary statistics of "GS as a share of GDP" are shown in table 3A.1. We are aware of the GDP differences between these countries, but this variable is a good proxy of the *saving effort* of each country.

Table 3A.1 **Summary statistics: Genuine savings as share of GDP 1870–2019**

Country	Mean	Median	Standard Deviation	Min	Max
USA	0.0811	0.0805	0.0615	−0.0916	0.261
Great Britain	0.0549	0.0603	0.0541	−0.120	0.145
Germany	0.113	0.131	0.113	−0.595	0.212
Australia	0.0655	0.0694	0.0417	−0.0480	0.190
France	0.118	0.138	0.0980	−0.254	0.256
Switzerland	0.175	0.175	0.0874	−0.0341	0.447
Argentina	0.0354	0.0324	0.0268	−0.0117	0.100
Brazil	0.0577	0.0439	0.0761	−0.125	0.262
Chile	−0.0375	−0.0362	0.0931	−0.314	0.166
Colombia	0.0469	0.0629	0.0898	−0.124	0.211
Mexico	−0.00298	0.0334	0.123	−0.437	0.171
Costa Rica	0.102	0.110	0.0563	−0.0526	0.189
Japan	0.0981	0.0666	0.0823	−0.0448	0.282
New Zealand	0.175	0.174	0.0286	0.123	0.231
Norway	0.0207	0.0448	0.207	−0.684	0.368
The Philippines	0.0897	0.0937	0.0367	−0.00327	0.186
Portugal	0.0684	0.0768	0.112	−0.311	0.250
Sweden	0.0800	0.0892	0.0861	−0.0669	0.223
Uruguay	0.154	0.0967	0.155	−0.105	0.691

Total Factor Productivity

We calculate TFP assuming a standard Cobb-Douglas production function with capital and labor measured in person-hours.

$$Y = AL^{(\alpha)}K^{1-\alpha}$$

where Y equals income, L is labor (measured in person hours) and K is the capital stock. A denotes TFP which is estimated as a residual from this calculation. Trend TFP was used to estimate the value of exogenous technological progress.

Trend TFP is estimated using a Kalman filter.

Social Cost of Carbon under Price Variation

As we discuss in section 3.4, our SCC estimates are based on a linear discount rate, using the latest models that have measured the potential damage of further CO_2 emissions (see table 3.1).

As the accumulated carbon in the atmosphere is lower in the first half of the 20th century, we initially use a lower constant SCC for this period. As the emissions increase in the latter 20th century, the accumulated carbon in the atmosphere and the decreased capacity of the atmosphere to absorb excess carbon emission lead us utilize a higher SCC in line with the literature, as discussed above.

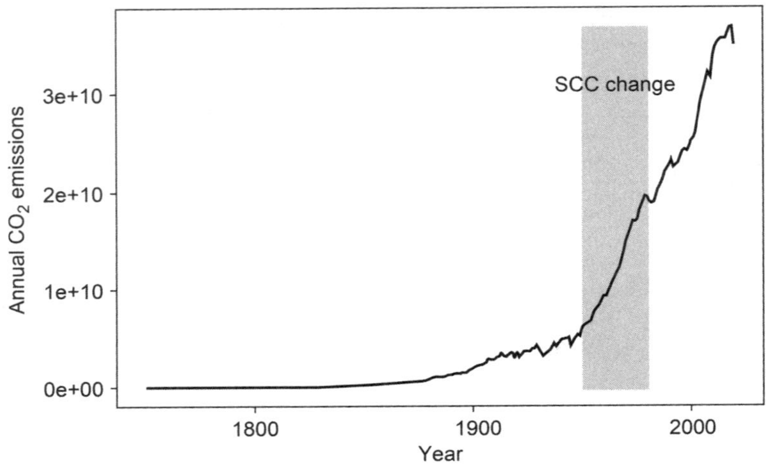

Figure 3A.1 CO_2 historical emissions

As we highlight in the main text, the difference between the estimates based on a discount rate of 2 percent are marginal. This is due to the fact that the amount of CO_2 emissions in the first half of the 20th century are lower compared to the latter 20th century, as shown in figure 3A.1. To formalize our visual analysis, we performed a structural break test on CO_2 emissions (the data from in figure 3A.1). The results identify a clear break point in 1954. As a result of this, we do not believe that there is a reason (or noticeable difference) to estimate distinct SSCs for different time periods. Rather we use a linearly discounted SCC which gives a lower SSC for the earlier years of the 20th century.

Deflators

An important point raised relates to the appropriate deflator for this exercise. As the wealth and change in wealth relates to welfare it is argued that perhaps a consumer price index might be a more appropriate deflator for the series. CPIs by definition are consumer focused, whereas a GDP deflator includes prices of all goods and services that contribute to GDP.

While they differ in theory, in practice they tend to co-move as it is difficult to isolate changes in prices of purely consumer goods from wider price movements in the economy. However, the movements can be sharper for one or the other and it is not consistent across countries. We illustrate this explicitly using data from the United States and the United Kingdom from 1870 to present (see figure 3A.2).

The key issue is how this affects the genuine savings series for the respective countries. We highlight the case of the United States and United Kingdom,

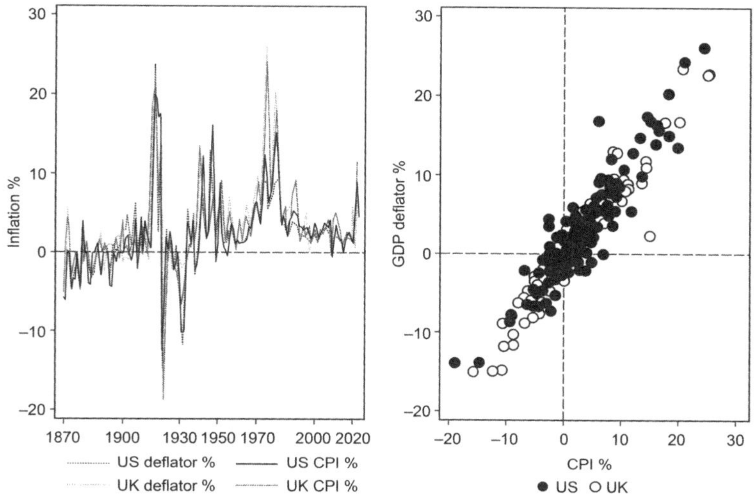

Figure 3A.2 Inflation in the United States and the United Kingdom, 1870–2022

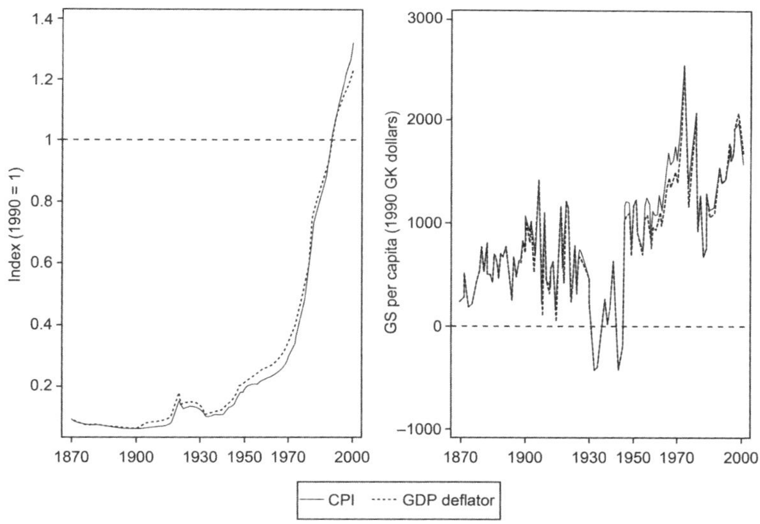

Figure 3A.3 Deflators and GS per capita, United States, 1870–2022

given their well-documented divergence between CPI and GDP deflators (Pessoa and Reenen 2013). In both cases there is a clear levels effect of deflating via a CPI vis-à-vis a GDP deflator. In the case of the United States, this results in a lower GS per capita on average when deflated by a GDP deflator, whereas in the United Kingdom, the GS per capita deflated by a CPI is lower on average (see figure 3A.4). However, in both the United States and

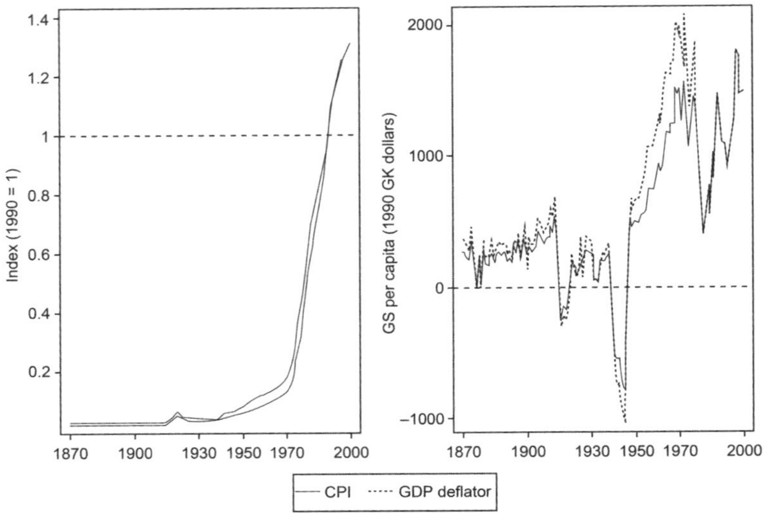

Figure 3A.4 Deflators and GS per capita, UK 1870–2022

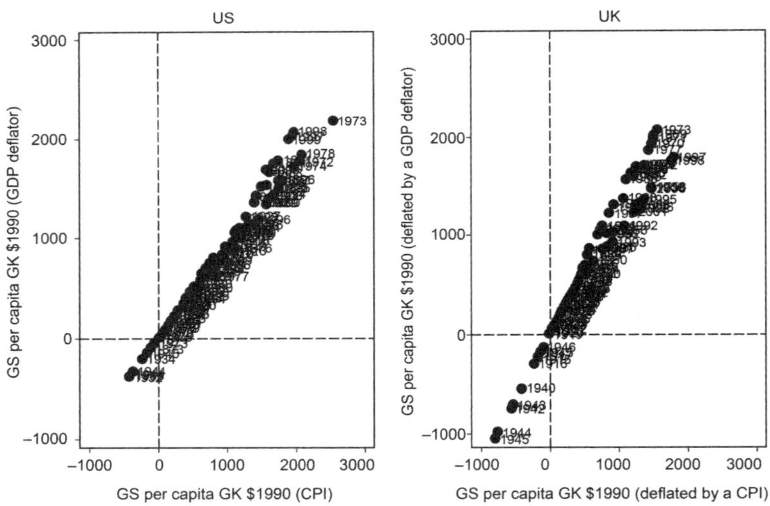

Figure 3A.5 Correlation between GS measures deflated by CPI and GDP deflator 1870–2000

the United Kingdom the underlying trends are similar; the choice of deflator does not lead to a divergence in terms of positive or negative GS in either context (see figure 3A.5).

Table 3A.2 highlights correlation coefficients between inflation as measured by CPIs and GDP deflators for the countries in our sample. While

Table 3A.2 **Correlation between GDP deflator and CPI %**

	1960–2022	pre-1990	Post-1990
Australia	0.936	0.953	0.618
Bolivia	1.000	1.000	0.735
Brazil	0.997	1.000	1.000
Cambodia	0.752	—	0.752
Chile	0.988	0.986	0.702
Colombia	0.873	0.838	0.830
Costa Rica	0.915	0.963	0.847
France	0.971	0.965	0.654
Germany	0.854	0.831	0.778
Japan	0.879	0.805	0.721
Mexico	0.981	0.986	0.855
New Zealand	0.938	0.844	0.530
Norway	0.489	0.811	0.561
Portugal	0.950	0.931	0.840
Spain	0.966	0.963	0.783
Sweden	0.934	0.887	0.846
Switzerland	0.895	0.795	0.866
UK	0.937	0.975	0.418
US	0.959	0.955	0.926
Uruguay	0.914	0.826	0.991
Venezuela	0.538	—	0.538

Source: World Bank (2023)

correlation is not perfect, their measures co-move. This suggests that, as with the United Kingdom and United States as depicted, there would be differences in levels depending on how the measures are deflated but that the underlying trends remain.

Data Availability

The data can be downloaded from the following link: https://www.genuinesavings.org/data. They are available in several formats (Stata, Gretl, Excel, csv and R) and the reference should be this paper if there are more than five countries used in the study. If the number of countries in your study is fewer than five, please use the list of references for each country available in the data set.

The code to reproduce the graphics and some of the estimations is available at further request: cristian.ducoing@ekh.lu.se.

Sources

Australia

The GS estimations for Australia used in this paper are from Greasley et al. (2017).

United Kingdom and United States

The GS estimations of Great Britain and United States are from Greasley et al. (2014) and Hanley et al. (2016).

Germany

The sources of the German data are described in Blum et al. (2019).

France and Switzerland

The GS estimates for these countries are based on Blum et al. (2017); the sources used are described extensively in the working paper linked to the book chapter (Blum et al. 2017). Please note that all statistics used for this study refer to European France, excluding Algeria and other (former) colonies.

Argentina, Brazil, Chile, Colombia, and Mexico

The GS estimates for these countries are based in Blum et al. (2017) and described extensively in the working paper linked to the book chapter (Blum et al. 2016).

Cambodia

The sources from these estimates are available at (Philippsen 2021).

Costa Rica

The sources from these estimates are available at (Pollak 2021).

Norway

The sources from these estimates are available at (Fink and Ducoing 2022).

The Philippines

The sources from these estimates are available at (Limjoco 2021).

Uruguay

The data sources for Uruguay are available in (Labat et al. 2018)

Venezuela

The data for the period 1942–1985 from (Rubio 2004) and the rest from (World Bank 2014).

References

Arrow, K., P. Dasgupta, L. Goulder, G. Daily, P. Ehrlich, G. Heal, S. Levin, K.-G. Maler, S. Schneider, D. Starrett, and B. Walker. 2004. "Are We Consuming Too Much?" *Journal of Economic Perspectives* 18 (3): 147–72.

Arrow, K. J., P. Dasgupta, L. H. Goulder, K. J. Mumford, and K. Oleson. 2012. "Sustainability and the Measurement of Wealth." *Environment and Development Economics 17* (03): 317–53.

Asheim, G. B. 1994. "Sustainability: Ethical Foundations and Economic Properties." World Bank Policy Research Working Paper *1302*.

Asheim, G. B., J. M. Hartwick, and R. Yamaguchi. 2023. "Sustainable Per Capita Consumption under Population Growth." *Resource and Energy Economics* 73: 101363.

Baier, S. L., G. P. Dwyer, and R. Tamura. 2006. "How Important Are Capital and Total Factor Productivity for Economic Growth?" *Economic Inquiry 44* (1): 23–49.

Bakker, G., N. Crafts, and P. Woltjer. 2019. "The Sources of Growth in a Technologically Progressive Economy: The United States, 1899–1941." *Economic Journal 129* (622): 2267–294.

Blum, M., C. Ducoing, and E. McLaughlin. 2017. "A Sustainable Century? Genuine Savings in Developing and Developed Countries, 1900–2000." In *National Wealth What Is Missing, Why It Matters*, edited by K. Hamilton and C. Hepburn, Chapter 5. Oxford Univ Press.

Blum, M., E. McLaughlin, and N. Hanley. 2019. "Accounting for Sustainable Development over the Long-Run:Lessons from Germany." *German Economic Review 20* (4): 410–46.

Bolt, J., and J. L. van Zanden. 2014. "The Maddison Project: Collaborative Research on Historical National Accounts." *Economic History Review 67*: 627–51.

Bolt, K., M. Matete, and M. Clemens. 2002. "Manual for Calculating Adjusted Net Savings." Environment Department, World Bank, 1–23.

Brandt, N., P. Schreyer, and V. Zipperer. 2013. "Productivity Measurement with Natural Capital." OECD Economics Department Working Papers No. 1092.

Bresnahan, T. F., and R. J. Gordon. 1996. *Introduction*. In *The Economics of New Goods*. Chicago: University of Chicago Press.

Broadberry, S., B. M. S. Campbell, A. Klein, and B. van Leeuwen. 2015. *British Economic Growth, 1270–1870*. Cambridge: Cambridge University Press.

Camacho, C. 2014. *Adjusted Net Savings and its Relationship with Future Well-being: Policy Implications for Latin America*. Msc thesis, TU Munich.

Clark, W. C., and A. G. Harley. 2020. "Sustainability Science: Toward a Synthesis." *Annual Review of Environment and Resources 45*: 331–86.

Cohen, F., C. J. Hepburn, and A. Teytelboym. 2019. "Is Natural Capital Really Substitutable." *Annual Review of Environment and Resources 44*: 425–48.

Costanza, R., and H. E. Daly. 1992. "Natural Capital and Sustainable Development." *Conservation Biology 6* (1): 37–46.

Costanza, R., R. d'Arge, R. De Groot, S. Farber, M. Grasso, B. Hannon, K. Limburg, S. Naeem, R. V. O'neill, J. Paruelo, et al. 1997. "The Value of the World's Ecosystem Services and Natural Capital." *Nature 387 (*6630): 253–60.

Dasgupta, P. 2001. *Human Well-Being and the Natural Environment*. Oxford: Oxford University Press.

Dasgupta, P. 2009. "The Welfare Economic Theory of Green National Accounts." *Environment and Resource Economics 42*: 3–38.

Dasgupta, P. 2021. *The Economics of Biodiversity: The Dasgupta Review*. London: HM Treasury.

Dasgupta, P., and G. Heal. 1974. "The Optimal Depletion of Exhaustible Resources." *Review of Economic Studies 41* (128): 3–28.

Deaton, A., and A. Heston. 2010. "Understanding PPPs and PPP-based National Accounts." *American Economic Journal: Macroeconomics 2* (4): 1–35.

Dietz, S., and E. Neumayer. 2007. "Weak and Strong Sustainability in the SEEA: Concepts and Measurement." *Ecological Economics 61*: 617–26.

EEA. 2014. "Costs of Air Pollution from European Industrial Facilities 2008–2012." Technical Report No 20/2014. Luxembourg: European Environment Agency.
Fankhauser, S. 1994. "The Social Costs of Greenhouse Gas Emissions: An Expected Value Approach." *Energy Journal 15* (2).
Feinstein, C. 1978. *Capital Formation in Britain*. Cambridge University Press.
Feinstein, C. H. 1972. *National Income, Expenditure and output of the United Kingdom, 1855–1965*. Cambridge University Press.
Feinstein, C. H., and S. Pollard, eds. 1988. *Studies in Capital Formation in the United Kingdom, 1750–1920*. Oxford University Press.
Fenichel, E. P., S. A. Levin, B. McCay, K. S. Martin, J. K. Abbott, and M. L. Pinsky. 2016. "Wealth Reallocation and Sustainability under Climate Change." *Nature Climate Change 6* (3): 237–44.
Fenichel, E. P., and J. Zhao. 2015. "Sustainability and Substitutability." *Bulletin Mathematical Biology 77*: 348–67.
Ferreira, S., and J. R. Vincent. 2005. "Genuine Savings: Leading Indicator of Sustainable Development?" *Economic Development and Cultural Change 53* (3): 737–54.
Ferreira, S., and M. Moro. 2011. "Constructing Genuine Savings Indicators for Ireland, 1995–2005." *Journal of Environmental Management 92* (3): 542–53.
Ferreira, S., K. Hamilton, and J. R. Vincent. 2008. "Comprehensive Wealth and Future Consumption: Accounting for Population Growth." *World Bank Economic Review 22* (2): 233–48.
Fink, J., and C. Ducoing. 2022. "Does Natural Resource Extraction Compromise Future Well-Being? Norwegian Genuine Savings, 1865–2018." *The Extractive Industries and Society 11*, 101127.
Gnégé, Y. 2009. "Adjusted Net Saving and Welfare Change.: *Ecological Economics 68*, 1127–139.
Goldewijk, K. K. 2014. *Environmental Quality since 1820*. Paris: OECD.
Gordon, R. J. 2016. *The Rise and Fall of American Growth*. Princeton University Press.
Greasley, D., E. McLaughlin, N. Hanley, and L. Oxley. 2017. "Australia: A Land of Missed Opportunities?" *Environment and Development Economics*, 674–98.
Greasley, D., N. Hanley, J. Kunnas, E. McLaughlin, L. Oxley, and P. Warde. 2014. "Testing Genuine Savings as a Forward-Looking Indicator of Future Well-Being over the (Very) Long-Run." *Journal of Environmental Economics and Management 67* (2): 171–88.
Hamilton, K., and C. Hepburn. 2017. *Introduction*. In *National wealth: What is missing, why it matters*, edited by K. Hamilton and C. Hepburn. Oxford, UK: Oxford University Press.
Hamilton, K., and M. Clemens. 1999. "Genuine Savings Rates in Developing Countries." *World Bank Economic Review 13* (2): 333–56.
Hanley, N., L. Dupuy, and E. Mclaughlin. 2015. "Genuine Savings and Sustainability." *Journal of Economic Surveys 29* (4): 779–806.
Hanley, N., L. Oxley, D. Greasley, E. McLaughlin, and M. Blum. 2016. "Empirical Testing of Genuine Savings as an Indicator of Weak Sustainability: A Three-Country Analysis of Long-Run Trends." *Environmental and Resource Economics* 63: 313–338. https://doi.org/10.1007/s10640-015-9928-7.
Hänsel, M. C., M. A. Drupp, D. J. A. Johansson, C. A. Frikk Nesje, M. C. Freeman, B. Groom, and T. Sterner. 2020. "Climate Economics Support for the UN Climate Targets." *Nature Climate Change 10*: 781–89.
Hartwick, J. 1977. "Intergenerational Equity and the Investing of Rents from Exhaustible Resources." *American Economic Review* 67 (5).

Höfeler, T. 2014. *Evaluating sustainable economic development in Latin America in historical perspective*. Msc thesis, TU Munich.
Inklaar, R., W. GU, and E. Diewert. 2023. "Deflation in the changing wealth of nations database." Technical report.
Iriarte, I. 2021. "Genuine Saving and Weak Sustainability: A Critical Approach to the Spanish Case in the Long Run (1955–2010)." *Cuadernos Económicos de ICE 101*.
Kaufman, N., A. R. Barron, W. Krawczyk, P. Marsters, and H. McJeon. 2020. "A Near-Term to Net Zero Alternative to the Social Cost of Carbon for Setting Carbon Prices." *Nature Climate Change 10* (11): 1010–1014.
Klenk, C. 2013. *Green accounting in a historical framework—The power of genuine saving rates as a forecasting instrument for future well-being*. Msc thesis, TU Munich.
Kunnas, J., E. McLaughlin, N. Hanley, D. Greasley, L. Oxley, and P. Warde. 2014. "Counting Carbon: Historic Emissions from Fossil Fuels, Long-Run Measures of Sustainable Development and Carbon Debt." *Scandinavian Economic History Review 62* (3): 243–65.
Labat, J., C. Román, and H. Willebald. 2018. "Genuine Savings and Sustainability in a Peripheral Economy. Uruguay in the Long Run, 1870–2014." Presented at World Economic History Congress, Boston, July 29–August 3, 2018. Lélé, S. M. 1991. "Sustainable Development: A Critical Review." *World Development 19* (6): 607–21.
Limjoco, Mary Lerma Ann. 2021. "Hints of Sustainable Development in the Philippines: Genuine Savings 1902–2018." Student Paper, Lund University.
Lindmark, M., and S. Acar. 2013. "Sustainability in the Making? A Historical Estimate of Swedish Sustainable and Unsustainable Development 1850–2000." *Ecological Economics 86*: 176–87.
Lindmark, M., N. T. Huong, and J. Stage. 2018. "Weak Support for Weak Sustainability: Genuine Savings and Long-Term Wellbeing in Sweden, 1850–2000." *Ecological Economics 145*: 339–45.
Maddison, A. 1992. "A Long-Run Perspective on Saving." *Scandinavian Journal of Economics 94* (2): 181–96.
Maddison, A. 2001. *The World Economy: a Millennial Perspective*. Paris: OECD.
Manuelli, R. E., and A. Seshadri. 2014. "Human Capital and the Wealth of Nations." *American Economic Review 104* (9): 2736–2762.
Markandya, A., and S. Pedroso-Galinato. 2007. "How Substitutable is Natural Capital?" *Environmental and Resource Economics 37* (1): 297–312.
McGrath, L., S. Hynes, and J. McHale. 2019. "Augmenting the World Bank's Estimates: Ireland's Genuine Savings through Boom and Bust." *Ecological Economics 165* (106364).
McGrath, L., S. Hynes, and J. McHale. 2021. "The Air we Breathe: Estimates of Air Pollution Extended Genuine Savings for Europe." *Review of Income and Wealth* 68 (1): 161–188.McGrath, L., S. Hynes, and J. McHale. 2024. "Advancing Testing of the Genuine Savings Hypothesis: The Use of Comprehensive Measures of Technical Change for Ireland." *Journal of Environmental Managmement 352*.
McLaughlin, E., C. Ducoing, and N. Hanley. 2024. "Challenges of Wealth-Based Sustainability Metrics: A Critical Appraisal." *Ecological Economics* 224.
McLaughlin, E., N. Hanley, D. Greasley, J. Kunnas, L. Oxley, and P. Warde. 2014. "Historical Wealth Accounts for Britain: Progress and Puzzles in Measuring the Sustainability of Economic Growth." *Oxford Review of Economic Policy 30*.
Mennig, P. 2015. *Genuine Savings and Future Well-Being in France, 1850–2000*. Msc thesis, TU Munich.

Mota, R. P., and T. Domingos. 2013. "Assessment of the Theory of Comprehensive National Accounting with Data for Portugal." *Ecological Economics 95*: 188–96.

Mota, R. P., T. Domingos, and Victor Martins. 2010. "Analysis of Genuine Saving and Potential Green Net National Income: Portugal, 1990–2005." *Ecological Economics 10* (15): 1934–1942.

Palumbo, M., J. Rudd, and K. Whelan. 2006. "On the Relationships between Real Consumption, Income, and Wealth." *Journal of Business & Economic Statistics 24*:1–11.

Pearce, D. 2002. "An Intellectual History of Environmental Economics." *Annual Review of Energy and the Environment 27*: 57–81.

Pearce, D. W., and G. D. Atkinson. 1993. "Capital theory and the measurement of sustainable development: an indicator of 'weak' sustainability." *Ecological Economics 8* (2): 103–8.

Pessoa, J. P., and J. V. Reenen. 2013. "Decoupling of Wage Growth and Productivity Growth? Myth and Reality." CEP Discussion Papers dp1246.

Pezzey, J. 1992. "Sustainable Development Concepts: An Economic Analysis." World Bank Economic Paper 2.

Pezzey, J. C. 2019. "Why the Social Cost of Carbon Will Always Be Disputed." *Wiley Interdisciplinary Reviews: Climate Change 10* (1): e558.

Pezzey, J. C. 2024. "Adjusted net savings needs further adjusting: Reassessing human and resource factors in sustainability measurement." *Journal of Environmental Economics and Management* 127: 102984.

Pezzey, J. C., and P. J. Burke. 2014. "Towards a More Inclusive and Precautionary Indicator of Global Sustainability." *Ecological Economics 106*: 141–54.

Pezzey, J. C., N. Hanley, K. Turner, and D. Tinch. 2006. "Comparing Augmented Sustainability Measures For Scotland: Is There a Mismatch?" *Ecological Economics 57* (1): 60–74.

Philippsen, Lina Madita. 2021. "Cambodia: The Pursuit of Sustainable Economic Development. Genuine Savings 1970–2019." Student Paper, Lund University.

Polasky, S., C. L. Kling, S. A. Levin, S. R. Carpenter, G. C. Daily, P. R. Ehrlich, G. M. Heal, and J. Lubchenco. 2019. "Role of Economics in Analyzing the Environment and Sustainable Development." *Proceedings of the National Academy of Sciences 116* (12): 5233–5238.

Pollak, Aurélie. 2021. "Testing the Long-Term Sustainable Development of a Central American Country: The Genuine Savings of Costa Rica between 1890 and 2015." Student Paper, Lund University.

Prados de La Escosura, L. 2021." Augmented Human Development in the age of Globalisation." *Economic History Review 74* (4): 946–75.

Qasim, M. 2017. "Sustainability and Wellbeing: A Scientometric and Biliometric Review of the Literature." *Journal of Economic Surveys 31* (4): 1035–1061.

Qasim, M., L. Oxley, and E. McLaughlin. 2020. "Genuine Savings As a Test of New Zealand Weak Sustainability." *Environment, Development and Sustainability 22* (1): 89–127.

Rennert, K., B. C. Prest, W. Pizer, R. G. Newell, D. Anthoff, C. Kingdon, L. Rennels, R. Cooke, A. E. Raftery, H. Sevcikova, and F. Erickson. 2021. "The Social Cost of Carbon: Advances in Long-Term Probabilistic Projections of Population, GDP, Emissions, and Discount Rates." *Brookings Papers on Economic Activity Fall 2021*, 223–75.

Rennert, K., F. Errickson, B. C. Prest, L. Rennels, R. G. Newell, W. Pizer, C. Kingdon, J. Wingenroth, R. Cooke, B. Parthum, et al. 2022. "Comprehensive Evidence Implies a Higher Social Cost of CO_2." *Nature* 610 (7933): 687–692.

Rubio, M. d. M. 2004. "The Capital Gains from Trade Are Not Enough: Evidence from the Environmental Accounts of Venezuela and Mexico." *Journal of Environmental Economics and Management 48* (3): 1175–191.

Schubert, A., and I. Láng. 2005. "The Literature Aftermath of the Brundtland Report 'Our Common Future': A Scientometric Study Based on Citations in Science and Social Science Journals." *Environment, Development and Sustainability 7* (1): 1–8.

SEEA. 1993. *Handbook of National Accounting: Integrated Environmental and Economic Accounting*. United Nations.

SEEA. 2003. *Handbook of National Accounting: Integrated Environmental and Economic Accounting 2003*. United Nations.

SEEA. 2014. *System of Environmental: Economic Accounting 2012—Central Framework*. United Nations.

Smith, A. 1981. [1776]. *An inquiry into the Nature and Causes of the Wealth of Nations*. Liberty Classics.

Solow, R. M. 1956. "A Contribution to the Theory of Economic Growth." *Quarterly Journal of Economics, 70* (1): 65–94.

Solow, R. M. 1974. "Intergenerational Equity and Exhaustible Resources." *Review of Economic Studies 41*: 29–45.

Stern, D. I., and R. K. Kaufmann. 1996. "Estimates of Global Anthropogenic Methane Emissions 1860–1993." *Chemosphere 33* (1): 159–76.

Stern, N. 2007. *Economics of Climate Change: The Stern Review*. Cambridge University Press.

Stern, N. 2022. "A Time for Action on Climate Change and a Time for Change in Economics. *Economic Journal 132*: 1259–1289.

Stiglitz, J. E. 1974. "Growth with Exhaustible Natural Resources: Efficient and Optimal Growth Paths." *Review of Economic Studies 41*: 123–37.

Tafunell, X. 2013. "Capital Formation in Latin America: One and a Half Century of Macroeconomic Dynamics." *CEPAL Review 109 (April)*.

Tafunell, X., and C. Ducoing. 2016. "Non-Residential Capital Stock in Latin America, 1875–2008: New Estimates and International Comparisons." *Australian Economic History Review 56*: 46–69.

Tol, R. S. 2003. "Is the Uncertainty about Climate Change Too Large for Expected Cost-Benefit Analysis?" *Climatic Change 56* (3): 265–89.

Tol, R. S. 2011. "The Social Cost of Carbon." *Annual Review of Resource Economics 3* (1): 419–43.

Tol, R. S. J. 2012. "On the Uncertainty About the Total Economic Impact of Climate Change." *Environmental and Resource Economics 53* (1): 97–116.

UNU-IHDP. 2012. *Inclusive Wealth Report 2012: Measuring Progress toward Sustainability*. Cambridge University Press.

UNU-IHDP. 2014. *Inclusive Wealth Report 2014: Measuring Progress toward Sustainability*. Cambridge University Press.

UNU-IHDP. 2018. *Inclusive Wealth Report 2018*. New York: United Nations.

US Government. 2021. "Technical Support Document: Social Cost of Carbon, Methane, and Nitrous Oxide Interim Estimates under Executive Order 13990." Technical report, Interagency Working Group on Social Cost of Greenhouse Gases, United States Government, Washington, DC.

Vincent, J. R. 2001. "Are Greener National Accounts Better?" Centre for International Development at Harvard University Working Papers 63.

Weitzman, M. 1997. "Sustainability and Technical Progress." *Scandinavian Journal of Economics 99* (1): 1–13.Weitzman, M. 1999. "Pricing the Limits to Growth." *Quarterly Journal of Economics 114* (2): 691–706.

Weitzman, M. 2003. *Income, Wealth, and the Maximum Principle*. Harvard University Press.
Weitzman, M. 2017. *A Tight Connection among Wealth, Income, Sustainability, and Accounting in an Ultra-Simplified Setting*. Oxford University Press.
World Bank. 2006. *Where is the Wealth of Nations? Measuring Capital for the 21st Century*. The World Bank.
World Bank. 2011. *The Changing Wealth of Nations: Measuring Sustainable Development in the New Millennium*. World Bank Publications.
World Bank. 2014. World development indicators (wdi).
World Bank. 2018. *The Changing Wealth of Nations 2018: Building a Sustainable Future*. The World Bank.
World Bank. 2021. *The Changing Wealth of Nations 2021: Managing Assets for the Future*. Washington, DC: International Bank for Reconstruction and Development/The World Bank.
World Bank. 2023. World Development Indicators. Accessed 2023–07–16. https://databank.worldbank.org/source/world-development-indicators.
World Commission on Environment and Development. 1987. Report of the World Commission on Environment and Development: Our Common Future (The Brundtland Report).
Yamaguchi, R., M. Islam, and S. Managi. 2019. "Inclusive Wealth in the Twenty-First Century: A Summary and Further Discussion of Inclusive Wealth Report 2018." *Letters in Spatial and Resource Sciences 12*: 101–11.

Comment Stefanie Onder

Measuring the sustainability of economic development has long been a concern for economists,[1] with two key indicators emerging as leading metrics: Comprehensive/Inclusive wealth (CW/IW) and Genuine/Adjusted Net Savings (GS/ANS). CW/IW measures the value of an economy's asset base, including produced, human, and natural capital as well as net foreign assets, which reflect the future consumption and well-being possibilities of a given nation. By measuring changes in wealth per capita over time, it provides policymakers with an important signal of how these future opportunities are changing. GNS/ANS is instead measuring how much an economy is, on balance, investing for the future by tracking net savings. Both metrics capture how assets are changing over time in positive (quality improvements and accumulation) and negative (depreciation and depletion) ways.

McLaughlin et al. (this volume) make a substantial contribution to this literature by producing historical GS estimates for a large group of devel-

Stefanie Onder was a senior environmental economist in the Environment, Natural Resources and Blue Economy (ENB) Global Practice at the World Bank when this comment was written, and is currently an assistant professor of economics at American University.

1. See Solow (1993), Dasgupta and Mäler (2000), Dasgupta (2001), and Arrow et al. (2004); as well as Fleurbaey and Blanchet (2013), Hamilton and Hartwick (2014), and Irwin et al. (2016) for excellent reviews.

oped and developing countries drawing on the ANS methodology developed by the World Bank (Hamilton and Clemens 1999). These GS estimates account for both the depletion of nonrenewable and renewable natural capital, the accumulation of human capital, technological progress, and greenhouse gas emission. Their results show that countries experience declines GNS despite a growth in income (as measured by Gross Domestic Product/GDP). These historical estimates can help us to trace the main trends in long run sustainability and provide important insights for future development policy. For example, natural resource rich countries have often based their economic development on the exploitation of their natural wealth. However, this will only be sustainable if net savings (as measured by GS/ANS) are not negative.

However, while in economic theory investment net of depreciation and depletion equals changes in wealth, in practice there are several factors that affect national wealth estimates that are omitted from GS/ANS calculations due to data limitations (World Bank 2021; Atkins and Venmans 2023). Data availability affects which assets can be included in the calculation in the first place, which is especially limiting when constructing a historical time series. For example, the World Bank's CW metric accounts for changes in the asset value of timber, agricultural land, marine fish stocks and several ecosystem services, while McLauglin et al. (this volume) can only account for net forest depletion. It is of course possible to address some of these concerns especially with more recent data, but care needs to be taken to ensure that any changes in CW correspond to (net) depletion or degradation of natural capital and ecosystem assets (Atkins and Venmans 2023).

Moreover, there are differences in measurement approaches for key assets, such as human and nonrenewable natural capital. For example, computations of GS/ANS typically use public expenditure in education as a proxy for human capital (following a cost-based approach) instead of the lifetime income or benefits-based approach used for CW. One key concern with such expenditure measures is that they only capture costs partially (UNECE 2016). That is, only direct expenditure on education and training by public actors is captured, but not by private individuals or entities, which can be substantial (Ferreira and Vincent 2005). Moreover, it does not account for the opportunity costs of education as well as depreciation. There are also differences in how depletion is valued for nonrenewable natural capital. GS/ANS computes the shadow price relative to the amount of resource extraction, while CW estimates hold the resource lifetime constant (Atkins and Venmans 2023). This can lead to substantial differences in the asset values, as ANS estimates the average resource asset value per physical unit, while CW estimates the present value of the last unit extracted.

Moreover, SNA conventions on how to measure savings and investments drive a further wedge between GS/ANS and CW (World Bank 2021). For

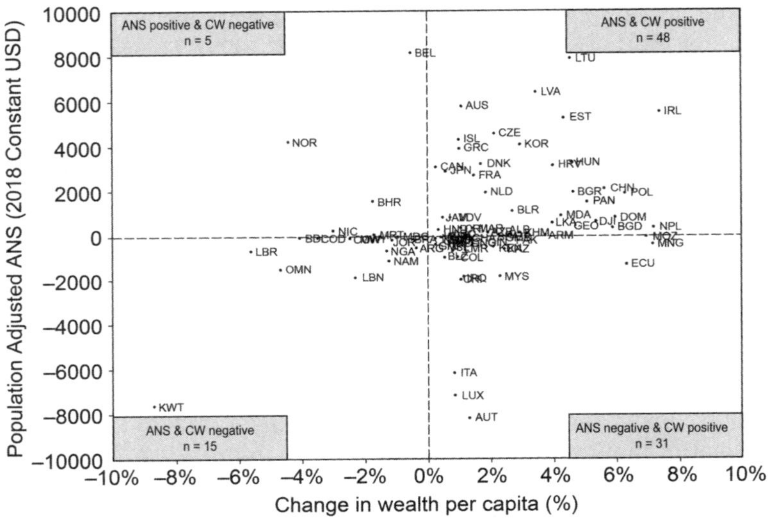

Figure 3C.1 Population-adjusted ANS vs. changes in wealth per capita, 2018
Source: World Bank staff calculations

example, new discoveries of subsoil assets are added to non-renewable natural capital wealth but not to GS/ANS (see also Atkins and Venmans 2023). In addition, changes in technology, world prices, or management all have impacts on the productivity of an asset or the volume of a resource to be exploited. These effects are captured only by wealth measures. For example, higher world prices for energy and minerals can make extraction for previously uneconomic resources feasible, thus increasing nonrenewable natural capital wealth. Similarly, a switch to higher value crops or improved irrigation technology will result in higher yields and, thus, higher values of agricultural land. Conversely, other exogenous factors that destroy or degrade assets, such as civil unrest or natural disaster, will reduce asset values but will not be recorded in ANS.

To illustrate the importance of these differences, figure 3C.1 maps population-adjusted ANS onto changes in CW per capita for 2018. While there is clearly a strong correlation for most countries, a third of countries recorded positive changes in CW per capita but negative population adjusted ANS. These differences are driven by omitted factors, such as changes in the value of agricultural land or new discoveries of minerals as well as improved measurement of human capital as part of the measurement for CW.

To provide a more comprehensive understanding of sustainability, GS/ANS and CW/IW should not be used in isolation but together. On the one hand, as long as CW/IW per capita does not decline over time, future generations will be at least as well off as current generations. This can be used as a simple criterion for weak sustainability. On the other, ANS/GS can provide policymakers with an understanding of the dynamics that drive the changes in wealth from one period to the next, capturing some (though not all) policy-induced dynamics. Corrective action can then be taken to ensure existing wealth is not squandered for short-term gains, but instead reinvested to finance future investment and, thus, economic development.

Acknowledgments

This work was carried out as part of the World Bank's *The Changing Wealth of Nations 2024: Revisiting the Measurement of Comprehensive Wealth* and was supported by the Global Program for Sustainability. For acknowledgments, sources of research support, and disclosure of the author's material financial relationships, if any, please see https://www.nber.org/books-and-chapters/measuring-and-accounting-environmental-public-goods-national-accounts-perspective/comment-tracing-sustainability-long-run-genuine-savings-estimates-1850-2018-onder.

References

Arrow, K., P. Dasgupta, L. Goulder, G. Daily, P. Ehrlich, G. Heal, S. Levin, K. G. Maler, S. Schneider, D. Starrett, and B. Walker. 2004. "Are we consuming too much?" *Journal of Economic Perspectives* 18 (3):147–172.

Atkins, G., and F. Venmans. 2023. "Wealth, Saving and Sustainability: A Discussion of Issues of Alignment Between 'Changing Comprehensive Wealth' and 'Adjusted Net Saving.'" Technical Report.

Dasgupta, P. 2001. *Human Well-Being and the Natural Environment*. New York: Oxford University Press.

Dasgupta, P., and K. G. Mäler. 2000. "Net National Product, Wealth, and Social Well-Being." *Environmental and Development Economics* 5 (1): 69–93.

Ferreira, S., and J. R. Vincent. 2005. "Genuine Savings: Leading Indicator of Sustainable Development?" *Economic Development and Cultural Change* 53 (3): 737–54.

Fleurbaey, M., and B. Blanchet. 2013. *Beyond GDP Measuring Welfare and Assessing Sustainability*. New York: Oxford University Press.

Hamilton, K., and J. M. Hartwick. 2014. "Wealth and Sustainability." *Oxford Review of Economic Policy* 30 (1): 170–87.

Hamilton, K., and M. Clemens. 1999. "Genuine Savings Rates in Developing Countries." *World Bank Economic Review* 13: 333–56.

Irwin, E. G., S. Gopalakrishnan, and A. Randall. 2016. "Welfare, Wealth, and Sustainability." *Annual Review of Resource Economics* 8: 77–98.

McLaughlin, E., C. Ducoing, and L. Oxley. "Tracing Sustainability in the Long Run: Genuine Savings Estimates 1850–2018." In *Measuring and Accounting for Environmental Public Goods: A National Accounts Perspective*, edited by Mary Bohman, Eli Fenichel, and Nicholas Z. Muller. Chicago, IL: University of Chicago Press. This volume.

Solow, R. 1993. "An Almost Practical Step towards Sustainability." *Resource Policy* 19 (3): 162–72.

UNECE (United Nations Economic Commission for Europe). 2016. *Guide on Measuring Human Capital*. New York and Geneva: United Nations.

World Bank. 2021. *The Changing Wealth of Nations 2021*. Washington, DC: The World Bank.

World Bank. 2024. *The Changing Wealth of Nations 2024: Revisiting the Measurement of Comprehensive Wealth*. Washington, DC: The World Bank. https://documents.worldbank.org/en/publication/documents-reports/documentdetail/099100824155021548/p17844617dfe6e0241ad251.

4

Microdata and the Valuation of Natural Capital

Jonathan Colmer and John Voorheis

4.1 Introduction

The theoretical basis for valuing natural capital and the ecosystem services they provide is well established (Weitzman 1976; Hartwick 1990; Heal 1998; Daily et al. 2000; Arrow et al. 2004; Nordhaus 2006; Arrow et al. 2012; Fenichel and Abbott 2014). However, despite substantial progress in our understanding of ecology and significant advances in quantifying natural capital, the valuation of natural capital has lagged behind.

How much society values the stock of natural capital and the flow of ecosystem services that it provides is ultimately an empirical question, the answer to which is critical for evaluating trade-offs between environmental conservation and use (Krutilla 1967; Fisher et al. 1972) and for assessing the question of whether society is following a sustainable economic program (Fenichel and Abbott 2014; Fenichel et al. 2018). The critical challenge to

Jonathan Colmer is an assistant professor in the Department of Economics at the University of Virginia.

John Voorheis is a principal economist in the Center for Economic Studies at the US Census Bureau.

Any opinions and conclusions expressed herein are those of the author(s) and do not reflect the views of the US Census Bureau. We thank Eli Fenichel, Nicholas Muller, Mary Bohman, Corbett Grainger, and seminar participants at the CRIW Conference on Natural Capital Accounting and US Census Bureau for helpful thoughts, comments, and discussion. We thank Surya Menon and Yolande Tra for research support. The Census Bureau has reviewed this data product to ensure appropriate access, use, and disclosure avoidance protection of the confidential source data used to produce this product (Data Management System (DMS) number: P-7505723, Disclosure Review Board (DRB) approval numbers: CBDRB-FY23-CES010-027). For acknowledgments, sources of research support, and disclosure of the authors' material financial relationships, if any, please see https://www.nber.org/books-and-chapters/measuring-and-accounting-environmental-public-goods-national-accounts-perspective/microdata-and-valuation-natural-capital.

valuing natural capital is determining the appropriate prices to use when evaluating these question. When there are missing or incomplete markets—as is often the case for many critical natural capital stocks—economists have to rely on nonmarket valuation approaches.

Addressing the challenge of valuing natural capital is pivotal to ongoing policy efforts and natural capital accounting. Credible valuation of natural capital is critical to the integration of environmental data into national economic accounts. Therefore, refining natural capital valuation methodologies is not just an academic exercise, but critical for providing evidence that can be used in frameworks that recognize and safeguard the value of the natural environment in policy-making and economic activity.

In this paper we consider the extent to which advances in the availability of microdata might help to relax some of the measurement constraints associated with the valuation of natural capital, and in turn open the door to new methodological and accounting frameworks that incorporate spatial and individual heterogeneity in valuations.

We first discuss some of the current conceptual challenges associated with natural capital accounting, and explore the potential role that microdata could play in helping to address these challenges. Second, using a new microdata infrastructure—the Environmental Impacts Frame (Voorheis et al. 2023)—we provide a case study to illustrate the empirical relevance of these challenges, in the form of evidence on the distribution of urban tree cover across individuals in the United States.

4.2 Conceptual Challenges

In this section we discuss several key conceptual challenges that natural capital accounting currently faces and discuss the potential role that microdata could play in helping to address these challenges.

4.2.1 Aggregation Bias and Natural Capital Accounting

To date natural capital accounting has focused largely on producing national accounts at the national level; however, such approaches make very strong assumptions about aggregation, commonly used in other accounting practices, which are unlikely to apply in the context of natural capital. A major conceptual challenge relates to the spatial context of natural capital.

Natural capital accounting has traditionally relied on a "law of one price." This is the approach taken when aggregating physical and financial capital stocks; however, unlike natural capital, physical and finanical capital stocks are generally tradable commodities that can be easily transported and exchanged, meaning that values can be aggregated using a common price. The assumption of a common price is more plausible in such settings because the location of physical or financial capital is less likely to affect its value. By contrast, many stocks of natural capital are immobile and depend critically on their location—natural capital is spatially dependent. If a stock of natural capital is concentrated in one area rather than another, the people living there will value it more highly than the national average (Addicott and Fenichel 2019). This relative scarcity will lead to a divergence between the total value of natural capital and the sum of its parts.

Spatially resolved microdata provides a platform with which to link spatially explicit natural capital stocks with detailed and comprehensive population and economic data. This can facilitate the definition and measurement of relevant economic jurisdictions, or "market extent," which in turn will facilitate the description, quantification, and valuation of natural capital across locations. This is critical because, as first noted by Smith (1993) differences in market extent are likely far more important than differences in marginal valuations.

4.2.2 Heterogeneity in Valuations within a Location

Concern about aggregation bias extends to heterogeneity in how individuals value natural capital within a market. While working with more spatially granular data can help to mitigate heterogeneity across locations, aggregation bias remains if there is heterogeneity in valuations across individuals within a location. Such differences in valuations may arise, for example, due to differences in income or preferences.

Here, confidential microdata provide descriptive details on the distribution of income, wealth, race and ethnicity, age, and other socioeconomic characteristics that will aid researchers and policymakers in understanding how the population within a "natural capital" jurisdiction varies compares to other jurisdictions. This will help to understand the extent to which marginal valuations of natural capital may vary between jurisdictions, as well as the potential for heterogeneity in valuations within a jurisdiction.

4.2.3 Missing Markets

The previous two conceptual challenges presume that accounting prices for natural capital are available or identifiable. In practice, identifying the appropriate prices needed is the core challenge associated with any natural capital valuation or natural capital accounting exercises.

The main constraint is the absence of observable prices for nonmarket goods and services. Even if prices for a given stock of natural capital were observed at two points in time, the prices used to value a change in wealth must by constant and formed as a convex combination of the two observed prices (Fenichel et al. 2016, 2018).

Restricted-use microdata provide no direct solution to this problem; however, by providing comprehensive economic and sociodemographic context at the individual level, combined with spatially explicit information on quantities of natural capital stocks, they provide necessary information about the economic program. When combined with appropriate methodologies and research designs, such data facilitate the identification of marginal valuations based on the actual choices and trade-offs that individuals and society make (Fenichel and Hashida 2019). Further, large sample sizes mean that heterogeneity in valuations can in principle be recovered when significant heterogeneity in populations exists within or between natural capital jurisdictions.

4.3 The Environmental Impacts Frame

While advances in technology have improved our understanding of *where* natural capital is located, there remain large gaps in our understand about *who* benefits from natural capital, as well as the consequences for health and well-being. As discussed above, the benefits of natural capital are unlikely to be evenly distributed across individuals within a population, resulting in misleading inferences when using aggregated data sources.

To help mitigate these constraints, we have developed a new prototype microdata infrastructure to facilitate individual-level analyses in the United States—the Census Environmental Impacts Frame (EIF). The EIF uses confidential Census Bureau microdata drawn from surveys, administrative records, and decennial censuses to provide detailed panel data on demographics, economic circumstances, and address-level residential histories for nearly all residents of the United States from the late 1990s forward. These rich microdata (containing more than six billion observations) present new opportunities to advance our understanding of the environmental conditions people face, why differences in exposure to environmental conditions arise, and the distributional consequences of exposure to hazards and amenities in the United States.

The EIF is a modular infrastructure, rather than a single combined file. There are two core modules constructed from confidential data at the Census Bureau: a demographic "spine," which contains basic demographic information, such as race, age, sex, date, place of birth, and date of death, for the relevant universe of individuals, and an annual residential history file for individuals in the spine, allowing researchers to track individuals over time and space.[2]

The EIF exists to facilitate the description and analysis of exposure to environmental amenities and hazards at the individual level. The core components described above—the demographic spine and the residential histories—provide the foundation for an exciting and extensive research agenda. Using the EIF, it is possible to incorporate and analyze any environmental data that can be geospatially resolved. As such, the EIF allows researchers to develop a systematic and comprehensive understanding of environmental exposures at a high spatial resolution over a relatively long time series. In the

2. See Voorheis et al. (2023) for more details on how these modules are constructed.

following section we leverage the EIF to highlight the conceptual challenges discussed and illustrate how the EIF could be used to alleviate (at least in part) some of these issues.

4.4 Urban Tree Canopy in the United States

Urban tree canopy cover—the layer of leaves, branches, and stems that cover land surfaces in urban areas—is an important variety of natural capital in the United States. Urban trees have been argued to provide many important benefits: absorbing carbon dioxide; providing shade and lowering air temperatures; supporting stormwater infrastructure by absorbing large amounts of water and reducing runoff; improving air and water quality; providing wildlife habitats that increase local biodiversity; and providing aesthetic, social, mental health, and cultural benefits.

We incorporate high-resolution data on urban tree canopy cover from the National Land Cover Database (NLCD) into the Environmental Impacts Frame for the year 2016. The NLCD provides satellite-derived data on tree cover at a 30 × 30 m grid and reports the share of each pixel that is covered in by tree canopy. Because this resolution is in many cases smaller than individual parcels, we aggregate the NLCD data to the census block level, and assign this block-level average canopy measure to each individual's location in the 2016 EIF as their exposure to canopy.

Figure 4.1 displays the distribution of canopy cover across the United States. As discussed in section 4.2.1, when natural capital is heterogenous across locations and immobile (as trees are wont to be), a common price cannot be used. Trees are locally non-excludable and have a relatively low marginal cost associated with providing services such as cooling and pollution abatement. This has the additional implication that, all else equal, trees might generate more natural capital services in in more densely populated areas.[3] We see that there is substantial spatial variation in canopy cover across the United States, and so the accounting price may vary substantially.

However, much of this variation may conflate regional differences. Given the density of population in urban areas, understanding variation in urban canopy cover is of particular interest. To avoid comparisons between rural and urban tree cover, we restrict our analysis to Core-Based Statistical Areas (CBSAs), geographic areas defined by the Office of Management and Budget (OMB) that contain urban areas and highly integrated adjacent communities. Using this data we provide a systematic description of how urban tree canopy cover varies across space and individuals and relate what we observe to the conceptual issues rasied in section 4.2.

We first provide systematic evidence on how much variation in canopy cover exists across and within-CBSAs in the United States and how within-

3. Of course, forests and larger agglomerations of trees create different services.

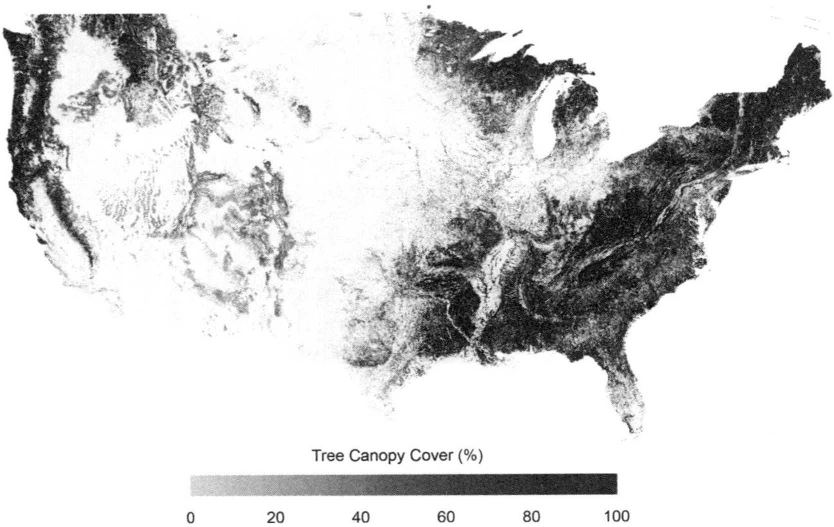

Figure 4.1 Tree canopy cover in the United States

Source: NLCD

Notes: This figure shows tree canopy coverage in the contiguous United States for the year 2016. Data is derived from multi-spectral satellite imagery. The raster data is available at a 30 meter resolution but aggregate to a 480 meter resolution in the figure for visualization purposes. Each 30 m grid cell reports the estimated share of land that is covered by tree canopy. Percent coverage increases visually in the figure from light to dark.

CBSA variation in canopy cover correlates with with several key measures of environmental quality. We document that there is substantial variation in urban tree canopy cover across the United States. The between-census block-group standard deviation in urban canopy cover is 18.73. The 90–10 gap is 47.33—an individual living in a census block-group at the 90th percentile of the urban canopy distribution has canopy cover that is 47.33 percentage points higher than an individual living at the 10th percentile of the urban canopy distribution. We show that there is substantial variation in canopy cover even with CBSAs. The within-CBSA standard deviation is 14.05. The within-CBSA 90–10 gap is 31.21—an individual living in a census block-group at the 90th percentile of their CBSA's urban canopy distribution has canopy cover that is 31.21 percentage points higher than an individual living in a census block-group at the 10th percentile of their CBSA's urban canopy distribution (figure 4.2).

Second, we show that this variation in urban canopy cover is associated with meaningful variation in exposure to a number of socioeconomically important margins of environmental quality. One important margin is the role that canopy plays in reducing surface temperatures. Temperatures can vary substantially over short distances due to differences in land cover, which

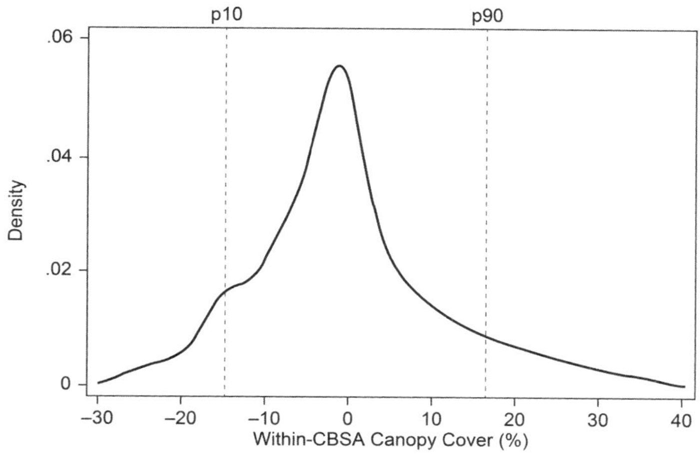

Figure 4.2 The within-CBSA distribution of tree canopy coverage in the United States

Source: NLCD

Notes: This figure presents a kernel density plot of the within-CBSA distribution of tree canopy coverage for the contiguous United States in 2016. The left dashed line is the 10th percentile of the within-CBSA distribution (-14.59). The right dashed line is the 90th percentile of the within-CBSA distribution (16.61). The within-CBAS 90–10 gap is 31.21 percentage points.

affects local surface energy balance—a phenomenon known as the urban heat island effect (Grimmond 2007). Pavement and concrete reflect less sunlight and absorb more heat than natural landscapes, such as trees and vegetation. Consistent with this we document that there is a strong negative association between canopy cover and surface temperature within CBSAs. On average, individuals living in census block-groups with 10 percentage point more canopy cover than their CBSA mean are exposed to summertime surface temperatures that are 3.5°F (approximately one standard deviation) lower than the CBSA mean (figure 4.3a). Chakma et al. (2023a) document the existence of peristent racial disparities in surface temperatures, canopy cover, and imperviousness and show that these disparities exist at every percentile of the national income distribution. Chakma et al. (2023b) show that the mortality effects of temperature are much higher in neighborhoods with greater imperviousness and that half of the black-white gap in temperature-driven mortality can be explained by differences in imperviousness.

We also estimate a strong negative correlation between canopy and flood risk. Urban tree canopy cover reduces flood risk by intercepting rainfall through the collection of water on branches and leaves, increasing the soil's capacity to absorb and retain water, and by physically slowing down the flow of water. All of these considerations reduce the burden on drainage systems.

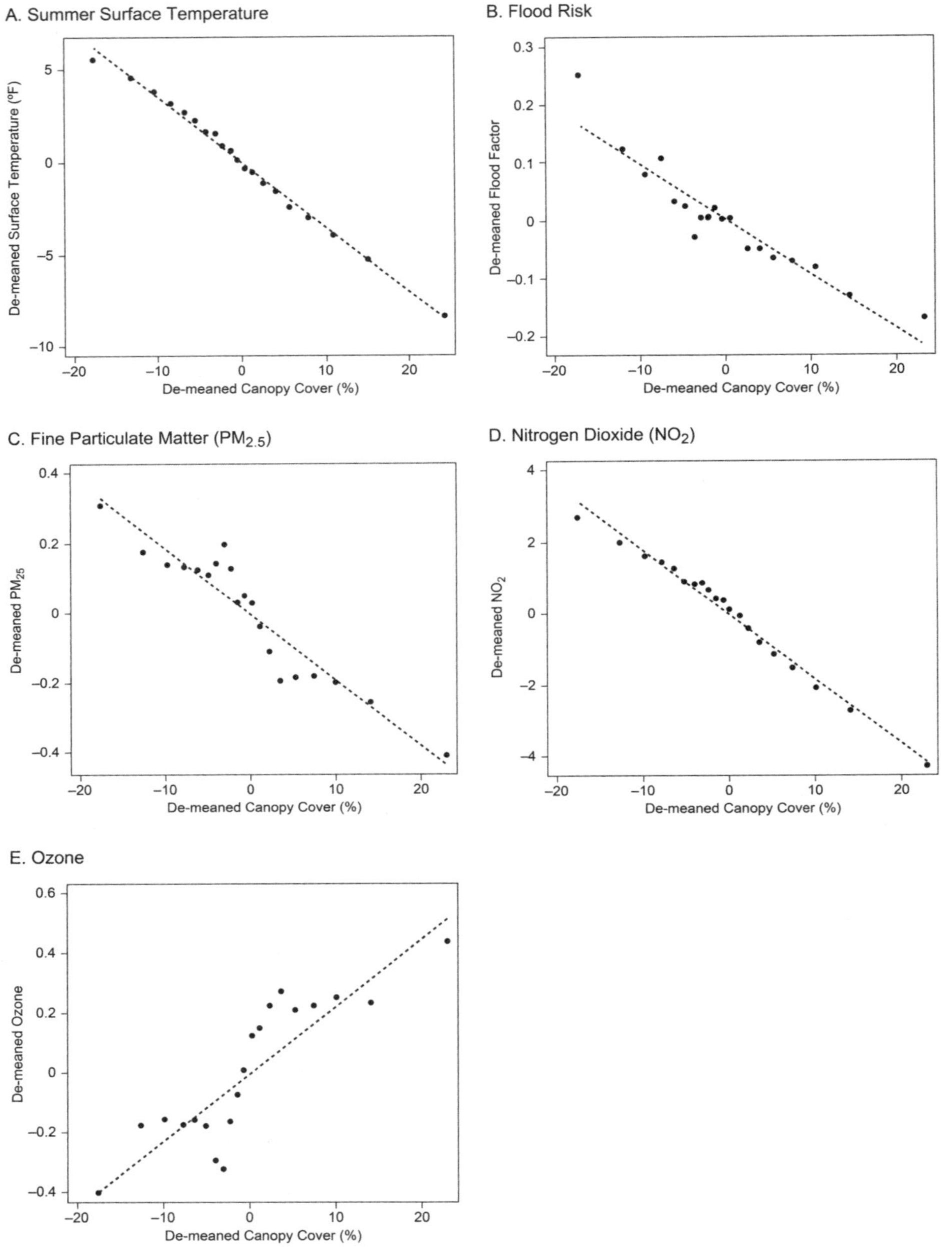

Source: NLCD, Landsat, First Street Foundation Floodfactor, the Environmental Impacts Frame, Di et al. (2020), Requia et al. (2020), and van Donkelaar et al. (2021).

Notes: These figures report the bivariate relationship between within-CBSA variation urban tree canopy cover and within-CBSA variation exposure to environmental risks in 2016. The unit of analysis for the underlying analysis is an individual.

We estimate that, on average, individuals living in census block-groups with 10 percentage points more canopy cover than their CBSA mean are exposed to a flood risk score that is 0.1 points (approximately one standard deviation) lower than their CBSA mean (figure 4.3b). Wing et al. (2022) calculate that annualized US flood losses are currently US$32.1 billion on average and are projected to rise to US$40.6 billion by 2050 under the RCP4.5 scenario.

Finally, in Figures 4.3c, 4.3d, and 4.3e we explore the relationship between urban canopy cover and different types of air pollution. In figure 4.3c we estimate a strong negative correlation between canopy cover and fine particulate matter ($PM_{2.5}$). Fine particulate matter consists of extremely small airborne particles (30 times smaller than the diameter of a human hair), often generated from combustion sources, that can penetrate deep into the lungs and bloodstream, posing significant health risks. Urban canopy has the potential to affect $PM_{2.5}$ concentrations through direct air filtration (leaves and bark trap and absorb $PM_{2.5}$ particles from the air), and cooling (cooler air can potentially hold fewer particles and reduces energy demand). On average, we estimate that individuals living in census block-groups with 10 percentage points more canopy cover than their CBSA mean are exposed to fine particulate matter that is 1.89 micrograms per cubic meter ($\mu g/m^3$) (approximately one standard deviation) lower than the CBSA mean. This association reflects a non-trivial difference in exposure. Deryugina et al. (2019) estimate that a 1 $\mu g/m^3$ increase in $PM_{2.5}$ exposure for one day causes 0.69 additional deaths per million elderly individuals over the following three days. This estimate likely reflects a lower bound. Deryugina and Reif (2023) estimate that the long-run effects of acute exposure are higher and calculate that the effect of chronic exposure on life expectancy are seven to eight times larger than the long-run effects of an acute exposure. Colmer et al. (2021) estimate that reductions in early childhood $PM_{2.5}$ exposure are associated with substantial increases in later-life W-2 earnings and document that disparities in exposure play a non-trivial role in shaping broader patterns of economic opportunity and inequality in the United States.

In figure 4.3d we also estimate a strong negative correlation between urban canopy cover and nitrogen dioxide (NO_2). NO_2 is a highly reactive gas, which forms primarily from the burning of fossil fuels. It contributes directly to smog, reacts with sunlight and other compounds in the atmosphere to form secondary pollutants such as ozone, and acts like a catalyst to transform primary emissions into secondary particulates, increasing the total amount of particulate matter in the air. Similar to particulate matter, urban canopy cover can affect NO_2 concentrations through direct air filtration and cooling. We estimate that, on average, individuals living in census block-groups with 10 percentage points more canopy cover than their CBSA mean are exposed to nitrogen dioxide concentrations that are 1.81 parts per billion (approximately one standard deviation) lower than the CBSA mean. These are meaningful differences. Meng et al. (2021) estimate that, on average, a 10$\mu g/m^3$ increase in previous day ambient NO_2 concentration was associated with a 0.46 percent increase in all-cause mortality.[4] Khreis et al. (2017) conduct a meta-analysis of 21 studies and generate a summary estimate for the likelihood of developing asthma at some point during childhood. They calculate an odds ratio of 1.05 per $4\mu g/m^3$, i.e., a 5 percent increase in risk.

In figure 4.3e we estimate the opposite relationship—a strong positive correlation between urban canopy cover and ozone concentrations. Ozone forms through complex chemical reactions between nitrogen oxides (NOx) and volatile organic compounds (VOCs) in the presence of sunlight. The consequences of urban canopy cover for ozone is unclear. On the one hand, trees absorb nitrogen dioxide, primary components of ozone. By lowering air temperature, tree cover could also reduce the efficiency of ozone formation. On the other hand, trees directly emit natural volatile organic compounds (VOCs), a critical percursor to ozone formation. Our empirical pattern suggests that, all else constant, the VOC channel is dominant in our context. We estimate that, on average, individuals living in census block-groups with 10 percentage points more canopy cover than their CBSA mean are exposed to ozone concentrations that are 0.22 parts per billion (approximately one standard deviation) lower than the CBSA mean. The epidemiological literature tilts toward larger damages from fine particulates and NOs vs. ozone (Turner et al. 2016, Qian et al. 2017), but without a more detailed comparison of dose response functions that account for the complex relationships between pollutants, it is unclear whether the increased damages from ozone would be offset by improvements in $PM_{2.5}$ and NOx.

These facts are helpful for documenting, at least in part, the potential economic value associated with urban canopy cover. However, showing how quantities vary does not provide any insight into the valuation of this form of natural capital or the extent to which valuations may vary within a location. An important margin that may shape differences in valuations is income. Natural capital Engel curves, if they existed, would tell us how demand varies with income holding prices and preferences fixed. However, absent prices, Engel curves cannot be estimated for nonmarket goods and services. Instead, we explore the extent to which canopy cover exposure varies with income, a revealed preference, but reduced form and likely inconsistent approximation for how demand may vary throughout the income distribution.

A common approach to evaluating the role the income plays in shaping differences in environmental quality is to use a place-based average of the household income; however, the use of even granular place-based data severely limits what one can learn about the potential for differences in willingness to pay for natural capital within locations. In our existing and

4. Assuming 1 atmosphere of pressure (1,013.25 hPa) and an average temperature of 12°C, we convert $\mu g/m^3$ into parts per billion (ppb), using a conversion factor of $1.967\mu g/m^3 = 1$ ppb. $10\mu g/m^3 = 5.085$ ppb.

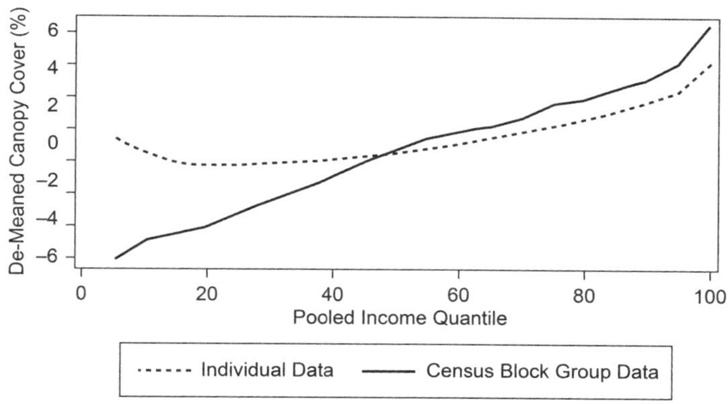

Figure 4.4 Aggregation bias and the canopy–income relationship
Source: NLCD and the Environmental Impacts Frame.
Notes: This figure shows how within-CBSA variation in canopy cover varies across the individual-level national income distribution (dotted line) and the distribution of census block-group average income per capita (solid line). We document a much flatter canopy-income profile when using the distribution of individual income than when using the distribution of census block-group average income per capita, indicating that there are other place-based factors correlated with place-based income that result in biased inferences about the importance of income in shaping exposure to urban canopy cover.

ongoing work we repeatedly document that substantial variation in income within even narrowly defined geographies results in misleading inferences being made about people when using place-based data (Chakma et al. 2023a; Colmer et al. 2023; Voorheis et al. 2023)—a problem known as aggregation bias. Here, we illustrate this in the context of the relationship between income and canopy cover. In figure 4.4, we show that within-commuting zone variation in canopy cover exposure is relatively flat through the first half of the individual-level national income distribution before increasing moderately at higher income levels. Individuals at the 90th percentile of the individual-level income distribution experience canopy cover that is 2.7 percentage points higher than individuals at the 10th percentile of the individual-level income distribution. By contrast, using the distribution of income per capita across locations, we see that there is a much stronger association between place-based average income and canopy cover. We estimate that individuals living in neighborhoods at the 90th percentile of the block-group income distribution experience canopy cover that is 8.6 percentage points higher than individuals living in neighborhoods at the 10th percentile of the block-group income distribution, more than tripling the individual-level gap. This is largely driven by differences in the relationship in the bottom half of the income distributions. These differences imply that there are other neighborhood-level factors or amenities correlated with income at the neighborhood level that are not as strongly correlated with the individual-level income distribution. Using place-based data results in a potentially incorrect interpretation of the canopy cover–income relationship. If one were to personify places, rather than using person-level data, one would come to vastly different inferences about the empirical relevance of income for predicting canopy cover exposures.

That there is less variation in expsoure to canopy cover within the individual-level income distribution suggests that within-location heterogeneity in income may not be a first-order determinant of willingness-to-pay for natural capital in this context. We caveat again, however, that these simple relationships do not convey direct information on willingness-to-pay, or the extent of heterogeneity in willingness-to-pay within census blocks; nevertheless, this finding suggests that the scope for heterogeneity along margins of income are more limited than one may infer from place-based data. This is not because there is limited heterogeneity in income within census block-groups—within-location heterogeneity is what leads to differences in the two canopy–income relationships (figure 4.4). By contrast, it suggests that there may be little scope for individual income as an important determinant of demand for natural capital. Colmer et al. (2023) provide causal evidence that even large changes in individual income lead to only small changes in demand for air quality. Whether this is because the true marginal willingness to pay for air quality is low, or because information frictions or other market failures distort revelead measures of marginal willingness to pay, remains unclear.

This highlights the third conceptual challenge that natural capital valuation faces—missing markets. Microdata are not able to do anything directly to address this constraint. Accounting prices are not observed and so can't be "provided" in the same way that data on earnings or housing prices can be made available. The granular variation provided by microdata does, however, create opportunities to credibly estimate accounting prices in a systematic and comprehensive way. This is beyond the scope of this paper, but the application of thoughtful research designs and/or structural models could be used to identify not only average accounting prices or willingness to pay estimates, but also distributions of these economic quantities.

4.5 Conclusion

In this paper we have raised the prospect of leveraging microdata (and in particular a new restricted-access environmental microdata infrastructure being developed at the Census Bureau) as an input to improve and expand measurement inputs necessary for natural capital accounting exercises. The availability of new microdata products creates opportunity for researchers to expand methodologies and accounting frameworks with individual-level data in mind.

We provide several illustrations of how microdata can help to address conceptual issues and inform natural capital accounting exercises. Restricted-access microdata can be helpful in defining the extent of the relevant economic jurisdictions when engaging in nonmarket valuation exercises, and address issues of heterogeneity in valuation within locations. Combined with appropriate research designs and structural models, restricted-access microdata containing individual-level information about income, wealth, locational choices, alongside information on exposure to natural capital, can be used to learn about willingness to pay for natural capital, as well as heterogeneity in willingness to pay. By facilitating the production of new facts and necessary structural estimates, microdata have the potential to improve the natural capital accounting endeavor by grounding estimates in the experiences and well-being of individuals, providing new and improved evidence which can inform decisions around how to manage the relationships between people, businesses, and the environment.

References

Addicott, Ethan T., and Eli P. Fenichel. 2019. "Spatial Aggregation and the Value of Natural Capital." *Journal of Environmental Economics and Management* 95: 118–32.

Arrow, Kenneth, Partha Dasgupta, Lawrence Goulder, Gretchen Daily, Paul Ehrlich, Geoffrey Heal, Simon Levin, Karl-Göran Mäler, Stephen Schneider, David Starrett, et al. 2004. "Are We Consuming Too Much?" *Journal of Economic Perspectives* 18 (3): 147–72.

Arrow, Kenneth J., Partha Dasgupta, Lawrence H. Goulder, Kevin J. Mumford, and Kirsten Oleson. 2012. "Sustainability and the Measurement of Wealth." *Environment and Development Economics* 17 (3): 317–53.

Chakma, T., J. Colmer, and J. Voorheis. 2023a. "Heat Disparities in the United States." Working Paper.

Chakma, T., J. Colmer, and J. Voorheis. 2023b. "The Causes and Consequences of Urban Heat Islands." Working Paper.

Colmer, Jonathan, John Voorheis, and Brennan Williams. 2021. "Air Pollution and Economic Opportunity in the United States." Working Paper.

Colmer, Jonathan, Suvy Qin, John Voorheis, and Reed Walker. 2023. "Income, Wealth, and Environmental Inequality in the United States." Mimeo.

Daily, G., T. Soderqvist, S. Aniyar, K. Arrow, P. Dasgupta, P. R. Ehrlich, C. Folke, A. Jansson, B. Jansson, N. Kautsky, S. Levin, J. Lubchenco, K. Mäler, D. Simpson, D. Starrett, D. Tilman, and B. Walker. 2000. "The Value of Nature and the Nature of Value." *Science* 289 (5478): 395–96.

Deryugina, Tatyana, and Julian Reif. 2023. "The Long-run Effect of Air Pollution on Survival." NBER Working Paper No. 31858. Cambridge, MA: National Bureau of Economic Research.

Deryugina, Tatyana, Garth Heutel, Nolan H. Miller, David Molitor, and Julian Reif. 2019. "The Mortality and Medical Costs of Air Pollution: Evidence from Changes in Wind Direction." *American Economic Review* 109 (12): 4178–4219.

Di, Qian, Heresh Amini, Liuhua Shi, Itai Kloog, Rachel Silvern, James Kelly,

M. Benjamin Sabath, Christine Choirat, Petros Koutrakis, Alexei Lyapustin, Yujie Wang, Loretta J. Mickley, and Joel Schwartz. 2020. "Assessing NO2 Concentration and Model Uncertainty with High Spatiotemporal Resolution across the Contiguous United States Using Ensemble Model Averaging." *Environmental Science & Technology* 54 (3): 1372–1384.

Fenichel, Eli P., and Joshua K. Abbott. 2014. "Natural Capital: From Metaphor to Measurement." *Journal of the Association of Environmental and Resource Economists* 1 (1/2).

Fenichel, Eli P., and Yukiko Hashida. 2019. "Choices and the Value of Natural Capital." *Oxford Review of Economic Policy* 35 (1): 120–37.

Fenichel, Eli P., Joshua K. Abbott, Jude Bayham, Whitney Boone, Erin MK Haacker, and Lisa Pfeiffer. 2016. "Measuring the Value of Groundwater and Other Forms of Natural Capital." *Proceedings of the National Academy of Sciences* 113 (9): 2382–2387.

Fenichel, E. P., J. K. Abbott, and S. D. Yun. 2018. "The Nature of Natural Capital and Ecosystem Income." In *Handbook of Environmental Economics*, edited by V. K. Smith, P. Dasgupta, and S. Pattanayak, 85–142. Elsevier.

Fisher, A. C., J. V. Krutilla, and C. J. Cicchetti. 1972. "The Economics of Environmental Preservation: A Theoretical and Empirical Analysis." *American Economic Review* 62 (4): 605–19.

Grimmond, Sue. 2007. "Urbanization and Global Environmental Change: Local Effects of Urban Warming." *Geographical Journal* 173 (1): 83–88.

Hartwick, John M. 1990. "Natural Resources, National Accounting and Economic Depreciation." *Journal of Public Economics* 43 (3): 291–304.

Heal, Geoffrey M. 1998. *Valuing the Future: Economic Theory and Sustainability*. Columbia University Press.

Khreis, Haneen, Clare Kelly, John Tate, Roger Parslow, Karen Lucas, and Mark Nieuwenhuijsen. 2017. "Exposure to Traffic-Related Air Pollution and Risk of Development of Childhood Asthma: A Systematic Review and Meta-Analysis." *Environment International* 100: 1–31.

Krutilla, John V. 1967. "Conservation Reconsidered." *American Economic Review* 57 (4), 777–86.

Meng, Xia, Cong Liu, Renjie Chen, Francesco Sera, Ana Maria Vicedo-Cabrera, Ai Milojevic, Yuming Guo, Shilu Tong, Micheline de Sousa Zanotti Stagliorio Coelho, Paulo Hilario Nascimento Saldiva, et al. 2021. "Short Term Associations of Ambient Nitrogen Dioxide with Daily Total, Cardiovascular, and Respiratory Mortality: Multilocation Analysis in 398 Cities." *BMJ* 372.

Nordhaus, William D. 2006. "Principles of National Accounting for Nonmarket Accounts." In *A New Architecture for the U.S. National Accounts*, edited by Dale W. Jorgenson, J. Steven Landefeld, and William D. Nordhaus. Chicago: University of Chicago Press.

Qian, Di., Yan Wang, Antonella Zanobetti, Yun Wang, Petros Koutrakis, Christine Choirat, Francesca Dominici, and Joel D. Schwartz. 2017. "Air Pollution and Mortality in the Medicare Population." *New England Journal of Medicine* 376 (26): 2513–2522.

Requia, Weeberb J., Qian Di, Rachel Silvern, James T. Kelly, Petros Koutrakis, Loretta J. Mickley, Melissa P. Sulprizio, Heresh Amini, Liuhua Shi, and Joel Schwartz. 2020. "An Ensemble Learning Approach for Estimating High Spatiotemporal Resolution of Ground-Level Ozone in the Contiguous United States." *Environmental Science & Technology* 54 (18): 11037–11047.

Smith, V. Kerry. 1993. "Nonmarket Valuation of Environmental Resources: An Interpretive Appraisal." *Land Economics* 69 (1): 1–26.

Turner, M. C., M. Jerrett, C. A. Pope III, D. Krewski, S. M. Gapstur, W. R. Diver, B. S. Beckerman, J. D. Marshall, J. Su, D. L. Crouse, and R. T. Burnett. 2016.

"Long-Term Ozone Exposure and Mortality in a Large Prospective Study." *American Journal of Respiratory and Critical Care Medicine* 193 (10): 1134–42.
van Donkelaar, Aaron, Melanie S. Hammer, Liam Bindle, Michael Brauer, Jeffery R. Brook, Michael J. Garay, N. Christina Hsu, Olga V. Kalashnikova, Ralph A. Kahn, Colin Lee, Robert C. Levy, Alexei Lyapustin, Andrew M. Sayer, and Randall V. Martin. 2021. "Monthly Global Estimates of Fine Particulate Matter and Their Uncertainty." *Environmental Science & Technology* 55 (22): 15287–15300.
Voorheis, J., J. Colmer, K. Houghton, E. Lyubich, M. Munro, C. Scalera, and J. Withrow. 2023. "Building the Prototype Census Environmental Impacts Frame." NBER Working Paper No. 31189. Cambridge, MA: National Bureau of Economic Research.
Weitzman, Martin L. 1976. "On the Welfare Significance of National Product in a Dynamic Economy." *Quarterly Journal of Economics* 90 (1): 156–62.
Wing, Oliver E. J., William Lehman, Paul D. Bates, Christopher C. Sampson, Niall Quinn, Andrew M. Smith, Jeffrey C. Neal, Jeremy R. Porter, and Carolyn Kousky. 2022. "Inequitable Patterns of US flood risk in the Anthropocene." *Nature Climate Change* 12 (2): 156–62.

Comment Corbett Grainger

Can we improve estimates of the value of natural capital by using high-resolution data on the population and the distribution of environmental amenities? Under what circumstances does the spatial unit of analysis affect our estimates of the value of natural capital? In their chapter, Colmer and Voorheis (this volume) use high-resolution data from the census, paired with remotely sensed estimates of tree canopy cover, to illustrate the potential importance of individual-level data in such valuation applications.

In this comment, I discuss how high spatial resolution, individual-level data could be important in natural capital applications. There are two interrelated factors that I will focus on: the degree of variation of the environmental good over space, and the extent to which demand for the environmental good varies with population characteristics.

Heterogeneity over Space

Some amenities vary significantly even within a small geographic area. Air pollution and urban tree canopy, two examples from Colmer and Voorheis (this volume), both vary significantly between cities but also within a given

Corbett Grainger is an associate professor in the Agricultural and Applied Economics Department at the University of Wisconsin-Madison.

The author thanks Eli Fenichel, Nicholas Muller, Mary Bohman, Jonathan Colmer, and John Voorheis for helpful discussions and comments. I also thank seminar participants at the CRIW Conference on Natural Capital Accounting. For acknowledgments, sources of research support, and disclosure of the author's material financial relationships, if any, please see https://www.nber.org/books-and-chapters/measuring-and-accounting-environmental-public-goods-national-accounts-perspective/comment-microdata-and-valuation-natural-capital-grainger.

urban area. The degree of variation within a Core-Based Statistical Area (CBSA) will depend on the application, but for urban canopy cover, there can be significant heterogeneity even within a census tract or block-group.

Other amenities may vary more *between* locations. The amount of land in forestry or agriculture, for example, will vary significantly between counties but less within a city block. Similarly, some environmental amenities such as lakes, coastal beaches, and urban parks may have coverage that varies within a tract or block-group, but the geographic coverage is continuous and well defined. In contrast, urban canopy cover is patchy, with significant variation even within a city block.

With air pollution, some pollutants vary significantly even within an urban block (e.g., black carbon), whereas others are better categorized as varying regionally (Apte et al. 2017).

As other work has shown (Voorheis et al. 2023), the variation of demographic characteristics is also a critical consideration when looking at exposure to environmental amenities or disamenities like pollution. In many cases, income may vary more *within* a census tract than *between* census tracts.

Why does this matter? As Colmer and Voorheis illustrate, the assignment of exposure or access to an environmental amenity could be highly local. One person may live in a location with a high level of urban canopy while their neighbor may have little. And the degree of coverage affects a variety of outcomes, from cooling effects to buffering against exposure to air pollution.

In situations where we are interested in quantifying *who* has access to an environmental amenity or *who* is exposed to a disamenity such as pollution, it is critical that we understand how population and environmental characteristics vary over space. The EIF data, combined with high-resolution environmental data, allow researchers and policymakers to better understand who has access/exposure to environmental goods and services.

Heterogeneity and Valuation

Individuals value environmental goods and services for a variety of reasons (use, non-use, and option values), and economists have developed a set of tools based on revealed and stated preferences to estimate values of such nonmarket goods. Although Colmer and Voorheis do not estimate the value of canopy cover, they illustrate the importance of understanding how the distribution of natural capital could affect its value.

There has long been a debate about the scale of analysis in hedonic applications. For example, Grainger (2012) compares tract-level and county-level estimates of the impact of improvement in air quality. In these applications, the spatial scale of estimation matters when pricing environmental goods or bads. In Grainger (2012), he argues that pollution reductions are targeted *within* nonattainment counties, so impacts near monitors in violation will experience larger pollution reductions (following Auffhammer et al. 2009).

In the case of Superfund site cleanups, Greenstone and Gallagher (2008) find no significant impact on housing prices at the tract level. Gamper-Rabindran and Timmins (2013) revisit this analysis using finer-scale data and find that effects of cleanups are positive but localized.

With urban canopy cover in Colmer and Voorheis, however, there is still significant *within-block* variation in canopy cover. Colmer and Voorheis illustrate that even block-group-level analysis could lead to significant aggregation bias, which would likely bias any hedonic estimates of the value of canopy cover.

Demand for environmental goods and services is generally a function of income, so there may not be "one price" to apply in natural accounting exercises. As such, understanding the income-demand relationship (i.e., Engel curves) would be critical if individual data on exposure or access were used to develop estimates of the value of natural capital.

Implications

The EIF data illustrated by Colmer and Voorheis, and discussed at length in Voorheis et al. (2023), will undoubtedly prove to be useful in a variety of important applications. I'll conclude with a few observations regarding the practical implications of the data described here.

Characterizing the Distribution of Exposure

As illustrated in their canopy example, assigning exposure at the individual and aggregating to the population leads to very different conclusions than assigning exposure based on percentiles of the distribution of median income at the block or tract level. If researchers or policymakers are concerned with the distribution of exposure to environmental amenities, this has important implications.

Place-Based Policies vs. Targeted Policies

Some environmental amenities vary more at the local level than others. As Colmer and Voorheis show, the *within-block* variation in canopy cover is significant, and that has implications when assigning exposure to individuals and aggregating. Other environmental amenities do not exhibit such dramatic heterogeneity at a fine spatial scale. Regional air pollution, for example, or access to conserved land, vary more between blocks.

It is also worth noting that the degree of targeting in policy also varies, depending on the specific application. For pollution from a point source such as a refinery, there may be directed policies to reduce exposure at the neighborhood level. Other policies may have impacts that cause changes in natural capital at higher levels of geography. In both cases, there may be aggregation bias when illustrating the distribution of exposure by income. But many policies are place based, and environmental justice communities are defined spatially, not as collections of individuals dispersed over large areas, so in some cases the "right" metric may indeed be characterized by median income, the proportion of households under the poverty line, or the proportion of the population from underrepresented groups.

Natural Capital Accounts and Microdata

In summary, as Colmer and Voorheis point out, adding Engel curves to data on individual exposure to an environmental amenity could help when aggregating to the value of an amenity over space. In many empirical applications, willingness to pay is a function of income but also varies by other demographic characteristics (age, race, ethnicity, education). In these types of applications, should the value of the natural capital take into account all observable characteristics of individuals when aggregating across population and over space? There remain questions about how microdata can be utilized and when they *should* be utilized in developing natural capital accounts, and I hope that future research will continue pushing this forward.

References

Apte, J. S., K. P. Messier, S. Gani, M. Brauer, T. W. Kirchstetter, M. M. Lunden, J. D. Marshall, C. J. Portier, R. C. Vermeulen, and S. P. Hamburg. 2017. "High-Resolution Air Pollution Mapping with Google Street View Cars: Exploiting Big Data." *Environmental Science & Technology* 51 (12): 6999–7008.

Auffhammer, M., A. M. Bento, and S. E. Lowe. 2009. "Measuring the Effects of the Clean Air Act Amendments on Ambient PM10 Concentrations: The Critical Importance of a Spatially Disaggregated Analysis." *Journal of Environmental Economics and Management 58* (1): 15–26.

Colmer, J., and J. Voorheis. "Microdata and the Valuation of Natural Capital." In *Measuring and Accounting for Environmental Public Goods: A National Accounts Perspective*, edited by Mary Bohman, Eli Fenichel, and Nicholas Z. Muller. Chicago, IL: University of Chicago Press. This volume.

Gamper-Rabindran, S., and C. Timmins. 2013. "Does Cleanup of Hazardous Waste Sites Raise Housing Values? Evidence of Spatially Localized Benefits." *Journal of Environmental Economics and Management 65* (3): 345–360.

Grainger, C. A. 2012. "The Distributional Effects of Pollution Regulations: Do Renters Fully Pay for Cleaner Air?" *Journal of Public Economics 96* (9–10): 840–852.

Greenstone, M., and J. Gallagher. 2008. "Does Hazardous Waste Matter? Evidence from the Housing Market and the Superfund Program." *Quarterly Journal of Economics 123* (3): 951–1003.

Voorheis, J. L., J. M. Colmer, K. A. Houghton, E. Lyubich, M. Munro, C. Scalera, and J. R. Withrow. 2023. "Building the Prototype Census Environmental Impacts Frame." NBER Working Paper No. 31189. Cambridge, MA: National Bureau of Economic Research.

5 The Value and Configuration of Coastal Natural Capital

Ethan T. Addicott

5.1 Introduction

The increasing availability of data has enabled operational ecosystem accounts (*SEEA EA* 2021) that track physical quantities and, ideally, the economic value of natural assets. The United States, for example, will assemble natural capital accounts and attempt to disentangle the contribution of natural assets to various sectors of the economy in the coming decade (Office of Science and Technology Policy et al. 2023). In the absence of market prices, systematic physical accounts of natural assets can serve as proxies for monetary accounts to describe the changes in the economic value of natural assets. However, physical indicators can also provide poor indices of the state of the environment if they aggregate units of natural capital generating different bundles of ecosystem services. For example, measuring physical stocks of a tree species distributed across a woodland with stocks of the same species planted more sparsely in urban areas masks important heterogeneity in the services these trees provide in situ. Using such mea-

Ethan T. Addicott is a lecturer in economics at the University of Exeter Business School, and a member of the Land, Environment, Economics and Policy (LEEP) Institute at the University of Exeter.

Data provided by Zillow through the Zillow Transaction and Assessment Dataset (ZTRAX). More information on accessing the data can be found at http://www.zillow.com/ztrax. The results and opinions are those of the author(s) and do not reflect the position of Zillow Group. This work was supported in part by Connecticut SeaGrant and the Knobloch Family Foundation. Many thanks to Justin Contat for helpful comments and discussion throughout, organizers and participants in the NBER CRIW Measuring and Accounting for Environmental Public Goods, and colleagues at Yale, the University of Exeter, and the LEEP Institute. For acknowledgments, sources of research support, and disclosure of the author's material financial relationships, if any, please see https://www.nber.org/books-and-chapters/measuring-and-accounting-environmental-public-goods-national-accounts-perspective/value-and-configuration-coastal-natural-capital.

surements as proxies for service flows will overstate urban noise mitigation services (Fletcher et al. 2022) and understate the habitat provisioning services for woodland fauna. Policy based on misleading indices, in turn, can compromise progress toward sustainability.

Here, I use beach sand as an example to explore the heterogeneity in value flows from natural assets along the US East Coast. I build on previous work from North Carolina (Addicott 2022) and Florida that characterizes the marginal value of coastal beach attributes, and provide an additional empirical example from Connecticut. I present summaries of the three case studies as evidence that associated service flows stemming from different configurations of natural assets drive heterogeneity in their economic value. Accounting for heterogeneity in service flows from natural assets can improve the quality of environmental-economic accounts, assist with targeting of policy interventions to mitigate impacts of climate change and sea level rise, and identify important omitted variables in determining natural asset values. In the discussion, I use the 2022 FEMA Ecosystem Service Value Updates as an example where recognizing service flow heterogeneity for coastal assets can improve policy and adaptation investments going forward (FEMA 2022).

Coastal areas are useful exemplars of the heterogeneity in service flows and values for natural assets because of their policy relevance and value. Coasts are on the front lines of the climate crisis, and understanding factors important for valuing coastal natural assets can inform high-impact decisions. The sustainability of coastal cities will depend on making effective adaptation decisions in the face of climate risk. Rising seas and more frequent storms imperil the intertwined produced and natural assets along coasts. While seawalls and other produced capital investments can help protect coastal properties from rising seas (Yohe et al. 1996), so too can robust beach-dune ecosystems. However, the value of natural capital assets—like sandy beaches and dune systems—and their associated ecosystem service flows are not well characterized. Consequentially, unmeasured natural assets and ecosystem services may, in practice, receive zero weight by planners and lead to inefficient policy decisions.

Coastal planners are tasked with assessing the cost-effectiveness of adaptation strategies in the face of coastal erosion and sea level rise. It is not sufficient to know the direct costs of seawall construction or dune restoration because of linkages between produced and natural assets (Rouhi Rad et al. 2021). There is evidence, for example, that produced defensive expenditures in coastal areas might diminish the resilience of coastal beaches and therefore their value (Berry et al. 2013). An informed link between the configuration of coastal beach sand and ecosystem service provision will improve independently assessed values for produced and natural solutions to climate risks and aid planners' decisions in the coastal zone. If we can value natural assets more accurately, then we will be in a better position to assess the costs and benefits of different policy responses.

Sand, in contrast to fish stocks or bird populations, is immobile (of its own accord). It is relatively homogeneous and substitutable. Despite the simplifying features of beach sand, aggregating sand values along the US East Coast using a benefits-transfer approach would be ill advised when there are the systematic differences in capitalization rates and service flows demonstrated here that are otherwise unaccounted for. Given this, other, more complicated assets (e.g., populations of migratory species or acres of wetland) require careful attention when included in natural capital accounts to avoid aggregation bias. The upside is that the data and methods to capture the extent, condition, and value of ecosystems at high resolution are increasingly available, obviating extensive reliance on poor physical indices or benefits transfer for policymaking.

Case Study I summarizes key results from Addicott (2022) from North Carolina. Case Study II focuses on inlets in Florida. For these first two study areas, beaches and the coastline are synonymous. All coastline in the sample is sandy. In Case Study II: Florida, I restrict the sample to portions of the coastline where the beach is interrupted at an inlet. This partition of the coastline interrupts the flows of sand along the shore and the case provides suggestive evidence that the interrupted service flows impact the capitalized value of beach sand in coastal properties. The third case study provides new evidence of the heterogeneity in the value of coastal beach sand along the US East Coast.

In Case Study III: Connecticut, I highlight pocket beaches where being adjacent to the coast is not synonymous with being adjacent to a beach. A mix of public and private access beaches, each with varying angles along the coast (e.g., east-facing compared to south-facing) and at a higher latitude, provide results for the capitalization of beach sand in coastal properties that are characteristically different from the other two case studies.

In each case study, I derive estimates of the marginal capitalization of beach width in coastal property values using the hedonic property value method. The literature on hedonic pricing of environmental amenities provides ample evidence that context is important for valuation (e.g., White and Leefers 2007). This paper shows that high-resolution geophysical, remotely sensed data can be used to scale up valuation efforts that otherwise faced the challenge of limited data (Barbier 2012; Mooney et al. 2004). By leveraging remotely sensed data for each of the three case studies along the US East Coast, I show that more accurate measures of the value of natural assets are attainable to inform policymaking (e.g., via cost-benefit analysis) and that these measures reflect important heterogeneity within cross-sections of the coast and between coastal areas. The estimates I provide assume a time-invariant hedonic price schedule and that the configuration of coastal assets are important and salient for bidders and buyers of the properties included in the sample. Identification strategies in each case study vary according to the available data and applicable tools for each setting. While the fixed-effects specifications are cross-sectional in nature, the results support the key idea that the arrangement of the portfolio of natural and produced assets along the coast drives differential provision of services and hence heterogeneity in natural asset values.

The remainder of the paper is organized as follows. Sections 5.2 and 5.3 provide background, describing the context of beach-dune ecosystems along the US East Coast, previous efforts in the literature to value coastal beach sand, and the data for the analysis. Sections 5.4–6 present case studies using hedonic property valuation of beach sand to illustrate the spatial distribution of values for an otherwise homogeneous asset. Section 5.7 offers discussion toward improved national accounts of natural assets.

5.2 Background and Setting

Coastal beaches are on the front lines of global change. Natural processes in coastal zones, and the services they generate, vary non-linearly across time and space (Barbier et al. 2008). Winds, tides, currents, waves, and eddies arrange and rearrange produced and non-produced assets in the coastal zone from ocean plastic and seaweed to nutrients and grains of sand. Sand exists above and below the surface of the ocean and contributes to the provision of spatially dependent services, like coastal protection and recreation, and disservices, like impeded coastal navigation (as a sand bar or shoal).

Sea level rise, storm damage, and climate change motivate increased attention to coastal beaches; however, they have long been featured prominently in the recreation demand and non-market valuation literatures (Bell and Leeworthy 1986, 1990; Landry and Hindsley 2011; McConnell 1977; Parsons and Powell 2001). While this literature focuses on coastal beaches as amenities that produce a single service—either recreation or coastal protection—more recently, sandy beaches have been studied as inputs to the production of multiple service flows (Addicott 2022; Dundas 2017). When an additional unit of sand is allocated to beach width, this sand provides recreation opportunities to beachgoers as well as coastal protection services to the owners of nearby property. Beach sand allocated to coastal dunes and their attributes (i.e., width, height, location) protects from flooding and windstorm-induced property damage through interactions with beach width.

The hedonic property valuation method has been used to estimate the value of beaches capitalized in nearby property values at specific beach locations around the world. These values are then used to assess the cost-effectiveness of widening beaches through beach nourishment (Parsons and Powell 2001), principally motivated by recreation values (Edwards and Gable 1991) or erosion/coastal protection (Landry et al. 2003; Pompe and Rinehart 1994). The hedonic property method is used and expanded upon in the case studies that follow because of the availability of property data (via e.g., ZTRAX and CoreLogic) and high-resolution environmental data.

These data can be used to value an environmental amenity through property transactions (Gindelsky et al. 2022; White and Leefers 2007). Benefits transfer is one option for elevating these estimates to inform natural capital accounts of coastal assets. This paper contributes to our understanding of how the capitalized value of natural assets can be reliably estimated across space when given reliable data. The case studies illustrate the degree to which the configuration of sand, within a cross-section of beach and along different arrangements of properties and coastline, can imperil the wide external validity of the hedonic approach when unaccounted for. In coastal areas where beaches are periodically nourished, property values and beach width are codetermined. Gopalakrishnan et al. (2011) first tackled this endogeneity resulting from nourishment decisions and find that their instrumental variables estimate (using distance to the continental shelf as an instrument for beach width) for the marginal value of beach width is six times larger than the OLS estimate.

The three case studies demonstrate different ways to configure sand—the asset of interest—along coastlines and with respect to coastal properties. I address how sand may be valued differently when varying (1) its configuration from offshore to onshore at a specific location; and (2) its configuration across locations along the coast. The three configurations of beach sand considered here are contiguous stretches of beach sand with prominent dunes (NC), inlet areas (FL), and pocket beaches (CT) (figure 5.1). I define these

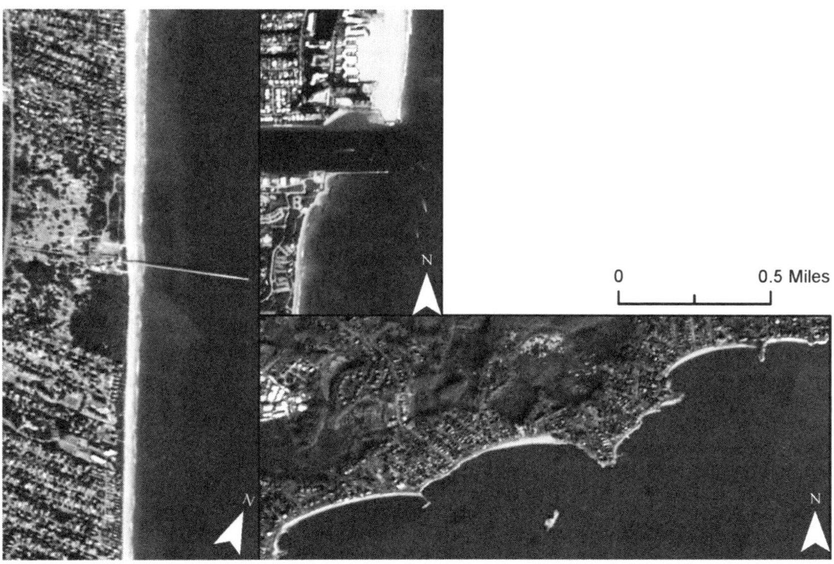

Figure 5.1 Three coastal configurations

Notes: Far Left: Dare County, North Carolina. Top Right: Broward County, Florida. Bottom Right: New Haven County, Connecticut. Images © 2017, 2018 Planet Labs PBC.

sand configurations on a macro scale. Since coasts are dynamic systems, I use beach measures as close to the time of sale as the data allow with the idea that beach width/dune features do change but are slow variables relative to property transactions. The Connecticut pocket beach example adds important richness to the previously explored Florida and North Carolina cases. Whereas in North Carolina and Florida public beaches are ubiquitous with access points well-distributed, in Connecticut, pocket beaches may or may not have public amenities and access.

5.3 Data and Methods

The data for these analyses include economic and biogeophysical data for all coastal counties in North Carolina and Connecticut as well as the surrounding area[1] of six inlets[2] on the Atlantic coast of Florida. The economic data are property transactions data and housing characteristics for sales of properties within 10 km of the coastline from 2008–2017 derived from parcel-level tax and deed data from CoreLogic (for North Carolina counties) and 2004–2022 from Zillow's ZTRAX data for Connecticut and Florida (2020).

The geophysical data were derived from the USGS Coastal LiDAR Dataset,[3] Connecticut Department of Energy & Environmental Protection GIS Open Data, and PlanetLabs (Team Planet 2017). USGS LiDAR data record dune features at high resolution and beach slope. The dune feature data consist of the horizontal position and elevation of the dune crest, dune toe, and shoreline on a five-meter grid. The dune toe is the point on the dune with the maximum increase in slope. This high-resolution information allows me to include a continuous measure of beach attributes into the hedonic property value framework.

5.4 Case Study I: North Carolina

In North Carolina, sandy beaches line almost the entire Atlantic coast of the state. For this sample, proximity (or adjacency) to the coast implies proximity (adjacency) to a sandy beach. Previous work by Gopalakrishnan et al. (2011) demonstrates that the capitalization of an additional foot of beach width for coastal properties is about 1 percent of property transaction prices. Due to the frequency of beach nourishment projects—which

1. Adjacent to the shoreline (200 meters inland) and within a 600-meter buffer of the inlet centroid.

2. Boca Raton, Ft. Pierce, Jupiter, Lake Worth, Ponce de Leon, and South Lake Worth.

3. LiDAR-derived Beach Morphology (Dune Crest, Dune Toe, and Shoreline) for US Sandy Coastlines, US Geological Survey site located at https://coastal.er.usgs.gov/data-release/doi-F7GF0S0Z/.

artificially widen beaches—along North Carolina's coast, beach width is an endogenous variable. Replicating the approach from Gopalakrishnan et al. (2011), I use distance to the continental shelf (an isobath) as an instrument for beach width. Distance to an undersea isobath, or contour line, is plausibly exogeneous and only impacts the bidder's decision insofar as it mediates beach width. I confirm their estimates and go on to show that beach sand configured as dune features capitalizes into property values differently than when allocated to a marginal foot of beach width (Addicott 2022). I elicit marginal values for different attributes of beach-dune ecosystems and attribute the values to service and amenity flows—namely coastal protection, recreation, and viewsheds.

For all case studies, I estimate similar first-stage semi-log hedonic models. For this case study, the P_{ij} is the 2017 CPI-adjusted sale price of property i located in county j, X_{ij} are characteristics of the property, including flood risk and the number of blocks away from the ocean, w_{ij} is the beach width at the closest coastal profile to each property, D^h and D^w are the dune width and dune height for the dune associated with the closest coastal profile:

$$(1)\quad ln\,ln(P_{ij}) = \alpha X_{ij} + \beta_1 w_{ij} + \beta_2 D^h_{ij} + \beta_3 D^w_{ij} + \tau_1 SaleMonth_{ij} + \tau_2 SaleYear_{ij} + \delta_1 County_j + \delta_2 BlocksfromOcean_{ij} + \epsilon_{ij}$$

Within each cross-shore slice of coast, from the closure depth at which nearshore sand fluctuations attenuate, to the far side of a coastal dune, the allocation and configuration of beach sand contribute to different suites of ecosystem services. As a result, the asset value of a unit of beach sand depends on where along the coastal profile it is located. In addition, the configuration of produced capital—the height of coastal properties—interacts with coastal dunes such that properties taller than dune can have valuable viewsheds obstructed by a marginal increase in dune height. Therefore, for these homes, taller dunes provide a viewshed reduction hand-in-hand with an increase in coastal protection.

In my preferred specification, an additional foot of beach width capitalizes at about 1 percent of property values and a marginally taller dune or marginally wider dune capitalize in property values differently depending on whether the property's viewshed is fully blocked by the dune (i.e., the property is shorter than the dune). Figure 5.2 presents the key result from Addicott (2022) as exposition for the following novel cases. The figure shows that the marginal capitalization in terms of feet of beach width/dune height/dune width depends on whether a property's viewshed is fully blocked by a dune. For properties with a fully blocked viewshed, a marginally taller dune does not provide an additional viewshed disamenity in the same way as it would for a property with an unobstructed view of the shore. I find that the marginal value of a foot of dune height for coastal protection is approxi-

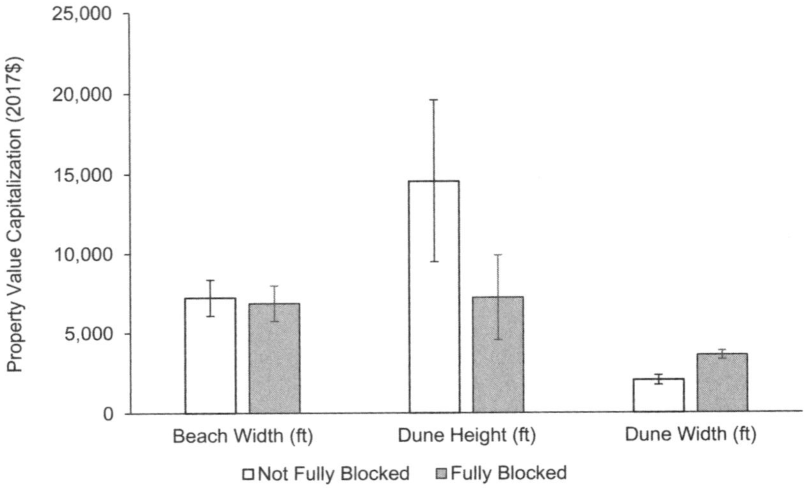

Figure 5.2 Summary of capitalization of coastal attributes in property values from Addicott (2022) across properties with fully blocked and not fully blocked viewsheds. Error bars represent 95% CI. See Addicott (2022) tables 1 and 5 for corresponding summary statistics and regression tables.

mately \$12,200/ft; however, that additional foot of dune height imposes a viewshed disamenity of over twice that magnitude (approx. −\$28,900/ft). Whereas the marginal value of beach width is uniformly positive for fully blocked and not fully blocked properties, the marginal value of dune height is not. In addition, depending on the shape of the dune and coastal profile, different volumes of sand will be needed to realize the horizontal or vertical foot of dune or beach. These volumetric results are presented in Addicott (2022).

I emphasize here as a starting point that the value of beach sand within a cross-section of beach depends on the configuration of coastal natural and produced capital (beaches, buildings, and dunes). A uniform investment in a volume of beach sand will realize different levels of ecosystem services depending on the dimensions of the coastal profile and the location along the (cross-shore) profile where the sand is allocated. Taking the framework from this setting and comparable high-resolution remotely sensed data to inlet areas in Florida and pocket beaches in Connecticut, I consider the heterogeneity in the capitalization of beach width elsewhere along the coast.

5.5 Case Study II: Florida

Whereas in the North Carolina case study the stretches of beach considered were contiguous, in Florida I focus on the interruption of the coastline

Table 5.1 **Summary statistics by inlet side**

	Full sample (1)	North of Inlet (2)	South of Inlet (3)
Sale Price	1,121,914	1,037,294	1,294,479
	(1,219,885)	(1,092,342)	(1,430,657)
Bedrooms	2.74	2.57	3.10
	(0.992)	(0.726)	(1.316)
Bathrooms	2.94	2.76	3.31
	(1.215)	(0.892)	(1.632)
Dist. to Shore	607.77	452.46	924.51
	(480.5)	(375.0)	(515.5)
Building Sq. Ft.	2,666.20	2,402.32	3,204.32
	(2,078.3)	(1,535.1)	(2,810.0)
Beach Width (Ft.)	112.37	98.07	144.04
	(54.15)	(33.38)	(74.30)
N	3,249	2,180	1,069

Notes: Standard deviations in parentheses.

by inlets. Inlets are a particularly important configuration of coastal sand in that they embody produced/natural asset substitution. For one, inlets allow vessels to navigate between the ocean and inland waters. On the other hand, they also interrupt the north to south flow of sand that would otherwise occur in their absence. As a result, inlet areas in Florida are managed via sand bypass, human-mediated sand transfers from the sand-rich side of an inlet to the sand-poor side.

Using property sales from 2004–2020 around five inlet areas in Florida, I show that inlets deserve special consideration for understanding the marginal value of coastal natural capital. There are two results to support this. First, controlling for structural characteristics, properties on the sand-starved side of inlets sell for less than properties on the sand-fed side. Second, beach width capitalizes at a higher rate on the sand-fed side of inlets than on the sand-starved side.

Table 5.2 presents both results using a similar hedonic first stage to Case Study I; however, here there is a more limited sample of property transactions for coastal adjacent homes within one half mile of the midpoint of six coastal inlets on Florida's east coast: Boca Raton Inlet, Ft. Pierce Inlet, Jupiter Inlet, Lake Worth Inlet, Ponce de Leon Inlet, and South Lake Worth Inlet. Again, as in Addicott (2022) and Gopalakrishnan et al. (2011) an additional foot of beach width capitalizes in coastal properties at about 1 percent of their value all else equal. Column 2 includes an indicator for whether a coastal property is located on the sand-starved south side of an inlet area. This indicates there is a 22.4 percent discount for properties on the sand-starved south side of inlets. While the inlet area fixed effects help

Table 5.2 **Florida inlet regression results**

Dependent variable: Log Sale Price (2017$)	(1)	(2)	(3)	(4)
Bedrooms	0.638***	0.644***	0.628***	0.548***
	(0.061)	(0.061)	(0.061)	(0.062)
Bedrooms Sq. Ft.	−0.088***	−0.086***	−0.083***	−0.077***
	(0.009)	(0.009)	(0.009)	(0.009)
Bathrooms	0.258***	0.268***	0.268***	0.305***
	(0.059)	(0.058)	(0.058)	(0.058)
Bath Sq. Ft.	−0.013	−0.012	−0.012	−0.018*
	(0.007)	(0.007)	(0.007)	(0.007)
Building Sq. Ft.	2.34e-04***	2.25 e-04***	2.21 e-04***	2.19 e-04***
	(1.40e-05)	(1.41e-05)	(1.40e-05)	(1.39e-05)
Beach Width (Ft.)	0.008***	0.009***	0.018***	0.019***
	(0.001)	(0.001)	(0.002)	(0.002)
1(South)		−0.224***	0.276*	0.028
		(0.046)	(0.108)	(0.116)
1(South) × Beach Width (Ft.)			−0.014***	−0.015***
			(0.003)	(0.003)
Annualized Bypass (Cu. Ft.)				2.67e-06***
				(4.79e-07)
Constant	10.99***	10.89***	10.64***	10.69***
	(0.140)	(0.140)	(0.148)	(0.147)
N	3249	3249	3249	3249
R^2	0.555	0.560	0.566	0.572

Notes: Standard errors in parentheses. All columns include inlet area, sale year, and season of year fixed effects.

* $p < 0.05$, ** $p < 0.01$, *** $p < 0.001$

address non-time-varying unobservable characteristics in each inlet area, the results here are not causal—merely illustrative of the difference in property transactions values for properties sited on the south side of inlets across 19 inlets on the state's east coast. Ideally, an event study using plausibly exogenous storm events could help address standard concerns with a cross-sectional hedonic approach.

Table 5.2, column 3 shows that an additional foot of beach width on the sand-starved south side of inlets capitalizes at a discount relative to an additional foot of beach width on the sand-fed north side of an inlet. One potential explanation for this difference in capitalization is that each of these inlets undergo regular sand-bypass transfers, moving sand from the north to the south side of the inlet. Column 5 controls for annualized sand supplements due to bypass at inlet sites. Narrower beaches on the south side of inlets, relative to the north side of inlets, realize greater quantities of transferred sand. These results suggest that human-mediated sand transfers and interruptions to the natural north-south flow of sand are important factors for determining the flows of benefits each unit of sand provides nearby property owners.

5.6 Case Study III: Connecticut

In Connecticut, the presence of pocket beaches means that properties can be adjacent to the coast without being near a sandy beach. Pocket beaches represent a different configuration of sand than the contiguous stretches of barrier island along the Florida or North Carolina coastlines, and may be enjoyed differently due to their structure.

Again, using a sample of property transactions, I estimate a first stage hedonic model to understand how pocket beaches capitalize into coastal property values. Table 5.3 shows capitalization estimates that include fixed effects by county, sale year, sale month, and nearest public beach. Column 5 clusters the standard errors at the county level.

Strikingly, these estimates for the marginal capitalization of beach width are smaller than the Florida and North Carolina case studies. Back-transforming to marginal capitalization from Column 6, a foot of beach width has a mean capitalization of $267/ft (95 pct CI $231-$303) in Connecticut. A back-of-the-envelope calculation using average cooling-degree days (27.25 percent ratio of cooling degree days between North Carolina and Connecticut) weights the capitalization in Connecticut to account for fewer warm beachgoing days since cooling degree days reflect the number of days the average temperature is above 75°F. However, the reweighted capitalization in Connecticut, $980/ft, still leaves a large gap compared to the $4,838/ft-$5,692/ft capitalization in North Carolina. One possible explanation for the smaller magnitude of capitalization is that beachgoing amenities and recreation opportunities associated with beach sand are seasonally limited and therefore the recreation services they provide command less of a premium in coastal property sales.

A second important feature of case study III is that the capitalization of beach width attenuates rapidly. Whereas in North Carolina the estimated market size for beach width extended as far out as three miles inland for some counties, in Connecticut the capitalization of beach width attenuates to zero for properties with centroids beyond 500 feet from the beach. Further, table 5.3 columns (3–6) introduce controls for distance to a public beach. The coefficients on this regressor in each of the specifications is greater than zero, suggesting that the premium for being within 500 feet of the beach can be offset by being too close to a public beach. Greater distances from public beaches, conditional on being near the coast, are associated with higher property values.

Table 5.3 Column 6 provides suggestive evidence that properties prone to inundation from sea level rise, in areas that have experienced past shoreline

Table 5.3 **Pocket beach sales regression results**

Log Sale Price (2017$)	(1)	(2)	(3)	(4)	(5)	(6)
Bedrooms	0.153***	0.239***	0.238***	0.236***	0.243***	0.248***
	(0.008)	(0.007)	(0.007)	(0.007)	(0.007)	(0.007)
Bedrooms Sq. Ft.	−0.011***	−0.028***	−0.028***	−0.028***	−0.028***	−0.029***
	(0.001)	(0.001)	(0.001)	(0.001)	(0.001)	(0.001)
Bathrooms	0.525***	0.366***	0.364***	0.363***	0.345***	0.338***
	(0.005)	(0.005)	(0.005)	(0.005)	(0.005)	(0.006)
Baths Sq. Ft.	−0.030***	−0.028***	−0.028***	−0.028***	−0.027***	−0.026***
	(0.001)	(0.001)	(0.001)	(0.001)	(0.001)	(0.001)
Ppty Sq. Ft.	6.259e-05***	9.727e-05***	9.730e-05***	9.473e-05***	9.338e-05***	9.434e-05***
	(1.167e-06)	(1.249e-06)	(1.246e-06)	(1.249e-06)	(1.234e-06)	(1.397e-06)
Beach Width (Ft.)	-8.215e-04**	5.403e-05*	1.885e-04***	1.807e-04***	1.586e-04***	4.552e-04***
	(I.724e-05)	(2.334e-05)	(2.372e-05)	(2.363e-05)	(2.330e-05)	(3.132e-05)
Coast Angle	−1.242e-03***	−4.322e-04***	−5.390e-04***	−6.244e-04***	−6.466e-04***	−4.585e-04***
	(3.983e-05)	(4.353e-05)	(4.397e-05)	(4.406e-05)	(4.318e-05)	(5.769e-05)
Dist to Public Beach (Ft.)			6.264e-05***	5.795e-05***	6.017e-05***	8.675e-05***
			(3.267e-06)	(3.289e-06)	(3.193e-06)	(4.028e-06)
Dist to Coast (Ft.)				4.680e-05***	5.750e-05***	7.671e-05***
				(1.902e-06)	(1.917e-06)	(2.300e-06)
1(Near Coast)					6.047e-01***	2.664e-01***
					(1.648e-02)	(7.951e-03)
1(Near Coast) X Coast Dist					−2.954e-03***	
					(2.122e-04)	
1(Near Coast) X Public Bch. Dist.					−7.759e-05***	
					(4.074e-06)	
SLR Shore Retreat (Ft.)						−2.087e-04***
						(2.733e-05)
Public Beach FE		X	X	X	X	X
N	197,940	197,940	197,940	197,940	197,940	148,309
R^2	0.526	0.632	0.633	0.634	0.642	0.662

Notes: Standard errors in parentheses. All columns include sale year, month of year, and county fixed effects. Number of stories and building vintage are also controlled. * $p < 0.05$, ** $p < 0.01$, *** $p < 0.001$.

retreat, sell at a discount. Shoreline retreat, or shore movement, data describe the net movement of the shoreline between 1880 and 2006 (O'Brien et al. 2014). This association has the same order of magnitude as the capitalization of a foot of beach width (per foot of long-term coastal retreat) and also the aspect (or angle) of the coast.

5.7 Discussion

Nonmarket valuation methods can be used to fill gaps in measurement of the value of ecosystem service flows from natural assets. Such economic tools provide policymakers with improvements to null/zero valued assets so that the value of natural assets are—at a minimum—partially accounted for in policy decision making. Whereas the nonmarket valuation literature includes estimates of the value of coastal natural assets and services, these estimates have typically required labor-intensive field data collection (e.g., Gopalakrishnan et al. 2011) and therefore were more limited in scope. The bespoke nature of nonmarket valuation studies means that scaling results for policy requires applying estimates from one context to similar, often neighboring locales. This process, known as benefits transfer, maximizes the application of outputs from costly data collection and analysis.

As an example, consider the United States Federal Emergency Management Agency (FEMA) policies for incorporating ecosystem services in the Benefit-Cost Analysis (BCA) process. The first ecosystem services policy was implemented in 2013 and allowed monetization of ecosystem services for riparian and green open space for BCA. The policy was updated in 2016 and again in 2022 to cover more land cover types and include more service flows. The policy favors values from meta-analyses as they are intended to be used for "streamlined" BCA as part of the agency's BCA toolkit and applicable to any project in the US. As values for land cover types and their associated ecosystem services are added or updated, zero-values for investments in natural assets and ecosystem services are improved and nature-based solutions are given credence in BCA. In the 2022 update, nine land cover types and 14 ecosystem services are considered, though not all combinations are populated with estimates. Beaches and dunes, for example, were assigned $223,840 (2021 USD) in aesthetic value per acre per year and $76,809/acre/year (2021 USD) for a total of $300,649/acre/year (2021 USD).

The three case studies presented here exemplify several points regarding FEMA's streamlined estimates of ecosystem service flows for BCA. The first is reflected in the fact that some land cover types are distinguished by more than just an ecological definition. Urban Green Open Space is distinguished from Rural Green Open Space. Coastal Wetland is distinguished from Inland Wetland. The latter distinction has to do with the configuration of natural assets in the land cover type across space. The former has to do with the relative configuration of produced and natural assets (i.e., rural vs. urban). The heterogeneity across estimates in Florida, North Carolina, and Connecticut support the idea that ecosystem service estimates should comport with *socio*ecological boundaries, tackling the differential provision of different service flows in different settings. The recreational service flows from of an acre of beach in the Northeast United States and in the Southeast United States over a year might vary seasonally with temperature, for example, and as a result, a similar differentiation to that used for green open space (rural vs. urban) may be justified.

5.7.1 Paths Forward for Natural Capital Accounting

Recently, remotely sensed data and the digitization of economic data—such as property characteristics and transactions—have replaced the need for labor-intensive data collection and enabled bespoke estimates to be generated at scale, reliably, and credibly, obviating the need for benefits transfer and enabling efforts to develop balance sheets of natural assets to track wealth changes.

The past focus on a particular place and service flow can now be broadened to develop a broad balance sheet of natural assets that is enabled by new remote sensing tools. Here, I demonstrated the spatial scalability of valuation tools for coastal natural capital that is enabled by reliable remotely sensed and economic data. Although repeat sales over a time series of remotely observed coastal characteristics are not used here, future work should focus on the repeatability of this valuation pipeline, making use of increasingly spatially and temporally resolved data. However, as the North Carolina case study exemplifies, the mapping between the suite of services and the portfolio of natural and produced assets that produce them is an important consideration for appropriately attributing values to context-specific service flows. Natural assets within ecosystems provide different flows of benefits. The classification of units and the definition of the sampling grid must be carefully decided on an asset-by-asset basis.

Future work expanding to isolated coastal communities in Georgia and lakeside dunes in Michigan will help reveal how different configurations of natural and produced assets generate different service flows in context. A Michigan dunes case study would move the work away from the US East Coast and consider the recreation, viewshed, and protection roles dunes and beach sand provide to properties exposed to climate impacts on lakeshores rather than the Atlantic seaboard. Whereas estimates for this project reflect economic values embedded in property values, this does not capture the value of coastal beach sand in more remote areas. Other approaches, for example travel cost methods, could be used to identify use values in these contexts.

Understanding the attribution of natural capital assets to various services flows, and how they are captured in existing accounts, will not only aid ecosystem accounting efforts but also help determine optimal investment decisions as natural capital is depreciated. While different portfolios of assets can provide the same service flows, the per unit value of the assets would be different, thereby driving aggregation bias in accounts. The function of natural assets is context dependent, and arbitrage of natural assets can be costly (Addicott and Fenichel, 2019). With high transactions costs, the exchange value of the services they provide are also context dependent and spatially heterogeneous.

Appendix

Table 5A.1 **Summary statistics for connecticut property transactions**

Variable	Obs	Mean	Std. Dev.	Min	Max
Sale Price (2017$)	145,271	436,507	341,526	82,915	1,398,300
Bedrooms	145,271	2.88	1	0	5
Bathrooms	145,271	2.09	.92	0	5
Property Sq Feet	145,271	2,897.22	2067.45	285	3,69364
Beach Width (ft.)	145,271	145	65.65	33.09	543.44
Near (Coast Dist < 330ft)	145,271	.05	.22	0	1
Dist to Beach (ft)	145,271	4,211.73	2,952.95	.11	13,054.62
Dist to Public Beach (ft)	145,271	4,454.45	2,884.66	9.27	13,168.81
SLR Shore Movement (ft)	145,271	16.3	57.01	−311.87	699.25
Dist to Coast (ft)	145,271	1,603.18	1345.52	.01	5,546.56
Angle of Nearest Coast	145,271	153.29	36.2	33.08	356.38

References

Addicott, E. T. 2022. "Many Assets, Many Services: Valuing Beaches, Buildings, and Dunes in Coastal North Carolina." WP.

Addicott, E. T., and E. P. Fenichel. 2019. "Spatial Aggregation and the Value of Natural Capital." *Journal of Environmental Economics and Management* 95: 118–32. https://doi.org/10.1016/j.jeem.2019.03.001.

Barbier, E. B. 2012. "Progress and Challenges in Valuing Coastal and Marine Ecosystem Services." *Review of Environmental Economics and Policy* 6 (1): 1–19.

Barbier, E. B., E. W. Koch, B. R. Silliman, S. D. Hacker, E. Wolanski, J. Primavera, E. F. Granek, S. Polasky, S. Aswani, and L. A. Cramer. 2008. "Coastal Ecosystem-Based Management with Nonlinear Ecological Functions and Values." *Science* 319 (5861): 321–23.

Bell, F. W., and V. R. Leeworthy. 1986. *An Economic Analysis of the Importance of Saltwater Beaches in Florida*. (No. FLSGP-T-86-003), Report / Florida Sea Grant College; FL-SGR-82. NOAA Florida Sea Grant, Gainesville, Florida.Bell, F. W., and V. R. Leeworthy. 1990. "Recreational Demand by Tourists for Saltwater Beach Days." *Journal of Environmental Economics and Management* 18 (3): 189–205.

Berry, A., S. Fahey, N. Meyers. 2013. "Changing of the guard: adaptation options

that maintain ecologically resilient sandy beach ecosystems." *Journal of Coastal Research* 29, 899–908.
Dundas, S. J. 2017. "Benefits and Ancillary Costs of Natural Infrastructure: Evidence from the New Jersey Coast." *Journal of Environmental Economics and Management* 85: 62–80.
Edwards, S. F., and F. J. Gable. 1991. "Estimating the value of beach recreation from property values: an exploration with comparisons to nourishment costs." *Ocean and Shoreline Management* 15: 37–55.
FEMA Ecosystem Service Value Updates. 2022. Federal Emergency Management Agency. https://www.fema.gov/sites/default/files/documents/fema_ecosystem-service-value-updates_2022.pdf.
Fletcher, D. H., J. K. Garrett, A. Thomas, A. Fitch, P. Cryle, S. Shilton, and L. Jones. 2022. "Location, Location, Location: Modelling of Noise Mitigation by Urban Woodland Shows the Benefit of Targeted Tree Planting in Cities." *Sustainability* 14 (12): Article 12. https://doi.org/10.3390/su14127079.
Gindelsky, M., J. G. Moulton, and S. A. Wentland. 2022. "Valuing Housing Services in the Era of Big Data: A User Cost Approach Leveraging Zillow Microdata." In *Big Data for Twenty-First-Century Economic Statistics*, edited by Katharine G. Abraham, Ron S. Jarmin, Brian Moyer, and Matthew D. Shapiro, 339–70. Chicago, IL: University of Chicago Press. https://doi.org/10.7208/chicago/9780226801391-014.
Gopalakrishnan, S., M. D. Smith, J. M. Slott, and A. B. Murray. 2011. "The Value of Disappearing Beaches: A Hedonic Pricing Model with Endogenous Beach Width." *Journal of Environmental Economics and Management* 61 (3): 297–310. https://doi.org/10.1016/j.jeem.2010.09.003.
Landry, C. E., and P. Hindsley. 2011. "Valuing Beach Quality with Hedonic Property Models." *Land Economics* 87 (1): 92–108. https://doi.org/10.3368/le.87.1.92.
Landry, C. E., A. G. Keeler, and W. Kriesel. 2003. "An Economic Evaluation of Beach Erosion Management Alternatives." *Marine Resource Economics* 18: 105–127. https://doi.org/10.1086/mre.18.2.42629388.
McConnell, K. E. 1977. "Congestion and Willingness to Pay: A Study of Beach Use." *Land Economics* 53 (2): 185–95. https://doi.org/10.2307/3145923.
Mooney, H. A., A. Cropper, and W. Reid. 2004. "The Millennium Ecosystem Assessment: What Is It All About?" *Trends in Ecology & Evolution* 19 (5): 221–24. https://doi.org/10.1016/j.tree.2004.03.005.
O'Brien, K., C. Deep, J. Stocker, U. Clear, B. Hyde, U. Clear, J. Barrett, and C. S. Grant. 2014. *Analysis of Shoreline Change in Connecticut*. (No. CONN-S-14-001). NOAA Connecticut Sea Grant, New London, CT.
Office of Science and Technology Policy, Office of Management and Budget, and Department of Commerce. 2023. *National Strategy to Develop Statistics for Environmental-Economic Decisions*. White House.
Parsons, G. R., and M. Powell 2001. "Measuring the Cost of Beach Retreat." *Coastal Management* 29 (2): 91–103.
Pompe, J. J., and J. R. Rinehart. 1995. "Beach Quality and the Enhancement of Recreational Property Values." *Journal of Leisure Research* 27: 143–154. https://doi.org/10.1080/00222216.1995.11949739.
Rouhi Rad, M., W. (Vic) Adamowicz, A. Entem, E. P. Fenichel, and P. Lloyd-Smith. 2021. "Complementarity (Not Substitution) between Natural and Produced Capital: Evidence from the Panama Canal Expansion." *Journal of the Association of Environmental and Resource Economists* 8 (6): 1115–146. https://doi.org/10.1086/714675.
System of Environmental-Economic Accounting—Ecosystem Accounting (SEEA

EA). 2021. White cover publication, pre-edited text subject to official editing. United Nations. https://seea.un.org/ecosystem-accounting.
Team Planet. 2017. *Planet Application Program Interface: In Space for Life on Earth* [Computer software].
White, E. M., and L. A. Leefers. 2007. "Influence of Natural Amenities on Residential Property Values in a Rural Setting." *Society and Natural Resources* 20 (7): 659–67.
Yohe, G., J. Neumann, P. Marshall, and H. Ameden. 1996. "The economic cost of greenhouse-induced sea-level rise for developed property in the United States." *Climatic Change* 32: 387–410. https://doi.org/10.1007/BF00140353.

Comment Justin C. Contat

Before one can make an economically informed decision about a natural asset like coastal capital, one first must be able to quantify and value the asset. For example, a potential homebuyer might view a property's location and access to the coast as a positively valued amenity and want to know the market valuation of such features when comparing different properties. As another example, introductory economics tells us that a government (or social planner) cannot know whether there is too much natural resource harvesting (e.g., timber, fish) taking place without first knowing the amount and associated (social marginal) dollar value of the resource being harvested. Additionally, placing a value on natural assets is also itself of direct interest, particularly if one is trying to measure the size of an economy taking natural resources into account. This is the rationale for the United Nation's 2021 System of Environmental-Economic Account's (SEEA) Ecosystem Account framework. However, as with all other nonmarket goods, placing a value on such assets is a challenging exercise. Alternative methods like stated or revealed preference must be used in the absence of any direct observations of price.

In this paper Ethan Addicott contributes to a growing empirical literature by valuing coastal capital in the United States using information from sales of nearby homes, decomposing the value of a property into environmental and non-environmental components. Viewing coastal capital as environmental amenities that are bundled with a home purchase (e.g., beach width, distance from home to shore, angle of coast, tidal protections, direct waterway access), the idea is to value the coastal assets by determining how they are capitalized into home prices. This approach has been used before in the real estate and urban economics literatures to study the effects of environmental features like sea level rise risk (Bernstein et al. 2019) and pollution exposure (Currie et al. 2015), as well as also non-environmental features like

Justin C. Contat is a senior economist at the Federal Housing Finance Agency.

school quality (Bayer et al. 2007), among many others. Such an approach requires both environmental and non-environmental data. The environmental data used by the paper are not commonly found in this setting; this is one of the first applications of high-resolution laser imaging, detection, and ranging (LiDAR) to value coastal environmental characteristics. This is surprising, as such data are open access, easily accessible, and available for many regions in the United States, meaning it may be the standard for future work in this space. In contrast, the non-environmental data used by the paper are more commonly found in the literature, including traditional housing characteristics (bedrooms, bathrooms, square footage, age, location, etc.) and date of transaction. These variables are commonly sourced using real estate listings, often from a Multiple Listing Service (MLS) or a similar platform.

After carefully connecting the data sources, the main finding is that there is substantial heterogeneity in the value of coastal capital. Not only are there differences across markets in the type and number of coastal characteristics, but there is also evidence that coastal characteristics may be valued differently holding the type and number of coastal characteristics fixed. To give an example, consider the fact that dunes are not present in all coastal markets. Even within coastal markets that have dunes, homes are likely to have different dune characteristics; some homes may experience taller dunes that obstruct views of the ocean while others do not. As another example, consider that beach width is likely valued differently depending upon elevation of the home and distance to the beach. The immediate implication of the results is that a one-size-fits-all approach to valuing coastal capital is likely to miscalculate its true value. Care is needed to distinguish the type and amount of capital when making value calculations.

Despite substantial empirical efforts, common challenges remain for hedonic valuation: sorting and unobserved heterogeneity. Various strategies have been developed to address each of these issues (e.g., Bakkensen and Ma 2020; Francke and Van de Minne 2021, respectively). Careful attention should be paid to ensure coastal amenities like beach views and healthy coastal ecosystems are disentangled from coastal disamenities like flood risk and sea level rise. For example, are the individuals who purchase homes those who value coastal amenities the most, care about coastal disamenities the least, or some combination of the two? Are there other unobserved home characteristics driving home prices which are correlated with coastal characteristics? From a methodological point of view, these are in principle able to be at least partially addressed.

Looking ahead, one avenue for future research could study the effects of sea level rise by asking how the values of characteristics (and the characteristics themselves) change over time. While the current focus is largely on static, long-run effects, documenting market dynamics like these opens a new set of questions. In particular, the interaction between realized climate change, beliefs about climate change, and coastal asset capitalization over time could help inform policy regarding coastal development. Future researchers working in this area can use this paper and others like it as an example of how to answer such an important question as, How should one value a natural asset?

Disclaimer: The views expressed here are solely those of the author and not necessarily those of the Federal Housing Finance Agency (FHFA) or the US government. Any errors or omissions contained herein are the sole responsibility of the author.

For acknowledgments, sources of research support, and disclosure of the author's material financial relationships, if any, please see https://www.nber.org/books-and-chapters/measuring-and-accounting-environmental-public-goods-national-accounts-perspective/comment-value-and-configuration-coastal-natural-capital-contat.

References

Bakkensen, L. A., and L. Ma. 2020. "Sorting over Flood Risk and Implications for Policy Reform." *Journal of Environmental Economics and Management* 104: 102362.

Bayer, P., F. Ferreira, and R. McMillan. 2007. "A Unified Framework for Measuring Preferences for Schools and Neighborhoods." *Journal of Political Economy* 115 (4): 588–638.

Bernstein, A., M. T. Gustafson, and R. Lewis. 2019. "Disaster on the Horizon: The Price Effect of Sea Level Rise." *Journal of Financial Economics* 134: 253–72.

Currie, J., L. Davis, M. Greenstone, and R. Walker. 2015. "Environmental Health Risks and Housing Values: Evidence from 1,600 Toxic Plant Openings and Closings." *American Economic Review* 105 (2): 678–709.

Francke, M., and A. Van de Minne. 2021. "Modeling Unobserved Heterogeneity in Hedonic Price Models." *Real Estate Economics* 49 (4): 1315–1339.

6

Accounting for Environmental Activity
Measuring Public Environmental Expenditures and the Environmental Goods and Services Sector in the United States

Dennis Fixler, Julie L. Hass, Tina Highfill, Kelly Wentland, and Scott Wentland

6.1 Introduction

During the 20th century, the national economic accounts had largely focused on measuring the economy and its conventional components, like consumption or investment expenditures as parts of Gross Domestic Product (GDP). While the United States and many other countries' governments had produced various economic statistics earlier in the 20th century, it was not until the last half of the century when most countries coalesced around a common set of accounting principles and standards for measuring aggregate economic activity and its component parts, namely the United Nation's

Dennis Fixler is chief economist of the US Bureau of Economic Analysis.
Julie L. Hass is an international consultant for environmental statistics and accounts, and a consultant to the US Bureau of Economic Analysis.
Tina Highfill is a research economist at the US Bureau of Economic Analysis.
Kelly Wentland is an associate professor of accounting in the Costello College of Business at George Mason University.
Scott Wentland is a research economist at the US Bureau of Economic Analysis.
We thank members of an interagency group, the Policy Working Group for Natural Capital Accounting and Environmental-Economic Statistics, for feedback on prior work. We also thank participants of the *9th IMF Statistical Forum on Measuring Climate Change* in 2021 and the *28th Meeting of the London Group on Environmental Accounting* in 2022, as this paper was adapted/updated from prior work presented at these meetings. We thank our conference discussant, David Evans, for thoughtful comments on a prior draft. Finally, we are grateful for Gary Cornwall's help with compiling and organizing the raw Refinitiv ESG data from the data platform. For acknowledgments, sources of research support, and disclosure of the authors' material financial relationships, if any, please see https://www.nber.org/books-and-chapters/measuring-and-accounting-environmental-public-goods-national-accounts-perspective/accounting-environmental-activity-measuring-public-environmental-expenditures-and-environmental.

System of National Accounts (SNA).[1] The most well-known of these official estimates, GDP, provides one measure of a country's economy—the market value of all final goods and services in a country over a given period of time. Generally, these aggregate statistics are critical for tracking a nation's economic growth and performance over time. Yet, as the economy changes, national statistical offices (NSOs) that produce these statistics must also continually adapt to the needs of decision-makers in the public and private sectors by developing new accounts. For instance, 21st-century environmental challenges and policy demands have spurred rapidly expanding interest in environmental-economic accounts, which would track the stocks and flows of environmental (natural capital) assets, ecosystem services, and aspects of the economy related to environmental protection, preservation, and natural resource management.[2]

While the US government reports a vast amount of information on the environment and the economy across its federal statistical system, it does not yet construct the cohesive suite of environmental-economic accounts proposed by statistical standards from the international community,[3] as official work on these types of accounts was halted in the 1990s.[4] In recent years, the United States has, however, developed pilot accounts as part of a multiagency research effort to explore the feasibility of constructing accounts using existing data. This included SEEA-based pilot accounts for water (Bagstad et al. 2020), land (Wentland et al. 2020; Wentland et al. 2023), air emissions (Chambers 2023), and various ecosystem services (Warnell et al. 2020; Heris et al. 2021). We extend this research effort by constructing a pilot environmental goods and services sector (EGSS) account, drawing new insights about this sector. Further, we also document measurement and classification challenges that would be relevant for a more comprehensive implementation, both in the United States and abroad.

Environmental activity accounts include a set of functional satellite

1. See Coyle's (2015) book *GDP: A Brief but Affectionate History* for a more detailed history of GDP measurement, the national economic accounts, and what is (and is not) measured in these accounts.

2. For more on the nature of these challenges and policy relevance of environmental-economic accounts, see Obst and Vardon (2014), Vardon et al. (2016), Boyd et al. (2018), and Hein et al. (2020).

3. The US Bureau of Economic Analysis (BEA) does, however, produce thematic satellite accounts for Outdoor Recreation and the Marine Economy. They both provide timely and useful statistics for specific aspects of the economy, but this industry-specific approach accounts for only part of the role that environmental activity plays in the US economy and is narrower in scope than the suite of System of Environmental-Economic Accounting Central Framework (SEEA)-based accounts. For more information on the current accounts that are constructed by the BEA, see: https://www.bea.gov/data/special-topics. We return to discuss background on SEEA accounts in the next section.

4. For a summary of this effort by the BEA and recommendations for the future of environmental economic accounts in the US, see: National Research Council. 1999. *Nature's Numbers: Expanding the National Economic Accounts to Include the Environment*. Washington, DC: The National Academies Press. https://doi.org/10.17226/6374.

accounts that quantify transactions in the economy undertaken to protect, rehabilitate, or preserve the environment.[5] To be clear, output like solar panels, wind turbines, catalytic converters, and forest management expenditures are already a part of the economy as traditionally measured in the National Income and Product Accounts, but are not currently disaggregated in the US accounts to areas relevant for understanding the size and scope of environmental-economic activity. Collectively, these accounts would comprise three areas of environmental activities in the economy: (1) environmental protection expenditures (EPE) and resource management expenditures; (2) environmental taxes and subsidies; and (3) environmental goods and services sector (EGSS). The scope of this paper concentrates on the last area, including a breakout quantifying gross output across both private and public sectors.[6] While preliminary, the pilot estimates we construct in this paper provide the first accounting of the size and growth of the EGSS in the United States across two recent periods (2015 and 2019). This includes information about the relative size of its components, and the estimates are broken down by categories consistent with international guidelines. We then discuss how a preliminary EGSS account can provide new insights into the supply and use of products for environmental protection and resource management in the US economy.

This paper contributes to the economic measurement literature by advancing practical solutions to a number of key classification and valuation issues faced by users of either the North American Industry Classification System (NAICS) or the European Nomenclature of Economic Activities (NACE) system, building on prior efforts within the US government (described in the next section) that set out to measure the "green economy" or "green jobs" in ways that predated the SEEA CF. Methodologically, our research marks the first time the United States has constructed this type of account following the prevailing methods and scope outlined in chapter 4 of SEEA CF for classifying environmental goods and services, which is key for both international comparability and consistency with our own national economic accounts. A common thread through prior research efforts in the United States on environmental-economic accounting is that little is known about how far we can get with existing data until we actually try to construct an account (Bagstad et al. 2021). Thus, our goals in constructing this pilot account are to illustrate some solutions to common problems facing NSOs while also posing new questions and challenges for the international community

5. More specifically, according to the SEEA CF manual, these accounts quantify and value "economic activities whose primary purpose is to reduce or eliminate pressures on the environment or to make more efficient use of natural resources" (SEEA CF §1.30).

6. Recent work in the United States has developed other pilot accounts for areas of the environment as part of a multi-agency research effort to explore the feasibility of constructing accounts using existing data. This included pilot accounts for water (Bagstad et al. 2020), land (Wentland et al. 2020; Wentland et al. 2023), air emissions (Chambers 2023), and various ecosystem services (Warnell et al. 2020, Heris et al. 2021).

to consider. As part of this process, both in this study and prior research, we learn more about the limitations of existing data and catalog multiple issues that would need to be remedied prior to being produced as a formal statistical product that would be of comparable quality to official estimates in the National Income and Product Accounts (NIPA). These include data gaps of existing official (government) data sources and limitations to private sector Environmental, Social, and Governance (ESG) disclosures that offer firm-level expenditures and revenues related to environmental goods and services (e.g., environmental R&D).

Though the scope of this NBER-CRIW volume focuses on measuring and accounting for environmental public goods in particular, this research also fits into a broader strategy of the US government to develop natural capital accounts over the next decade or so. In 2023, an interagency group led by the White House's Office of Science and Technology Policy (OSTP), Office of Management and Budget (OMB), and Department of Commerce (DOC) released the first national strategy for developing natural capital and environmental-economic statistics.[7] This strategy recommends the development of environmental activity accounts at the initial phase (Phase I) of a long-term plan to produce a full suite of SEEA-based environmental-economic accounts to complement the NIPA. Understanding the landscape of the data and the accompanying accounting challenges are necessary prerequisites for producing timely, high-quality accounts measuring economic activities that are undertaken to protect, rehabilitate, or preserve the environment. Further, as private sector accounting standards evolve to account for environmental expenditures and revenues, this research may also offer insights for how private sector data might be used by the national accounts in the future and the limitations of firm-level ESG data in their current form.

6.2 Background

6.2.1 Satellite Accounts and Statistical Standards: The System of National Accounts (SNA), Classification of Environmental Protection Activities (CEPA), and System of Environmental-Economic Accounts Central Framework (SEEA CF)

The System of National Accounts (SNA)—the international statistical standard that governs the prevailing national economic accounting methodology—provides guidance for extensions or satellite accounts that move away from a focus about *what* is purchased to *why* or *for what purpose* do these outlays occur. Specifically, in chapter 29 of the 2008 System

7. National Strategy to Develop Statistics for Environmental-Economic Decisions: A US System of Natural Capital Accounting and Associated Environmental-Economic Statistics, 2023. https://www.whitehouse.gov/wp-content/uploads/2023/01/Natural-Capital-Accounting-Strategy-final.pdf.

of National Accounts (SNA 2008), it presents extensions to the system of national accounts that support the development of satellite accounts.[8] As a further step toward standardizing collection and dissemination of economic information related to the environment, the UN Statistical Commission adopted two new manuals as statistical standards: the System of Environmental-Economic Accounting (SEEA) Central Framework (2012—SEEA CF) and Ecosystem Accounting (2021—SEEA EA).[9] These serve to complement the SNA and extend the scope of the national accounts by measuring the assets and services flowing from the environment. To do this, the manuals prescribe methods for producing satellite accounts or supplementary environmental-economic statistics to complement the core SNA accounts by using a common accounting and valuation framework.[10] Specifically, SEEA accounts measure physical flows and monetary values of environmental-economic activities, assets, and ecosystem services, including land, water, fisheries, timber, mineral resources, and other types of natural resources. According to the UN Statistical Division, as of 2020,[11] at least 90 countries compile or produce at least one account using the accounting approaches prescribed by the SEEA CF or SEEA EA. Many countries use these to support public and private decision-making along with international reporting on global conventions/agreements like the UN Framework Convention on Climate Change, Convention to Combat Desertification, and Sustainable Development Goals (SDGs).[12]

Extending from prior work on classifying environmental protection and resource management expenditures,[13] the fourth chapter of the SEEA CF

8. Specifically, the SNA defines the scope of this account as measuring the following: "environmental taxes, property income and property rights, and environmental protection, natural resource use and management expenditures" (SNA2008, §29.110).

9. Only a portion of the latter manual, SEEA EA, was approved by the UNSC as a statistical standard, designating the chapters on valuation of ecosystem services as still experimental and in need of further development. When it was up for approval, experts from numerous national statistical offices voiced objections to the valuation methods in the manual (e.g., see Brown et al. 2021), agreeing with the UNSC, as the SEEA EA chapters included valuation methods seen as incompatible with the SNA framework, among other criticisms.

10. For more information about BEA's current satellite accounts, see: https://www.bea.gov/resources/learning-center/what-to-know-special-topics.

11. For more information, see: https://seea.un.org/content/frequently-asked-questions#How_many_countries.

12. The UN and non-governmental institutions like the International Monetary Fund (IMF) also use information from these accounts for a variety of purposes, like global climate change indicators and to track international progress on the environment for the purposes of policy analysis. See the IMF's Climate Change Indicators Dashboard which came online in April 2021: https://climatedata.imf.org/.

13. Prior to the 2008 SNA or 2012 SEEA CF, numerous countries had classified economic activity as "environmental" in their national accounts, or they produced some variant of an environmental industry satellite account prior to the adoption of the SEEA CF. Initially, the Classification of Environmental Protection Activities (CEPA) was established in the late 1980s to serve this purpose, with a focus on pollution and environmental protection. Eventually, a focus on natural resource management led to the development of the Classification of Environmental Activities (CEA). The CEA has two parts: Part I focuses on environmental protection, and Part II on resource management.

now serves as the methodological foundation of environmental activity accounts, which includes guidance on how to produce satellite accounts for environmental protection expenditures, environmental goods and services sector (EGSS), and tax and subsidy accounts. A common theme across environmental activity satellite accounts, whether they are SEEA-based or some variation of its predecessors (CEPA or national versions), is that they focus on measuring economic activity that is already within the scope of the current NIPA. Compared to other environmental-economic accounts, this is relatively "low-hanging fruit" for countries like the United States which are developing new accounts, given that the valuation of these transactions is already being measured by national statistical offices and folded into more aggregated statistics. In contrast, valuing other environmental assets, flows, or ecosystems services outside these accounts often involves difficult valuation challenges due to the unique and heterogeneous nature of many natural capital assets, which the academic literature has tackled in a variety of settings and applications (e.g., Muller 2009; Fenichel and Abbott 2014; Banzhaf et al. 2016; Cavender-Bares et al. 2022). Hence, rather than a valuation challenge, the principal methodological challenge for environmental activity accounts is to classify and decompose activity for environmental purposes that has already been valued in the accounts.

6.2.2 What Is Environmental Activity? Some Conceptual Classification Challenges

Before turning to the environmental classifications and what other countries do in a practical sense, it is important to explain more precisely what economic activity we are trying to describe conceptually. The SEEA CF provides the following guidance for deciding whether a given transaction's scope is categorically environmental or not. It is based on the concept of main or primary purpose. The SEEA CF explains this concept as follows:

> *4.11 The scope of environmental activities encompasses those economic activities whose primary purpose is to reduce or eliminate pressures on the environment or to make more efficient use of natural resources.*
>
> *4.12 These various activities are grouped into two broad types of environmental activity: environmental protection and resource management. Environmental protection activities are those activities whose primary purpose is the prevention, reduction and elimination of pollution and other forms of degradation of the environment . . .*
>
> *4.13 Resource management activities are those activities whose primary purpose is preserving and maintaining the stock of natural resources and hence safeguarding against depletion.* (SEEA CF 2012, §4.11–4.13)

Determining the primary purpose needs to follow general principles of classification. That is, its purpose is consistent with the definitions of the two types of environmental activity: environmental protection and resource management. This includes a wide range of activities in the economy such as: waste treatment and disposal; hydroelectric, nuclear electric, solar electric, wind electric, geothermal, and biomass electric power generation; sewage treatment facilities; materials recovery facilities; septic tank and related services; expenses of environmental, conservation and wildlife organizations; and environmental consulting services. See appendix table 6A.1 for a more complete list.

In practice, a Department/Ministry of Transportation might claim that all output for railroads were "environmental expenditures," for example. Their argument might be that the trains reduced the use of road and air transportation, and thus the air emissions from these modes of transportation. Therefore, all expenditures for the railroads should be classified as part of the environmental goods and services sector (EGSS). Based on the application of the "primary purpose" principle, a national statistical office would likely evaluate this claim and conclude that, although this may have been one of the results of the expenditures on the railroads, the *primary* purpose of the expenditures for railroads was rail transport and not primarily for environmental protection. Thus, the total expenditures on railroads would not be included in the environmental protection expenditure statistics of the government sector as developed by the national statistical office.[14] This example (via exception) helps illustrate the broader rule from the SEEA CF that, from a national accounts perspective, it is not sufficient to be *related* to environmental protection or resource management, but its *primary purpose* must be oriented toward these ends. From an accounting standpoint, drawing a line is necessary, given that virtually any economic activity is in some way *related* to the environment somewhere along the supply chain or in its use. For the purposes of this paper, however, we take the standards and definitions as given, leaving the debate about where these definitional lines should be drawn to others.

The example above highlights an important challenge for the United States and other countries implementing environmental activity accounts using existing, repurposed statistics: the context through which one set of statistics or estimates was initially developed may not have been initially constructed to be consistent with the guidance regarding the "primary purpose" principle or other principles set forth in the SNA and SEEA CF. Therefore, it requires expertise in national accounting to sort through the initial purpose and accounting guidelines of, for example, the North American Product Classification System (NAPCS) products codes associated with NAICS industries to determine whether these definitions are sufficiently close to the scope of the corresponding expenditure for a formal environmental activity account line item. In the rail example above, if the federal

14. It is worth noting, however, that expenditures of the Department/Ministry of Transport that did have a primary purpose of environmental protection, such as the construction of noise barriers along railway lines and roads, would be included.

budgeting policymakers include all rail infrastructure expenditures in their definition of environmental protection expenditures on a balance sheet line item, it is necessary that this type of difference is flagged so that a roadmap for constructing the formal accounts would include recommendations for separating out these kinds of expenditures in the underlying source data to be more consistent with SNA and SEEA CF guidelines and principles.

6.2.3 Environmental Activity Accounts—SEEA Central Framework and Its Predecessors

Methodologies and corresponding statistics describing the Environmental Goods and Services Industry/Sector (EGSS), also called the Environment Industry (or "Green Economy"), have been developed by both national and international institutions. The OECD and Eurostat developed the first compilation manual in 1999.[15] Building on this work, Eurostat then developed several iterations of a Classification for Resource Management Activities (CReMA),[16] which helped inform the SEEA CF's CEA although categories for aquatic and mineral resources were not part of the CReMA. Eurostat has since published a number of manuals and guidelines for EGSS statistics (e.g., see Eurostat 2009, 2016a, 2016b). Along with a number of other countries around the world, the EU and the European Statistical System (ESS) member countries now produce a regular set of environmental-economic accounts, including an environmental goods and services sector (EGSS) account,[17] environmental protection expenditure accounts (EPEA),[18] and environmental tax statistics.[19] In fact, since 2017, EGSS statistics are now required to be reported annually for countries of the ESS using standardized questionnaires. Statistics Canada, on the other hand, has taken a slightly different approach in definitions and categories (see Statistics Canada 2024).

6.2.4 A Brief History of the US Experience with "Green" Classification

The US government has long collected rich data on economic activity at product and industry levels, which follow NAPCS and NAICS. This fine-

15. OECD (1999). The Environmental Goods and Services Industry: Manual for Data Collection and Analysis, Paris: OECD Publication Services. https://doi.org/10.1787/9789264173651-en,

16. Earlier work on resource management classification was pioneered by Istat, the Italian national statistical office, using techniques from government budget analysis. See Ardi, Carolina and Frederico Falcitelli (2007) "The Classification of Resource Use and Management Activities and expenditure—CRUMA."

17. See "Glossary: Environmental goods and services sector (EGSS)" from Eurostat: https://ec.europa.eu/eurostat/statistics-explained/index.php?title=Glossary:Environmental_goods_and_services_sector_(EGSS).

18. See "Environmental protection expenditure accounts" from Eurostat: https://ec.europa.eu/eurostat/statistics-explained/index.php?title=Environmental_protection_expenditure_accounts.

19. See "Environmental tax statistics" from Eurostat: https://ec.europa.eu/eurostat/statistics-explained/index.php?title=Environmental_tax_statistics.

grained, detailed data make it possible for US statistical agencies like BEA to compile industry breakdowns of economic activity (e.g., GDP by industry), input-output accounts, and satellite accounts organized around a specific theme (e.g., Outdoor Recreation, Marine Economy). Other US agencies like the Bureau of Labor Statistics (BLS) and the Census Bureau have used this data and/or this classification system for a variety of purposes, including earlier initiatives to measure the "Green Economy" or "Green Jobs" that predate the standards and definition in the SEEA CF, briefly described below.

One of the notable predecessors to the SEEA EGSS was undertaken by a partnership among the US Census Bureau, Environmental Protection Agency (EPA), and the International Trade Administration (ITA). In 1998, the Census Bureau published the results from its Survey of Environmental Products and Services (SEPS), conducted on behalf of the EPA and ITA.[20] Specifically, they defined the environmental industry as "the manufacture of products, performance of services and the construction of projects used, or that potentially could be used, for measuring, preventing, limiting, or correcting environmental damage to air, water, and soil." The definition also included services related to the removal, transportation, storage, or abatement of waste, noise, and other contaminants. As we noted in the example in section 6.2.2 above, a key departure from prior efforts and the SEEA CF is the extent to which transportation is included, particularly if its primary purpose is not environmental. Nevertheless, they found that 49 industries (4-digit SIC) met their definitional requirements for produced environmental goods and services: 24 in manufacturing, 22 in services, and 3 in construction. The survey's reference year was 1995. Overall, the results from SEPS estimated the green industry to be $102.8 billion in revenue in 1995, employing 774,000 employees. Tables further categorized the revenue by specific products and services and by media (e.g., air, water, solid waste, energy conservation, etc.).[21]

More than a decade ago, BLS launched a closely related initiative in the United States to measure the number of jobs associated with the environment, so-called "green jobs." Officially titled the "Measuring Green Jobs Initiative," BLS collected data in the early 2010s for two reference years (2010, 2011). The initiative had three components: Green Goods and Services (GGS), Green Goods and Services occupation survey (GGS-OCC), and Green Technologies and Practices (GTP). The GGS measured employment

20. For more information, see "Survey of Environmental Products and Services," prepared for the Environmental Protection Agency and the International Trade Administration, US Department of Commerce, by the Bureau of the Census, February 1998. https://www.epa.gov/sites/default/files/2017-08/documents/ee-0413_acc.pdf.

21. A more recent study by Census and EPA researchers matched SEPS microdata to data from the Annual Survey of Manufactures and surrounding Census of Manufactures. See Becker and Shadbegian (2009).

associated with the production of green goods and services from sampled establishments, which included breakdowns by industry. They identified 325 industries (6-digit NAICS) as potential producers of green goods and services.[22] The GGS identified occupational employment and wages in establishments that produced green goods and services. They defined employment related to GGS that benefited the environment or conserved natural resources. To do this, BLS linked data provided to the existing BLS Occupational Employment and Wage Survey (OEWS) with the same establishment's response to the Green Goods and Services industry survey.[23] Finally, the GTP collected information on more than 35,000 business establishments on their use of green technologies and practices. They defined green technologies and practices as "those that make their establishment's production processes more environmentally friendly or use fewer natural resources."[24]

Around the same time the BLS initiative began, the Economics and Statistics Administration (ESA) of the US Department of Commerce issued a report, "*Measuring the Green Economy,*" in 2010.[25] ESA's report defined green products and services as "those with a predominant function of conserving energy and other natural resources, or reducing pollution," providing options for both a "narrow" interpretation and a "broad" interpretation of the underlying activity. The "narrow" definition identified 497 green products/services among the 22,000 overall products/services, while the "broad" interpretation included 732 green products/services, which included products/services where the extent to which they were "green" was more ambiguous. Lists of these products and services appear in appendix 1 of the ESA report. Overall, the report concluded that "green products and services comprised 1 percent to 2 percent of the total private business economy in 2007," with the 1 percent ($371 billion) corresponding to the "narrow" definition and 2 percent ($516 billion) corresponding to the more expansive "broad" definition of green products and services. To illustrate how sensitive the figures are to classification choices, we take a similar approach to this effort by offering both a narrower, more conservative estimate of EGSS and

22. For more information, see "Green Goods and Services" from the US Bureau of Labor Statistics: https://www.bls.gov/ggs/.

23. See "Green Goods and Services Occupations" from the US Bureau of Labor Statistics, www.bls.gov/ggsocc/home.htm.

24. See also "Green Technologies and Practices" from the US Bureau of Labor Statistics, www.bls.gov/gtp/home.htm. Ultimately, the BLS initiative was ended due to budget cuts. This was a critical effort that illustrated tremendous challenges in defining and measuring a new sector of the economy that did not, at the time, have a widely accepted definition or production boundary.

25. "Measuring the Green Economy," US Department of Commerce, Report of the Office of Policy and Strategic Planning, April 10, 2010, https://www.commerce.gov/data-and-reports/reports/2010/04/measuring-green-economy. See the report at https://www.commerce.gov/sites/default/files/migrated/reports/greeneconomyreport_0.pdf and Appendix at https://www.commerce.gov/sites/default/files/migrated/reports/appendix2_0.pdf.

a broader definition that is inclusive of partial categories. We return to this point in the next section.

6.3. Classifying Environmental Activities for the EGSS—Methodology

6.3.1 Methodological Approach

The previous US and international studies, manuals, and the SEEA CF statistical standard were used as references for developing a list of environmental products and services that could be directly used with the BEA's most detailed internal SUTs. This process required several iterations between the SEEA-compliant Eurostat lists of industries and products, the pre-SEEA US studies—especially the ESA report—evaluated as to which portions were SEEA-compliant, and the various classification conversion keys (NACE/ISIC to/from NAICS, CPA/CPC to/from NAPCS, and older US classifications to the current classifications). Once lists of environmentally relevant NAICS-2017 industries and NAPSC-2017 services and products were identified, the next step was to take theses industry, product, and service lists and match them to the internal BEA supply and use table (SUT) product and services categories. The internal BEA SUT product and services categories were then evaluated, based on their description, to be either totally relevant, partially relevant,[26] or irrelevant related to the environment. The environmentally relevant SUT categories were then coded according to CEPA/CReMA categories as summarized in appendix A.

One of the foundational accounting goals of the SNA, and by extension the SEEA CF and SEEA EA, is that economic accounts produced by national statistical offices should be comparable as they are anchored to a common statistical standard. For this reason, and the fact that the existing methods used in the European statistical system are SEEA-compliant and updated annually,[27] these served as our initial starting point for identifying the SEEA-relevant NAICS and NAPCS categories. Since environmental goods and services change over time due to new technologies and the exclusion of outdated technologies, using the most updated lists of indicative

26. To be clear, "partially relevant" here means that part of this industry/product category contains activities where their *primary purpose* is environmental, as opposed to a partial or secondary purpose criterion. We discuss this coding in greater detail in sections 6.3.3 and 6.3.4.

27. See *Commission Implementing Regulation (EU) 2015/2174 of 24 November 2015* from EUR-Lex: https://eur-lex.europa.eu/legal-content/EN/TXT/?uri=uriserv%3AOJ.L_.2015.307.01.0017.01.ENG. This approach is possible only due to a legal reporting requirement under Regulation (EU) No. 2015/2174, which directed the development of an indicative compendium of environmental goods and services and economic activities for the European statistical system. These lists outline where the relevant activities and products for the EGSS can be identified in the European statistical system. European countries that report to Eurostat often base their work on these lists.

goods and services was a useful starting point. We then used the prior US projects (described in section 6.2.4 above) to help identify environmental activities more precisely in the US statistical systems and develop the final list of environmental goods and services we use for constructing the estimates.

The final step in the development of the list of the SUT product and services categories was to use secondary information to estimate a percent value for the partial categories. The Eurostat compilation manuals were helpful in proposing potential secondary sources—such as the production of organic crops, energy saving appliances, and electric vehicles. In addition, the budgets of relevant government institutions were examined and used as secondary sources for identifying specific, relevant services provided by the government. This was important especially for identifying resource management activities, which is a main activity of some government agencies. Estimating the environmental portion of partial or mixed categories was one of the key challenges for constructing EGSS estimates; and, for reasons we discuss further in section 6.5 below, this is an important area for additional development in future work.

6.3.2 Challenges with Translating NACE/ISIC to NAICS

A fundamental challenge with drawing on the European experience is the imperfect mapping of product and industry classifications across these systems. There are well-trotted conversion tables for industry classifications, i.e., between NACE/ISIC and NAICS, which can be helpful in this process. However, the environmentally relevant portions of the NACE that need to be matched with NAICS can often be easier to find comparing the verbiage of the categories directly (using keyword searches for example), given that the activities of interest may be found in other categories than what are referenced in the conversion tables. One example of this is the renewable environmental product "fuel wood." This would be in both NACE 02.20 and 16.10, and the partial activity covering only fuel wood would need to be determined using additional information. NAICS-based product codes developed by BEA from the NAPCS, on the other hand, have only one product: "Firewood and fuel wood containing fuel binder manufacturing." In this instance, the NAICS-based classification system makes it easier to identify this product within US data, which more cleanly aligns with the SEEA CF defined boundary.

Another example where the NAICS classification is more specific, and thus more cleanly aligns with the SEEA CF definition, is environmental consulting services. NACE classifies this in 74.9 as "Other professional, scientific and technical activities n.e.c." This means that the environmental portion of this NACE needs to be separated out from other activities, likely necessitating supplementary data to estimate the proportion that is specific to environmental activity. NAICS, on the other hand, has a separate six-digit category, 541620, as "Environmental Consulting Services." In other cases, sometimes the terminology is altogether different between the classifications, where the NACE verbiage makes the classification more straightforward. For example, the term *biofuels* can be found in the European lists but not in the BEA SUT product lists. In this case, the United States uses the narrower term *fuel ethanol* in the product classification rather than the broader term, biofuels. With 6,000 to 10,000 categories in each of the different classifications, finding and classifying the relevant industries, products, and services is a massive undertaking, which we summarize here.[28]

While the methodologies of prior US "green" classification efforts were all different (e.g., EPA and BLS used surveys, ESA used a type of supply-use table [SUT] approach, and Brookings-Battle [2011] used secondary sources), we should note that these initiatives and surveys were helpful in identifying the industries and products in a US context because they had grappled with classifying activities within the same industry/product system. The report provided by the ESA (ESA 2010) was especially helpful because there was an extensive appendix with lists that identified green products and services. Although, we should reiterate that, while useful, the definition used by the ESA is not the same as the definition of Environmental Goods and Services in the SEEA CF, so it could not be used without careful consideration. But, as a starting point, it was still very helpful, given the lack of extended description of the NAPCS.[29]

6.3.3 Coding Environmental Activities and Supplemental Data Sources

One of the core issues with classifying environmental activity is that some economic activity does not neatly fit into a finite classification system. In many cases, a particular good or service product/industry category may have a purpose that only partially fits the definition in the SEEA CF, or there is some ambiguity as to the extent a set of goods/services with a particular production or industry cost fits within the appropriate boundary. We thus developed a three-part coding system to identify the environmental portion of the

28. The other challenge related to the US version of the product classification, NAPCS, is the lack of a description of the product code classification; there is only the name of the group—no extended description. Canada's NAPCS has an extensive description of each of the items (North American Product Classification System (NAPCS) Canada, 2017 Version 2.0, Released October 11, 2018 and updated April 12 2019, https://www150.statcan.gc.ca/n1/en/pub/12-003-x/12-003-x2018001-eng.pdf?st=tKE6fxSC; North American Industry Classification System (NAICS) Canada 2022 Version 1.0, Released January 27, 2022, https://www.statcan.gc.ca/en/subjects/standard/naics/2022/v1/index), but this does not currently exist for US data.

29. Currently, only the US Department of Commerce International Trade Administration (ITA), analyzing data purchased from Environmental Business International, Inc. (EBI), regularly publish data covering the US environmental technologies industry. Although the focus is primarily on export potential, there are also estimates of the total revenues of environmental technologies (See "Environmental Technologies Industry Overview" from the International Trade Administration, https://www.trade.gov/environmental-technologies-industry-overview). This would be a subset of the total EGSS.

NAPCS/NAICS category, and every product category was coded drawing on comparisons to corresponding NACE categories coded by the European statistical system as well as our own expertise. If the whole category was environmentally relevant the category was coded 1, partially relevant was 2, and not relevant or outside the boundary was 3. For all categories coded 1 and 2, we further coded it according to the CEPA and CReMA classifications currently used by Eurostat for comparability. This additional coding allowed for splitting the commodities according to environmental domains, which is useful for understanding the breakout of this activity across domains.[30] In the next section, we discuss the data we used to assist with classifying activities into these categories and the different advantages and challenges we face with using this data for these classifications.

6.3.4 Methodology: A Satellite Account Approach

Our method for constructing a pilot EGSS account follows BEA's satellite account approach, which aims to decompose portions of the US economy related to a particular activity or purpose. This approach relies on using detailed internal data pulled from the BEA's supply and use tables (SUTs). Supply and use tables contribute input-output accounts that the BEA produces for the public, which reflect how industries interact with each other and the rest of the economy. Supply tables track the total value of goods and services available in the domestic economy whereas use tables convey how the supply of goods and services is used. These tables break out industry output for the entire US economy into more than 5,300 distinct product categories, which is advantageous for our purposes.[31]

We use SUT data from 2015 and 2019 as these have the finest level of detail given they draw from the most recent benchmark years available at the time we constructed the estimates below. Hence, we provide estimates of gross output for 2015 and 2019 in both producer and purchaser values. The purchaser values include trade margins, or the value added by wholesalers and retailers in the distribution of a commodity from producers to final purchasers and the transport costs paid separately by the purchaser in taking delivery of goods. All values are in current-dollar or nominal terms, meaning there is no adjustment for inflation.[32]

The relatively fine product-level detail of the internal SUTs data allows

30. See appendix A for a table listing of identified product categories and source data details.

31. For reference, the United Kingdom's environmental activity accounts draw from their SUTs, which have 112 industries and 112 products. In this regard, the US data are among the finest, most detailed source data in the world for the product/industry categories underlying its SUTs.

32. For real values, future work would need to develop a more specific price index for this particular basket of goods and services. For example, if we deflated the nominal values by a GDP price index, it would remove a common inflation trend, but it would not provide a true real value of expenditures—that would require activity-specific price indexes which do not currently exist.

the BEA to more precisely disaggregate US economic activity into different activities that are not easily identifiable under standard industry classifications, such as NAICS, to be able to assess how they contribute to gross output and value added.[33] While official BEA satellite accounts often include estimates of gross output by NAICS industry, we instead use the CEPA/CReMA output category to present our gross output estimates, similar to other BEA satellite accounts that present gross output by activity.[34] This also facilitates comparability with the European statistical system and countries, an important benefit with a pilot account, given they use the CEPA/CReMA categories. Presenting the EGSS estimates by industry as well would require translating commodity-level data to industries, which is outside of the scope of these preliminary estimates. Despite the fact that the United States has very fine product categories relative to many other countries, the product categories were not initially devised with the EGSS in mind. Hence, as noted above, one of the chief data challenges for the United States (as well as most other countries) is that there are many mixed categories that contain both non-environmental and environmental output.[35]

For this EGSS account, we estimate gross output for environmental goods and services by first identifying relevant commodities (goods and services) within the SUTs as described in the prior subsection for categories 1 (those wholly in the environmental classification) and 3 (those outside the environmental classification). For those coded 2 (where categories are partially environmentally relevant), we leverage data from other sources to identify the environmentally relevant portion of that category. We provide several examples of this process here to help make the unique challenges with classification for category 2 clearer. For instance, the vintage of SUT data we use in this study does not differentiate between organic agriculture and conventional crop production. We use the NASS Survey,[36] which col-

33. Gross output represents the market value of the goods and services, reflecting both the value of goods and services that are used in other production processes (intermediate inputs) and the value of goods and services purchased by end-use consumers (final products). Value added or gross domestic product (GDP) represents just the value of final products. BEA's growing suite of satellite accounts currently includes: travel and tourism; arts and culture; the marine economy; the space economy; and outdoor recreation. See Special Topics from the BEA: https://www.bea.gov/data/special-topics.

34. Some satellite accounts also present gross output by activities that are salient to data users as opposed to just industry alone. For example, the outdoor recreation satellite account provides estimates of gross output by type of recreational activity, such as boating or bicycling, that includes production from all industries producing these commodities.

35. Recently, BEA has been working on converting its internal categories to be better aligned with the most recent version of the NAPCS classification system. However, this will take some time to complete. Though there are correspondence tables that BEA uses, and only the environmental portion of some of the categories is needed here, there are still instances where the official conversion is not appropriate. There are similar issues using the Eurostat CPC/CPA to NAPCS and ISIC/NACE to NACE matching.

36. See organic agricultural surveys from the National Agricultural Statistics Service of the US Department of Agriculture: https://www.nass.usda.gov/Surveys/Guide_to_NASS_Surveys/Organic_Production/index.php.

lects detailed crop production and sales data from certified organic farms. This detailed crop level information is then matched to the respective BEA product to develop the percentage of the total production that is considered environmental (organic) in its purpose. Most of the agriculture products in the BEA system were able to be matched to the USDA certified organic crops, including wheat, corn, rice, rye, soybeans, potatoes, lettuce, tomatoes, apples, grapes, strawberries, milk, broilers and chickens, eggs, etc. Further, appliances and other durable goods may not separate out Energy Star (or similar energy-saving appliances) from conventional ones.[37] We used EPA data for sales of Energy Star labeled appliances (both industrial and household) to estimate the portion of appliance sales that are energy efficient versus conventional sales. We then used fuel-efficient vehicle sales to identify the portion of fuel-efficient (hybrid and electric) vehicles that were manufactured in distinction from conventional vehicle sales.

Another commingled activity (in category 2) is research and development (R&D) where a portion of R&D may be undertaken for environmental protection (CEPA 80) or resource management (CReMA 150). We used microdata from Refinitiv's ESG data set,[38] which includes firm-level information from public and private companies regarding their environmental R&D expenditures, to see if it could provide insights into the portion of R&D firms typically engage in that is for environmental purposes versus more traditional purposes. While these data are often paired with other financial data for determining firm ESG scores, we instead use the raw expenditure information reported by firms for environmental R&D, which is more relevant for purposes of quantifying this activity. Unfortunately, we found that only a very small subset of firms provides detailed environmental R&D expenditures, as environmental R&D is not (yet) a required disclosure by the SEC for public companies. Thus, it was not broad enough coverage to extrapolate this information to the SUT values, and we do not incorporate environmental activity for CEPA 80 and CReMA 150 in our estimates. We return to this point in the discussion section below.

37. Energy Star ratings are binary by nature, requiring varying thresholds of energy savings (depending on the product) over some minimum standard. One complicating factor these examples highlight is that some products that are more environmentally friendly (in the sense that their purpose is to conserve energy or protect environmental resources) than their more traditional counterparts on the market; yet, SEEA prescribes that we count the entire product rather than the portion or marginal value of the product that is environmental-related in its purpose. We follow international conventions on this issue by counting the full product/service, but we revisit this point in our discussion in section 6.5.3 below regarding how to consider partial categories in the future. Another complicating factor for future versions of this account might be if regulations change such that certain products are required to be uniformly above an Energy Star standard and the baseline/minimum products are outlawed.

38. For more information on this data, see: https://www.refinitiv.com/en/financial-data/company-data/esg-data.

6.3.5 Alternative Scenarios and Sensitivity Tests

In some cases, source data were not available to separate economic activity for Environmental Goods and Services (EGS) where the product categories were too coarse and included both environmental and non-environmental commodities. To explore how sensitive the estimates are to the exclusion of these categories that may be partially relevant, we present tables under two scenarios. In the first scenario, we exclude EGS where we do not have sufficient source data to estimate the portion of the commodity (or group of commodities in particular product category) that are "environmental" in their primary purpose. This is a more conservative approach to estimating output of this sector that wholly and unambiguously aligns with the definition of environmental activity in the SEEA CF. In the second scenario, we estimate the environmental share as 10 percent as a way to give some weight to these relevant commodities that were designated as partially relevant. This is still a somewhat conservative approach, but it accomplishes two objectives. First, it ensures we account for at least some of the relevant EGS in our estimates, albeit assuming that the partial category is at least 10 percent relevant. Second, and most importantly, it is a sensitivity check for illustrating the relative magnitude of the categories designated as partially relevant. If the gap between these two scenarios turns out to be very large, it would be evidence that partially relevant categories might be the primary driver of the overall size of the account. If the gap is small, partially relevant categories could still be economically important, but it would provide some confidence that the conservative approach of including unambiguous categories is a reasonable starting point for EGSS estimates.[39]

There are two additional caveats to consider when reviewing these estimates. First, in practice, gross output is composed of sales or receipts, other operating income, commodity taxes, and inventory change. For this paper, we did not have the source data to estimate inventory change for the EGSS. This exclusion, however, is unlikely to substantially impact our results (based on BEA's experience with other satellite accounts), but we leave further exploration of this issue for future work. The second consideration is the potential for double-counting electricity and/or heat produced from renewable sources. To the extent that energy produced from renewable sources

39. One coarse analogy for this approach might be instructive. Suppose we have a bunch of rooms in a zoo, and we are trying to add up how much the animals weigh. In many of the rooms, we can see into them fine and measure how much they weigh. But, suppose there is a dark room, and we can hear that there might be either elephants or mice in there (or both), but we do not know in what proportion. If we knew how much the room weighed (or how much 10 percent of the room weighed), we would have a sense of whether there are elephants in there. And, if so, perhaps we should focus more of our future efforts on shining light in that particular room to find out for sure. Or, if not, additional effort into shining light in there may not change our total estimates much, and we prioritize accordingly.

is used in the production of other environmental goods and services (as part of intermediate consumption), our estimates would double-count the value of that energy use. There may also be double-counting if government purchases include high levels of environmental products that are identified separately such as, for example, electric vehicles (EVs). The total sales of EVs are identified and separated from other vehicles but who purchases these EVs is not identified. If both the entire budgets of certain government agencies/departments are included, those agencies' purchases of EVs would be double-counted. Double-counting of government transfers and subsidies are avoided since these are already balanced out of the SUTs, which is one of the advantages of using the SUT methodology.

6.4 Results

6.4.1 Summary of the US Environmental Goods and Services Sector (EGSS)—Overall

Our first set of results summarizes the pilot estimates for the US environmental goods and services sector (EGSS) under two sets of assumptions to assess the sensitivity of our method. Specifically, table 6.1a shows gross output estimates of environmental goods and services in both producer and purchaser values for 2015 and 2019 by CEPA/CReMA category under the first scenario (excluding EGS where we do not have source data to estimate the precise "environmental" portion of the product category). We divide each year's EGSS output into three columns (Producer Value, Margins, and Purchaser Value) across 16 different categories along the rows, containing aggregations of EGS by CEPA category (14 of which come from the relevant CEPA/CReMA categories, one "Mixed" category that includes cross-category activity, and one "Unclassified" category).[40] The totals for each column are tallied along the bottom row. Overall, the estimates in table 6.1a (columns 3 and 6) show EGSS in purchaser values accounted for $620.6 billion of US gross output in 2015, growing to $724.5 billion in 2019. This translates to about 1.9 percent of total US gross output in both years. Nominal growth for the EGSS averaged 3.8 percent over the period, slightly slower than the overall US growth rate of output of 4.2 percent.

One insight gained from this exercise is that table 6.1a provides new

40. The producer price is the amount receivable by the producer inclusive of taxes on products, except deductible value added tax and exclusive of subsidies on products. The purchaser price is the amount payable by the purchaser. This includes trade margins realized by wholesalers and retailers (by definition, their output) as well as transport margins (that is, any transport charges paid separately by the purchaser) and non-deductible VAT. The SNA defines a trade margin as "the difference between the actual or imputed price realized on a good purchased for resale and the price that would have to be paid by the distributor to replace the good at the time it is sold or otherwise disposed of" (2008 SNA, §6.146). See also the SNA manual or BEA's online glossary (https://www.bea.gov/help/glossary) of terms for definitions other terms.

Table 6.1a **Estimates of gross output for environmental goods and services (EGSS) (in millions $)**

		2015 EGSS Gross Output			2019 EGSS Gross Output		
CEPA/CReMA	CEPA/CReMA category	Producer Value (1)	Margins (2)	Purchaser Value (3)	Producer Value (4)	Margins (5)	Purchaser Value (6)
10	Protection of ambient air and climate	$2,976	$2,686	$5,662	$2,611	$4,513	$7,124
20	Wastewater management	$84,384	$1,370	$85,754	$95,508	$2,192	$97,700
30	Waste management	$126,204	$27,298	$153,502	$152,873	$33,605	$186,478
40	Protection and remediation of soil, groundwater and surface water	$7,581	$3,626	$11,207	$12,379	$7,810	$20,189
60	Protection of biodiversity and landscapes	$79,665	$0	$79,665	$93,494	$0	$93,494
70	Protection against radiation	$1,765	$484	$2,249	$2,950	$981	$3,931
90	Other environmental protection	$6,160	$0	$6,160	$6,798	$0	$6,798
100	Management of water	$103,391	$1,802	$105,193	$122,391	$2,228	$124,618
110	Management of forest resources	$2,185	$0	$2,185	$4,357	$0	$4,357
111	Management of forest areas	$3,537	$0	$3,537	$3,578	$0	$3,578
112	Minimization of the intake of forest resources	$339	$0	$339	$368	$0	$368
120	Management of wild flora and fauna	$4,072	$0	$4,072	$3,378	$0	$3,378
131	Production of energy from renewable sources	$53,131	$2,323	$55,454	$56,824	$3,097	$59,920
132	Heat/Energy saving and management	$27,077	$41,878	$68,955	$30,119	$40,190	$70,309
Mixed	Mixed	$31,101	$709	$31,810	$35,941	$702	$36,644
Unclassified	Unclassified	$3,910	$898	$4,808	$4,711	$928	$5,639
Yearly Totals		**$537,479**	**$83,074**	**$620,553**	**$628,280**	**$96,246**	**$724,526**

Note: Scenario 1—Includes product categories that align fully with EGS definitions or where supplemental data can be used to estimate the EGS component. Excluding partial categories of EGSS where we do not yet have source data to estimate the “environmental” portion of the commodity.

estimates of the magnitudes of each CEPA/CReMA domain for the US economy, highlighting the relative prominence of some categories like waste management and management of water, in particular. Waste management represented the largest category in both years, responsible for just over one-quarter of the EGSS purchaser value total. Management of water was the second largest category, followed closely by wastewater management and protection of biodiversity and landscapes. These four categories accounted for about 70 percent of total EGSS production in 2015 and 2019 in terms of purchaser value. This result is relatively common when compared to other EGSS accounts internationally. For example, in 2015 and 2019 in the EU-27 countries, waste management accounted for 26–27 percent of Gross Value Added (GVA) of the environment industry, and wastewater management accounted for 12–15 percent. One takeaway from this exercise is that the makeup of the environmental goods and services sector may look different in aggregate than preconceived notions of solar panels, electric cars, and other more high-profile green technologies. While these types of transactions are important components of EGSS output, and may grow in prominence over time, one takeaway is that water/resource management and waste management activities factor in more prominently in the most recent years for which we have data.[41]

Table 6.1b is organized the same way as table 6.1a, but shows gross output estimates under the second scenario, where we use 10 percent as the environmental portion for mixed commodity categories that we do not have source data to precisely separate environmental-specific activities from output whose purposes are more conventional or non-environmental. There are many commodity categories in the internal SUT data that contain a subset of output whose primary purpose is environmental. Yet, without supplemental data to separate these out, it is difficult to discern *ex ante* whether the output from these categories is large. However, table 6.1b provides evidence that our primary results in table 6.1a that leave out many of these partial product categories are likely a reasonable starting point for these pilot accounts. Specifically, when we compare the bottom row of both tables, the overall effect is to add about $12 billion to the producer values and $14 billion to the purchaser values for each year. This modest increase represents initial evidence that the partial categories do not contain an overwhelming bulk of the EGSS output. That is, the conservative approach used by table 6.1a is not *too* conservative by only including product categories that are unambiguously regarded as environmental in their primary purpose. We return to this issue of using additional data in our discussion section below.

41. If markets for solar panels, electric cars, and others high-profile green products continue to outpace growth in other categories, the relative proportions by category reported in these tables could look much different in the future.

Table 6.1b **Estimates of gross output for environmental goods and services (EGSS) (in millions $) (Scenario with 10% environmental portion)**

		2015 EGSS Gross Output			2019 EGSS Gross Output		
CEPA/CReMA	CEPA/CReMA category	Producer Value (1)	Margins (2)	Purchaser Value (3)	Producer Value (4)	Margins (5)	Purchaser Value (6)
10	Protection of ambient air and climate	$2,976	$2,686	$5,662	$2,611	$4,513	$7,124
20	Wastewater management	$84,384	$1,370	$85,754	$95,508	$2,192	$97,700
30	Waste management	$126,494	$27,390	$153,884	$153,281	$33,744	$187,025
40	Protection and remediation of soil, groundwater and surface water	$9,771	$3,626	$13,397	$14,592	$7,810	$22,402
60	Protection of biodiversity and landscapes	$79,665	$0	$79,665	$93,494	$0	$93,494
70	Protection against radiation	$1,765	$484	$2,249	$2,950	$981	$3,931
90	Other environmental protection	$6,160	$0	$6,160	$6,798	$0	$6,798
100	Management of water	$103,391	$1,802	$105,193	$122,391	$2,228	$124,618
110	Management of forest resources	$4,873	$835	$5,708	$6,686	$845	$7,531
111	Management of forest areas	$3,537	$0	$3,537	$3,578	$0	$3,578
112	Minimization of the intake of forest resources	$566	$55	$622	$565	$59	$624
120	Management of wild flora and fauna	$4,422	$9	$4,431	$3,877	$11	$3,889
131	Production of energy from renewable sources	$55,617	$2,571	$58,188	$59,190	$3,239	$62,429
132	Heat/Energy saving and management	$27,208	$41,915	$69,123	$30,233	$40,223	$70,456
Mixed	Mixed	$34,411	$1,076	$35,487	$39,539	$1,044	$40,583
Unclassified	Unclassified	$4,544	$960	$5,504	$5,113	$994	$6,107
Yearly Totals		**$549,784**	**$84,779**	**$634,563**	**$640,407**	**$97,882**	**$738,288**

Note: Scenario 2—Beginning with Table 6.1a as a baseline, for a sensitivity analysis we use a placeholder of 10% for EGSS for partial categories without source data to estimate the "environmental" portion of the commodity.

6.4.2 Public and Private Sector Breakout of the EGSS in the United States

In our second set of tables (tables 6.2 and 6.3), we separate government output from the EGSS to shed new light on the magnitude of government expenditures relative to non-government output in this sector. This is an explicit step toward better measuring and accounting for environmental public goods, a key goal of this NBER-CRIW volume, by tallying output at all levels of government that are environmental in their primary purpose. Tables 6.2 and 6.3 show the government portion of the gross output in the EGSS for 2015 and 2019, respectively, separating out producer value, margins, and purchaser value as in table 6.1a and table 6.1b. The government portions represent the share of total gross output attributable to government spending.[42] Government spending can represent production by the government sector, such as the federal government's budget for wildland fire management, or procurement of goods and services, such as government purchases of Energy Star equipment. The "government portion of environmental margins" in the tables are the margins associated with government purchases of goods and services. Since intermediate inputs are not typically separately identified as government production in the SUT data, our estimates likely underestimate the government portion of EGSS output.[43]

Overall, the results from tables 6.2 and 6.3 (bottom row, columns 4 and 6) show the public sector accounted for about 27 or 28 percent of the EGSS in 2019 and 2015, respectively. Alternatively, we depict the results from table 6.3 in figure 6.1 below. This proportion of public sector output, however, varies widely by category—as some categories are either fully or almost entirely composed of government expenditures (like those associated with forest management or management of wild flora/fauna). Other categories fall on the other side of the spectrum and are dominated by the private sector, which include the energy-related categories and protection against radiation. The largest categories, those related to management of water, wastewater, and waste, are dominated by the private sector in the United

42. The value of non-market government output is typically valued in the SNA by sum of costs. However, it is possible for there to be both non-market and market output. Paragraph 6.132 in the SNA states, "Government units and NPISHs may be engaged in both market and non-market production. Whenever possible, separate establishments should be distinguished for these two types of activities, but this may not always be feasible. Thus, a non-market establishment may have some receipts from sales of market output produced by a secondary activity: for example, sales of reproductions by a non-market museum. However, even though a non-market establishment may have sales receipts, its total output covering both its market and its non-market output is still valued by the production costs. The value of its market output is given by its receipts from sales of market products, the value of its non-market output being obtained residually as the difference between the values of its total output and its market output. The value of receipts from the sale of non-market goods or services at prices that are not economically significant remains as part of the value of its non-market output."

43. For example, hydroelectric power generation is an intermediate input and is not separately identified as government or private production in the SUT data, so we did not allocate any of this value to government.

Table 6.2 **2015 Environmental goods and services sector (EGSS) output by type—public sector vs. private sector output (in millions $)**

		2015 EGSS Gross Output					
CEPA/ CReMA	CEPA/CReMA category	Government Portion of EGSS Gross Output (Producer Value) (1)	Government Portion of Margins (2)	Government Portion of EGSS Gross Output (Purchaser Value) (3)	Public Sector % of Total EGSS Gross Output (Purchaser Value) (4)	Private Sector EGSS (Purchaser Value) (5)	Private Sector % of Total EGSS Gross Output (Purchaser Value) (6)
10	Protection of ambient air and climate	$2,098	$267	$2,366	*41.8*	$3,296	*58.2*
20	Wastewater management	$41,629	$0	$41,629	*48.5*	$44,125	*51.5*
30	Waste management	$16,834	$0	$16,834	*11.0*	$136,668	*89.0*
40	Protection and remediation of soil, groundwater and surface water	$1,607	$0	$1,607	*14.3*	$9,600	*85.7*
60	Protection of biodiversity and landscapes	$79,665	$0	$79,665	*100.0*	$0	*0.0*
70	Protection against radiation	$128	$24	$152	*6.8*	$2,097	*93.2*
90	Other environmental protection	$1,235	$0	$1,235	*20.0*	$4,925	*80.0*
100	Management of water	$18,632	$3	$18,635	*17.7*	$86,558	*82.3*
110	Management of forest resources	$2,185	$0	$2,185	*100.0*	$0	*0.0*
111	Management of forest areas	$3,537	$0	$3,537	*100.0*	$0	*0.0*
112	Minimization of the intake of forest resources	$339	$0	$339	*100.0*	$0	*0.0*
120	Management of wild flora and fauna	$3,031	$0	$3,031	*74.4*	$1,041	*25.6*
131	Production of energy from renewable sources	$23	$0	$23	*0.0*	$55,431	*100.0*
132	Heat/Energy saving and management	$1,123	$378	$1,501	*2.2*	$67,454	*97.8*
Mixed	Mixed	$2,823	$0	$2,823	*8.9*	$28,987	*91.1*
Unclassified	Unclassified	$20	$1	$22	*0.4*	$5,518	*99.6*
Yearly Totals		**$174,908**	**$674**	**$175,582**	***28.3***	**$445,702**	***71.7***

Note: This table divides the portion of the EGSS estimates from Table 6.1a into public and private sector output for 2015.

Table 6.3 **2019 Environmental goods and services sector (EGSS) output by type—public sector vs. private sector output (in millions $)**

		2019 EGSS Gross Output					
CEPA/ CReMA	CEPA/CReMA category	Government Portion of EGSS Gross Output (Producer Value) (1)	Government Portion of Margins (2)	Government Portion of EGSS Gross Output (Purchaser Value) (3)	Public Sector % of Total EGSS Gross Output (Purchaser Value) (4)	Private Sector EGSS (Purchaser Value) (5)	Private Sector % of Total EGSS Gross Output (Purchaser Value) (6)
10	Protection of ambient air and climate	$2,611	$809	$3,420	*48.0*	$3,704	*52.0*
20	Wastewater management	$43,790	$0	$43,790	*44.8*	$53,910	*55.2*
30	Waste management	$15,642	$0	$15,642	*8.4*	$170,836	*91.6*
40	Protection and remediation of soil, groundwater and surface water	$2,351	$0	$2,351	*11.6*	$17,838	*88.4*
60	Protection of biodiversity and landscapes	$93,494	$0	$93,494	*100.0*	$0	*0.0*
70	Protection against radiation	$65	$14	$79	*2.0*	$3,852	*98.0*
90	Other environmental protection	$788	$0	$788	*11.6*	$6,010	*88.4*
100	Management of water	$22,480	$2	$22,482	*18.0*	$102,136	*82.0*
110	Management of forest resources	$4,357	$0	$4,357	*100.0*	$0	*0.0*
111	Management of forest areas	$3,578	$0	$3,578	*100.0*	$0	*0.0*
112	Minimization of the intake of forest resources	$368	$0	$368	*100.0*	$0	*0.0*
120	Management of wild flora and fauna	$3,177	$0	$3,177	*94.0*	$201	*6.0*
131	Production of energy from renewable sources	$21	$0	$21	*0.0*	$59,899	*100.0*
132	Heat/Energy saving and management	$469	$139	$608	*0.9*	$69,701	*99.1*
Mixed	Mixed	$2,763	$0	$2,763	*7.5*	$33,881	*92.5*
Unclassified	Unclassified	$104	$11	$115	*1.8*	$6,366	*98.2*
Yearly Totals		**$196,056**	**$976**	**$197,032**	**27.2**	$528,336	**72.8**

Note: This table divides the portion of the EGSS estimates from Table 6.1a into public and private sector output for 2019.

States in 2015 and 2019; but, because of their overall magnitude in the EGSS overall, these three categories still constitute a large proportion of the overall public expenditure on the EGSS (about $82 billion of the $197 billion in gross EGSS output by the public sector in 2019). These relative proportions also appear in the lower panel of figure 6.1 (panel B), which underscores this point more visually.

Comparisons across years underscore the necessity for building out a longer time series of data points. For example, the government portion of CEPA 10 (protection of ambient air and climate) category in 2015 represented 41.8 percent of output, but in 2019 it was 48 percent.[44] While these

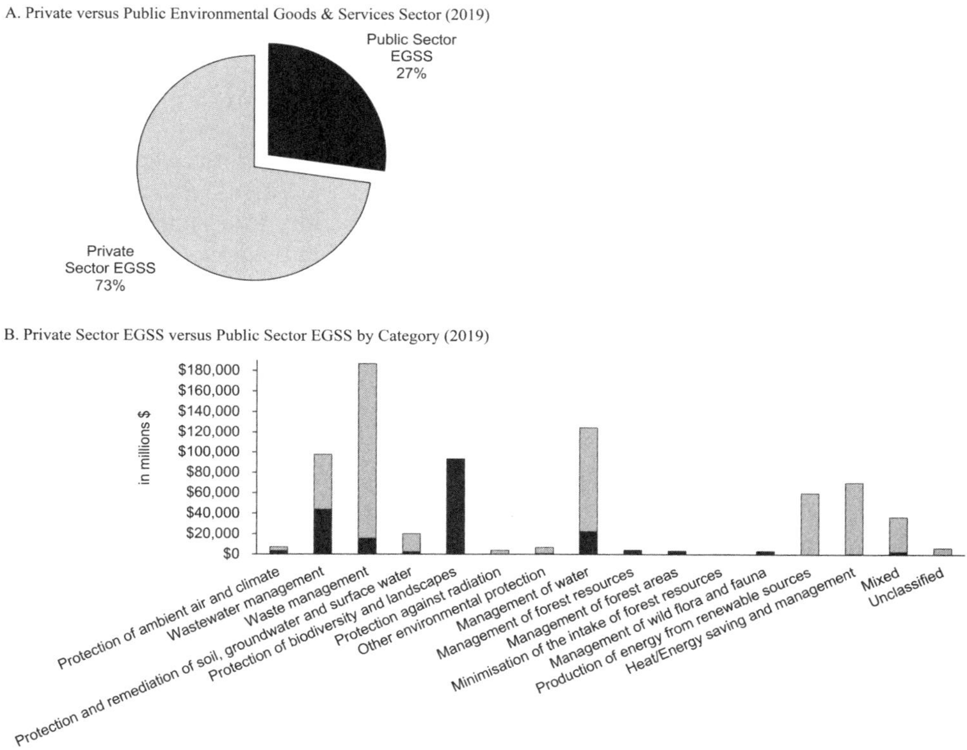

Figure 6.1 Private versus public environmental goods and services sector

Notes: The results above come from table 6.3—EGSS Gross Output (Purchaser Value, Scenario 1) by CEPA/CREMA Category. Figure 6.1 panel A reports the breakout of the private vs. public portions of the EGSS. Panel B then presents this breakout by category. The private sector is depicted in gray, and the Public Sector is depicted in black.

44. There was also a large jump in margins for some categories, like protection of air and climate, which raises a similar question regarding whether some of these changes over time are sustained increases or one-off outliers.

tables represent a proof-of-concept and not a comprehensive time series, the results motivate the need for a fuller time series to make the data more complete for users. For example, production of a longer time series of EGSS could indicate whether a shift like we see with CEPA 10 is part of a longer trend over time or merely represents an outlier for a particular year.

Finally, when developing environmental activity accounts, such as EGSS, it can be helpful to compare the monetary flows to the owner of the natural resources to see if there is some agreement between the expenditures identified and the ownership of the resources. For example, in the eastern parts of the United States, the forests used for timber production are primarily owned and managed by private individuals and companies. In contrast, many of the forest areas in the West and Alaska are owned by federal and state government agencies.[45] That management of forest resources in tables 6.2 and 6.3 only shows figures for government output, which suggests that further work is needed to identify the private contributions to this activity. That the protection of biodiversity and landscapes is shown as solely a government activity is also not so surprising, given that this is where the management activities of the national parks, wilderness areas, and wildlife sanctuaries would be found.[46] Agricultural production, for example, may include landscape protection like planting trees as wind barriers and other soil-preserving practices that may not be accounted for in the pilot estimates. These are just a few examples of how knowledge about the physical environment, the roles and responsibilities of the various levels of government (federal, state, and local), and the role of the private sector need to be considered and matched before the EGSS statistics can be more comprehensive in its scope. Future work would need to include a greater focus on the roles of government.[47]

45. Western states have a much higher proportion of public lands compared to the eastern United States. For a more detailed breakdown on public land management, see for example "Public Land Statistics 2020" from the Bureau of Land Management, US Department of the Interior, Volume 205, June 2021, https://www.blm.gov/sites/default/files/docs/2021-08/PublicLandStatistics2020_1.pdf.

46. On the other hand, that the majority of water management is located in the private sector may indicate that government expenditures are underrepresented. Water management in the western states is very important, and seven state agreements regulate the use of the water in the Colorado River Basin, for example. The Bureau of Reclamation plays a prominent role in the management of this Basin. Future work might identify government activity at finer scales using supplemental data, which would improve the estimates of the EGSS.

47. We should also provide the caveat that there are conceptual issues that complicate the distinction between the public and private sector in a complex economy like the United States'. The US economic system itself is mixed (like most economies around the world), as the public sector plays a prominent role in the United States' market economy, as both regulator and direct producer of output. For the purposes of national accounts, we draw the distinction by institutional unit producing the output. Even if a regulation from the public sector requires a private sector firm to make investments in environmental protection, for example, it would count as private sector gross output (or an intermediate good allocated to the private sector). So, when we split "protection of ambient air and climate" among private and public sectors, the current standards do not require (nor would the data allow) us to answer *why* private sector units are doing this.

6.4.3 International Comparisons: Are These Estimates Reasonable?

We can also compare these pilot estimates of the US EGSS to their counterparts in Europe. A recent Eurostat publication[48] stated that the environmental economy as a whole was 2.3 percent of the 2018 GDP of the EU-27. This includes market output, ancillary or final and non-market production. If only market output is considered, the contribution to 2018 EU-27 GDP was 1.2 percent. In this current study of the US EGSS, only gross output is developed so the figures are not directly comparable. Despite this, overall, we find the comparison of the reported magnitudes to be reasonable, given that differences will remain due to measurement differences (e.g., our preliminary, incomplete estimation of partial categories) and underlying differences in the economies. For this proof-of-concept, pilot account to transition to production of an official account, numerous challenges would need to be overcome, including filling data gaps and addressing key classification issues. We discuss some of these in the next section.

6.5 Discussion

One of the purposes of this project is to push the existing data as far as possible, exploring what is currently feasible and what issues remain. In this section, we discuss several remaining challenges that would need to be overcome prior to production of an official EGSS account, including data gaps and classification/methodological issues. The subsections below are not intended to be exhaustive, but they are meant to illustrate the types of challenges facing the United States and other countries implementing an EGSS account, along with potential solutions and practical considerations.

6.5.1 Classification Alignment, Data Gaps, and Other Issues

The first issue, which was discussed at some length above, is a well-known issue with constructing satellite accounts based on NAPCS/NAICS (or CPA/NACE or CPC/ISIC) classifications—the definitions of the product and industry categories do not perfectly align with the underlying account being constructed. In some examples above, a category might contain multiple products, where only a subset has a purpose that is primarily environmental. In the case of organic farming, an example we discussed above, one can estimate what proportion of the reported agricultural products are organic using alternative data sources (e.g., the US Department of Agriculture's Organic Survey). In other cases, the alternative data source might be less clear cut or more difficult to access. To be conservative, we explored how our estimates might change if we assigned a low percentage (10 percent proportion) to these categories. If the United States were to produce a formal

48. See "Environmental economy—statistics by Member State" from Eurostat (June 29, 2022), https://ec.europa.eu/eurostat/statistics-explained/index.php?title=Environmental_economy_%E2%80%93_statistics_by_Member_State.

account to the standards BEA produces other National Income and Product Accounts (NIPAs), then it would require extensive work in estimating these partial product/industry categories. This would require additional source data from government agencies (in some cases, special data collections or internal data) and the private sector. In other cases, simple statistics and tabulations from alternative data may not be sufficient, as it may also require more sophisticated statistical analysis or modeling based on that data. This is not a problem unique to the United States, as numerous countries around the world face similar challenges to align product/industry categories with environmental purposes.

One way to address misalignment of product/industry categories is to alter the survey collection process or identify data that could stand in for firm-level or entity-level microdata. In fact, the US EPA and US Census used to survey firms regularly on their pollution abatement costs and expenditures (PACE) starting in the 1970s and continuing until 2005.[49] A recent trend for statistical agencies in the United States, however, has been to find ways to shed their reliance on costly surveys that firms and individuals find increasingly burdensome. Agencies like BEA and the US Census Bureau have progressively found ways to incorporate big data and administrative data as supplements to, or in some cases replacements for, traditional survey data.[50] Hence, if the United States would begin devoting significant resources to constructing official environmental-economic accounts in the coming years, there may be opportunities to employ these 21st-century approaches using existing data. By exploring additional ways data sources that already exist (i.e., "nontraditional data" that are collected for some other purpose but that may be of sufficient quality to be used for statistical purposes) and, to the extent that gaps remain, subsequently deploying more limited (less burdensome) surveys may fill those gaps. For example, if there are ways the economic census could be altered to address some of the key data gaps, one avenue to mitigate these gaps would be for BEA to work with the Census Bureau and other agencies on subsequent revisions to survey collections such that the underlying SUT data (and other government data) would better align with environmental classifications. Some key mixed categories could be disaggregated further to provide cleaner breaks of environmental and conventional, non-environmental output along the lines of its primary purpose.

49. See "Pollution Abatement Costs and Expenditures: 2005 survey" from the US Environmental Protection Agency, https://www.epa.gov/environmental-economics/pollution-abatement-costs-and-expenditures-2005-survey#History.

50. For a summary of some of these big data efforts by the BEA, see Moyer and Dunn (2020). For a summary of uses of nontraditional data sources across the US government and academia for economic measurement, see Abraham et al. (2022), Editor's Introduction, *Big Data for 21st Century Economic Statistics: The Future Is Now*. National Bureau of Economic Research.

The imperfect alignment of NAPCS/NAICS can also be addressed, at least in part, as part of the ongoing NAPCS/NAICS revision cycle. These classification systems are continuously revised over time to accommodate changing aspects of the economy. However, to this point, since the United States does not yet formally produce SEEA-based accounts, this revision process has not had a focus on altering classifications in ways to better align some of these definitions with SEEA explicitly. We cannot speak for our partnering countries like Canada and Mexico, however, as they may (or may not) have been actively prodding revisions in this direction. If the United States were to fund the regular production of environmental activity accounts, BEA would need to cooperate with the BLS, Census Bureau, and others on the White House Office of Management and Budget (OMB)–led Economic Classification Policy Committee (ECPC) to explore how NAPCS/NAICS could be altered in future revision cycles to better align with collection and classification related to environmental activity. We should note that this is a careful, deliberate process, as what revisions are made would need to maintain current levels of usability and quality for existing users of NAPCS/NAICS (like the NIPA accounts). The process could take several years, at least.[51]

The United States may also need to consider whether there are important areas that are included in the Classification of Environmental Activities (see Table 4.1 in SEEA CF) but which are excluded from the CEPA/CReMA classification developed for the European Statistical System. For example, the management of aquatic resources and management of mineral resources have not been explicitly part of the CEPA/CReMA system in prior years. The BEA has already developed Marine Satellite Accounts, so that the management of aquatic resources—including, for example, the relevant work of the National Oceanic and Atmospheric Administration (NOAA)—would seem to be a logical extension of the EGSS for the United States. Both Canada and the United Kingdom have developed country specific classifications for this area of statistics, and future iterations of the US EGSS would likely consider additional categories needed for domestic users in addition to the categories developed by the international institutions.[52]

51. The proposed production timelines for the OSTP-OMB-DOC *national strategy* for various environmental-economic accounts extend many years into the future. One reason for this, among many, is that the deliberative processes altering source data collections can take years in the US federal statistical system. Likewise, the revision process to potentially alter NAPCS/NAICS categories relevant for environmental activity accounts would also extend years into the future.

52. Other areas for improvements include working with the US Forest Service to identify ways to identify timber harvest quantities from sustainably managed forests and expenditures related to sustainable forest management; and isolating US production of Energy Star appliances and electric and hybrid vehicles rather than total sales in the United States which include imported products.

6.5.2 Environmental R&D and the Limitations of Firm-Level Environmental, Social, and Governance (ESG) Data

We briefly mentioned in section 6.3.3 that, due to data limitations, we omit environmental R&D from the EGSS tables presented in this paper. In this subsection, we discuss in greater depth why this is an important omission and how limitations of firm-level ESG data present challenges for filling this data gap. Indeed, the lessons we learned from examining these data more closely may have broader implications for how national statistical offices (NSOs) use these data in the future (or how these data might evolve to be more useful for national accounts).

R&D expenditures represent a critical component of our economy and are likely an important omission in the initial pilot version of this EGSS account, given the long history of research linking R&D activity, innovation, and economic growth (see, for example, Stokey 1995; Ulku 2007; Aghion and Jaravel 2015). Yet, this omission is not unique in the development of national economic accounts. Historically, R&D has been a difficult issue for the national accounts given that the intangibility of its output has been difficult to measure. In fact, it was not until the BEA's comprehensive revision back in 2013 that R&D was incorporated into the investment component of GDP. The incorporation came after several iterations of a R&D satellite account—the first one being created in 1994.[53]

R&D output is now in the supply-use data (i.e., purchases of R&D are capitalized in the SUTs since they are recorded as investments) and is also part of GDP. It is not, however, broken down by function in a way that is directly useable for the purposes of the EGSS pilot account.[54] As part of this pilot study, we therefore investigated supplemental data to estimate the proportion of total R&D that is undertaken for primarily an environ-

53. Several iterations of the satellite account were needed to resolve some fundamental measurement questions such as, What is the output? How can R&D expenditures be transformed into an R&D capital stock? How should the output of R&D be valued? And how fast does R&D capital depreciate? For an excellent review, see "The Evolving Treatment of R&D in the US National Economic Accounts" by Carol E. Moylan and Sumiye Okubo, Bureau of Economic Analysis, March 2020, https://www.bea.gov/system/files/2020-04/the-evolving-treatment-of-rd-in-the-us-national-economic-accounts.pdf.

54. The discussion in this section focuses on environmental R&D in the private sector, but there is potentially important data related to public sector R&D as well. For example, the NCSES NSF Federal budget statistics include an environmental function (Table 11, https://ncses.nsf.gov/pubs/nsf23324/assets/data-tables/tables/nsf23324-tab011.pdf) and an energy function (Table 10, https://ncses.nsf.gov/pubs/nsf23324/assets/data-tables/tables/nsf23324-tab010.pdf), which includes energy efficiency and other relevant topics (https://ncses.nsf.gov/pubs/nsf22316/#section9397). See also Boroush (2022) for a broader discussion of these statistics, including data sources and methods. The government performs an R&D function, but it also funds private sector activity. Although the R&D function can be separately identified, these could be double-counted since the budgets of relevant agencies have already been included in the estimates. As a result, the use of the NSF R&D statistics for government expenditures needs to be considered carefully so as to not introduce double-counting.

mental purpose. One potential source of non-traditional data is firm-level disclosures in their annual reports (10Ks) and supplemental/voluntary environmental, social, and governance (ESG) disclosures.[55] According to a recent report by KPMG, 96 percent of the largest (and 80 percent of large and mid-cap) firms around the world already publicly report on sustainability (KPMG 2020).[56] To help evaluate the coverage and availability of current (voluntary) private industry information on environmental activity, BEA purchased a database from Refinitiv's ESG Bulk Data that captures detailed firm-level environmental disclosures from across the globe (for 106 countries) over 2002–2021. While much of the ESG data used in academic studies correspond to firm-level environmental category scores (e.g., climate change risk scores) produced by various vendors, Refinitiv is presently the only data vendor that offers a centralized database on monetized estimates of environmental activity, such as environmental R&D expenditures, environmental fines, and environmental provisions, which are the most relevant for the national accounts.[57]

While proprietary, Refinitiv pulls information from a number of different public documents in which firms report ESG information: annual reports, CSR or sustainability reports, company websites, NGO websites, stock exchange filings, and news sources. For US firms in this global database, we linked these records with Compustat North America based on the firm's CUSIP supplemented by its ticker and year to be able to compare the degree of environmental R&D expenditures reported in Refinitiv relative to the overall annual R&D expenditures reported by the firm in its annual 10-K filings following US GAAP. Overall R&D expense and other financial statement information for US firms come from Compustat. We report descriptive statistics of environmental R&D reporting in appendix B.[58]

In appendix B, we report an array of descriptive statistics to help illustrate

55. Under US GAAP, firms generally expense R&D whereas in the NIPAs R&D is capitalized following SNA standards (Rassier 2014). While environmental R&D expenditures are not (currently) a required disclosure for US GAAP, US firms more generally follow an expensing approach (in line with US GAAP) rather than a capitalization approach when reporting these values.

56. The large firms sample (labeled G250) is based on the world's 250 largest companies by revenue as defined in the Fortune 500 ranking of 2019. The large and mid-cap firm sample (labeled N100) is based on a worldwide sample of 5,200 that represent the top 100 companies by revenue in each of the 52 countries and jurisdictions captured in the study.

57. ESG data vendors, like MSCI, Sustainalytics, and others generally provide ratings or scores and a number of indicators or (binary) flags that contribute to these ratings. But, they do not provide monetized environmental expenditure and revenue values for firms that are relevant for evaluating environmental goods and services accounts.

58. We had initially considered developing a regression model to predict environmental R&D based on existing firm data in the Refinitiv data and linked firm characteristics from Compustat; then, we would evaluate the proportion of environmental R&D for a broader, more representative sample of firms. As we show in appendix B, the US data for environmental R&D are very limited. If firm reporting on this information increases to where prediction models would be more relevant, this could be an interesting avenue for future research.

the potential landscape for public disclosures about environmental activity in private industry as a resource for populating national accounts. Several takeaways from these statistics are important to this discussion. First, in line with the conclusions from KPMG report discussed above, we find that a substantial number of firms around the world report at least some type of environmental activity to the public and a large proportion of the reported activity corresponds with US firms (roughly 50 percent) (see panel A of table 6B.1 in the appendix).[59] Further, we observe that the extent of reported environmental activity has increased over time (see figure 6B.2 panel A). For example, the number of firms captured in the global Refinitiv data reporting relevant environmental data globally in 2002, 2010, and 2021 was 982, 7,106, and 12,587, respectively (shown in figure 6B.2 panel A).

Additional (untabulated) summary statistics also reveal a couple of key limitations of the private sector data's potential as a resource for national accounts, particularly for environmental R&D. First, only a very small percent of the global database provides monetized values that correspond to EGSS activities like environmental R&D expenditures (e.g., CEPA 80). For example, only about 3 percent of observations with environmental activity actually report environmental R&D expenditures. Further, only 1 percent of the global database provides the firm's country information in addition to the environmental R&D expenditure to be able to evaluate which country would include the activity in its national accounts.[60] Second, when we examine the small sample of US firms that did report environmental R&D expenditures and benchmark this with the R&D expense reported by these firms for US GAAP (table 6B.1 panel B), we identify some additional concerns regarding whether the nature of these activities falls within the definitional scope relevant for a national account. For example, we observe that about 12 percent (13 percent) reported environmental R&D expenditure values that exceeded (exactly equaled) their overall GAAP annual R&D expense whereas the remaining 74 percent report environmental R&D expenditures less than the firm's GAAP annual R&D expense.[61] The types of firms that report a very high amount of environmental R&D relative to GAAP annual

59. Appendix table 6B.1 panel A reports that 49.4 percent (50,351 out of 101,925 firm-year observations) of reporting in the Refinitiv global detail file over the period is for US firms.

60. A total of 3,368 out of the 123,169 firm-year observations provide environmental R&D expenditures (3,368/123,169 = 2.7 percent) but only 1,160 firm-years provide a country address attached with the disclosure (1,160/123,169 firm-years = 0.9 percent). While not broken out in table 6B.1, it is worth noting that this is not unique to environmental R&D expenditure coverage. The percentage of the database with other monetized environmental costs like environmental fines and environmental expenditures, while higher than environmental R&D expenditures, is still relatively small (8.5 and 10.9 percent, respectively).

61. Appendix table 6B.1 panel B shows that out of 105 US firm-years with available environmental R&D expenditure and GAAP annual R&D expenditure data available in Compustat North America, 13 observations (12 percent) had an environmental value greater than the annual GAAP value, 14 (13 percent) had values that were equal, and 78 (74 percent) had environmental values less than their annual GAAP R&D expenditure value.

R&D expense could represent differences in definitional distinctions for how US firms report their environmental values (e.g., a firm could allocate more overhead or labor costs to R&D than what GAAP would consider as R&D). Alternatively, it could represent different horizons for how environmental values are reported in public disclosures (e.g., if firms only provide forward-looking, multi-year expenditure values rather than annual values). Each of these considerations presents challenges with using voluntary, private sector environmental disclosures for national accounts, not only for the United States but also NSOs abroad that might consider this kind of data for national accounts purposes.

Overall, our investigation of the Refinitiv global data offers a few lessons regarding the use of firm-level data in constructing environmental activity accounts. First, the current data reported by US firms for their environmental R&D are very limited and only disclosed by a small percentage of public firms, making extrapolations from such a small sample problematic. The rate of growth in reporting on this data over time, however, presents the possibility that the data may be more representative in future years (figure 6B.2 panel A).[62] Second, an additional limitation of private sector data is that currently ESG disclosures are largely voluntary where much of the information is not standardized and the information is not harmonized around a common set of definitions and classifications.[63] From a national accounts perspective, these data would be most useful when the accounting definition in the firm-level disclosure is sufficiently aligned with the SEEA/NIPA accounting definitions. In other words, even if there would eventually be rich/representative enough data reported with ESG disclosures,[64] if the accounting definitions are sufficiently far apart, then their usefulness would still be limited for national statistical offices.

More recently, US accounting standard setters and regulators have laid out plans to consider environmental disclosure standards and requirements for US firms. One notable example came in March 2022, when the Securities and Exchange Commission (SEC) released a climate-disclosure proposal

62. That said, in appendix figure 6B.2 panel A, we present the number of firms reporting environmental R&D expenditures over time and observe that the degree of reporting for the expenditure has remained relatively small, suggesting that it is not a particular subperiod examined that explains lower reporting by US firms. Further, in figure 6B.2 panel B, we break out environmental detail reporting by industry (based on two-digit NAICS) to verify that the low reporting for environmental R&D expenditures is not particular to a specific type of industry and observe similarly low levels of reporting for this expenditure in different industry classifications.

63. For example, recent work by Berg et al. (2022) raises concerns with the noisiness of ESG ratings and scores. This is one reason why we emphasize using the underlying expenditure data, as it is not clear how these scores would be of use for the national accounts.

64. We should note that there are different conventions in the literature that define "ESG" activities and the reporting of those activities. We follow Christensen et al. (2021, 1,179), and use the terms *ESG*, *CSR*, and *sustainability* interchangeably while recognizing that there are subtle differences in these terms. In particular, we define ESG activities as those that "assess, manage, and govern" a firm's impacts on society and the environment. Further, we define reporting as "measurement, disclosure, and communication" about these activities.

targeting an initial effective date in December 2022. The proposed rules would have required SEC registrants (both domestic and foreign private issuers) to phase in disclosures on climate-related financial statement metrics and emissions information in firm registration statements and annual reports. The proposal received more than 5,000 public comments that debated the legality of the proposal and different aspects of the disclosure requirements.[65] The original proposal required that any climate costs that are 1 percent or more of each line item of a company's financial statements (e.g., like R&D expense, SEC 2022, 135) would have to be reported.[66]

While weighing in on the private industry climate disclosure debate falls outside the scope of this paper, our analysis from examining private sector ESG data suggests that if environmental information reported by firms (whether mandated or voluntary) becomes more standardized and commonly reported, its usefulness to statistical agencies will directly relate to how well the accounting used by firms aligns with the SEEA CF and SNA. From a public goods perspective, if firm environmental disclosures are highly compatible with national accounts information in a standardized way, it would aid their broader use by policymakers in the national accounts.[67]

6.5.3 Future Challenges and Concluding Remarks

Overall, while this pilot effort identifies an important list of challenges to consider for potential EGSS accounts, it also shows that there are reasonable, tangible avenues for tackling these challenges. The data gaps discussed above are significant, though not insurmountable if production of official environmental activity accounts are sufficiently funded in the United States. Further, future work could expand the scope of the EGSS to incorporate other aspects of this sector besides output to fill out a more complete picture of the "green economy" (as prior efforts had called it). For example, funding for an official satellite account might also produce measures of GDP (value added), employment, and compensation in this sector. Using BEA's established satellite account module would also allow for adding in inventories and removing double-counting of electricity produced from renewable

65. The discussion of comments on the proposal is based on a Harvard Law School Forum discussion and related review of the comments on SEC climate rulemaking by the Commonwealth Climate and Law Initiative, which prepared a summary classification of more than 1,000 comments made by "trade associations, politicians, NGO and third sector entities, companies, investors and academics, as well as lawyers, professional organizations, regulators and standards bodies" (Williams and Eccles 2022).

66. However, the proposal did not specifically address how to treat "expensed or capitalized costs that are *partially* incurred towards the climate-related events and transition activities (e.g., the expenditure relates to research and development expenses that are meant to address both the risks associated with the climate-related events and other risks)" (SEC 2022, 138–139).

67. See also Vardon et al. (2016) and Keith et al. (2017) for additional discussion of the use of environmental-economic accounts information for policymakers and natural resource management.

sources and help address a number of other issues discussed above. Taken together, the results of our proof-of-concept EGSS account show that quantifying the EGSS would not only be feasible (conditional on resources to fill aforementioned data gaps) but would also offer a potentially valuable part of a suite of accounts that could help further our understanding of the intersection of the environment and the economy in the 21st century.

Looking forward, another challenge is a conceptual one. Like the other pilot accounts cited above, this study largely takes the SEEA Central Framework and other international standards as given, applying their principles and methods to US data. As these standards evolve over time to incorporate new/revised methods and periodically change their scope, standard setters may reevaluate key measurement issues we discussed earlier in the paper. For example, we noted in the description of our current methodology that energy saving appliances and electric cars are part of the EGSS. This binary, "in-out" treatment of these products is consistent with international standards. Yet should the *full* product be considered environmental, even if the overall product fits the primary purpose criterion? For example, if two luxury cars are both plug-in electric vehicles but one has higher-end features that have nothing to do with environmental protection (e.g., nicer interior or a fancier sound system), should the marginal difference in value between those cars be included in the EGSS account? Prior academic work in environmental economics has attempted to disentangle the environmental component from output (e.g., Shadbegian and Gray 2005; Färe et al. 2007), but the data and methodological demands to disentangle these components may be insurmountable to do at scale for an entire economy currently. Or, if a once-considered environmental product becomes the only option (via regulation or otherwise), do we classify it differently going forward? Future standard setters, potentially armed with better data and more developed methods to tackle these nuances, may revisit these issues in the years ahead.

Disclaimer: Any views expressed here are those of the authors and not necessarily those of the Bureau of Economic Analysis, US Department of Commerce, or the US government.

Appendix A

Table 6A.1 Environmental goods and services identified in BEA supply-use tables

Products in the Supply-Use Tables	Environmental portion	Data used to isolate environmental portion	CEPA/ CReMA
Agriculture products by type	Certified organic agriculture products	US Dept of Agriculture Certified Organic Surveys for 2015 and 2019; Value of Sales. See below for link	40
Forestry and logging	Timber harvested from sustainably managed forests	n/a (see note)	110
Game preserves	Portion that is for protection and not only for hunting	n/a	120
Support activities for agriculture and forestry	Portion of support activities that is for certified organic agriculture and sustainable forestry	n/a	40
Electric power generation from: Hydroelectric, Nuclear electric, Solar electric, Wind electric, Geothermal, and Biomass	All	Supply-use tables	131
Water supply services	All	Supply-use tables	100
Sewage treatment facilities	All	Supply-use tables	20
Construction and maintenance of: - Sewage and waste disposal structures; - water supply structures; - conservation and development facilities; - sewer facilities	All	Supply-use tables	20 & 30 100 160 20
Construction and maintenance of electric utilities structures	Renewable energy structures and facilities portion	n/a	131
Durable goods manufacturing	Energy star appliances	EPA ENERGY STAR® Unit Shipment and Market Penetration Report Calendar Year 2015, 2019 Summary	132

Durable goods manufacturing (cont.)	Electric vehicles	US Department of Energy, Energy Efficiency & Renewable Energy, Alternative Fuels Data Center: https://afdc.energy.gov/data/ Calculated as number of HEV+PEV+AltFuel vehicles sold in US as percent of total number of Light Duty Vehicles produced in USA	10
	Various products including diverse insulation products; mineral wool; firewood; diverse repair and rebuilding works; solar energy collectors; air source heat pumps	Supply-use tables	Diverse: 132 30 10
	Various products including particle board—portion that reduces virgin materials; products made from wastes; construction papers for insulation; sealed insulating glass products; fabricated steel plate containers for trash (only); turbine generators—those used in hydropower plants	n/a	Diverse: 30 132 10
Non-durable goods manufacturing	Various products including fuel ethanol, water treatment compounds, plastic water and sewer pipe, water pipe, sewer pipe, tire retreading	Supply-use tables	Diverse: 10 20 100
	Various products including plastic drain, waste and vent pipe; latex foam products for insulation	n/a	
Testing Laboratories	There are many different types of testing laboratories, need portion that tests environmental media such as water, soil, air, etc.	n/a	Mixed
Environmental Consulting Services	All	Supply-use tables	Mixed
Waste Collection	All	Supply-use tables	30
Waste Treatment and Disposal	All	Supply-use tables	30

(*continued*)

Table 6A.1 (continued)

Products in the Supply-Use Tables	Environmental portion	Data used to isolate environmental portion	CEPA/ CReMA
Remediation Services	All	Supply-use tables	40
Materials Recovery Facilities	All	Supply-use tables	30
Septic tank and related services	All	Supply-use tables	20
All other miscellaneous waste management services	All	Supply-use tables	30
Expenses of Environment, Conservation and Wildlife Organizations (tax exempt)	All	Supply-use tables	160
Tax exempt receipts of Environment, Conservation and Wildlife Organizations (tax exempt)	All	Supply-use tables	160
Sales of scrap and refuse of manufactured goods	All	Supply-use tables	30
Federal nondefense government services	*US EPA* *US Dept of Agriculture:* - Forest Service; *US Dept of Interior:* - Bureau of Land Management; - Bureau of Ocean Energy Management; - Bureau of Reclamation; - Fish and Wildlife Service; - US Geological Survey; - Wildland Fire Management; - National Park Service - Office of Surface Mining Reclamation and Enforcement; - Natural Resource Damage Assessment and Restoration Program;	Public budget documents for 2017 & 2021 which show the 2015 & 2019 actual figures. US Environmental Protection Agency: See Budget in Brief documents (link below) Forest service: https://www.fs.usda.gov/about-agency/budget-performance Dept of Interior Agencies: https://www.doi.gov/bpp/budget-justifications	Diverse: 110, 111, 40, 60, 120, 140

State & Local government services: - Agriculture and natural resources; - Parks and recreation; - Water utilities; - Sewerage systems	All	Supply-use tables	20 100
Sales of scrap and refuse of manufactured goods	All	Supply-use tables	20

Note: n/a means environmental portion could not be ascertained so these products were excluded from the estimates in tables 6A.1, 6.2, and 6.3. For table 6B.1, the environmental portion of these products was estimated to be 10 percent of total output.

USDA Certified Organic Survey Data: https://www.nass.usda.gov/Surveys/Guide_to_NASS_Surveys/Organic_Production/

US EPA Budget documents: https://www.epa.gov/planandbudget/archive

Code list for CEPA/CReMA categories—based on SEEA-CF CEA classification:

10: Protection of ambient air and climate
20: Wastewater management
30: Waste management
40: Protection and remediation of soil, groundwater and surface water
50: Noise and vibration abatement
60: Protection of biodiversity and landscapes
70: Protection against radiation
80: Research and development (R&D)
90: Other environmental protection
100: Management of water
110: Management of forest resources
111: Management of forest areas
112: Minimization of the intake of forest resources
120: Management of wild flora and fauna
130: Management of fossil energy resources
131: Production of energy from renewable sources
132: Heat/Energy saving and management
133: Minimization of the intake of fossil resources as raw material
140: Management of minerals
150: Research and development (R&D)
160: Other resource management

Appendix B

Table 6B.1 Private industry public environmental information

Panel A—Sample construction for the US environmental R&D sample (N = firm-year observations)

Description	*N* excluded	*N* remaining
Refinitiv global environmental detail file for 2002–2021		123,169
Require firms to have country information (by address) to identify US firms	21,244	101,925
Limit to US firms	51,574	50,351
[a] To put this into perspective, there are 163,832 US firm-years in Compustat North America (Compustat NA) for the same period. This suggests it is likely that roughly 31% of large US public firms both report some form of detailed environmental information publicly and have environmental information captured in the Refinitiv detail file.		
Limit to firms with non-missing values of environmental R&D expenditures	50,186	165
[b] For comparison, there are 61,898 US firm-years in Compustat NA in this period with GAAP R&D in Compustat NA. This suggest a much smaller % of large US public firms both report environmental R&D expenditures and have this information captured in the Refinitiv detail file (about 0.3%).		
[c] Coverage for other monetized US environmental values are also relatively small (environmental fines (*N*: 1,771 (1.1% of 163,832 in Compustat NA)); environmental expenditures (*N*: 2,261 (1.4% of 163,832 in Compustat NA))).		
Require non-missing and non-zero values of GAAP R&D expense ("XRD") in Compustat NA to calculate environmental R&D as a % of GAAP annual R&D expense	60	105

Panel B—Distribution of environmental R&D expenditure firm-year observations reported for US firms as a % of GAAP annual R&D expense

	N	1%	5%	10%	25%	50%	75%	90%	95%	99%	Mean
All	105	0.04	0.50	13.62	23.51	50.39	100.00	109.25	172.00	250.00	64.94
If > 100%	13	100.03	100.03	101.38	116.25	157.50	191.30	250.00	283.95	283.95	165.48
If = 100%	14	100.00	100.00	100.00	100.00	100.00	100.00	100.00	100.00	100.00	100.00
if < 100%	78	0.03	0.49	0.50	19.37	37.99	66.67	85.82	99.38	99.99	41.90

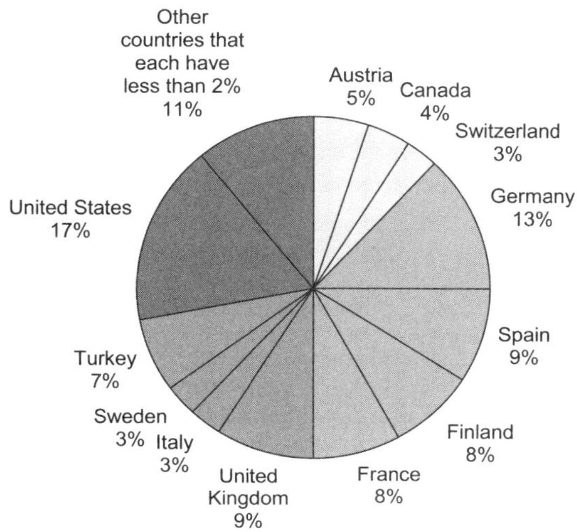

Figure 6B.1 Percent of OECD firm-year observations with non-missing environmental R&D expenditures in Refinitiv

Figure 6B.1 presents the percent of observations with non-missing environmental R&D expenditure values by country represented in Refinitiv's Global Environmental Detail File. The US provides the largest portion by country of non-missing values, which suggests the low reporting of environmental R&D is not driven by lower than normal reporting of this information in the US in particular.

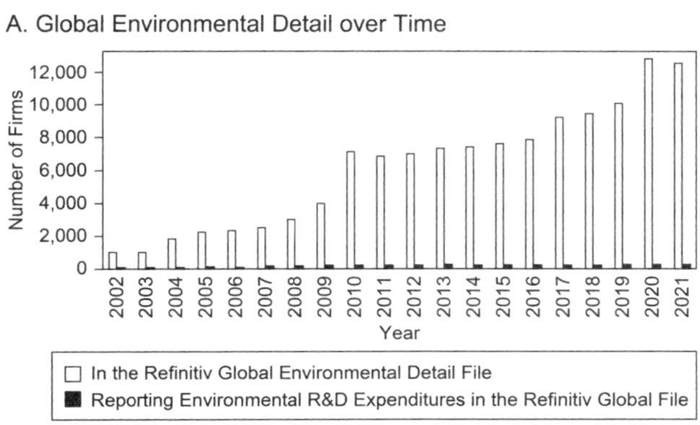

Figure 6B.2 Global environmental detail over time and by industry

Figure 6B.2 Panels A and B present stratifications of the number of firms in the Refinitiv global environmental detail file and those presenting non-missing environmental R&D over time and across industries, respectively. In Panel A, the number of firms in Refinitiv with environmental detail is increasing over time but the environmental R&D expenditure reporting has remained relatively low. Panel B shows that a large portion of firms in the Refinitiv environmental detail file is outside manufacturing and services (in the "Other" classification) but that the extent of firms reporting environmental R&D expenditures in the "Other" classification is also relatively low, similar to the other manufacturing and services industries. Overall, the low reporting of environmental R&D expenditures does not appear to correspond with a particular period or industry sector.

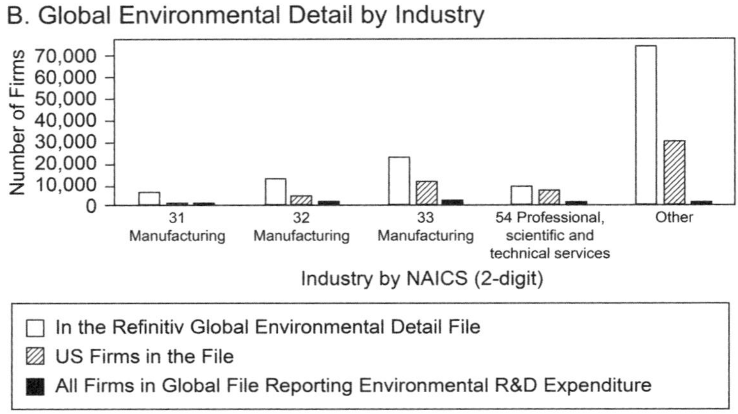

Figure 6B.2 (continued)

References

Abraham, K. G., R. S. Jarmin, B. Moyer, and M. D. Shapiro. 2022. "Introduction: Big Data for Twenty-First-Century Economic Statistics: The Future Is Now." In *Big Data for Twenty-First-Century Economic Statistics*, edited by Katharine G. Abraham, Ron S. Jarmin, Brian C. Moyer, and Matthew D. Shapiro. Chicago, IL: University of Chicago Press.

Aghion, P., and X. Jaravel. 2015. "Knowledge Spillovers, Innovation and Growth." *Economic Journal* 125 (583): 533–73.

Bagstad, K. J., J. C. Ingram, C. D. Shapiro, A. La Notte, J. Maes, S. Vallecillo, C. F. Casey, P. D. Glynn, M. P. Heris, J. A. Johnson, and C. Lauer. 2021. "Lessons Learned from Development of Natural Capital Accounts in the United States and European Union." *Ecosystem Services* 52: 101359.

Bagstad, K. J., Z. H. Ancona, J. Hass, P. D. Glynn, S. Wentland, M. Vardon, and J. Fay. 2020. "Integrating Physical and Economic Data into Experimental Water Accounts for the United States: Lessons and Opportunities." *Ecosystem Services* 45: 101182.

Banzhaf, H. S., D. Burtraw, S. C. Criscimagna, B. J. Cosby, D. A. Evans, A. J. Krupnick, and J. V. Siikamäki. 2016. "Valuation of Ecosystem Services in the Southern Appalachian Mountains." *Environmental Science & Technology* 50 (6): 2830–2836.

Becker, R. A., and R. J. Shadbegian. 2009. "Environmental Products Manufacturing: A Look inside the Green Industry." *BE Journal of Economic Analysis & Policy* 9 (1).

Berg, F., J. F. Koelbel, A. Pavlova, and R. Rigobon. 2022. "ESG Confusion and Stock Returns: Tackling the Problem of Noise." NBER Working Paper No. 30562.

Boroush, M., National Center for Science and Engineering Statistics (NCSES). 2022. *Sizable Growth in Federal Budget Authority for R&D Evident for the FYs 2017–21 Period; Further Increase Proposed for FY 2022*. InfoBrief NSF

22–322. Alexandria, VA: National Science Foundation. https://ncses.nsf.gov/pubs/nsf22322/.

Boyd, J. W., K. J. Bagstad, J. C. Ingram, C. D. Shapiro, J. E. Adkins, C. F. Casey, C. S. Duke, P. D. Glynn, E. Goldman, M. Grasso, J. L. Hass, J. Johnson, G. Lange, J. Matuszak, K. Miller, S. Posner, C. Rhodes, F. Soulard, M. Vardon, F. Villa, B. Voigt, and S. A. Wentland. 2018. "The Natural Capital Accounting Opportunity: Let's Really Do the Numbers." *BioScience* 68 (12): 940–43.

Brookings-Battle. 2011. Sizing the clean economy: a national and regional green jobs assessment. Washington, DC.

Brown, N., A. Femia, D. Fixler, O. G. Pedersen, S. C. Kaumanns, G. P. Oneto, S. Schürz, F. N. Tubiello, and S. Wentland. 2021. "Statistics: Unify Ecosystems Valuation." *Nature* 593 (7859): 341.

Cavender-Bares, J. M., E. Nelson, J. E. Meireles, J. R. Lasky, D. A. Miteva, D. J. Nowak, W. D. Pearse, M. R. Helmus, A. E. Zanne, W. F. Fagan, and C. Mihiar. 2022. "The Hidden Value of Trees: Quantifying the Ecosystem Services of Tree Lineages and Their Major Threats across the Contiguous US." *PLOS Sustainability and Transformation* 1 (4): e0000010.

Chambers, M. 2023. "Proof of Concept for a U.S. Air Emissions Physical Flows Account." BEA Working Paper (WP2023–2).

Christensen, H., L. Hail, and C. Leuz. 2021. "Mandatory CSR and Sustainability Reporting: Economic Analysis and Literature Review." *Review of Accounting Studies* 26: 1176–248.

Coyle, D. 2015. *GDP: A Brief but Affectionate History, Revised and Expanded Edition*. Princeton University Press.

Eaglesham, J., and P. Kiernan. 2023. "SEC Considers Easing Climate-Disclosure Rules After Investor Pushback." *Wall Street Journal*, February 3. https://www.wsj.com/articles/sec-considers-easing-climate-disclosure-rules-after-investor-pushback-11675416111.

Eurostat, European Commission. 2009. The environmental goods and services sector: a data collection handbook. Luxembourg: European Communities.

Eurostat, European Commission. 2016a. Environmental goods and services sector and accounts manual. Luxembourg: European Union.

Eurostat, European Commission. 2016b. Environmental goods and services sector accounts: practical guide. Luxembourg: European Union.

Färe, R., S. Grosskopf, and C. A. Pasurka Jr. 2007. "Pollution Abatement Activities and Traditional Productivity." *Ecological Economics* 62 (3–4): 673–82.

Fenichel, E. P., and J. K. Abbott. 2014. "Natural Capital: From Metaphor to Measurement." *Journal of the Association of Environmental and Resource Economists* 1 (1/2): 1–27.

Hein, L., K. J. Bagstad, C. Obst, B. Edens, S. Schenau, G. Castillo, F. Soulard, C. Brown, A. Driver, M. Bordt, and A. Steurer. 2020. "Progress in Natural Capital Accounting for Ecosystems." *Science* 367 (6477): 514–15.

Heris, M., K. J. Bagstad, C. Rhodes, A. Troy, A. Middel, K. G. Hopkins, and J. Matuszak. 2021. "Piloting Urban Ecosystem Accounting for the United States." *Ecosystem Services* 48: 101226.

Keith, H., M. Vardon, J. A. Stein, J. L. Stein, and D. Lindenmayer. 2017. "Ecosystem Accounts Define Explicit and Spatial Trade-Offs for Managing Natural Resources." *Nature Ecology & Evolution* 1 (11): 1683–1692.

KPMG. 2020. "The Time Has Come: The KPMG Survey of Sustainability Reporting 2020." December. https://assets.kpmg/content/dam/kpmg/xx/pdf/2020/11/the-time-has-come.pdf.

Moyer, B. C., and A. Dunn. 2020. "Measuring the Gross Domestic Product (GDP):

The Ultimate Data Science Project." *Harvard Data Science Review* 2 (1). https://doi.org/10.1162/99608f92.414caadb.
Muller, N. Z. 2009. "Using Hedonic Property Models to Value Public Water Bodies: An Analysis of Specification Issues." *Water Resources Research* 45 (1).
Obst, C., and M. Vardon. 2014. "Recording Environmental Assets in the National Accounts." *Oxford Review of Economic Policy* 30 (1): 126–44.
Ramonas, A., and A. Iacone. 2022. "SEC Climate Rules Pushed Back Amid Bureaucratic, Legal Woes." *Bloomberg Law*, October 19. https://news.bloomberglaw.com/securities-law/sec-climate-rules-pushed-back-amid-bureaucratic-legal-woes.
Rassier, D. 2014. "Treatment of Research and Development in Economic Accounts and in Business Accounts." *Survey of Current Business* March: 1–8.
Shadbegian, R. J., and W. B. Gray. 2005. "Pollution Abatement Expenditures and Plant-Level Productivity: A Production Function Approach." *Ecological Economics* 54 (2–3): 196–208.
Statistics Canada. 2024. 2022 Annual Survey of Environmental Goods and Services. Record number: 1209.
Stokey, N. L. 1995. "R&D and Economic Growth." *Review of Economic Studies* 62 (3): 469–89.
Ulku, H. 2007. "R&D, Innovation, and Growth: Evidence from Four Manufacturing Sectors in OECD Countries." *Oxford Economic Papers* 59 (3): 513–35.
United Nations, European Commission, Food and Agriculture Organization of the United Nations, International Monetary Fund, Organisation for Economic Co-operation and Development, and The World Bank. 2014a. System of Environmental-Economic Accounting 2012: Central Framework. (SEEA CF). New York: United Nations.
United Nations, European Commission, Food and Agriculture Organization of the United Nations, Organisation for Economic Co-operation and Development, and The World Bank. 2014b. System of Environmental-Economic Accounting 2012: Experimental Ecosystem Accounting. (SEEA-EEA). New York: United Nations.
United Nations, European Commission, International Monetary Fund, Organisation for Economic Co-operation and Development, and World Bank. 2009. System of National Accounts 2008. (SNA2008). New York: United Nations.
U.S. Securities and Exchange Commission. 2022. "Proposed Rule: Enhancement and Standardization of Climate-Related Disclosures for Investors." March 21. https://www.sec.gov/rules/proposed/2022/33–11042.pdf.
Vardon, M., P. Burnett, and S. Dovers. 2016. "The Accounting Push and the Policy Pull: Balancing Environment and Economic Decisions." *Ecological Economics* 124: 145–52.
Warnell, K. J., M. Russell, C. Rhodes, K. J. Bagstad, L. P. Olander, D. J. Nowak, R. Poudel, P. D. Glynn, J. L. Hass, S. Hirabayashi, and J. C. Ingram. 2020. "Testing Ecosystem Accounting in the United States: A Case Study for the Southeast." *Ecosystem Services* 43: 101099.
Wentland, S. A., Z. H. Ancona, K. J. Bagstad, J. Boyd, J. L. Hass, M. Gindelsky, and J. G. Moulton. 2020. "Accounting for Land in the United States: Integrating Physical Land Cover, Land Use, and Monetary Valuation." *Ecosystem Services* 46: 101178.
Wentland, S., J. Moulton, and G. Cornwall. 2023. "For What It's Worth: Measuring Land Value in the Era of Big Data and Machine Learning." BEA Working Paper (WP2023–4).
Williams, C., and R. Eccles. 2022. "Review of Comments on the SEC Climate Rulemaking." Harvard Law School Forum on Corporate Governance. November 23. https://corpgov.law.harvard.edu/2022/11/23/review-of-comments-on-sec-climate-rulemaking/.

Comment David A. Evans

Fixler et al. (this volume) construct a pilot environmental goods and service sector (EGSS) account for 2015 and 2019. Along the way, the authors carefully identify various conceptual and measurement challenges associated with constructing the account for the United States. I provide some background on how the study fits into the *National Strategy to Develop Statistics for Environmental-Economic Decisions* (hereafter *national strategy*) (OSTP et al. 2023) that is discussed in the introduction to this volume. Further, I identify some potential uses of the EGSS account and conclude with a simple caution about the interpretation of the size of the sector.

The study represents an early effort to begin to fulfill Recommendation 3(a) of the *national strategy* to "[i]ncorporate the internationally agreed System of Environmental-Economic Accounts [SEEA] to guide development of U.S. natural capital accounts and environmental-economic statistics. . . ." Research supporting this strategy is an important budget priority (EOP 2023). Specifically, the paper and the pilot EGSS follows the intention "to adopt the concepts, definitions, and classifications recommended in the SEEA CF [Central Framework] and EA [Ecosystem Accounting], with exceptions for improvements and alternative interpretations for specific U.S. institutions and context."

The pilot EGSS account is informed by the SEEA-CF and applies Classification of Environmental Protection Activities (CEPA) and Classification of Resource Management Activities (CReMA) aggregations that are used by the European Union Statistical Agencies to identify activities within the sector. The pilot EGSS measures gross output across private and public sectors, and therefore reflects a mix of final goods, intermediates, and government expenditures. The pilot account is constructed from supply-use data compiled by the BEA that is supplemented by additional data sources. These data sources are used to parse broader sector output levels to identify the portion suitable for inclusion in the EGSS.

The value of an EGSS account goes beyond an annual compiling of the bottom-line estimate of the size of the sector that may be of interest to policymakers. Having a US account of the size and composition of the EGSS that generally aligns with the approach in other countries also allows for comparisons to other countries. Furthermore, as familiarity with an EGSS account increases, including how its size and composition have changed over time and learning more about its internal relationships, market models can be leveraged to understand how policies directly impacting one set of activities in the sector influence the others. For example, partial equilibrium and economy-wide models can be used to evaluate how policies to increase renewable energy may affect air pollution control activities in

David A. Evans is a senior economist at the National Center for Environmental Economics of the US Environmental Protection Agency.

both the power and industrial sectors, the amount of investment in energy-efficient equipment, and the cost of providing environmental management (e.g., wastewater management). Furthermore, these market simulation tools and econometric studies can be used to evaluate how government investments in these activities influence private investment in this sector (Boushey 2023).

The existence of such an account also highlights the possibilities for deeper exploration of the sector including the value of complementary data collections (e.g., Becker and Shadbegian 2009; Nestor and Pasurka 1995a). Pairing components of the EGSS and complementarity data collections can improve our understanding of the relationship between the sector, as well as other sectors that provide inputs that support environmental activities, and sectors that consume their output, opening up additional research questions (e.g., Nestor and Pasurka 1995b). Components of the EGSS may also be used to evaluate more complete measures of productivity that directly or indirectly account for changes in environmental quality—e.g., changes in expenditures in subsectors relative to changes in emission; it is up to decision-makers to weigh the benefits and costs of developing and maintaining such accounts—but there clearly is significant value in understanding the scale of activities that contribute to a broader perspective on the quality of life (Diamond 2023; Department of Finance Canada 2021).[1]

Finally, it is important to acknowledge what the EGSS is *not* measuring. It neither measures the total cost of environmental protection nor the environmental benefit from the activities included in the EGSS. For example, the activities included may produce multiple services (e.g., output of renewable generators) and therefore does not measure the cost of protection as the authors discuss, particularly in the concluding section. That a measure of expenditures to provide public goods is not a measure of the social benefit of those expenditures, even on the margin, is self-evident. Fortunately, other ongoing studies are attempting to estimate the benefits of environmental quality and the value of natural resources, including research by some of the authors, to support the recommendations of the *national strategy*. And that all said, the EGSS helps fulfill the need to grasp the scale of the activities and investments that protect and support natural capital, the quality of which fundamentally influences our well-being (Krutilla 1967).

The views expressed herein are the author's and do not necessarily represent those of the USEPA. This comment was informed by helpful discussions with the organizers, authors, Wade Davis, Andrew Schreiber, and especially Carl Pasurka. For acknowledgments, sources of research support, and disclosure of

1. Additional policy uses, and associated research questions, of an EGSS account and similar efforts to understand this sector are identified in Eurostat (2009, 24) and Pasurka and Steurer (1995, 6).

the author's material financial relationships, if any, please see https://www.nber.org/books-and-chapters/measuring-and-accounting-environmental-public-goods-national-accounts-perspective/comment-accounting-environmental-activity-measuring-public-environmental-expenditures-and.

References

Becker, Randy A., and Ronald J. Shadbegian. 2009. "Environmental Products Manufacturing: A Look Inside the Green Industry." *BE Journal of Economic Analysis & Policy* 9 (1).

Boushey, Heather. 2023. *The Economics of Public Investment Crowding in Private Investment*. The White House Blog, August 16. https://www.whitehouse.gov/briefing-room/blog/2023/08/16/the-economics-of-public-investment-crowding-in-private-investment/.

Department of Finance Canada. 2021. *Measuring What Matters: Toward a Quality of Life Strategy for Canada*. April 19. Government of Canada. https://www.canada.ca/en/department-finance/services/publications/measuring-what-matters-toward-quality-life-strategy-canada.html.

Diamond, Ian. 2023. "The Future of Economic Statistics." Speech to the Royal Society, March 9. https://www.ons.gov.uk/news/news/thefutureofeconomicstatisticsaspeechbysiriandiamondnationalstatisticiantotheroyalsociety9march2023.

Eurostat. 2009. "The Environmental Goods and Services Sector." https://ec.europa.eu/eurostat/documents/3859598/5910217/KS-RA-09-012-EN.PDF.

Executive Office of the President (EOP). 2023. *Multi-Agency Research and Development Priorities for the FY 2025 Budget*. Washington, DC: The White House. https://www.whitehouse.gov/wp-content/uploads/2023/08/M-23-20.pdf.

Fixler, Dennis, Julie L. Hass, Tina Highfill, Kelly Wentland, and Scott Wentland. "Accounting for Environmental Activity: Measuring Public Environmental Expenditures and the Environmental Goods and Services Sector in the United States." In *Measuring and Accounting for Environmental Public Goods: A National Accounts Perspective*, edited by Mary Bohman, Eli Fenichel, and Nicholas Z. Muller. Chicago, IL: University of Chicago Press. This volume.

Krutilla, John V. 1967. "Conservation Reconsidered." *American Economic Review* 57 (4): 777–86.

Nestor, D., and C. Pasurka. 1995a. "Alternative Specifications for Environmental Control Costs in a General Equilibrium Framework." *Economics Letters* 48 (3–4): 273–80.

Nestor, D., and C. Pasurka. 1995b. "Environment-Economic Accounting and Indicators of the Economic Importance of Environmental Protection Activities." *Review of Income and Wealth* 41 (3): 265–87.

OSTP, OMB, and DOC. 2023. *National Strategy to Develop Statistics For Environmental-Economic Decisions: A U.S. System of Natural Capital Accounting and Associated Environmental-Economic Statistics*. Edited by the Office of Science and Technology Policy, Office of Management and Budget, and Department of Commerce. Washington, DC: The White House.

Pasurka, C., and A. Steurer. 1995. "Assessing the Environmental Industry Integration of Demand and Supply Side Data." *Meeting of the OECD Informal Working Group on the Environmental Industry*. OECD.

7

Natural Capital Accounting on Forested Lands in the United States
An Application to the Colorado River Basin

Travis Warziniack, Ken Bagstad, Michael Knowles, Christopher Mihiar, Arpita Nehra, Charles Rhodes, Leslie Sanchez, Christopher Sichko, and Charles B. Sims

7.1 Introduction

In January 2023, the US government released a strategy to develop natural capital accounts for the nation (hereafter, the national strategy).[1] The national strategy outlines a 15-year plan to move from experimental and pilot accounts to what are called production-grade statistics. The timeline is intentionally long, recognizing that the methods and data for doing so still need to be developed for many natural resources. With a focus on the Colorado River Basin, this study initiates the development of natural capital accounts for forested lands in the United States that are suitable for forward-looking economic analysis and examines gaps in data, information, and science that might be needed for forest accounts in the United States.

To the extent feasible, the United States will follow standards in the

Travis Warziniack is a research economist with the USDA Forest Service.
Ken Bagstad is a research economist with the US Geological Survey.
Michael Knowles has retired as an ecologist with the USDA Forest Service.
Christopher Mihiar is a research economist with the USDA Forest Service.
Arpita Nehra is a postdoctoral researcher in the Forestry and Environmental Resources Department at North Carolina State University.
Charles Rhodes was an economist with the US Geological Survey when this chapter was written.
Leslie Sanchez is a research economist with the USDA Forest Service.
Christopher Sichko is a research agricultural economist with the Economic Research Service of the US Department of Agriculture.
Charles B. Sims is an associate professor of economics at the University of Tennessee, Knoxville.

1. "National Strategy to Develop Statistics for Environmental-Economic Decisions: A U.S. System of Natural Capital Accounting and Associated Environmental-Economic Statistics." Office of Science and Technology Policy, Office of Management and Budget, Department of Commerce, January 2023. https://www.whitehouse.gov/wp-content/uploads/2023/01/Natural-Capital-Accounting-Strategy-final.pdf.

United Nations System of Environmental-Economic Accounting (SEEA), which is the accepted international standard for environmental-economic accounting (United Nations et al. 2014; United Nations Statistical Commission 2021). SEEA formalizes relationships between natural capital and human economic benefits and provides a means to map, quantify, and value them. The SEEA approach is primarily characterized by the quantification of stocks of environmental or ecosystem assets,[2] changes in assets, and flows from these assets that benefit humanity—echoing the same stocks-and-flows design in national economic accounts.

Forest accounts in the national strategy are to be developed as Phase 2 statistics, meaning that the methodology is still being refined and validated and that the statistics are likely to rely on results from Phase 1 accounts (air emissions, land, marine, and water). Currently, only some of the benefits of forests fit into economic accounting methodologies such as Gross Domestic Product (GDP). These benefits are typically private; statistics on timber output and forest sector employment, for example, are readily available. Other benefits from forests—usually public benefits, such as clean drinking water and carbon storage, which are shared by society—do not fit into historic accounting methods but are nonetheless important for human and ecosystem health and well-being. In some cases, existing data allow forest account development including those related to forest extent and condition. In others, ecosystem service values cannot be calculated effectively due to data and methodological limitations.

Our goal is to create the first set of natural capital accounts for forests and demonstrate how they can interact with economic models to capture the integrated ecological processes that constitute a forest and the ecosystem services they provide. Existing research on the benefits of forests tends to focus on single ecosystem services (IPBES 2019; Muttaqin et al. 2019; Ojea et al. 2012; Pereira et al. 2018; Wang and Fu 2013) without considering interactions within the forest system. Failing to account for the joint production of ecosystem services in a forest and the links between ecological and economic systems overlooks the potential for ecosystem externalities and can lead to inaccurate measurements of economic value (Apriesnig et al. 2022; Crocker and Tschirhart 1992). We address these limitations by integrating a general equilibrium economic model with a set of ecological production functions estimated from data to examine jointly produced ecosystem services from forests in the United States. Computable general equilibrium (CGE) models require specific representations of economies, and in this case, interactions with the natural world. CGE models can offer forward-looking analyses of changes in natural capital by accounting for changes in local and national markets due to changes in the natural system. Specifically, we model market-

2. Following SEEA definitions, environmental assets, ecosystem assets, and ecosystem services are defined in the Data and Methods sections below.

based environmental services (timber) and nonmarket ecosystem services (NMES) (water purification and carbon storage).

This work builds on previous efforts to model the relationships among market services, NMES, and joint production technologies, in which NMES enhance the provision of market commodities (Fisher et al. 2009; Kragt and Robertson 2014; Nalle et al. 2004; Sims et al. 2014). Such studies use an ecological-economic production possibilities frontier, which shows trade-offs and complementarities between market goods and NMES and between different NMES (Bekele et al. 2013; J. Cavender-Bares et al. 2015; Polasky et al. 2005; White et al. 2012). Private firms therefore have some incentive to provide NMES that support their supply chain even though the market assigns no direct value to them (Wossink and Swinton 2007), either through direct provision of NMES or by supporting policies that provide NMES on public lands (Kragt and Robertson 2014; Kroeger and Casey 2007; Swinton et al. 2007). Because NMES outside of a firm's supply chain are likely to be ignored by that firm and thus be underprovided, ignoring complementarities between production technologies and economy-wide benefits leads to the under-provision of NMES.

This work also builds on the work incorporating ecosystem services in general equilibrium models. Das et al. (2005) used a multiregional CGE model to show how reducing timber production in the US Pacific Northwest can impact other timber production regions of the country, particularly the southern United States. The Forest and Agricultural Sector Optimization Model (FASOM) is a national model of the US timber industry used to measure the potential impacts of carbon policies (Adams 1996; Alig et al. 2002). More recent work has integrated ecological production relationships to allow for an analysis of a broader range of ecosystem services (Allan et al. 2019; Banerjee et al. 2020; Jendrzejewski 2020; Ochuodho and Alavalapati 2016; Warziniack et al. 2011; 2014; 2017). These models show that the value of the ecosystem service depends on the availability of other factors of production and whether those factors are substitutes or complements to the ecosystem service (Warziniack et al. 2011).

7.1.1 Study Area

We develop methods that are applicable to forests throughout the United States and operationalize them with a case study of the Upper Colorado River Basin (UCRB). The Colorado River and its tributaries provide water to a semi-arid region that includes seven southwestern US states and portions of northern Mexico. The river basin is a complex network that covers an area of 243,000 square miles, spanning 1,450 miles from the Rocky Mountains to the Gulf of California (figure 7.1). The water of the Colorado River reaches 30 million people, including the people of Denver, Las Vegas, Los Angeles, and Phoenix. The basin is divided into the Upper and Lower Colorado River Basin at Lee's Ferry in northern Arizona. The UCRB

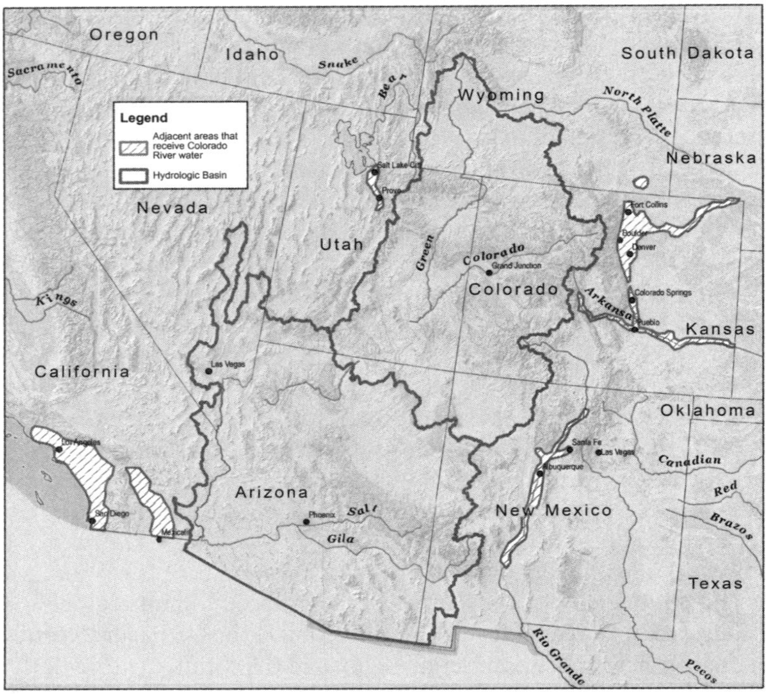

Figure 7.1 Map of the Colorado River Basin

encompasses parts of Colorado, Utah, Wyoming, and areas of northern Arizona and New Mexico. The Lower Colorado River Basin includes the remainder of Arizona and parts of southern California and Nevada.

The Colorado River is significant for both the number of people reliant on it for drinking water and because the region faces some of the worst water shortages in the United States (Heidari et al. 2021). Initial studies of the river's flows put annual river capacity between 15 and 17.5 million acre-feet (MAF), and early allocations of water rights required the Upper Basin states to deliver no less than 75 MAF for any period of 10 consecutive years to the Lower Basin states. More recent estimates put the average annual flow of the Colorado River at Lee's Ferry closer to 12.3 MAF, with recent drought years being much lower. In 2023, basin states agreed on a 13 percent reduction in water use through 2026 in an attempt to avert serious disaster.

Our model measures the impact of land use change on timber production, drinking water provision, and carbon storage—ecosystem services that one might assume *a priori* to drive much of the story for the region—across a broad set of tree species. The biggest driver of decreased forestland is expansion of developed land, and land use change in the UCRB is projected to be low compared to other US regions due to the limited number of urban centers in the area and the ownership distribution. Our results show that loss of carbon stored in forests is the greatest impact from projected land use change, but damage is mitigated by extensive public management in the case study region. Furthermore, most forest reductions occur outside of municipal source watersheds resulting in limited impacts to drinking water provision—highlighting the spatial link between water intakes and forests. Lastly, timber market activity impacts are low in the UCRB which may be attributed to the low merchantable quality of timber that limits market activity in the UCRB. Although the magnitude of our estimated impacts are low in this region, our approach demonstrates the value of environmental-economic accounting by elucidating the trade-offs relevant to a regional context, revealing the pivotal role of land ownership and market activity on natural capital accounting.

A key takeaway of our results is that the value of forest natural capital is likely to vary substantially across the country, and for some types of ecosystem services, those values, or the threats to them, may be relatively small. Our study area contains large amounts of federal land that is both protected from development pressure and the dominant source of drinking water (Liu et al. 2021). While our estimated timber market impacts are closely tied to the size of the regional timber industry, our drinking water results point to the value of the region's public lands in protecting drinking water sources from the threat of development.

This paper proceeds as follows: Section 7.2 describes the data and gives an overview of the methods, with additional detail included in the appendices. Section 7.3 presents the results for the forest extent accounts, estimates of forest carbon, and impacts of land use on ecosystem services from forests. Section 7.4 discusses the results in the context of the broader literature. Section 7.5 concludes.

7.2 Data and Methods

Herein, we create pilot natural capital accounts for forests in the United States, operationalized around a case study for the Upper Colorado River Basin (UCRB). We create two types of accounts: (1) asset accounts for timberland; and (2) service accounts for timber harvest, water purification, and carbon storage. We demonstrate the usefulness of these natural capital accounts for impact and policy analysis by examining the effects of land use change on the regional economy and forest ecosystem services. We create forest extent accounts using US Forest Service Forest Inventory Analysis (FIA) Program data (USFS 2021). We then examine the impacts of land use change based on projections from the US Environmental Protection Agency's (EPA) Integrated Climate and Land-Use Scenarios (ICLUS) (US EPA 2017) to drive impacts in a computable general equilibrium model.

This section describes the main data and modeling methods. Additional methods underlying the forest asset accounts and computable general equi-

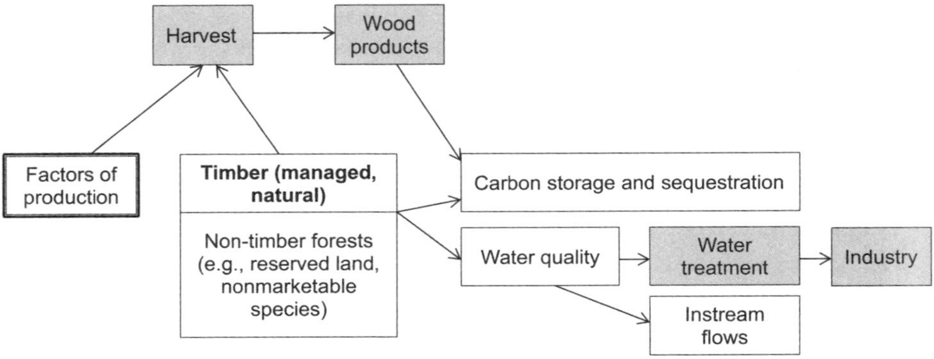

Figure 7.2 Conceptual model of ecosystem services in general equilibrium. Changes in the area of forests managed for timber reduce the supply of forested land available for harvest. This loss impacts downstream industries, such as the wood products industry. The model also includes changes to water quality, water treatment costs, and carbon storage. Linkages are included between economic and ecological systems in the computable general equilibrium model used to measure economic impacts.

librium (CGE) model are in appendix A. Figure 7.2 provides a conceptual overview of our approach where the dark boxes represent marketed goods and services, and the light boxes indicate nonmarket ecosystem services. Forest resources (timber and non-timber forests) produce nonmarket products like carbon storage and water quality and are combined with factors of production (e.g., capital and labor) to produce marketed products like timber. Water quality affects downstream economic activity such as the cost of water treatment and its suitability for industrial water use. Increased costs for water treatment and similar indirect uses of forest benefits can be viewed as ecosystem externalities—forest loss impacts water usage via hydrologic processes internal to the ecosystem but external to the economy. In other words, the ecosystem externality implies that forest accounts are incomplete (they are missing service accounts) and are therefore undervalued.

7.2.1 Asset Accounts for Forest Extent

Data for forest extent and condition are available from the US Forest Service's Forest Inventory and Analysis (FIA) program. FIA maintains the largest continuous body of forest inventory data in the world, including data on forest type, ownership, forest health, and forest condition. These data are the basis for land management, policy decision-making, and national assessments that evaluate the current and future conditions of US forests and grasslands, including greenhouse gas reporting.

For this study, we begin with estimates for timberland area (yellow box in figure 7.2) aggregated for each state in the conterminous United States from the FIA database and grouped by forest type, then focus on the UCRB to

Table 7.1 **Extent of timberland in the conterminous United States by forest type group (in 1000s of acres)**

Forest Type Group	2017	2018	2019	2020	2021	2017–2021 (% Δ)
Alder/Maple	2,639.0	2,637.6	2,641.1	2,641.1	2,641.1	0.1%
Aspen/Birch	20,797.9	20,727.5	20,647.8	20,634.6	20,707.8	−0.4%
California Mixed Conifer	6,293.6	6,274.9	6,268.6	6,268.6	6,268.6	−0.4%
Douglas-Fir	34,723.0	34,773.9	34,730.4	34,730.4	34,730.4	0.0%
Elm/Ash/Cottonwood	24,129.2	24,004.3	23,135.3	23,198.0	23,055.2	−4.5%
Exotic Hardwoods	1,313.0	1,341.9	1,324.1	1,337.9	1,342.8	2.3%
Exotic Softwoods	603.3	579.0	602.7	599.0	605.4	0.3%
Fir/Spruce/Mtn. Hemlock	21,836.8	21,748.5	21,646.4	21,646.4	21,646.4	−0.9%
Hemlock/Sitka spruce	4,205.9	4,213.2	4,219.3	4,219.3	4,219.3	0.3%
Loblolly/Shortleaf Pine	61,345.9	61,551.1	61,814.3	62,082.9	61,052.5	−0.5%
Lodgepole pine	9,388.9	9,280.3	9,315.9	9,315.9	9,315.9	−0.8%
Longleaf/Slash Pine	12,387.8	12,307.2	12,194.4	12,229.8	12,225.9	−1.3%
Maple/Beech/Birch	43,497.6	43,321.0	43,225.9	43,231.9	43,191.8	−0.7%
Non-Stocked	9,814.8	9,909.2	10,043.7	10,005.1	9,945.5	1.3%
Oak/Gum/Cypress	23,072.1	23,051.7	22,972.7	22,922.3	22,554.9	−2.2%
Oak/Hickory	136,224.3	135,698.2	134,403.8	134,088.7	132,443.7	−2.8%
Oak/Pine	26,707.9	26,342.1	26,055.0	26,046.1	25,672.2	−3.9%
Other Eastern Softwoods	2,127.2	2,157.5	2,119.2	2,093.3	2,044.9	−3.9%
Other Hardwoods	3,205.7	3,265.9	3,309.5	3,369.0	3,367.4	5.0%
Other Softwoods	1.0	1.0	0.8	0.8	0.8	−19.6%
Other Western Softwoods	1,700.7	1,687.0	1,701.3	1,701.3	1,701.3	0.0%
Pinyon/Juniper	115.3	109.6	109.1	117.1	113.8	−1.3%
Ponderosa Pine	21,286.5	21,164.8	21,240.3	21,251.3	21,251.3	−0.2%
Redwood	679.5	678.7	689.4	689.4	689.4	1.5%
Spruce/Fir	14,290.6	14,315.4	14,374.6	14,376.3	14,313.5	0.2%
Tanoak/Laurel	1,682.6	1,678.4	1,660.1	1,660.1	1,660.1	−1.3%
Tropical Hardwoods	367.1	370.2	371.3	371.3	371.3	1.1%
Western Larch	1,597.1	1,629.9	1,636.3	1,636.3	1,636.3	2.5%
Western Oak	2,422.5	2,372.9	2,404.1	2,404.1	2,404.1	−0.8%
Western White Pine	102.7	108.1	105.3	105.3	105.3	2.5%
White/Red/Jack Pine	9,238.9	9,284.9	9,346.7	9,342.8	9,351.7	1.2%
Woodland Hardwoods	73.7	71.1	40.4	40.4	40.4	−45.1%
Total Timberland Area	497,871.9	496,656.9	494,350.0	494,357.0	490,671.3	−1.4%

demonstrate a method for integrating a forest extent asset account with a CGE model of the economy. Timberland is defined as accessible and non-reserved forestland with potential growth of at least 20 cubic feet/acre/year. The FIA began annual inventories in the early 2000s; however, inventory periods vary by state. Annual inventories for the Pacific states, including California, which is heavily dependent on Colorado River Basin water, did not begin publishing annual inventories until 2017, hence the choice of 2017 as the first year in table 7.1.

7.2.2 Service Accounts for Carbon Storage and Water Purification

The FIA's Big Data, Mapping, and Analytics Platform (BIGMAP) raster layers were utilized for carbon storage estimates and forest extent for the year 2018 by forest-type group (USFS 2021). International reporting through the US National Greenhouse Gas Inventory also relies on FIA's carbon estimates, and these data will play a vital role in future development of forest-related natural capital accounts in the United States. BIGMAP includes carbon pools for live biomass, dead biomass, and organic biomass in soils at 30 m spatial resolution. Here, we focus on impacts on the live biomass pool, though impacts occur in other pools as well. Therefore, our estimates should be viewed as conservative.

Water provision estimates are based on drinking water intake data from the US Environmental Protection Agency's Safe Drinking Water Information System (SDWIS) (US EPA 2017) and spatially joined to watersheds in the conterminous United States (CONUS) using fourth-level hydrological unit codes (HUC) in the National Hydrography Dataset (US Geological Survey 2016). The SDWIS database includes information on intake location, type of water source, and the population served by the intake. Intakes were filtered to create a subset that serves community water systems and that uses surface water. Of the 5,375 intakes within the study area boundaries, 22.8 percent (1,303 intakes) are in forests.[3]

7.2.3 Changes in Accounts Due to Land Use Change

We employ land use projections from the US Environmental Protection Agency's Integrated Climate and Land-Use Scenarios (ICLUS) project for the period between 2020 and 2100 (US EPA 2017). ICLUS's spatially explicit projections of land use and population are based on Intergovernmental Panel on Climate Change (IPCC) scenarios and pathways, of which we use Relative Concentration Pathway (RCP) 8.5, Shared Socioeconomic Pathway (SSP) SSP5, and the HADGEM2_ES general circulation climate model.

ICLUS baseline data are layered with the 2018 Forest Inventory Analysis BIGMAP data to form the reference which is summarized by forest extent and total carbon stored in each UCRB state for the year 2018 by forest type group. ICLUS projection rasters are then applied to each BIGMAP layer to calculate the change in forest area and carbon storage due to new land development on land that was forested in 2018.

7.2.4 Integrating Natural Capital Accounts with the Economic Model

Natural capital accounts are integrated into the economic analysis through a CGE model following Warziniack (2014) and described in more detail in

3. Forested lands are derived from 2019 NLCD data and defined as deciduous forest (NLCD category 41), evergreen forest (NLCD category 42), and mixed forest (NLCD category 43).

appendix A. We consider six production sectors: (1) forestry and logging; (2) wood products manufacturing; (3) agriculture; (4) power generation; (5) water treatment; and (6) a catchall miscellaneous sector for all other goods. The model is extended to include the impacts of changes in forest cover from ICLUS projections and impacts on carbon storage and drinking water costs from forest loss in those projections. The foundation for a CGE model is a social accounting matrix (SAM). The SAM shows the flow of expenditures from industry to industry in the production process, payments to factors of production, household expenditures, and government activities.

Ideally, the SAM would include the value of nature that goes into the production process, but SAM and CGE models with fully integrated ecosystem services are rare, as one would have to calibrate a snapshot of the economy with values of nature in the production process and returns from nature to households. In the case of forests, nascent research calculates the value of land in the production of timber, using either the allocated land value (ALV) or bare land value (BLV) (Harris et al. 2018). Following this approach, we assume the ALV is included in the value of capital stock in the forestry sector and create a separate factor of production for timberland.

It may be that natural resources are not directly used by firms, but rather are complementary to the production process. As is the case for drinking water, improvements in environmental quality serve not to increase output but to decrease costs. Impacts to drinking water costs are included through impacts from land use change on sediment and turbidity in rivers, streams, and reservoirs with drinking water intakes. We assume the percentage of a watershed that is forested is inversely proportional to water treatment costs following Warziniack et al. (2017) such that a 1 percent decrease in the baseline forest cover increases the amount of sediment in the watershed's streams and reservoirs by 3 percent, and every 1 percent increase in turbidity increases the costs of treating drinking water by 0.19 percent. These costs are modeled through a multiplicative impact factor $\Delta_k = [1 - (f_k / f_{k0})]\varphi$, where f_{k0} and f_k are the initial and final forest covers in watershed k, and φ is a parameter measuring the percent increase in treatment costs due to reductions in forest cover, set equal to 0.57 (3 × 0.19).

The primary impacts on carbon storage from land use change are captured directly by the loss of forests projected by ICLUS and the carbon stored in that forest. Land transitioning out of forests goes into a developed use, and we assume the stock of carbon from those trees is lost forever. Secondary impacts are captured in the CGE model through the land market, in which loss of timberland raises the costs of forestry and logging, which increases costs to the wood products industry. Janowiak et al. (2017) estimate that more than 2,600 million metric tons of carbon were stored in harvested wood products in 2015, and Christensen et al. (2021) estimate that harvested wood products from California forests alone sequestered 0.8 MMT CO_2e per year, accounting for $1.4 billion in total sales. Based on the California data, we assume carbon fluxes from wood products are on average 6 kg per dollar of output. For a detailed treatment of carbon stored in wood products, see Baker et al. (2023).

Economic data in the SAM is based on a benchmark 2012 data set from IMPLAN (IMPLAN 2012) for all counties in the UCRB. The industry sectors were aggregated from IMPLAN's 440 sectors to 6: (i) forestry and logging; (ii) wood products manufacturing; (iii) agriculture; (iv) power generation; (v) water treatment; and (vi) miscellaneous. We collapse IMPLAN households into one representative household. The federal government's interactions in the model were kept distinct while city, county, and state governments were aggregated into a single state and local government agent. Given the importance of trade flows into and out of the region, foreign trade and domestic trade were modeled separately. IMPLAN's employee compensation account was used to construct the labor account. Capital was found as the summation of proprietary income and other property income. Final balancing was done by minimizing least squares differences between regional supplies and demands.

Elasticities of substitution in CGE models have a strong effect on measuring economic impacts. Armington elasticities that determine the ability to substitute locally produced goods with imports are especially interesting in the context of natural resources for two reasons. First, benefits from ecosystem services tend to be very local, with little substitution from other regions. Drinking water provision, at least on the scale of large basins, has limited substitution possibilities with other domestic sources and virtually no substitute possibilities with international sources. Similarly, forest products, due to their bulk and importance in local supply chains, are also mostly processed within the region of harvest. Second, it is likely that impacts on natural resources affecting one region are affecting other regions that might serve as substitutes. Here, the driving force behind the economic analysis was the conversion of forested land to development. Conversion of forests is occurring throughout the United States, particularly in the southern United States where much of the US timber production is located. If similar impacts are occurring among trade partners, substitution possibilities might be limited. We examine sensitivity to changes in Armington elasticities by varying their value from 3.2 (the median value found in a review of the literature by Feenstra et al. 2018), to half that value (1.6) for the forest products and water sectors.

7.3 Results

Carbon stocks and suitability of timber depend on forest type, the distribution of which is shown in figure 7.3 across the UCRB. Table 7.2 shows the beginning stocks in forests and forest carbon in 2018 and projected changes by 2100. A more detailed summary of US timberland area for 2017–2021

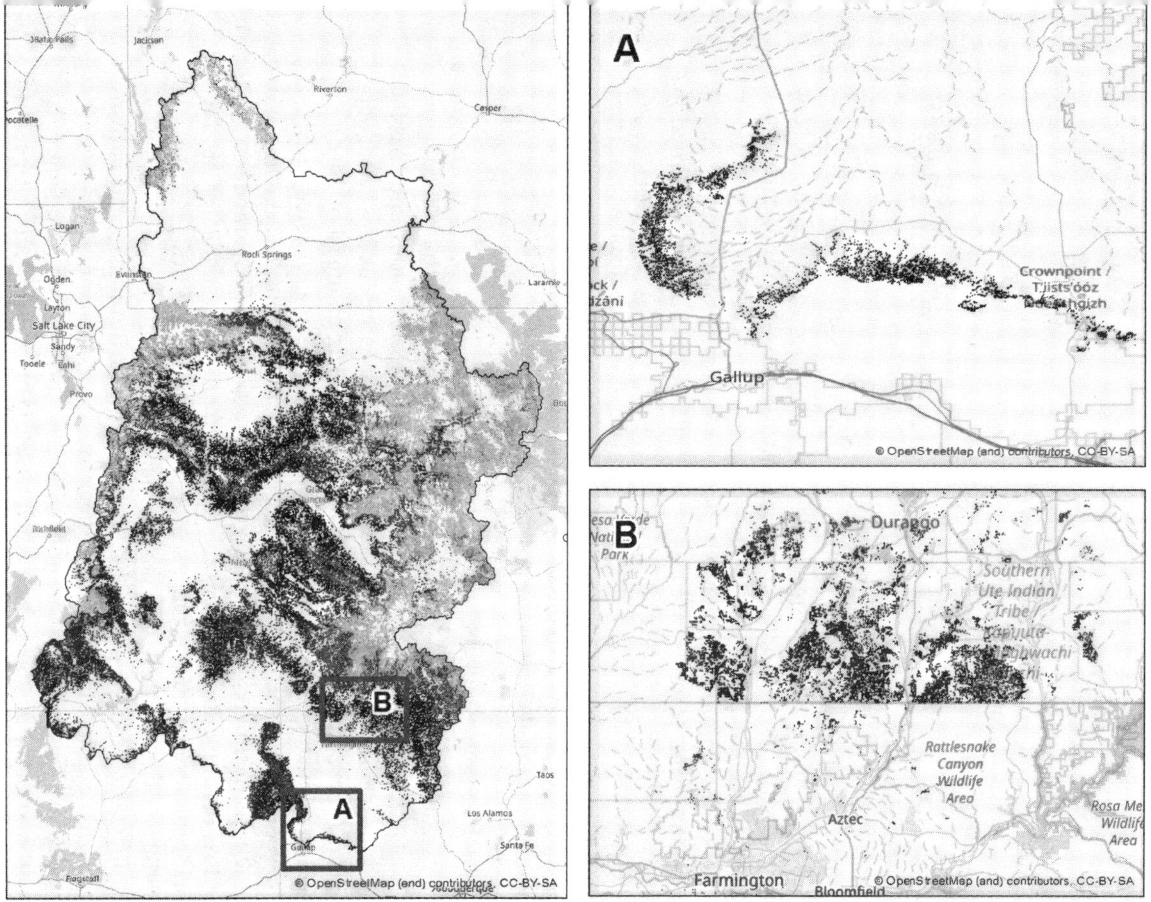

Figure 7.3 Forest type distribution in the Upper Colorado River Basin (UCRB). The left panel shows forestland extent by forest type group distributed across the UCRB. Panel A is the area of forestland lost to development by 2100 resulting from growth out of Gallup, NM. Panel B shows the area of forestland loss projected to occur south of Durango, CO, and north of Farmington, NM.

Table 7.2 **Forest extent, carbon stocks, and projected changes for the Upper Colorado River Basin**

State	Forests		Forest carbon	
	Extent 2018 (acres)	Change 2100 (acres)	Carbon 2018 (tons)	Change 2100 (tons)
Colorado	34,007,386	−46,789	254,026,421	−240,632
New Mexico	17,913,072	−215,788	146,344,068	−762,794
Utah	24,988,973	−48,377	117,383,671	−184,003
Wyoming	15,941,418	−16,556	122,788,823	−100,928
Total	**92,850,849**	**−327,510**	**640,542,983**	**−1,288,357**

is presented in appendix B. The dominant forest types in the UCRB region are pinyon juniper and fir-spruce. The largest projected losses are in New Mexico, with almost 216,000 acres of forest and 763,000 tons of carbon lost between 2018 and 2100.

Across the region, there is an expected loss of over 327,500 acres of forests to development, leading to a loss of 1.3 million tons of carbon stored in forests. We allocated forest and carbon loss evenly across the analysis period, such that about 4,000 acres of forest and 15,700 tons of carbon storage are lost each year. To put the annual loss in perspective, the lost carbon is equivalent to the average emissions of 3,400 passenger cars per year (based on an average of 4.6 metric tons per car) (EPA 2023).

7.3.1 Economic Impacts

Development-driven forest loss implies economic growth for the region, at least as growth is traditionally defined ignoring externalities, and possible short-term gains for the forest industry as those trees are cut down. Impacts measured here are the losses associated with land use change, both in direct effects to industry sectors like timber and indirect effects associated with loss of carbon storage and declines in water quality. Projections of forest loss and reductions in timberland have two direct effects in the CGE model. First, the loss of timberland reduces the amount of forest available for production in the forestry and logging sector. Second, loss of forests changes the condition of the region's watersheds, increasing sediment in the waterways and increasing the cost of treating drinking water. Both losses have downstream impacts, most obviously in the wood products manufacturing sector by reducing logs available for inputs, but also through broadscale impacts on all users who face increased water prices. The present value of general equilibrium impacts is calculated using a 2.25 percent discount rate, the US government rate for discounting water and land projects (Federal Register 2022).

Table 7.3 **Present value of economic impacts of forest loss in the Upper Colorado River Basin**

Type of impact	Armington elasticity 3.2	Armington elasticity 1.6
Reductions in timberland	$1.13 million	$2.15 million
Impacts to water treatment costs	$80,000	$90,000
Carbon from forest loss	$28 million	$28 million
Total impact	**$29.21 million**	**$30.24 million**

The total economic impact from 327,500 acres of forests (about 0.4 percent loss in timberland) in the UCRB, as measured by the CGE model, has a present value of $2.24 million using an Armington elasticity of 1.6, indicative of fewer substitution possibilities. This loss includes $2.15 million associated with reductions in timberland and $90,000 from impacts to water treatment costs (table 7.3). The wood products industry sees an annual decrease of $2 million by 2100, compared to a total sector output of $183 million. The forestry and wood products sectors together contribute only 1 percent of total output to the regional economy, so that even with some highly local impacts, capital and labor are readily employed by other sectors, resulting in minor general equilibrium impacts to the prices of factors and goods.

Table 7.3 shows the sensitivity of impacts to substitution elasticities. The relatively localized nature of the forest sector leads to larger economic losses than would occur if the economy was more integrated with other regions. Allowing more substitution with supplies outside of the region (increasing the Armington elasticity to 3.2) decreases economic losses by $1.03 million. There are no good estimates in the literature of what such elasticities should be for ecosystem services, though these results show their importance and a need for future work.

Economic impacts on carbon occur outside the CGE model based on the ICLUS projections and are thus additive to the damages discussed above. We use the interim value of $51 per metric ton of CO_2 from the Interagency Working Group on Social Cost of Greenhouse Gases.[4] If forest loss occurs at roughly equal rates between years, the present value of the lost carbon between 2020 and 2100 equals $28 million. Secondary impacts from lost carbon stored in wood products are negligible by comparison. Model esti-

4. "Technical Support Document: Social Cost of Carbon, Methane, and Nitrous Oxide: Interim Estimates under Executive Order 13990," Interagency Working Group on Social Cost of Greenhouse Gases, United States Government, February 2021, https://www.whitehouse.gov/wp-content/uploads/2021/02/TechnicalSupportDocument_SocialCostofCarbonMethaneNitrousOxide.pdf.

mates show a $94,000 decrease in the wood products industry. At 6 kg per dollar, that amounts to a reduction in carbon stored in wood products of 564 kg of carbon.[5]

The timing of damages and role of discounting has considerable effects on the above damage estimates. If the 327,500 acres of forest loss were to occur within a single year, the undiscounted economic damages would be roughly $127,000 owing to the relatively small size of the forest and wood products sectors in the regional economy. Carbon impacts would be much larger, where a decrease of 1.3 million tons of carbon stored in forests results in an undiscounted value of $76.5 million.

7.4 Discussion

Our results demonstrate how a set of natural capital accounts can interact with economic models. However, they rely on several assumptions about substitution possibilities between goods, among factors of production, and between the natural and built environments. Many of these factors are well studied in the literature. Values for land have been an active area of research for a long time (North and Thomas 1973). Other ecosystem service values, ranging from the ability of forests to provide recreation and purify the air, to more complex interactions between forest health, fire risk, and air pollution impacts from wildfire, are noticeably missing from this analysis—more complicated models could certainly be built. The advantage of CGE models is that they prompt discussion about what has been left out of the model as much as what has been included.

Questions arise about the generalizability of such models and how they work together with bottom-up models like those proposed by Fenichel et al. (2016) and Warnell et al. (2020). Aggregated models, such as CGE models, are designed to examine large impacts on large economic systems. Defining features of CGE models include substitution possibilities and changes in prices. When changes in the natural system cause significant changes in local and national markets, CGE models can offer a forward-looking analysis of changes in natural capital and the impacts of actions that preserve natural capital. Spatial and sectoral economic data, however, are often limited, necessitating the use of county-level economic data for aggregated economic sectors. These might not be appropriate assumptions for many natural resources. The impact of forest loss to water treatment, for example, is a highly localized problem, affecting a particular water system serving a limited population in a market with regulated prices. New York City's Catskill water collection system, perhaps the most popular example linking forests to drinking water, spent about $1.4 billion in land acquisitions and pollution reductions in the upstream watershed that ultimately saved the city

5. $\$94{,}000 * (6\text{kg}/1\$) = 564$ kg carbon.

from needing a $6 billion treatment facility (Grolleau and McCann 2012). With a customer base of roughly 9 million people, that amounts to a $500 savings per customer over the life of the project—real savings, but not likely to have a significant impact on regional wages. In such cases, the use of local partial equilibrium studies might be more appropriate.

Our results, while primarily for demonstration purposes, are in line with the rest of the literature examining ecosystem services from forests. Cavender-Bares et al. (2022) examine nonmarket values from trees throughout the United States. They find the value associated with air pollution removal and carbon storage far exceeds the value derived from wood products. The reality of these values is already playing out in land markets throughout the country. In November 2022, Oak Hill Advisors and partners paid $1.8 billion for 1.7 million acres of forest as an investment in future carbon offset markets from forests (Dezember 2022). Such direct investments by firms and through Real Estate Investment Trusts (REITs) are becoming more common.

7.5 Conclusion

The effects of deforestation are widespread, ranging from direct changes on the forest industry, to indirect impacts on water treatment, to costs associated with decreased carbon stocks. Among the impacts in our case study, we find the largest to be from lost carbon, overwhelming all other impacts. Given the relatively small size of the forestry sector in the region and the large amount of public land in the region, small economic impacts associated with timber production and drinking water provision are perhaps not surprising. Over a third of Colorado is in federally preserved lands, and those lands are the source of 80 percent of Colorado residents' drinking water, for example.[6] The largest amount of development in the study area is projected to happen on grazing land, not on forests. The small size of the impacts on the timber industry speaks to the small size of the regional forestry sector, but the small size of the impacts on drinking water speaks to the large value of the region's public lands on decreasing threats of deforestation in source watersheds.

Forests in the United States involve a complicated mix of private investments in public land and public benefits from private land. Among the 310 million hectares of US forests, 41 percent are publicly owned, with the federal government being the largest public owner (31 percent) (Oswalt et al. 2019). The percentage of public ownership varies throughout the country. At the upper end, roughly 75 percent of forests in parts of the Rocky Mountain region[7] are publicly owned. At the lower end, roughly 20 percent of

6. According to the Colorado Department of Public Health and Environment, (accessed 12/12/2023). https://www.cohealthmaps.dphe.state.co.us/cdphe_swap_protection_planning/.
7. Includes AZ, CO, ID, KS, MT, NE, NV, NM, ND, SD, UT, and WY.

forests in the southern United States[8] are publicly owned (Congressional Research Service 2021; Oswalt et al. 2019). The mix of private and public interests and private and public ownership of US forests highlights the need for a better accounting of the benefits and costs of forest management.

Disclaimer: The findings and conclusions in this report are those of the author(s) and should not be construed to represent any official US government determination or policy. This research was supported in part by the US Department of Agriculture and US Geological Survey. Any use of trade, firm, or product names is for descriptive purposes only and does not imply endorsement by the US government.

For acknowledgments, sources of research support, and disclosure of the authors' material financial relationships, if any, please see https://www.nber.org/books-and-chapters/measuring-and-accounting-environmental-public-goods-national-accounts-perspective/natural-capital-accounting-forested-lands-united-states-application-colorado-river-basin.

Appendix A

Computable General Equilibrium Model

Most parameters of the model are found through calibration as in Ballard et al. (1985) and de Melo et al. (1992). The calibration routine sets benchmark input and output prices equal to one (by constant returns to scale and the units of the initial data being in value terms). Using all first-order conditions from profit maximization, cost minimization, utility maximization, and benchmark data and prices, most parameters apart from the elasticities of substitution are found. Estimates of elasticities of substitution are taken from the literature and given in the computer code. The household is assumed to have an elasticity of substitution between consumption goods of 0.9. All general equilibrium calculations were made with the General Algebraic Modeling System (GAMS) software package using the PATH solver.

The model includes several types of goods:

- Import and export goods: Domestically produced goods are exported out of the region, and goods from the same industries are imported. The set of traded goods is the same as the set of domestically produced goods, thus traded goods are also indexed with j. The price received for exports is PE_j; the price paid for imports is PM_j.
- Armington goods: Goods consumed by households and goods used as intermediate inputs by firms are Armington composites (Armington

8. AL, AR, FL, GA, KY, LA, MS, MT, NC, OK, SC, TN, TX, and VA.

1969), which are aggregates of domestically produced and imported goods. No Armington good exists that is not either produced locally or imported, thus Armington goods are also indexed with j. The price paid for Armington composite good j is PX_j.

- Primary factors: Primary factors of production are inputs that are not produced and generally include capital and labor. The set of primary factors of production is indexed $f \in F$, and each factor is paid price PF_j.

The human-produced composite is produced following a standard structure for modeling firms in CGE models. Taxes of type t are paid as a fixed share of output at rate, $atax_{tj}$, such that

$$(1) \qquad TAX_{tj} = atax_{tj} DY_j .$$

After-tax output is produced with intermediate inputs and a value-added composite of primary factors. Let $V_{jj,j}$ be the level of intermediate inputs from firm *jj* to firm *j* and VA_j be the level of value-added composite used by firm *j*. This nest is assumed to be Leontief, such that

$$(2) \qquad V_{jj,j} = aint_{jj,j} DY_j$$

$$(3) \qquad VA_j = ava_j DY_j .$$

The Leontief assumption implies costs, CV_j, can be written

$$(4) \qquad CV_j = \sum_t atax_t CV_j + \sum_{jj} aint_{jj,j} PX_{jj} + ava_j CVA_j .$$

The value-added composite includes capital and labor, combined using a constant elasticity of substitution CES production function $VA_j = \psi_j[\delta_j K_j^{-\rho_j} + (1-\delta_j)L_j^{-\rho_j}]^{-1/\rho_j}$, where $\sigma_j = [1/(1+\rho_j)]$ is the elasticity of substitution between labor and capital and ψ_j is an efficiency parameter. The firm's optimal mix of capital and labor is found by minimizing the unit cost of producing the value-added component,

$$(5) \quad CVA_j(PF_K, PF_L) = min_{K_j,L_j}\{PF_K * K_j + PF_L * L_j : VA_j(K_j, L_j) = VA_j\}.$$

The demand functions for capital and labor are therefore

$$(6) \qquad K_j = VA_j \left(\frac{\delta CVA_j}{PF_K} \right)^{\sigma_j} \psi_j^{\sigma_j - 1}$$

$$(7) \qquad L_j = VA_j \left(\frac{(1-\delta) CVA_j}{PF_L} \right)^{\sigma_j} \psi_j^{\sigma_j - 1}.$$

Using the price index for CES functions, we close this nest by

$$(8) \qquad CVA_j = \frac{1}{\psi_j} \left(\delta_j^{1/(1+\rho_j)} PF_K^{\rho_j/(1+\rho_j)} + (1-\delta_j)^{1/(1+\rho_j)} PF_L^{\rho_j/(1+\rho_j)} \right)^{1+(1/\rho_j)}.$$

Household Behavior

The allocation of expenditures between consumptive goods follows standard CGE procedures. Households choose consumption levels HX_{jh} to minimize the cost of achieving utility level $\underline{C}$. The mathematical expression of this optimization is

$$(9)\quad \text{Min } PX_j HX_{jh} \text{ s.t. Min } PX_j HX_{jh} \text{ s.t. } \underline{C} = C(HX_{1h}, HX_{2h}, \ldots, HX_{Jh}).$$

The first order conditions require

$$(10)\quad \frac{(\partial C / \partial HX_{jh})}{(\partial C / \partial HX_{ih})} = \frac{PX_j}{PX_i}.$$

Appendix B

Timberland Extent by State Based on Forest Inventory Analysis Data

Table 7B.1

Colorado

Forest Type Group	Forest Code	Extent 2018 (acres)	Extent Change 2021 (acres)	Carbon 2018 (tons)	Carbon Loss 2100 (tons)
Other East Soft	170	1	—	5	—
Pinyon Juniper	180	9,858,458	26,110	43,599,681	111,035
Douglas Fir	200	2,916,915	3,068	26,743,792	27,293
Ponderosa	220	2,628,786	4,626	18,722,279	32,158
Fir Spruce Mountain Hemlock	260	8,726,629	2,018	99,914,321	20,740
Lodgepole	280	1,295,146	572	11,418,973	4,936
Other West Soft	360	507	0	2,019	1
Cali, Mixed	370	11	—	68	—
Oak Hickory	500	191	0	867	1
Elm Ash Cottonwood	700	5	—	16	—
Aspen Birch	900	5,487,125	4,960	41,803,802	27,834
Other Hardwoods	960	2	—	8	—
Woodland Hard	970	3,092,859	5,433	11,817,235	16,626
Non-Stocked	999	751	2	3,355	7
Totals		34,007,386	46,789	254,026,421	240,632

Table 7B.2

New Mexico

Forest Type Group	Forest Code	Extent 2018 (acres)	Extent Change 2021 (acres)	Carbon 2018 (tons)	Carbon Loss 2100 (tons)
Pinyon Juniper	180	17,904,731	199,187	69,416,768	619,882
Douglas Fir	200	1,598	2,369	16,724,716	25,270
Ponderosa	220	4,469	6,629	39,050,429	57,220
Fir Spruce Mountain Hemlock	260	896	2,446	11,237,231	28,869
Lodgepole	280	55	195	490,844	1,653
Other West Soft	360	0	0	38	1
Cali, Mixed	370	0	—	4	—
Oak Hickory	500	0	—	1,000	—
Elm Ash Cottonwood	700	0	—	8	—
Aspen Birch	900	625	1,907	5,723,752	14,617
Other Hardwoods	960	0	—	2	—
Woodland Hardwoods	970	689	3,050	3,646,930	15,260
Non-Stocked	999	9	4	52,346	21
Totals		17,913,072	215,788	146,344,068	762,794

Table 7B.3

Utah

Forest Type Group	Forest Code	Extent 2018 (acres)	Extent Change 2021 (acres)	Carbon 2018 (tons)	Carbon Loss 2100 (tons)
Pinyon Juniper	180	16,307,209	33,391	61,806,758	118,508
Douglas Fir	200	901,516	1,433	7,645,063	10,515
Ponderosa	220	341,742	1,706	2,111,948	7,759
Fir Spruce Mountain Hemlock	260	2,306,237	528	20,208,806	4,417
Lodgepole	280	441,652	40	3,907,685	336
Other West Soft	360	20,633	9	97,167	21
Cali, Mixed	370	14	—	101	—
Oak Pine	900	2,187,565	3,244	12,263,124	16,397
oak Hickory	970	2,481,086	8,026	9,335,220	26,046
Non-Stocked	999	1,320	1	7,799	4
Totals		24,988,973	48,377	117,383,671	184,003

Table 7B.4

Wyoming

Forest Type Group	Forest Code	Extent 2018 (acres)	Extent Change 2021 (acres)	Carbon 2018 (tons)	Carbon Loss 2100 (tons)
Spruce Fir	120	229	—	925	—
Other East Soft	170	1	—	1	—
Pinyon Juniper	180	348,969	407	970,795	827
Douglas Fir	200	1,981,580	3,573	15,872,290	26,448
Ponderosa	220	1,819,013	2,943	8,174,900	9,243
Fir Spruce Mountain Hemlock	260	6,069,434	2,961	53,383,951	24,688
Lodgepole	280	4,433,351	3,721	38,215,023	27,508
Other West Soft	360	111,959	155	569,665	1,007
Oak Hickory	500	1,730	24	3,775	26
Elm Ash Cottonwood	700	29	—	57	—
Aspen Birch	900	1,122,241	2,555	5,470,866	10,593
Other Hardwoods	960	14	—	21	—
Woodland Hardwoods	970	48,360	208	114,690	567
Non-Stocked	999	4,508	10	11,865	21
Totals		15,941,418	16,556	122,788,823	100,928

References

Adams, D. M. 1996. The Forest and Agricultural Sector Optimization Model (FASOM): Model Structure and Policy Applications, Vol. 495. US Department of Agriculture, Forest Service, Pacific Northwest Research Station.

Alig, R. J., D. M. Adams, and B. A McCarl. 2002. "Projecting impacts of global climate change on the US forest and agriculture sectors and carbon budgets." *Forest Ecology and Management* 169 (1-2): 3–14.

Allan, G., D. Comerford, K. Connolly, and P. McGregor. 2019. "Incorporating natural capital into A computable general Equilibrium model for Scotland." In *27th International Input-Output Association Conference & 9th Edition of the International School of IO Analysis.*

Apriesnig, J. L., T. W. Warziniack, D. C. Finnoff, H. Zhang, K. D. Lee, D. M. Mason, and E. S. Rutherford. 2022. "The Consequences of Misrepresenting Feedbacks in Coupled Human and Environmental Models." *Ecological Economics* 195: 107355. https://doi.org/10.1016/j.ecolecon.2022.107355.

Armington, P. S. 1969. "The Geographic Pattern of Trade and the Effects of Price Changes." (Structure géographique des échanges et incidences des variations de prix) (Estructura geográfica del comercio y efectos de la variación de los precios). *Staff Papers (International Monetary Fund)* 16 (2): 179–201. https://doi.org/10.2307/3866431.

Baker, J. S., G. Van Houtven, J. Phelan, G. Latta, C. M. Clark, K. G. Austin, O. E. Sodiya, S. B. Ohrel, J. Buckley, L. E. Gentile, and J. Martinich. 2023. "Projecting US Forest Management, Market, and Carbon Sequestration Responses to a High-Impact Climate Scenario." *Forest Policy and Economics* 147: 102898.

Ballard, C. L., J. B. Shoven, and J. Whalley. 1985. "General Equilibrium Computations of the Marginal Welfare Costs of Taxes in the United States." *American Economic Review* 75 (1): 128–38.

Banerjee, O., K. J. Bagstad, M. Cicowiez, S. Dudek, M. Horridge, J. R. Alavalapati, et al. 2020. "Economic, land use, and ecosystem services impacts of Rwanda's Green Growth Strategy: An application of the IEEM+ ESM platform." *Science of The Total Environment* 729: 138779.

Bekele, E. G., C. L. Lant, S. Soman, and G. Misgna. 2013. "The Evolution and Empirical Estimation of Ecological-Economic Production Possibilities Frontiers." *Ecological Economics* 90 (1–9).

Cavender-Bares, J., S. Polasky, E. King, and P. Balvanera. 2015. "A Sustainability Framework for Assessing Trade-Offs in Ecosystem Services." *Ecology and Society* 20 (1).

Cavender-Bares, J. M., E. Nelson, J. E. Meireles, J. R. Lasky, D. A. Miteva, D. J. Nowak, W. D. Pearse, M. R. Helmus, A. E. Zanne, W. F. Fagan, C. Mihiar, N. Z. Muller, N. J. B. Kraft, and S. Polasky. 2022. "The Hidden Value of Trees: Quantifying the Ecosystem Services of Tree Lineages and Their Major Threats across the Contiguous US." *PLOS Sustainability and Transformation* 1 (4): e0000010. https://doi.org/10.1371/journal.pstr.0000010.

Christensen, G. A., A. N. Gray, O. Kuegler, N. A. Tase, and J. Groom. 2021. *AB 1504 California Forest Ecosystem and Harvested Wood Product Carbon Inventory: 2019 Reporting Period*. U.S. Department of Agriculture, Pacific Northwest Research Station; California Department of Forestry and Fire Protection, Fire and Resources Assessment Program; Groom Analytics, LLC.

Congressional Research Service. 2021. *U.S. Forest Ownership and Management*. Washington, DC: Congressional Research Service. https://crsreports.congress.gov/product/pdf/IF/IF12001.

Crocker, T. D., and J. Tschirhart. 1992. "Ecosystems, Externalities, and Economies." *Environmental and Resource Economics* 2 (6): 551–67.

Das, G. G., J. R. Alavalapati, D. R. Carter, and M. E Tsigas,. 2005. "Regional impacts of environmental regulations and technical change in the US forestry sector: a multiregional CGE analysis." *Forest Policy and Economics* 7 (1): 25–38.

de Melo, J. D., D. G. Tarr, and D. W. Tarr. 1992. *A General Equilibrium Analysis of US Foreign Trade Policy*. Cambridge, MA: MIT Press.

Dezember, R. 2022. "Wall Street Firm Makes a $1.8 Billion Bet on Forest Carbon Offsets." *Wall Street Journal*, November 2. https://www.wsj.com/articles/wall-street-firm-makes-a-1-8-billion-bet-on-forest-carbon-offset-11667390624.

Federal Register. 2022. Change in Discount Rate for Water Resources Planning. *Federal Register* 87 (23). https://www.govinfo.gov/content/pkg/FR-2022-02-03/pdf/2022-02295.pdf.

Feenstra, R. C., P. Luck, M. Obstfeld, and K. N. Russ. 2018. "In search of the Armington elasticity." *Review of Economics and Statistics* 100 (1): 135–150.

Fenichel, E. P., J. K. Abbott, J. Bayham, W. Boone, E. M. K. Haacker, and L. Pfeiffer. 2016. "Measuring the Value of Groundwater and Other Forms of Natural Capital." *Proceedings of the National Academy of Sciences* 113 (9): 2382–2387. https://doi.org/10.1073/pnas.1513779113.

Fisher, B., R. K. Turner, and P. Morling. 2009. "Defining and Classifying Ecosystem Services for Decision Making." *Ecological Economics* 68 (3): 643–53. https://doi.org/10.1016/j.ecolecon.2008.09.014.

Grolleau, G., and L. M. J. McCann. 2012. "Designing Watershed Programs to Pay Farmers for Water Quality Services: Case Studies of Munich and New York City." *Ecological Economics* 76: 87–94. https://doi.org/10.1016/j.ecolecon.2012.02.006.

Harris, A. B., and C. N. S. MAI. 2018. "Land Value Differentials Resulting from Variability between the Sales Comparison and Income Approaches in Timberland Valuation." *Appraisal Journal* 86 (3): 192–205.

Heidari, H., M. Arabi, and T. Warziniack. 2021. "Vulnerability to Water Shortage under Current and Future Water Supply-Demand Conditions across US River Basins." *Earth's Future* 9 (10): e2021EF002278.

IMPLAN® model. 2012. Data, using inputs provided by the user and IMPLAN Group LLC, IMPLAN System (data and software), 16905 Northcross Dr., Suite 120, Huntersville, NC 28078 www.IMPLAN.com

IPBES. 2019. *Summary for Policymakers of the Global Assessment Report on Biodiversity and Ecosystem Services of the Intergovernmental Science-Policy Platform on Biodiversity and Ecosystem Services*. IPBES Secretariat. https://doi.org/10.5281/zenodo.3553579.

Janowiak, M., C. Swanston, and T. Ontl. 2017. *Carbon Benefits of Wood-Based Products and Energy*. U.S. Department of Agriculture, Forest Service, Climate Change Resource Center.

Jendrzejewski, B. 2020. "Bioeconomic modelling–An application of environmentally adjusted economic accounts and the computable general equilibrium model." *Land use policy* 92: 104431.

Kragt, M. E., and M. J. Robertson. 2014. "Quantifying Ecosystem Services Trade-Offs from Agricultural Practices." *Ecological Economics* 102: 147–57. https://doi.org/10.1016/j.ecolecon.2014.04.001.

Kroeger, T., and F. Casey. 2007. "An Assessment of Market-Based Approaches to Providing Ecosystem Services on Agricultural Lands." *Ecological Economics* 64 (2): 321–32. https://doi.org/10.1016/j.ecolecon.2007.07.021.

Liu, N., P. V. Caldwell, G. R. Dobbs, C. F. Miniat, P. V. Bolstad, S. A. C. Nelson, and G. Sun. 2021. "Forested Lands Dominate Drinking Water Supply in the Conterminous United States." *Environmental Research Letters* 16 (8): 084008. https://doi.org/10.1088/1748–9326/ac09b0.

Muttaqin, M. Z., I. Alviya, M. Lugina, F. A. U. Hamdani, and Indartik. 2019. "Developing Community-Based Forest Ecosystem Service Management to Reduce Emissions from Deforestation and Forest Degradation." *Forest Policy and Economics* 108: 101938. https://doi.org/10.1016/j.forpol.2019.05.024.

Nalle, D. J., C. A. Montgomery, J. L. Arthur, S. Polasky, and N. H. Schumaker. 2004. "Modeling Joint Production of Wildlife and Timber." *Journal of Environmental Economics and Management* 48 (3): 997–1017. https://doi.org/10.1016/j.jeem.2004.01.001.

North, D., and R. Thomas. 1973. *The Rise of the Western World: A New Economic History*. Cambridge, UK: Cambridge University Press.

Ochuodho, T. O., and J. R. Alavalapati. 2016. "Integrating natural capital into system of national accounts for policy analysis: An application of a computable general equilibrium model." *Forest Policy and Economics* 72: 99–105.

Ojea, E., J. Martin-Ortega, and A. Chiabai. 2012. "Defining and Classifying Ecosystem Services for Economic Valuation: The Case of Forest Water Services." *Environmental Science & Policy* 19–20: 1–15. https://doi.org/10.1016/j.envsci.2012.02.002.

Oswalt, S. N., W. B. Smith, P. D. Miles, and S. A. Pugh. 2019. "Forest Resources of the United States, 2017: A Technical Document Supporting the Forest Service 2020 RPA Assessment." General Technical Report WO-97. Washington, DC: U.S.

Department of Agriculture, Forest Service, Washington Office. https://doi.org/10.2737/WO-GTR-97.
Pereira, P., I. Bogunovic, M. Muñoz-Rojas, and E. C. Brevik. 2018. "Soil Ecosystem Services, Sustainability, Valuation and Management." *Current Opinion in Environmental Science & Health* 5: 7–13. https://doi.org/10.1016/j.coesh.2017.12.003.
Polasky, S., E. Nelson, E. Lonsdorf, P. Fackler, and A. Starfield. 2005. "Conserving Species in a Working Landscape: Land Use with Biological and Economic Objectives." *Ecological Applications* 15 (4): 1387–1401. https://doi.org/10.1890/03-5423.
Sims, C., D. Aadland, J. Powell, D. C. Finnoff, and B. Crabb. 2014. "Complementarity in the Provision of Ecosystem Services Reduces the Cost of Mitigating Amplified Natural Disturbance Events." *Proceedings of the National Academy of Sciences of the United States of America* 111 (47): 16718–16723. https://doi.org/10.1073/pnas.1407381111.
Swinton, S. M., F. Lupi, G. P. Robertson, and S. K. Hamilton. 2007. "Ecosystem Services and Agriculture: Cultivating Agricultural Ecosystems for Diverse Benefits." *Ecological Economics* 64 (2): 245–52. https://doi.org/10.1016/j.ecolecon.2007.09.020.
United Nations, European Union, Food and Agriculture Organization of the United Nations, International Monetary Fund, Organisation for Economic Co-operation and Development, and The World Bank. 2014. *System of Environmental-Economic Accounting 2012 Central Framework*. https://unstats.un.org/unsd/envaccounting/seearev/seea_cf_final_en.pdf.
United Nations Statistical Commission. 2021. *System of Environmental-Economic Accounting–Ecosystem Accounting*. https://seea.un.org/ecosystem-accounting.
U.S. Environmental Protection Agency (EPA). 2017. *Updates to the Demographic And Spatial Allocation Models to Produce Integrated Climate and Land Use Scenarios (ICLUS)*. Final Report, Version 2. Washington, DC: U.S. Environmental Protection Agency.
U.S. Environmental Protection Agency (EPA). 2023. Tailpipe Greenhouse Gas Emissions from a Typical Passenger Vehicle, Office of Transportation and Air Quality, EPA-420-F-23-014, June.
USFS. 2021. *Big Data, Mapping, and Analytics Platform*. U.S. Department of Agriculture, Forest Service. https://fia-usfs.hub.arcgis.com.
U.S. Geological Survey. 2016. *USGS National Watershed Boundary Dataset (WBD) Downloadable Data Collection*. National Geospatial Data Asset Watershed Boundary Dataset.
Wang, S., and B. Fu. 2013. "Trade-Offs between Forest Ecosystem Services." *Forest Policy and Economics* 26: 145–46. https://doi.org/10.1016/j.forpol.2012.07.014.
Warnell, K. J. D., M. Russell, C. Rhodes, K. J. Bagstad, L. P. Olander, D. J. Nowak, R. Poudel, P. D. Glynn, J. L. Hass, S. Hirabayashi, J. C. Ingram, J. Matuszak, K. L. L. Oleson, S. M. Posner, and F. Villa. 2020. "Testing Ecosystem Accounting in the United States: A Case Study for the Southeast." *Ecosystem Services* 43: 101099. https://doi.org/10.1016/j.ecoser.2020.101099.
Warziniack, T. 2014. "A General Equilibrium Model of Ecosystem Services in a River Basin." *Journal of the American Water Resource Association* 50 (3): 683–95.
Warziniack, T., C. H. Sham, R. Morgan, and Y. Feferholtz. 2017. "Effect of Forest Cover on Water Treatment Costs." *Water Economics and Policy* 3 (04): 170006.
Warziniack, T., D. Finnoff, J. Bossenbroek, J. F. Shogren, and D. Lodge. 2011. "Stepping stones for biological invasion: a bioeconomic model of transferable risk." *Environmental and Resource Economics* 50: 605–627.
White, C., B. S. Halpern, and C. V. Kappel. 2012. "Ecosystem Service Tradeoff Analysis Reveals the Value of Marine Spatial Planning for Multiple Ocean Uses."

Proceedings of the National Academy of Sciences 109 (12): 4696–4701. https://doi.org/10.1073/pnas.1114215109.
Wossink, A., and S. M. Swinton. 2007. "Jointness in Production and Farmers' Willingness to Supply Non-marketed Ecosystem Services." *Ecological Economics* 64 (2): 297–304. https://doi.org/10.1016/j.ecolecon.2007.07.003.

Comment Andie M. Creel

Natural capital enables the production of market goods and services and the provision of nonmarket services that benefit, and sometimes are critical to, individuals' welfare. The United States is beginning to craft national accounts that track the stock of natural assets and their marginal values (i.e., price), following the UN-SEEA (United Nations et al. 2014; United Nations Statistical Commission 2021). Once populated, these accounts enable the calculation of exchange values, which are a good's price multiplied by its quantity. The difference in these exchange values through time will inform if an asset is being managed to achieve sustainable development because changes in exchange value approximate changes in welfare (Arrow et al. 2003). Sustainable development is non-declining welfare for future generations (World Commission on Environment and Development 1987).

William Nordhaus identified "the big five" of natural capital accounting as forest, soil, water, clean air, and climate (Nordhaus 2023). Mismanagement of these resources may seriously hinder sustainable development. Therefore, estimating these stocks and their values is pressing. These natural assets are in Phase I or II of the national strategy (Office of Science and Technology Policy, Office of Management and Budget, and Department of Commerce 2023).

Warziniack et al. (this volume) significantly contribute to the field by demonstrating methods that can lead to the population of forest natural capital accounts, one of the "big five." They apply their methods at a substantial scale, estimating the stock of forest land and the cost of deforestation expected under projected management of the Upper Colorado River Basin (UCRB). Thirty million people live in the UCRB, nearly 10 percent of the US population.

Warziniack et al. (this volume) use the US Forest Service Forest Inventory Analysis to determine the current stock of forests and carbon storage. They use the US Environmental Protection Agency's Integrated Climate and Land-Use Scenarios (ICLUS) for their modeled land-use changes. Land-use changes are based on the International Panel on Climate Change projec-

Andie M. Creel is a PhD student in Natural Resource Economics at the Yale School of the Environment.

tions. This demonstrates how federal agency data that have already been collected can be used to populate the national accounts.

Warziniack et al. (this volume) use a computable general equilibrium (CGE) model to estimate the benefits that forests provide through timber production, water purification, and carbon storage. The cost of deforestation is calculated by comparing deforestation projections from ICLUS to a counterfactual scenario where the stock of forest in the UCRB remains at its 2018 acreage.

By using a general equilibrium model, their estimated cost of deforestation considers forests' complements and substitutes. This consideration is critical for the correct valuation of natural resources that are enabling assets to market goods and those that have produced substitutes. Partial equilibrium results can be appropriate when the benefit of an ecosystem is only local (e.g., endangered species, Maher et al. 2020).

Warziniack et al. (this volume) predict that 327.5 thousand acres of forest in the UCRB will be lost to development by 2100. In 2018, there were 93 million acres. The present-value cost of total deforestation in 2100, compared to 2018 acreage, is $30.24 million. This result assumes deforestation will happen at a constant rate. The undiscounted cost of this loss of forest land is $76.5 million, which is a relevant upper bound if deforestation happens quicker than a constant rate.

Most of the cost of deforestation comes from losing carbon storage. This loss leads to a $28 million cost, which dominates the loss of timber production ($2.15 million) and water purification ($90,000). If concern follows costs, the primary concern about deforestation in the UCRB should be its implication on climate change. Future management policies should consider the loss from carbon storage as well as the loss of timber products while bearing in mind that the social costs of carbon are global and the cost to the timber industry will be felt the most by local communities.

The small cost of deforestation on water purification in the UCRB should not be extrapolated to other regions. This emphasizes why a significant contribution of Warziniack et al. (this volume) is methodological. The significant amount of public land in the UCRB decreases the cost of deforestation in the UCRB on water purification. More research is needed in other regions with different mixes of private and public forests, particularly the southeastern United States, which has a high share of private forests that are being deforested quickly.

It is important to consider how the results from benefit-cost analyses can overlap or differ from core statistics for the national accounts. Benefit-cost analyses compare one state of the world to a policy-relevant counterfactual. The results in Warziniack et al. (this volume) come from a benefit-cost analysis comparing projected deforestation to a counterfactual where forest acreage stays at its 2018 level at zero cost. Accountants calculate changes in exchange value. As mentioned, exchange value is the price of an asset multiplied by its quantity. Accountants evaluate if an asset is being managed sustainably by comparing the exchange value in one period to a prior one. In the case of Warziniack et al. (this volume), their counterfactual scenario is the same as the scenario accountants consider because they compare projected changes to the initial time period. This equivalence will not be valid for all benefit-cost analyses because it relies on the benefit-cost analysis's counterfactual to be the state of the world in the initial period at zero cost.

It is also important to highlight that the national accounts will require price-quantity pairs for environmental assets to calculate exchange values. Warziniack et al. (this volume) did not report a price, or marginal value, for an acre of lost forest in the UCRB. However, because their counterfactual is equivalent to the scenarios considered by accounts, I can calculate the average value for a lost acre of forest when I make the simplifying assumption that price is exogenous to quantity and that average value is a good approximation for marginal value. Both assumptions are common when populating national accounts.

Assuming a constant marginal value and a linear decline in forest acreage as Warziniack et al. (this volume) do, the change in exchange value between time-period 0 and T is

$$\Delta EV = \sum_{0}^{T} \left(\frac{1}{1+r}\right)^{t} * p * \Delta x_t,$$

where p is the marginal value of one acre of forest, r is the discount rate, Δx is the change in the stock of forests, t is the period, the initial time-period is 2018 and T is 82 (the year 2100). The change in equivalent variation from 2018 to 2100 is equivalent to the cost of deforestation from Warziniack et al. (this volume), \$30.24 million. The annual change in forest coverage is constant, and about 4,000 acres per year. The discount rate is 2.25.

I find that the results in Warziniack et al. (this volume) imply that the marginal value of one acre of forest is \$220.22 by solving for p.[1] This assumes that price is exogenous to the stock of forest, which should not be assumed if changes in the stock are large. The change in forest acreage projected by Warziniack et al. (this volume) is less than 1 percent.

Finally, as Warziniack et al. (this volume) discussed, using a CGE model prompts the conversation of what other services associated with forests have been left out and what assumptions are appropriate. This is a useful contribution to the field because future research can modify and build on their CGE model. An assumption worth relaxing may be that carbon lost from losing a stock of trees is lost forever because durable wood products can store carbon (Domke et al. 2020). Additional ecosystem services from forests identified by Warziniack et al. (this volume) are recreation and air purifi-

1. Assuming a constant percent change (–0.00425%) leads to nearly the same result, \$200.12 per acre lost.

cation. Additional services of interest to Phase II of the national strategy are how forests cool urban areas and stabilize soils (Office of Science and Technology Policy, Office of Management and Budget, and Department of Commerce 2023). Soil stabilization is partially captured by the value forests provide to water purification.

For acknowledgments, sources of research support, and disclosure of the author's material financial relationships, if any, please see https://www.nber.org/books-and-chapters/measuring-and-accounting-environmental-public-goods-national-accounts-perspective/comment-natural-capital-accounting-forested-lands-creel.

References

Arrow, Kenneth J., Partha Dasgupta, and Karl-Göran Mäler. 2003. "Evaluating Projects and Assessing Sustainable Development in Imperfect Economies." *Environmental and Resource Economics* 26 (4): 647–85. https://doi.org/10.1023/B:EARE.0000007353.78828.98.

Domke, Grant M., Sonja N. Oswalt, Brian F. Walters, and Randall S. Morin. 2020. "Tree Planting Has the Potential to Increase Carbon Sequestration Capacity of Forests in the United States." *Proceedings of the National Academy of Sciences* 117 (40): 24649–51. https://doi.org/10.1073/pnas.2010840117.

Maher, Samantha M., Eli P. Fenichel, Oswald J. Schmitz, and Wiktor L. Adamowicz. 2020. "The Economics of Conservation Debt: A Natural Capital Approach to Revealed Valuation of Ecological Dynamics." *Ecological Applications* 30 (6): e02132. https://doi.org/10.1002/eap.2132.

Nordhaus, William. 2023. "Keynote Adress." Presented at the Yale Climate, Environmental and Economic Growth Conference, New Haven, CT, November 10. https://egc.yale.edu/events/climate-environment-growth-2023.

Office of Science and Technology Policy, Office of Management and Budget, and Department of Commerce. 2023. "National Strategy to Develop Statistics for Environmental Economic Decisions." https://www.whitehouse.gov/wp-content/uploads/2022/08/Natural-Capital-Accounting-Strategy.pdf.

United Nations, Food and Agriculture Organization of the United Nations, International Monetary Fund, Organisation for Economic Co-operation and Development, and The World Bank. 2014. "System of Environmental-Economic Accounting 2012 Central Framework." https://unstats.un.org/unsd/envaccounting/seearev/seea_cf_final_en.pdf.

United Nations Statistical Commission. 2021. "System of Environmental-Economic Accounting–Ecosystem Accounting." https://seea.un.org/ecosystem-accounting.

Warziniack, T., K. Bagstad, M. Knowles, C. Mihiar, A. Nehra, C. Rhodes, L. Sanchez, C. Sichko, and C. Sims. "Natural Capital Accounting on Forested Lands in the United States: An Application to the Colorado River Basin." In *Measuring and Accounting for Environmental Public Goods: A National Accounts Perspective*, edited by Mary Bohman, Eli Fenichel, and Nicholas Z. Muller. Chicago, IL: University of Chicago Press. This volume.

World Commission on Environment and Development. 1987. *Our Common Future*. Oxford University Press.

8

Natural Capital Considerations for an Extension of the US Marine Economy Satellite Account

Jeffrey Wielgus, Monica Grasso, Charles Colgan, Jennifer Zhuang, Sarah Siegel, Joseph Conran, and Tadesse Wodajo

8.1 Introduction

The marine environment provides space and resources for a large number of economic activities. Some countries have developed satellite accounts[1] for the ocean based on the United Nations System of National Accounts (SNA), which provides valuable information on the role of oceans as providers of products for the economy. For example, the United States National Oceanic and Atmospheric Administration (NOAA) has developed the Marine Economy Satellite Account (NOAA 2022), or MESA, in collabo-

Jeffrey Wielgus is director of the Social Science & Performance Division at the National Oceanic and Atmospheric Administration (NOAA) Performance, Risk & Social Science Office.

Monica Grasso is chief economist at the National Oceanic and Atmospheric Administration.

Charles Colgan is the director of research for the Center for the Blue Economy (CBE) at the Middlebury Institute of International Studies at Monterey.

Jennifer Zhuang is an economist at Integrated Systems Solutions, Inc.

Sarah Siegel is an economist at the National Oceanic and Atmospheric Administration.

Joseph Conran is a senior economist in the Office of the Chief Economist at the National Oceanic and Atmospheric Administration.

Tadesse Wodajo is a senior economist at the Office of the Chief Financial Officer at the National Oceanic and Atmospheric Administration.

We are grateful to Mary Bohman, Eli Fenichel, Nick Muller, Andrew Scheld, Arnab Acharya, Jeff Adkins, and Doug Lipton for insightful suggestions that helped improve earlier versions of the manuscript. Errors and omissions remain solely the responsibility of the authors. We thank Alissa Miller-Gonzalez for compiling the data in table 8.3. The scientific results and conclusions, as well as any views or opinions expressed herein, are those of the authors and do not necessarily reflect the views of NOAA or the Department of Commerce. For acknowledgments, sources of research support, and disclosure of the authors' material financial relationships, if any, please see https://www.nber.org/books-and-chapters/measuring-and-accounting-environmental-public-goods-national-accounts-perspective/natural-capital-considerations-extension-us-marine-economy-satellite-account.

1. Satellite accounts provide statistics for a particular aspect of the economy. Data presented in satellite accounts are consistent with BEA's core statistics.

ration with the United States Bureau of Economic Analysis (BEA); and the Economics: National Ocean Watch (ENOW) data set.[2] These efforts are a substantive improvement in our ability to understand how marine industries and activities contribute to society.

However, these efforts do not account for specific environmental inputs and ecosystem services that support economic activities, or the manner and degree to which natural capital stocks are consumed or adversely affected by those economic activities (Colgan 2016; Fenichel et al. 2020; Hoagland et al. 2020). Applying the United Nations System of Environmental-Economic Accounts (SEEA) framework to understand the contributions of natural capital to activity in the marine environment would be a logical next step in characterizing the US marine economy. Other countries, including Portugal,[3] Norway,[4] and Canada,[5] are beginning the process of developing ecosystem accounts for the ocean by building upon efforts to create marine satellite accounts.

MESA identifies the activities of the marine economy and measures the output, value added, compensation, and employment associated with these activities at the national level. To make the contributions of natural capital to the marine economy visible, MESA can be extended by following the guidelines of the SEEA Central Framework (SEEA-CF),[6] which is an internationally agreed standard for accounting for environmental assets and their supply to and use in the economy. SEEA-CF provides guidance for accounting for non-produced, non-financial assets,[7] such as minerals and fisheries, in greater detail than the System of National Accounts (United Nations et al. 2014).

This paper considers an initial extension of MESA to include natural capital considerations by adopting key elements of SEEA-CF in pilot activities of the marine economy. It contributes to the implementation of the National Strategy to Develop Statistics for Environmental-Economic Decisions: A US System of Natural Capital Accounting and Associated Environmental

2. See "Economics: National Ocean Watch," from NOAA Office for Coastal Management, https://coast.noaa.gov/digitalcoast/data/enow.html.

3. See "Ocean Satellite Account 2016–2018, Methodological Report," July 2022, from Statistics Portugal, https://www.ine.pt/ngt_server/attachfileu.jsp?look_parentBoui=569531189&att_display=n&att_download=y.

4. See "Progress on Ocean Accounting in Norway," Paper for the 28th London Group Meeting in Siegburg, Germany, published June 21, 2023 by Statistics Norway, https://www.ssb.no/nasjonalregnskap-og-konjunkturer/nasjonalregnskap/artikler/progress-on-ocean-accounting-in-norway/_/attachment/inline/df99d004-df1a-4839-9639-aa4ca55e3705:742aef3b1dae70b406bc98831670f3d0d1143371/NOT2023-28.pdf.

5. See "Canadian Ocean Accounts: A Pilot Project," June 8, 2022, from the Global Ocean Accounts Partnership, https://www.oceanaccounts.org/canadian-ocean-accounts-pilot.

6. See SEEA Central Framework, System Environmental Economic Accounting, United Nations, https://seea.un.org/content/seea-central-framework.

7. These assets are defined as existing without human production but can be used in production. Examples are natural resources such as land, mineral and energy reserves, and non-cultivated biological resources.

Economic Statistics, which was released in 2023 by the White House Office of Science and Technology Policy, the White House Office of Management and Budget, and the Department of Commerce.[8]

The paper is organized as follows. Section 8.2 discusses MESA, and section 8.3 provides a general discussion of dependencies and impacts related to natural capital in MESA activities. The fourth section considers a more general plan for extending MESA based on elements of SEEA-CF to three pilot sectors. Finally, section 8.5 concludes and discusses possible challenges to the MESA extension as well as theoretical issues that will need to be addressed.

8.2 The US Marine Economy Satellite Account

An interest to create international statistical standards that would allow comparisons between national economies followed the formation of the United Nations (UN). The UN Statistical Office released the first System of National Accounts (SNA) in 1953 and has released multiple updates, with the most recent one in 2008, with support and input from other statistical agencies (European Commission et al. 2009).[9] The SNA provides standard recommendations to compile measures of economic activity and includes a strong statistical setup with internal consistency checks which allow for robust statistics. The recommendations describe a "coherent, consistent, and integrated" set of macroeconomic accounts that provide an overview of economic processes (European Commission et al. 2009, 1). The most well-known measure from the SNA is gross domestic product (GDP), but the accounts provide much more information about the economic state of a country at a certain point in time.

The SNA provides guidance for four types of accounts: (1) production accounts (to measure how much producers make and sell); (2) consumption and expenditure accounts (to measure how much households buy and consume); (3) accumulation accounts and balance sheets (to measure the change in assets and their value, i.e., wealth); and (4) supply and use or input-output tables (to describe the interconnections of how goods and services flow through the economy). The SNA also provides guidance to adjust for changes in price through time (United Nations et al., 2009).

The SNA does not explicitly focus on the marine-dependent portions of a nation's economy. In the United States, efforts to measure marine economic activities date back to the 1970s (e.g., Nathan Associates 1974). The

8. See "National Strategy to Develop Statistics for Environmental-Economic Decisions: A U.S. System of Natural Capital Accounting and Associated Environmental-Economic Statistics," The White House, January 2023, https://www.whitehouse.gov/wp-content/uploads/2023/01/Natural-Capital-Accounting-Strategy-final.pdf.

9. For the historical updates of the SNA, see https://unstats.un.org/unsd/nationalaccount/HistoricSNA.asp.

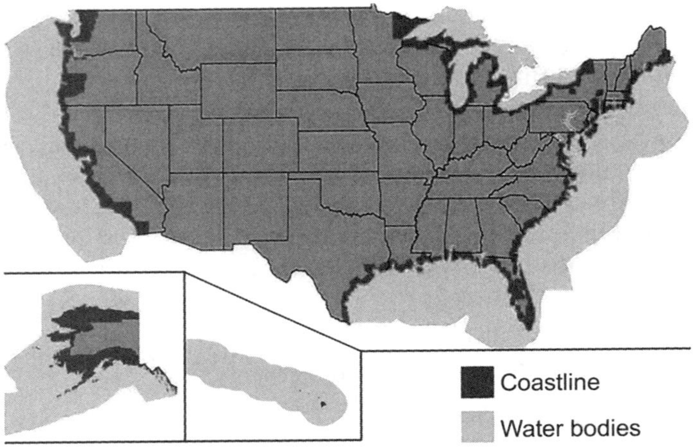

Figure 8.1 Geographical extent of the marine environment, whose contribution to the US economy is captured in the Marine Economy Satellite Account. Coastline areas capture shore-adjacent zip codes. (From Nicolls et al. 2020).

National Ocean Economics Program (NOEP) has produced time series data on marine economic activities since 1999 (Colgan 2013). Building upon the NOEP's methodology, the National Oceanic Atmospheric Administration (NOAA) started to develop and maintain the ENOW data set in 2011. ENOW focuses on six economic sectors: Living Resources, Marine Construction, Marine Transportation, Offshore Mineral Resources, Ship and Boat Building, and Tourism and Recreation.

The ENOW/NOEP approach provides a regional focus but gives limited detail on marine industries. To get a more comprehensive view of the marine economy, Congress directed NOAA and BEA to develop a satellite account for the US marine economy in 2017. First released in 2021 with data from 2014–2019, MESA is published annually in June. MESA provides data for a wide array of ocean activities because it uses the detailed input-output tables produced by BEA.

The United States is not the only country moving to the satellite accounts approach. Portugal (Statistics Portugal 2016), the United Kingdom (Stebbings et al. 2020), China (Wang and Wang 2019), and Norway (Randen et al. 2022) have also rolled out experimental satellite accounts recently. The Organisation for Economic Co-operation and Development (OECD) is also currently exploring an international ocean economy satellite account aiming to provide global totals and comparisons across countries (Jolliffe et al. 2021b).

MESA captures economic activity in the marine environment (figure 8.1), which is defined to include the US Exclusive Economic Zones of the Atlantic, Pacific, and Arctic Oceans (approximately 200 nautical miles off the US coast); the Gulf of Mexico; the Great Lakes (up to the international boundary with Canada); and major estuaries and embayments (e.g., the Chesapeake Bay and Puget Sound); as well as segments of inland river downstream from the major seaports that accommodate ocean-going vessels, even though they are located far from the coast (e.g., Portland, Oregon; New Orleans and Baton Rouge, Louisiana). The geographic scope is derived from the Coastal Zone Management Act of 1972, which assigned NOAA management of coastal resources and the Great Lakes (Nicolls et al. 2020).

There are four criteria as to whether an economic activity is included in MESA: (1) the activity takes place in the marine environment, as defined above (e.g., marine transportation); (2) it uses essential inputs from the marine environment (e.g., seafood processing); (3) it produces goods/services predominantly for use in the marine environment (e.g., marine navigational equipment); (4) it would not take place if not located in proximity to the coast (e.g., beach vacation rental property). Economic activities in the SNA that meet any of the four criteria above are identified and categorized into 29 marine industries in the following 10 sectors: Living Resources, Construction, Research and Education, Transportation and Warehousing, Professional and Technical Services, Offshore Minerals, Coastal Utilities, Ship and Boat Building, Tourism and Recreation, and National Defense and Public Administration.

Many activities along the coast are not solely marine related, and MESA uses a set of coefficients, or "partials," to estimate the portion that is specifically marine dependent. Partials are applied to the final demand categories of each good and service class in BEA's supply-use framework: personal consumption expenditure, exports, imports, government expenditure, inventory changes, and private fixed investment (Nicolls et al. 2020). If a good or service is not marine related, a partial of 0 is assigned to the category and it is excluded from MESA; if a good or service is entirely marine related, a partial of 1 is assigned to the category; finally, if one category includes both marine and non-marine components, a percentage is estimated to partially include the category in MESA. For example, for electric power generation, output is defined by identifying all electric power production within the national shoreline and calculating the gross megawatt hour (MWh) output for this as a share of the national MWh generated.

Data to estimate partials are collected by the private sector or government agencies, and sources include NOAA, BLS, Census Bureau, Department of Energy, Department of Defense, National Marine Manufacturers Association, the Baker Hughes oil field service company, and the DK Shifflet travel performance research firm, among others. To maximize consistency, the same sources are consulted from year to year. When data are available from more than one source, data released by government agencies are prioritized.

MESA reports statistics for both the customized set of groupings (the sectors and activities) that align better with natural "breakpoints" in the marine economy and the standard BEA industry groupings in the national accounts. The June 2023 release of MESA,[10] with 2021 data, showed that the US marine economy contributed $432 billion to the national GDP in 2021, generated $730 billion in gross output, and supported more than 2.3 million jobs. The marine economy accounted for 1.8 percent of national total gross output, 1.9 percent of total GDP, and 1.3 percent of total employment. Recovering from the effects of COVID-19 in 2020, the marine economy bounced back strongly in 2021 with 7.4 percent growth from 2020 to 2021 in real GDP, larger than the overall US economy's growth of 5.9 percent. The marine economy sectors with the highest growth in 2021 were Tourism and Recreation (27.3 percent growth in gross output to a level of $231.8 billion); Transportation and Warehousing (16.8 percent growth to $57.1 billion); and Living Resources (13.5 percent to $31.0 billion).

8.3 Natural Capital in MESA

Although the SNA has been in use for over half a century, there has long been criticism that the accounts, and especially GDP, do not provide a full representation of a society's well-being, including that linked to a healthy environment (Nordhaus and Tobin 1973). Alternatives have been proposed that help provide a greater context to societal welfare, including the Human Development Index and the Gross National Happiness Index, among many others (Fleurbaey 2009).[11] Nonetheless, in many of these proposed indicators there is no consideration of the economy's impact on the environment nor a systematic process to keep track of the environment's contribution to the economy. Furthermore, it is important to develop measures tracking changes and potential depletions of natural capital.

Initiatives to account for natural capital in the measurement and reporting of economic performance culminated in the development of SEEA in 1993, but it took two more decades for SEEA-CF to be adopted as a statistical standard by the United Nations Statistical Commission (United Nations et al. 2014). The goal of the framework is to provide a comprehensive view of the stocks and changes in stocks of environmental assets. SEEA-CF generally follows the SNA's accounting structures, which allow the integration of information on economic and environmental assets. MESA and ENOW provide SNA-consistent data on the annual flows of market-based values related to ocean activities. The investment part of the SNA's National Income Accounts includes both additions to capital stocks and reductions in capital stock values through consumption of fixed capital (depreciation) (BEA 2022). Extending concepts from the SNA framework, SEEA-CF

10. See "Marine Economy Satellite Account, 2020," BEA News Release BEA 22–24, June 9, 2022, https://www.bea.gov/sites/default/files/2022-06/mesa0622.pdf.

11. The Human Development Index is discussed in https://hdr.undp.org/data-center/human-development-index#/indicies/HDI, and the Gross National Happiness Index is discussed in https://www.grossnationalhappiness.com.

Table 8.1 **Major relationships or dependencies of MESA sectors with the marine environment**

MESA Sector	Resource Extraction	Ecosystem Health	Ecosystem Impacts	Ecosystem Management
Living Resources	X	X		
Offshore Minerals	X		X	
Tourism and Recreation		X		
Transportation and Warehousing			X	
Construction			X	
Ship and Boat Building			X	
Coastal Utilities			X	
National Defense and Public Administration				X
Research and Education				X
Professional and Technical Services				X

requires measuring both additions to capital stocks and reductions in the stocks.

The marine economic sectors captured in MESA can be classified into four types (with some overlapping categories) according to their connections with natural capital (table 8.1): (1) Living Resources and Offshore Minerals are sectors that depend on the extraction of natural resources from the ocean; (2) Living Resources and Tourism and Recreation are sectors that directly benefit from a healthy and sustainable marine environment; (3) Offshore Minerals, Transportation and Warehousing, Construction, Ship and Boat Building, and Coastal Utilities are sectors that do not heavily rely on the health of the natural ecosystems but may bring potential significant impacts to the environment; and (4) National Defense and Public Administration, Research and Education, and Professional and Technical Services are sectors that provide regulation, management, scientific and technological advances, and education on the uses of marine resources.

8.4 Pilots for an Initial Extension of MESA

An expansion of MESA to incorporate natural capital will help fill in the gaps to include the value of the stocks and the flows between economic activities and the natural environment. Consistent with SEEA-CF, this will include accounting for investments needed to reduce the damages to natural capital caused by each of the economic activities, as well as the value of damages attributable to other economic activities (residual damages). However, these measurements of the natural capital foundations of the ocean-related economy require a more complex process than the estimation of MESA. The data, for the most part, are not nearly as readily available, and the specific measure of natural capital is unique to each type of good or service in the ocean economy. Therefore, the MESA extension will start from major marine economic activities with a known relative abundance of statistics and an explicit relationship to environmental stocks and flows. The pilot marine activities considered here are offshore oil and gas exploration and production (a component of Offshore Minerals), commercial fishing (a component of Living Resources), and beach recreation (a component of Tourism and Recreation).

Offshore oil and gas exploration and production are one of the largest ocean-related contributors to the US GDP in the offshore mineral extraction sector (NOAA 2022). The value of the mineral reserves extracted and sold in the market is monitored in BEA's national accounts, statistics from the Department of Energy, and the private sector. The valuation of mineral reserves is a well-established field in mining and mineral economics, and the methodology is fairly straightforward.

Commercial fishing is the one economic activity that is found in virtually all the marine waters of the United States, from the Bering Sea to the Caribbean. For more than 50 years, NOAA has been maintaining a variety of time-series data on fisheries in the United States, including harvests, stocks, spawn and mortality rates, and overfishing status, and conducting in-depth research studies on both deep sea and coastal ecosystems that support fisheries. Some of these statistics, such as fish landing values, have been incorporated into BEA's models for the national accounts. Internationally, the SNA framework uses fish stocks as an example of natural assets that are in scope for the non-produced non-financial balance sheet. The basic approach for measuring fisheries-related natural capital is also well defined in the SEEA-CF.

While oil and gas are the largest contributors to GDP among ocean sectors, the largest sector in terms of employment is Tourism and Recreation (NOAA 2022). Beach recreation, extending from Maine to Hawaii, is the primary activity underlying this sector. The natural capital value of beaches is a function primarily of the value of beach use for recreation. This value has been studied using various versions of stated and revealed preference methods. For the purposes of promoting their coastal economies, some state and local tourism bureaus and industry associations keep active track of beach visits and consumer behavior statistics through regular surveys and tax reports in some areas, which provide a foundational understanding on the value of the natural environment for tourism and recreation.

The following discussion provides the conceptual basis for measuring natural capital in the three pilots and examples of data sources that we have identified to build pilot accounts.

8.5 Conceptual Basis for Pilot Accounts

8.5.1 Offshore Oil and Gas

8.5.1.1 Physical Account

Offshore oil and gas lying under the seabed between the seaward extent of the states' jurisdiction and the seaward extent of federal jurisdiction belong to the national government under the Law of the Sea Conventions (LOSC)[12] of 1958, 1964, and 1982. Under the US Outer Continental Shelf (OCS) Lands Act of 1954, as amended in 1978 (43 USC 29), the steward of that resource is the Department of the Interior, specifically the Bureau of Ocean Energy Management (BOEM). BOEM divides its jurisdiction into four areas: Atlantic, Gulf of Mexico, Pacific, and Alaska. The OCS Lands Act is based on the premise that the seabed oil and gas resources will be developed and sold in the market and that the private oil and gas industry is authorized to explore, develop, produce, and sell the oil and gas.

The offshore oil and gas accounts will be structured following guidance for mineral and energy asset accounts from SEEA-CF. The framework provides guidelines for developing physical and monetary accounts and focuses on clearly organizing the relevant information to highlight flows of extraction, depletion, and discoveries (SEEA-CF 5.169).

The scope of deposits included in the SEEA-CF mineral asset accounts are based on the United Nations Framework Classification for Fossil Energy and Mineral Reserves and Resources 2009, and are classified in three classes: Class A, commercially recoverable resources; Class B, potentially commercially recoverable resources; and Class C, non-commercial and other known deposits.[13] The scope and classifications of BOEM are aligned in spirit with SEEA's classifications. BOEM's resource classification includes undiscovered resources (equivalent to class C), contingent resources (class B), and reserves (class A).[14]

BOEM releases annual reports for reserves found in the Gulf of Mexico and Pacific OCS areas. There are also intermittent data on contingent resources as well as five-year reports on undiscovered resources. Thus, annual tables for the Gulf of Mexico and Pacific OCS areas can be developed for Class A (reserves) resources, and Class B and C data will be added as available.

Table 8.2 provides an example of an annual physical asset account using the 2013 estimates of oil in the Gulf of Mexico OCS area. The table matches the format of the physical account tables of SEEA-CF, but it has two additional rows: "unknown additions" and "unknown reductions." These rows were added to ensure transparency when fitting BOEM data into the SEEA format, as BOEM does not fully release information specifying the different reasons for additions and reductions in the stock. The exception is with

12. Although not yet a party to the treaty, the United States observes the LOSC as reflective of customary international law and practice.

13. See "United Nations Framework Classification for Fossil Energy and Mineral Reserves and Resources 2009," ECE Energy Series No. 39, United Nations, 2010, https://unece.org/DAM/energy/se/pdfs/UNFC/unfc2009/UNFC2009_ES39_e.pdf.

14. See "Classification and Methodology for Reserves Calculations" from the Bureau of Ocean Energy Management, US Department of the Interior, https://www.boem.gov/oil-gas-energy/resource-evaluation/classification-and-methodology-reserves-calculations, for more information on BOEM's classification and methodology for reserves calculations.

Table 8.2 **2013 Oil Gulf of Mexico OCS physical asset account (billion barrels)**

	Commercially Viable (A)	Potentially Commercially Viable (B)	Non-Commercial Other Known Deposits (C)
Opening stock	4.33	4.61	
+ Discoveries			
+ Upward reappraisals			
+ Reclassifications			
+ Unknown additions			
Total additions	0	0	
− Extractions	0.46		
− Catastrophic losses			
− Downward reappraisals			
− Reclassifications			
− Unknown reductions	0.19	1.32	
Total reductions	0.65	1.32	
Closing stock	3.68	3.29	35.01

Notes: Data sources for the table are from the following reports, which are available on BOEM's website (www.boem.gov): Estimated Oil and Gas Reserves Gulf of Mexico OCS Region December 31, 2019 (data for column A); Reports on Estimated Oil and Gas Reserves Gulf of Mexico OCS Region December 31, 2012 and 2013 (data for column B); and the Assessment of Technically and Economically Recoverable Hydrocarbon Resources of the Gulf of Mexico Outer Continental Shelf as of January 1, 2014 (data for column C).

production data, which are published annually and will be included under extractions.

8.5.1.2 Monetary Account

The monetary account of the mineral asset account is limited in scope to class A of minerals, which are those that are commercially recoverable. Thus, we are interested in valuing the offshore plots in which a lease has been sold and there is confirmed commercial progress. BOEM handles the sale and management of leases and has developed an auction system that works pursuant to the OCS Lands Act, which requires that winning bids must be considered "fair market value."[15] The Department of Interior developed a five-year program which sets a schedule under which BOEM offers for sale a defined group of 9 mi^2 blocks within an OCS planning area. The auction is called a lease sale because the winning bidder is given lease hold rights to the designated block; ownership of the undersea lands remains with the government, but the oil and gas become the property of the firm producing the resource. A lease gives the winner the right to drill for oil or gas (sub-

15. See "Fair Market Valuation Methodology" from the Bureau of Ocean Energy Management, US Department of the Interior, https://www.boem.gov/oil-gas-energy/resource-evaluation/fair-market-valuation-methodology, for a description of BOEM's fair market valuation methodology.

ject to environmental reviews) for up to five years, and this period may be extended. The use of the sealed bid auction processes is used to ensure that the bids are received in a fair market.

If oil and/or gas are discovered, the lease owner has the right to install development wells to extract oil or gas. Once the field development is complete, the lease owner may produce and sell the oil and gas. The lease owner is also responsible for transporting the oil and gas to shoreside processing via pipelines or tankers. The terms of the lease ownership call for three payments to be made to the government. A rental fee is charged per acre for each 5,700-acre block. The rental fee is paid regardless of any discoveries or drilling activity. A royalty is charged as a percentage of the gross value of all oil and gas sold. The royalty is charged only if oil or gas are found.

The bids in the sealed bid auction are for what amounts to an up-front payment of a share of the value of oil and in excess of the royalty and rental payments. Because it is a competitive market, the optimal bid for the company wishing to have the right to explore for and perhaps acquire producible reserves is considered remaining rents. The oil company, in other words, must pay to the government a substantial amount for an unknown (and at the time unknowable) right to possibly produce and sell oil. The only rational maximum bid is an amount that just leaves the company with the likelihood of a minimum return if oil is present. The lease sale system using bonus bidding identifies and measures the resource rent which is transferred from the oil company to the government as a competitive market price. Tracts that receive no bids or that receive bids below the BOEM minimum bid are not considered in the valuation of oil and gas resources. Any oil and gas they may contain is accounted for as undiscovered (unconfirmed) resources.

BOEM records provide a means to measure the capital value of the currently leased OCS lands.[16] Currently, there are no active leases in the Atlantic, nor are there any plans to sell land there, and Alaska reserve and leasing data are not available to the public. However, data are available for the Gulf of Mexico and Pacific regions.

This measure of the capital stock of offshore oil and gas can be updated every year to show changes in the stocks' values. This update will reflect changes in expected physical levels of oil and gas and expectations of prices as reflected in bonus bids.

The use of the bonus payments as a measure of capital value of offshore oil and gas raises a definitional question. Only some areas sold for exploration will actually yield oil and/or gas; the majority in fact will not. The bonus bid can be considered the market value of blocks with oil and gas (at the time of sale), while the payments where no hydrocarbons are found can

16. This information may be retrieved from the BOEM Data Center on the Bureau of Ocean Energy Management website https://www.data.boem.gov, "Leasing Information" subsite. Data are available for deposits that are being produced and the value of bonus payments paid for leases.

be considered a capital value of the seabed. Accounts need to separate the minerals from the lands. It should be noted that the lands may also have other capital value as habitat for fisheries, which should also be estimated in a complete capital account. These challenges are currently being investigated in the oil and gas pilot research phase.

8.5.1.3 Environmental Expenditures Account

The method above meets many of the needs for a capital asset valuation for oil and gas, but it lacks a consideration of important environmental issues. SEEA-CF environmental accounts ensure that goods and services that protect or improve the environment are identified and their value recognized. The environmental accounts cover two broad categories of environmental expenditures: resource management and environmental protection.

Expenditures on environmental protection are generally internal expenditures within organizations that are accounted for as "inputs" to the final produced goods. SEEA-CF calls for these expenditures to be separated from the standard accounts to explicitly measure environmental protection as a good or service. The environmental protection aspects of natural capital should include both those investments needed to reduce the extent of environmental damage caused by extraction of the oil and gas, and the value of residual damages that cannot be avoided. In the case of oil and gas, these can be grouped as operational environmental effects and investments and catastrophic effects.

Environmental impacts of oil and gas operations are well understood because of decades of experience in managing these effects under the authority of the OCS Lands Act, the Clean Air and Clean Water Acts, the Oil Pollution Act, and other federal (and state) environmental laws. Major effects of concern include small-scale oil spills (from transferring fuels), air emissions from venting and flaring of natural gas, and the impacts of disposal of drilling materials. There are also solid and domestic wastes typical of ship-bound operations. In general, all of these impacts are managed by the oil companies to the extent required by their permits of operation. The physical extent of possible versus actual pollutants should be documented from permitting records. It is unclear if the monetary expenditures on environmental protection are routinely accounted for.

While regulation of the environmental effects of OCS exploration and production results in extensive investment in environmental protection, there are known to be uncontrolled residual effects. These include oil spills that are small individually but are cumulatively quite significant. This is particularly the case in the transportation subsystems of OCS oil and gas. These residual effects have been extensively studied and to the extent possible will be accounted for in the pilot.

The final major element is the possibility of catastrophic oil spills. These are quite rare, as the most frequent causes of such events are understood and controls are put in place. However, as the Deepwater Horizon oil spill of 2010 showed, the right combination of individually low probability events can still result in a large disaster. The damages to the environment as well as to the fishing and other ocean industries were of an order of magnitude to exceed total bonuses paid in some years. Measuring the losses in environmental capital value from catastrophic oil spills is a major challenge for this project. The events are too large to be ignored but too infrequent to forecast. The development of an appropriate methodology will be an important part of the prototype project. An initial approach may be to adapt the stochastic simulation methodology that is used by DOI to estimate the probability of oil existing within a designated area, but this would be highly experimental research.

In addition to environmental protection expenditures, SEEA also calls for spending on resource management to be included in the accounts. For purposes of the prototype account, the OCS program management expenditures by BOEM can serve as a measure of resource management expenditures. Expenditures by other public agencies at the federal and state levels may also be included to the extent that distinct budgetary lines and expenditures can be identified.

8.5.2 Commercial Fishing

8.5.2.1 Physical Account

The commercial fisheries pilot will begin with the selection of an initial fishery to examine. NOAA recognizes over 450 distinct fish stocks, of which some 250 are designated as "high value."[17] Some stocks are shared with other countries and spread between state and federal waters. The natural capital estimate will attempt to determine the economic value of some subset of these stocks. It is expected that a portion of the capital stock will be removed each year as depletion from both natural and man-made causes. In a renewable resource such as fisheries, the critical natural capital question is whether there is a long-term reduction in exploitable stocks and output in the fishing industry. The usual assumption is that this reduction in the physical size of fisheries stocks is brought about by overfishing, that is, fishing beyond the biological reproduction rate such that removal exceeds population growth.

This question of sustainable exploitation of the resources is clearly an important issue. US fish stocks support a mix of unsustainable and sus-

17. These stocks make up about 80 percent of total landed value; see "Population Assessments: Fish Stocks," from NOAA Fisheries, https://www.fisheries.noaa.gov/topic/population-assessments/fish-stocks.

Table 8.3 **Illustration of some of the data available to build pilot physical and monetary natural capital accounts for the Atlantic scallop (*Placopecten magellanicus*) fishery**

	Physicial Account Data			Landings Data		
Year	Catch (MT)	Abundance (MT)	Fishing Mortality	Revenue ($US)	Landings (MT)	Unit ($/MT)
2022	—	—	—	426,491,119	12,873	33,131.34
2021	—	—	—	560,882,635	16,670	33,646.70
2020	—	—	—	347,202,577	15,916	21,814.89
2019	27,647	147,073	0.34	434,337,168	20,796	20,885.17
2018	26,433	173,494	0.23	411,546,653	20,179	20,394.80
2017	23,458	193,441	0.23	369,604,286	16,446	22,474.09
2016	18,439	188,876	0.23	303,898,576	11,235	27,048.00
2015	16,207	175,263	0.26	286,546,638	10,559	27,137.83
2014	15,343	132,925	0.25	297,522,810	10,645	27,950.13
2013	18,664	108,533	0.35	366,369,379	14,538	25,201.61
2012	25,915	113,215	0.40	389,320,756	17,776	21,901.69

Notes: Stock SMART was used for stock data, and NOAA's National Marine Fisheries Service provided scallop fishery landings data. The latest stock data available are from 2019, which is the data year for the most recent stock assessment, published in 2020. Catch refers to the total amount harvested by fishing vessels or gear, while landings refers to the portion of the catch that is brought to port or landed for commercial use.

tainable fisheries, so this will become an additional criterion in selecting the stocks to be examined. However, traditional issues of over exploitation are not the only source of possible long-term change in capital stocks. Climate change is expected to reduce the size of fish populations in some areas and increase populations in other areas as populations respond to changes in thermal and chemical properties of the ocean. In addition, indirect impacts across multispecies fisheries (e.g., prey responses when fishing for predatory species) commonly result in stock changes. Because capital value is the discounted present value of some future flows of values, incorporating expected impacts of climate change and ecological relationships will be important considerations across fisheries.

Due to these complexities, the initial commercial fisheries pilot will likely focus on a single-fishery, sedentary species fishery with a history of sustainable exploitation and harvest data. We will use data from NOAA's Stock SMART database,[18] which provides biomass estimates for fishery stocks as well as data on recruitment and fishing mortality. Stock assessment information from NOAA can be used to supplement Stock SMART data (table 8.3).

18. See "Stock SMART—Status, Management, Assessments & Resource Trends" from the NOAA Fisheries site: https://apps-st.fisheries.noaa.gov/stocksmart?app=homepage.

8.5.2.2 *Monetary Account*

Fish stocks from which fish are caught and sold are primary inputs to commercial fishery industries but are generally unpriced. The economic conceptual challenge with fisheries is to identify this unpriced value.

The discussion of asset valuation for fisheries in SEEA-CF focuses on market-based transactions used to secure the right to fish. Such transactions could include tradable fisheries permits or individual transferable quotas, the prices of which can be assumed to represent the resource rents that fishing enterprises are willing to surrender for the right to fish (Newell et al. 2005). For commercial fisheries in federal waters that are managed this way, quota prices, where available, will be used to estimate rents (e.g., see Holland et al. 2015).

In the absence of a market-based resource allocation system, or in cases where quota prices are not available, the method recommended is the residual value approach, which estimates the net present value of the implied resource rents accruing from holding or using the asset (Obst 2010). This method starts with the gross output value (i.e., the landed value) and works backward to remove the costs of inputs such as fuel, bait, and labor to yield an approximate value of the profits of fishing. These profits are a combination of the return to the capital invested in fishing activities and the return to the natural capital.

The empirical issues associated with a residual estimate of value for a specific fishery begin with data on the gross output values. These data are regularly maintained by state and federal fisheries agencies and are generally of high quality. However, the same is not true of the values of the various purchased inputs, which are not regularly measured in any economic statistics series. Labor in commercial fishing, for example, is not measured by standard wage data because crew on fishing vessels are, with some exceptions, treated as individual contractors and their labor compensation computed as a share of the catch value. Data on other variable costs such as ice, fuel, and bait may or may not be available, and there are limited data on the value of fishing vessels and gear. Some of these data may be available on an episodic basis for specific fisheries through various studies by NOAA's Fisheries Office in support of management decisions. Some fisheries such as the Atlantic scallop are relatively data-rich, but we are investigating potential ways of addressing challenges in data-sparse fisheries, including exploring if information from the National Accounts could be used to fill in gaps.

The residual value approach to estimate resource rent should be applied with caution, as there are potential estimation challenges that could include the vertical integration of companies that transfer profits to elsewhere in the supply chain, and barriers to entry that may produce quasi-rents that could be confounded with resource rents (Obst 2010). A comparison with values obtained through the analysis of quotas, where available, would help shed light on these potential drawbacks.[19]

8.5.2.3 Environmental Expenditures Account

Eight Regional Fishery Management Councils, established in 1976 under the Magnuson-Stevens Fishery Conservation and Management Act, oversee the management of fishery resources in federal waters of the United States. Each council develops region-specific management plans to prevent overfishing, rebuild fish stocks, and ensure the long-term health of US fisheries.[20]

For example, the New England Fisheries Management Council manages the Atlantic sea scallop under a variety of measures provided in the fishery's management plan. Allowable catch is determined based on stock estimates, and fishing permits are allocated to different fishing groups depending on historical catch. Additional management measures include crew-size limits, closures of certain areas to protect young scallops and reduce bycatch, and mandatory use of vessel monitoring systems. Certain fishing groups are allowed to participate in a program of individual catch quotas.[21] Management plans are publicly available and can be used to estimate resource management expenditures for fisheries.[22]

8.5.3 Beach Recreation

8.5.3.1 Physical Account

The physical account will help track changes due to natural erosion and accretion, and human impacts such as beach nourishment, which will increase beach areas, and infrastructure developments that could reduce beach extent. High-resolution remote sensing (e.g., see Addicott, this volume) as well as existing beach physical data can be used to measure the linear extent and area of the stock of beaches. Stock will be defined in the pilot in both linear extent and surface area from the top of the dune to mean low water.

8.5.3.2 Monetary Account

The natural capital value derived from recreational use of beaches accrues in part to the recreational users and in part to the businesses that supply services, such as lodging and recreational equipment sales and rentals. The

19. We thank Andrew Scheld for drawing attention to these potential challenges with the approach.

20. See the US Regional Fishery Management Councils site, https://www.fisherycouncils.org.

21. See the "Atlantic Sea Scallop" in the NOAA Fisheries Species Directory, https://www.fisheries.noaa.gov/species/atlantic-sea-scallop.

22. For illustration, the Fisheries Management Plan and supplementary information for the Atlantic sea scallop can be found at https://www.nefmc.org/management-plans/scallops.

recreational user value is normally taken as an unpriced benefit since few beaches have entrance fees, and other variables included in the willingness to pay for recreation need to be estimated. This unpriced benefit has been extensively studied by economists using both stated and revealed preference methods, as discussed below. The majority of these studies have been done in a few states, including Florida, California, and New Jersey, but estimates have tended to fall within a narrow enough range to be useful. The share of the beach value accruing to businesses supporting tourists is, like the value of fish stocks, a portion of the profits of the relevant businesses.

Although the estimation of beach values for recreational users has a substantial theoretical foundation in the literature, data on the number of users of beaches are not widely collected. The same public access that creates the unpriced benefit that has been so extensively explored also makes it difficult to measure the number of beach visitors (and visits). A further complication in estimating user values is that a significant portion of the studies of user benefits are done with stated preference studies using different methods (e.g., Landry et al. 2020; Lew et al. 2022). Such studies are well grounded in economic theory and methods, but the diversity of approaches raise questions about comparability of results (De Valck and Rolfe 2018; Glenk et al. 2020). These validity issues led the SEEA-CF and SEEA-Ecosystem Accounting standards to recommend against using stated preference studies and instead using market-price based valuation methods such as travel cost (e.g., Pascoe 2019).

The producer side of the capital value may be estimated from industry data in the national income accounts for selected industries. The Tourism and Recreation sector in the ENOW and MESA data provides basic information. For industries such as hotels, ENOW data include establishments located in shore adjacent zip codes, which will permit some localization of the relevant data.

Like commercial fisheries, natural capital estimation for beaches will require selection of case studies to estimate natural capital. In this case, the choice of case studies will be made from beaches for which adequate user volume data is available or where user benefit studies have been done, and where there is adequate localized data on relevant businesses.

8.5.3.3 Environmental Expenditures Account

Beach use is occasionally affected by closures related to water quality issues and business cycle reductions in tourism spending. The COVID-19 pandemic also generated beach closures. Like commercial fisheries, climate change is a threat to beach recreation through erosion of beaches or, in the case of some activities such as surfing, changes in water levels that alter recreation. The economic value of erosion on beaches, which reduces the available area and increases congestion, will be reviewed to determine if user values decline with changes in the physical nature of the beach. Beach cleanup expenditures, such as daily raking, may also be considered, and data availability is being investigated.

8.6 Discussion and Conclusions

In the United States, the development of the Marine Economy Satellite Account (MESA) and the Economics: National Ocean Watch (ENOW) database has provided a focus on the contribution of the ocean to the national and regional economies. Both of these efforts are based on conventional measurements for assessing relationships between the economy and the environment, and thus are limited in their assessment of the contribution of natural capital accounting to the economy. This paper has described a plan to extend MESA so that it begins to incorporate key aspects of the United Nations System of Environmental-Economic Accounts Central Framework (SEEA-CF) as a foundation to gain an understanding of the contributions of natural capital to economic activities in the marine environment.

Standard national income accounting based on the United Nations System of National Accounts (SNA), including MESA, measures flows of economic activity in a specific period. In contrast, accounting based on SEEA-CF includes measures of both stocks and flows of economic values. An extension of MESA would allow expanding the definition of "capital assets" to include natural resource assets and to account for their depreciation and depletion. Measurement of the natural capital foundations of the marine-related economy requires a significantly more complex process than the estimation of MESA because the data and methods are much more complex and, for the most part, not nearly as readily available. Thus, one way to begin the MESA extension is by developing pilots for three sets of ocean activities defined in MESA that are relatively data rich: offshore oil and gas, commercial fishing, and beach recreation. However, a number of challenges will need to be addressed. Table 8.4 summarizes links to MESA, analytical challenges, and environmental connections related to the pilots.

Challenges in the oil and gas pilot include capturing the extent of oil and gas resources, navigating contract complexities, and accurately valuing stocks. In addition, measuring the probabilistic risk of environmental factors, such as pollution, proves challenging. The government lease sale system introduces uncertainty, requiring SEEA to encompass environmental resource management in its accounting framework.

There are a number of questions that will need to be considered in the commercial fishing pilot. Changes in ocean chemistry and other climate-related impacts should be included in the stock-assessment process. In addition, fish stocks are sometimes well defined from a biological perspective, but traditional ideas of fish stocks have been significantly undermined by the presence of multi-species fisheries in which complex predator-prey and eco-

Table 8.4 Links to the Marine Economy Satellite Account (MESA), analytical challenges, and environmental connections associated with the three pilots for extending MESA to include natural capital considerations

Pilot	Links to MESA	Analytical Challenges	Environmental Connections
Offshore Minerals	Oil and Gas: - Resource Extraction - Ecosystem Impacts	Capturing geographic and quality extent; difficulties in measuring additions and reductions in stock; monetary valuation limited to subset of minerals; value of stock contingent on expected value at auction	MESA does not account for activities that protect or improve environment; protective expenditures not explicit; measuring losses of environmental capital due to catastrophic events is challenging
Commercial Fishing	Living Resources: - Resource Extraction - Ecosystem Health	Must consider both fishing and ecological reductions in stock; climate change projections should be integrated into forecasts to help properly value fish stocks	Fish stocks sensitive to ocean climate change and ecological interactions
Beach Recreation	Tourism and Recreation: - Ecosystem Health	MESA provides producer side of value but does not represent unpriced recreational user benefits; use and comparability of diverse valuation studies; need to include adjacent areas to account for lodging and other relevant producer surplus	Climate impacts may degrade usable area and quality of beaches; potential increase in cleanup costs subject to ocean and weather variability

system conditions have more influence on the total amount of fish available to be caught than the simple process of natural population change adjusted for the amount of fish caught. Trophic interactions can be captured in the shadow prices of prey and predator species (Yun et al. 2017). This will be explored further as part of the pilot.

Additional issues will need to be addressed for natural accounting in the commercial fisheries sector as a whole. Unique valuations will be required for a large number of fisheries that in some cases are shared with other countries and spread between state and federal waters. Discount rates present a number of theoretical and empirical issues, and resource dynamics are important in calculating effective discount rates (Fenichel and Abbott 2014; Fenichel et al. 2016; Hoagland et al. 2020). For fisheries, conservation that leads to stock increases for a renewable resource would lower the effective discount rate.

In the beach recreation pilot, recreational value for some of the case studies may need to be taken as an unpriced benefit since few beaches have entrance fees. Although methods for the estimation of beach values for recreational users have a substantial foundation in the literature, data on the number of users of beaches are not widely collected. A further complication in user values is that a significant portion of the studies of user benefits are done with stated preference studies, which are not recommended in SEEA.

There are now efforts to create SEEA accounts across 90 countries, including efforts in a number of them to develop ocean accounts.[23] Australia recently released experimental estimates for a National Ocean Account,[24] which include measures of extent, condition, and carbon stocks for mangroves and seagrasses. Also recently, Norway published a pilot ocean satellite account in the spring of 2022 and has released information on plans for developing an ocean account.[25] In January 2023, the United States launched the National Strategy to Develop Statistics for Environmental-Economic Decisions: A US System of Natural Capital Accounting and Associated Environmental Economic Statistics, which provides guidelines to create a national system for natural capital accounting. The work described in this paper will contribute to the national strategy and will benefit from the lessons learned by countries that are already conducting natural capital accounting for the oceans. The extension of MESA will be a first step to account for the

23. See "2022 Global Assessment Results" of the System of Environmental Economic Accounting, https://seea.un.org/content/2022-global-assessment-results.

24. See "Towards a National Ocean Account" released by the Australian Bureau of Statistics on August 25, 2022, https://www.abs.gov.au/articles/towards-national-ocean-account.

25. See "The Progress on Ocean Accounting in Norway," Paper to the 28th London Group Meeting held in Siegburg, Germany, published by Statistics Norway, https://seea.un.org/sites/seea.un.org/files/lg28_d1_s2_2_randen.pdf.

contribution of marine natural capital to the economy. It will also provide essential information for industries relying on the ocean.

The pilots we consider in this paper will shed light on data and research needs for the development of a consistent accounting system for marine natural capital. They will offer exploratory work to identify challenges and identify solutions to advance the implementation of the aforementioned US national strategy. Lessons learned in the pilots will be applicable to sectors of MESA that have similar uses and dependencies in regards to marine natural capital. Conceptually, the natural capital underlying each of these economic uses of the ocean is the same: the value that the natural environment contributes to creation of valuable goods and services through the application of labor and capital. But the nature of that capital is very different among the three, and this will necessitate further exploring how natural capital that supports one activity can be reduced or augmented by other activities, and how this interaction is reflected in the different accounts.[26]

The data gleaned in the MESA extension will also be useful for the eventual development of accounts for specific ecosystems, which will provide another layer of information to marine-dependent industries. A reduction in the health of ocean ecosystems will affect key industries such as commercial fishing and tourism. A decline in the healthy cover of coastal ecosystems such as mangroves will make coastal communities more prone to damages from natural disasters. Decision-makers at all levels will benefit from marine natural capital accounting data in helping to make a wide range of policy decisions.

References

Addicott, E. T. "The Value and Configuration of Coastal Natural Capital." In *Measuring and Accounting for Environmental Public Goods: A National Accounts Perspective*, edited by Mary Bohman, Eli Fenichel, and Nicholas Z. Muller. Chicago, IL: University of Chicago Press. This volume.

Bureau of Economic Analysis (BEA). 2022. Concepts and Methods in the U.S. National Income Accounts. Chapters 1–13, December. Also available from: https://www.bea.gov/resources/methodologies/nipa-handbook.

Colgan, Charles S. 2013. "The Ocean Economy of the United States: Measurement, Distribution, & Trends." *Journal of Ocean and Coastal Management* 7: 334–43.

Colgan, Charles S. 2016. "Measurement of the Ocean Economy from National Income Accounts to the Sustainable Blue Economy." *Journal of Ocean and Coastal Economics* 2.

De Valck, Jeremy, and John Rolfe. 2018. "Spatial Heterogeneity in Stated Preference

26. An example from the pilot activities is oil spills, which can be a byproduct of oil and gas extraction and can damage natural capital that supports recreation.

Valuation: Status, Challenges and Road Ahead." *International Review of Environmental and Resource Economics* 11 (4): 355–422.

European Commission, International Monetary Fund, Organisation for Economic Co-operation and Development, United Nations and World Bank. 2009. System of National Accounts 2008. New York. United Nations Publication, Sales No. E.08.XVII.29. https://unstats.un.org/unsd/nationalaccount/docs/SNA2008.pdf.

Fenichel, Eli P., and Joshua K. Abbott. 2014. "Natural Capital: From Metaphor to Measurement." *Journal of the Association of Environmental and Resource Economists* 1 (1/2): 1–27.

Fenichel, Eli P., Ethan T. Addicott, Kristine M. Grimsrud, Glenn-Marie Lange, Ina Porras, and Ben Milligan. 2020. "Modifying National Accounts for Sustainable Ocean Development." *Nature Sustainability* 3 (11): 889–95. https://www.nature.com/articles/s41893-020-0592-8.

Fenichel, E. P., Joshua K. Abbott, Jude Bayham, Whitney Boone, Erin M. Haacker, and Lisa Pfeiffer. 2016. "Measuring the Value of Groundwater and Other Forms of Natural Capital." *Proceedings of the National Academy of Sciences* 113 (9): 2382–2387.

Fleurbaey, Marc. 2009. "Beyond GDP: The Quest for a Measure of Social Welfare." *Journal of Economic Literature* 47 (4): 1029–1075.

Glenk, Klaus, Robert J. Johnston, Jürgen Meyerhoff, and Julian Sagebiel. 2020. "Spatial Dimensions of Stated Preference Valuation in Environmental and Resource Economics: Methods, Trends and Challenges." *Environmental Resource Economics* 75: 215–42. https://doi.org/10.1007/s10640-018-00311-w.

Hoagland, Porter, Di Jin, and Stace Beaulieu. 2020. "A Primer on the Economics of Natural Capital and Its Relevance to Deep-Sea Exploitation and Conservation." In *Natural Capital and Exploitation of the Deep Ocean*, pp. 25–52. Oxford University Press. https://doi.org/10.1093/oso/9780198841654.001.0001.

Holland, Daniel S., Eric Thunberg, Juan Agar, Scott Crosson, Chad Demarest, Stephen Kasperski, Larry Perruso, Erin Steiner, Jessica Stephen, Andy Strelcheck, and Mike Travis. 2015. "US Catch Share Markets: A Review of Data Availability and Impediments to Transparent Markets." *Marine Policy* 57: 103–10. https://doi.org/10.1016/j.marpol.2015.03.027.

Jolliffe, James, Claire Jolly, and Barrie Stevens. 2021a. "Blueprint for Improved Measurement of the International Ocean Economy: An Exploration of Satellite Accounting for Ocean Economic Activity." OECD Science, Technology and Industry Working Papers 2021/04. Paris: OECD Publishing. https://dx.doi.org/10.1787/aff5375b-en.

Jolliffe, James, Claire Jolly, and Barrie Stevens. 2021b. "Key Considerations for the Development of Internationally Comparable Statistics on Ocean Economic Activity." *Journal of Ocean and Coastal Economics* 8 (2): Article 6. https://doi.org/10.15351/2373–8456.1140.

Landry, Craig E., J. Scott Shonkwiler, and John C. Whitehead. 2020. "Economic Values of Coastal Erosion Management: Joint Estimation of Use and Existence Values with Recreation Demand and Contingent Valuation Data." *Journal of Environmental Economics and Management* 103.

Lew, Daniel K., Leif E. Anderson, Douglas W. Lipton, Tammy B. Murphy, and Kristy Wallmo. 2022. "Adherence to Best Practices for Stated Preference Valuation within the U.S. Marine Ecosystem Services Literature." *Journal of Ocean and Coastal Economics* 9 (1): Article 3. https://doi.org/10.15351/2373-8456.1159.

Nathan Associates. 1974. *Gross Product Originating from Ocean-Related Activities*. Washington DC: Bureau of Economic Analysis.

National Oceanic and Atmospheric Administration (NOAA). 2022. "NOAA Report on the U.S. Marine Economy." Charleston, SC: NOAA Office for Coastal Management. http://coast.noaa.gov/digitalcoast/training/econreport.html.

Newell, Richard G., Kerry L. Papps, and James N. Sanchirico. 2005. "Asset Pricing in Created Markets for Fishing Quotas." Discussion Papers 10639. Washington, DC: Resources for the Future.

Nicolls, William, Connor Franks, Teresa Gilmore, Rachel Goulder, Luke Mendelsohn, Edward Morgan, Jeffery Adkins, Monica Grasso, Kate Quigley, Jennifer Zhuang, and Charles Colgan. 2020. "Defining and Measuring the U.S. Ocean Economy." Bureau of Economic Analysis, U.S. Department of Commerce. https://www.bea.gov/system/files/2021-06/defining-and-measuring-the-united-states-ocean-economy.pdf.

Nordhaus, William D., and James Tobin. 1973. "Is Growth Obsolete?" In *The Measurement of Economic and Social Performance*, edited by Milton Moss. 509–64. New York, NY: National Bureau of Economic Research.

Obst, Carl. 2010. "Valuation of Assets: A Case Study on the Valuation of Fish Stocks." Outcome Paper for Global Consultation, Issue #12. United Nations Statistics Division, Department of Economic and Social Affairs. https://unstats.un.org/unsd/envaccounting/seearev/OCdocs/Outcome12.pdf.

Pascoe, Sean. 2019. "Recreational Beach Use Values with Multiple Activities." *Ecological Economics* 160: 137–44.

Randen, Trine H. B., Kristine Grimsrud, Tarik Ogbamichael, and Tor Kristian Ånestad. 2022. "Progress on Ocean Accounting in Norway." Paper for the 28th London Group meeting. Siegburg, Germany. https://seea.un.org/sites/seea.un.org/files/randen_1.pdf.

Statistics Portugal. 2016. "Satellite Account for the Sea—2010–2013, Methodological Report." December. Department of National Accounts, Statistics Portugal and Department of Strategy, Directorate-General for Maritime Policy. https://www.ine.pt/ngt_server/attachfileu.jsp?look_parentBoui=300613867&att_display=n&att_download=y.

Stebbings, Emily, Eleni Papathanasopoulou, Tara Hooper, Melanie C. Austen, and Xiaoyu Yan. 2020. "The Marine Economy of the United Kingdom." *Marine Policy* 116: 103905. https://doi.org/10.1016/j.marpol.2020.103905.

United Nations, European Union, Food and Agriculture Organization of the United Nations, International Monetary Fund, Organisation for Economic Co-operation and Development, and The World Bank. 2009. The System of National Accounts, 2008. New York. https://unstats.un.org/unsd/nationalaccount/docs/sna2008.pdf.

United Nations, European Union, Food and Agriculture Organization of the United Nations, International Monetary Fund, Organisation for Economic Co-operation and Development, and The World Bank. 2014. System of Environmental-Economic Accounting 2012—Central Framework. New York. United Nations Publication, Sales No. E.12.XVII.12. https://unstats.un.org/unsd/envaccounting/seearev/seea_cf_final_en.pdf.

Wang, Yixuan, and Nuo Wang. 2019. "The Role of the Marine Industry in China's National Economy: An Input–Output Analysis." *Marine Policy* 99: 42–49. https://doi.org/10.1016/j.marpol.2018.10.019.

Yun, Seong Do, Barbara Hutniczak, Joshua K. Abbott, and Eli P. Fenichel. 2017. "Ecosystem-Based Management and the Wealth of Ecosystems." *Proceedings of the National Academy of Sciences of the United States of America* 114: 6539–6544.

Comment Andrew M. Scheld

Quantifying and valuing natural capital is needed to provide a holistic view of economies and assess trade-offs between growth, development, and impacts to the natural environment. The marine environment is home to a variety of natural capital assets that provide a diverse array of valuable ecosystem services. Measurement and tracking of the value of marine natural capital has been acknowledged as important for some time, and several countries are beginning to develop ocean ecosystem accounts to complement existing national accounts. In the United States, ocean-based economic activity is wide ranging, including extraction of non-renewable and renewable natural resources; transportation, shipping, and trade; recreation; and research, education, and management. These activities depend on, and derive surplus value from, marine natural capital. “Natural Capital Considerations for an Extension of the US Marine Economy Satellite Account,” hereafter Wielgus et al. 2023, considers three pilot extensions of the existing Marine Economy Satellite Account (MESA) to incorporate information on natural capital stocks and value for offshore oil and gas, commercial fisheries, and beach recreation. These three industries are dominant sectors in the US ocean economy and represent renewable and non-renewable resources, as well as extractive and non-extractive uses. Piloting extensions across this diverse range of industries should facilitate progress in natural capital accounting more broadly as common challenges are encountered and standard approaches arrived at.

The United Nations System of Environmental-Economic Accounting Central Framework (UN SEEA-CF) discusses three approaches for estimating natural capital asset values: the appropriation method, where rent values are based on asset sales; the residual value method, where rent is estimated as gross revenues net costs; and the access price method, where resource use licenses are limited, freely traded, and the access price corresponds to rents. This range of valuation approaches is well represented in the pilot extensions to MESA considered in Wielgus et al. 2023. In offshore oil and gas, winning bids for exploration and extraction rights to specific areas of seabed convey information about expected resource rents and can be used in natural capital valuation. Bids are made under imperfect information however, leading to some divergence between payments and realized rents that should be further explored. For commercial fisheries, valuation approaches are proposed that include utilizing permit and quota transaction data from fisheries managed with limited access privilege programs as well as calculation of residual value (rent) by deducting fishing costs from landings revenues. In some instances, both methods may be able to be applied in the same fishery, which should

Andrew M. Scheld is the Moses D. Nunnally Associate Professor at the Virginia Institute of Marine Science at the College of William & Mary.

provide useful comparisons. When considering beach recreation, it is noted that a variety of studies have documented willingness-to-pay, however information on rates of beach use are less available and additional data collection may therefore be needed. In all instances, market distortions created through government policies, industry structure, or other factors should be carefully considered.

Quantifying natural capital values requires information on physical stocks. For both offshore oil and gas and commercial fisheries, federal agencies maintain information on stock levels, which could be used to develop physical accounts. The definition of natural capital stock for beach recreation is less straightforward and will require efforts to identify and measure those properties determined to define the stock, which is potentially an opportunity for advancement of natural capital accounting methodologies. Across applications, stock boundaries and structure can be influenced by exogenous environmental conditions and evolve over time in response to physical forcings. Discoveries and shifts in human use add further dynamics in physical asset levels. Intertemporal considerations will likely be important in developing natural capital accounts that facilitate comparisons over time.

Valuation of natural capital is critically important to understanding and informing pressing environmental-economic trade-offs. There remain a number of difficulties in operationalizing natural capital accounting, however. Wielgus et al. 2023 note several challenges associated with available data and proposed valuation methods, including data quality and coverage, the influence of confounding factors on resource rent estimates, and the complexity of ecosystems. In addition to these, the proper partitioning of value to avoid double counting should be considered important. Valuing final services exclusively is recommended in general, though complex interdependencies between habitats, biological or physical resources, and human activities may complicate this in practice. Despite these and other difficulties, progress in natural capital accounting is being made. The pilot extensions to MESA considered in Wielgus et al. 2023 represent substantial advances in natural capital accounting of US marine resources. Development of these and other natural capital accounts should be expected to provide many salient lessons and produce data that complement existing national accounts, ultimately facilitating increased consideration of marine natural capital values in ocean development and governance.

For acknowledgments, sources of research support, and disclosure of the author's material financial relationships, if any, please see https://www.nber.org/books-and-chapters/measuring-and-accounting-environmental-public-goods-national-accounts-perspective/comment-natural-capital-considerations-extension-us-marine-economy-satellite-account-scheld.

Author Index

Subject Index

Note: Page numbers followed by *f* or *t* refer to figures or tables, respectively.